The Similitude of Blossoms

Harvard East Asian Monographs, 172

The Similitude of Blossoms

A Critical Biography of Izumi Kyōka (1873–1939),
Japanese Novelist and Playwright

Charles Shirō Inouye

Published by the Harvard University Asia Center
and distributed by Harvard University Press
Cambridge (Massachusetts) and London, 1998

Printed in the United States of America

The Harvard University Asia Center publishes a monograph series and, in coordination with the Fairbank Center for East Asian Research, the Korea Institute, the Reischauer Institute of Japanese Studies, and other faculties and institutes, administers research projects designed to further scholarly understanding of China, Japan, Vietnam, Korea, and other Asian countries. The Center also sponsors projects addressing multidisciplinary and regional issues in Asia.

Library of Congress Cataloging-in-Publication Data
Inouye, Charles Shirō.
  The similitude of blossoms : a critical biography of Izumi Kyōka (1873–1939), Japanese novelist and playwright / Charles Shirō Inouye.
      p.   cm. -- (Harvard East Asian monographs : 172)
  Includes bibliographical references and index.
  ISBN 0-674-80816-9 (alk. paper)
    1. Izumi, Kyōka, 1873–1939.   2. Authors, Japanese--20th century--Biography.   I. Title.   II. Series.
  PL 809.Z9Z7396   1998
  985.6'342--dc21   98-35543
                                                                    CIP

Index by the author

⊗   Printed on acid-free paper

Last figure below indicates year of this printing
08 07 06 05 04 03 02 01 00 99 98

TO HOWARD HIBBETT AND

MURAMATSU SADATAKA

.

The twofold world of our ancestors has vanished like a mist. In this time
at the end of all time, we show respect for the dead by recording tales of
banished dreamers and by searching out the unfinished dreams
of those who have gone on.

*Orikuchi Shinobu, "To the Land of the Dead Mother,
to the Eternal Land—Vicissitudes of Trespass"
(Haha ga kuni e, tokoyo e—ikyō-ishiki no kifuku)*

I came to believe in a Great Memory passing on from
generation to generation. But that was not enough, for these images
showed intention and choice.

William Butler Yeats, "Anima Mundi"

Acknowledgments

I began thinking about Izumi Kyōka as an undergraduate at Stanford, enrolled in Makoto Ueda's course on modern Japanese literature. I read a short story that Edward Seidensticker had translated for Donald Keene's anthology, *Modern Japanese Literature*. At that time, "A Tale of Three Who Were Blind" was the only piece of Kyōka's work widely available in English; had it not been for Professor Seidensticker's fine rendering of that story, and for Professor Ueda's inspirational guidance, I might not have been prepared for what was to come.

I wrote a senior thesis on Nagai Kafū and then went as a Monbushō scholar to study in Japan with Noguchi Takehiko at Kōbe University, who immediately rejected my initial research proposal. He was of the opinion that there were plenty of other writers to think about other than the one I had in mind at the time. He happened to be writing about Kyōka and was planning to teach a seminar on the author's short fiction. It was in that course that I discovered for myself the genuineness that I had sensed in Seidensticker's translation. Here was an artist who knew what he was doing, someone wildly innovative yet true to his tradition and sincere about the possibilities of art.

Like Professor Ueda, Professor Noguchi proved to be a wonderful mentor. He was both an engaging teacher and a productive scholar who played as hard as he worked. Our backgrounds could not have been more different, but our aesthetic and intellectual interests meshed well. I should also mention my other teachers at Kōbe: Professors Soma and Ikegami. All three men were patient and encouraging. I thank them for teaching me the general contours of Japanese literature, and for allowing me to become one of the crowd. I also thank my colleagues at Kōbe Daigaku, especially Takakuwa Noriko, who has since become an important Kyōka scholar.

I wrote a master's thesis on Kyōka's plays and returned to the United States. Having earlier been a visiting scholar in America, Noguchi recommended that I continue my graduate studies with Howard Hibbett. Like my other mentors, Professor Hibbett had one foot in the Edo period and one in a more recent era. This breadth proved to be a crucial advantage as I began to look for the sources of Kyōka's roots in a "visual tradition," and as I now continue my search for early configurations of Japanese modernity. Howard proved to be an insightful critic and unfailing supporter, and it is to him that I dedicate this book. To my other teachers at Harvard—Gen Itasaka, Donald Shively, Haruko Iwasaki, and Edwin Cranston—I also owe my heartfelt thanks. Itasaka-sensei was always engaging. Professor Shively taught me the importance of accuracy in scholarship. Haruko shared my interest in Kyōka and has been a generous friend. Professor Cranston, who suffered through my hastily written dissertation, has continued over the years to be a common literary spirit. My thanks also to George Potter, Ho Ch'ien, Timothy Conner, Aoki Toshiyuki, and the others of the Harvard-Yenching Library staff who have provided me with access to that wonderful resource.

Grants from the Social Science Research Council and the Fulbright-Hayes made it possible for me and my family to spend some time in Tokyo to work on the dissertation that became the embryo for this book. I was fortunate enough to study with Muramatsu Sadataka, who was introduced to me through the graces of the late Tamae Kensuke. Professor Muramatsu is the "godfather" of Kyōka studies in Japan, having begun his lifelong study of the author and his work while Kyōka was still alive. He generously took me under his wing and introduced both me and Cody Poulton, who was there to work on the plays, to the members of the Kyōka Kenkyū Kai. This group took Cody and I seriously, even to the point of listening to us stumble through papers at their semi-annual meetings. For their support, I owe

thanks to all. But I especially want to thank Kasahara Nobuo, Tōgō Katsumi, Mita Hideaki, and Taneda Wakako for their conversations, articles,
and books. I also dedicate this book to Professor Muramatsu.

While in Tokyo, I relied upon the services of two institutions in particular: the Mita Information Center at Keiō University, and the Kindai Bunko
at Shōwa Women's College. Kyōka's personal library and manuscripts were
being held at Keiō, and access to these was crucial. My thanks to Shiraishi
Tsutomu and Tanaka Masayuki, who allowed me to use this collection on
an almost daily basis. (Mr. Shiraishi was even so kind as to take me on the
proverbial outing to Enoshima.) I would also like to thank Keiō University's
Matsumura Tomomi for introducing me to this resource and for assisting
my research in numerous ways. It would not be an exaggeration to say that I
could not have written this book were it not for Matsumura's help. In the
same breath, I give thanks to Yoshida Masashi, another careful and hardworking scholar, who helped me gain access to the excellent collection of
Meiji-period journals kept at Shōwa Women's College. I cannot count the
number of times I have prevailed upon him and the members of the staff of
the Kindai Bunko, especially Komatsu Hiroko, in my search for book reviews and articles written by Kyōka's contemporaries.

During this stay in Japan, I also consulted with a number of other scholars who deserve mention: Suzuki Jōzō, who showed me his magnificent collection of *kusazōshi*; Uda Toshihiko; Momokawa Takahito, who has become
a great friend; and the late Maeda Ai. As a testament to his intellectual vigor
and willingness to be helpful, Professor Ai visited with me regularly even
though he was already seriously ill. I never knew he had cancer until I received word of his death a few short months after our return to Cambridge.
I was ashamed to think that I had not been more sensitive to his physical
condition.

Upon returning to Harvard, a grant from the Reischauer Institute allowed me to write up my research, and a post-doctoral grant from the same
institute allowed me to begin the process of writing this book. I and my
family returned to Japan a few years later, this time to Kyōka's hometown of
Kanazawa. A grant from the Japan Foundation allowed us to live there for
several rainy months. I consulted numerous times with my colleagues there,
especially Yoshimura Hirotō and Kobayashi Teruya. As is true of Japanese
scholars in general, Professor Kobayashi's grasp of the details, such as the
bridges of the Asano River, was impressive and humbling. Nagae Teruyo,

who had been instrumental in helping me to get some of Kyōka's stories translated into English, was gracious and generous enough to allow us the use of her second home; and the warm hospitality of many others—the America-loving Tsuruga Hiroyuki, Uno Jirō, my fishing partner Nishimoto Yoichi, and Hayashi Takanobu, to name a few—made our stay a memorable one. My thanks also to Mayor Yamade, who took an interest in my work and has been consistent in his commitment to preserving Kyōka's legacy. Because of the kindness of so many, I can honestly say that my family came to appreciate Kanazawa more than Kyōka himself did.

Besides those already mentioned, a number of others helped in the final stages of this project. At Tufts, I was fortunate enough to be able to work under ideal conditions, taking time off occasionally to focus on the project. The chair of my department, Christiane Romero, has been an extraordinary advocate and colleague. I also thank Teruko Craig for her willingness to let me pursue a full research agenda while learning the ropes at Tufts. With their help, I was able to win a Mellon grant that gave me additional time for writing. Two readers for the Harvard Council on East Asian Studies, Joseph Murphy, Richard Torrance, and Cody Poulton evaluated the manuscript at various stages of its preparation. I thank them for their careful reading and useful suggestions. John Ziemer, my editor, has done an excellent job of tightening here and there, and of ensuring consistency and accuracy. Needless to say, any remaining factual errors or clumsiness of expression are my own.

Portions of this book have appeared in other publications: "Water Imagery in the Work of Izumi Kyōka," *Monumenta Nipponica*; "The 'Purely Japanese' Izumi Kyōka," *Japan Foundation Newsletter*; "Izumi Kyōka and Language," *Harvard Journal of Asiatic Studies*; *Tales of Mystery and Imagination: Japanese Gothic by Izumi Kyōka* (Takakuwa Bijutsu Insatsu, 1992); *The Tale of the Wandering Monk* (Limited Editions Club, 1995); and *Japanese Gothic Tales by Izumi Kyōka* (University of Hawaii Press, 1996). Because this is the first book in English to be written on the entire scope of Kyōka's life and works, and because only a few of the works discussed have been translated into English, I have had to include fairly detailed summaries of the author's work. For some readers, these recountings will be tedious. But I hope they will serve as a useful map for those struggling through the originals.

Finally, I wish to express my thankfulness to the members of my immediate family, especially Sibyl, for the many sacrifices she and our children have had to make because of this book. The project was a massive, protracted one. It took us to Japan twice, each time with a newly born baby, first Mie and then Leif. Although she would surely be embarrassed to hear me say this, Mie, now age twelve, read the entire book out loud so I could check the final proofs and prepare an index. A special father's thanks to her.

C.S.I.

Contents

Sixteen pages of photographs follow p. 118

The Similitude of Blossoms

Introduction

The famous Japanese critic Kobayashi Hideo (1902–83) outlined a number of issues crucial to an evaluation of Izumi Kyōka's (1873–1939) life and works.

Contemporary writers have in many ways tried to distance themselves from what Kyōka represented, and in fact have been successful in doing so. But will they be able to escape what he stood for? I ask this question because Kyōka was of all writers the most thorough with regard to the fundamental and difficult questions that surround the issue of what it means to be a writer. By this I do not mean to declare him to be the only writer. It is simply that in his case the questions are raised in an extremely pure form. The narrowness of his vision, his stubborn persistence, the patterns of his sensibility, these all came together in a fortunate way. They took shape with a purity that is rare for novelists, and even for poets.

By now you already anticipate the point that I wish to make. Kyōka's perfect faith in the power of words was his most distinguishing characteristic. It would not be an exaggeration to say that letters (*bunshō*) were his only god. Compared to Kyōka, today's novelists cannot be called believers. They negotiate a path between many gods and many idols.

Kyōka shut himself up within the world of words. Reality did not enter in. The realities and events of society, even the details of his own life, could have no place in his world unless they first cast off the life they had received in the real world and were reborn as beautiful words. He believed in the absolute value of linguistic images, and in certain inevitable relationships that he wished to perceive among them. Consequently, he felt convinced that the linguistic structure that he wove together from these images was everlasting. Not only is "The Heartvine" [his final story] devoid of all signs of contemporary life, but it also has no direct connection to Kyōka's experience either. We do not see his gray hair, nor his wrinkles. Even the ambiguous appearances of age do not figure in. Seen from the immutable youthfulness of this world of Kyōka's belief, words come to appear as the final mask of life's ephemerality, stained as they are with the trials of this floating world. That is the extent to which Kyōka's world is the truth made from lies.[1]

Kobayashi did not elaborate upon these issues. What does it mean, for example, to have "perfect faith in the power of words"? And with what qualifications can it be said that "reality did not enter" directly into Kyōka's "world of words"? If neither the "realities and events of society" nor the "details of [Kyōka's] own life" found a place unless they first "cast off the life they had received in the real world" in order to be "reborn as beautiful words," what was this process of rebirth or translation?

Throughout this well-known summation of Kyōka's accomplishments, Kobayashi made a distinction between the real and the imagined that is both a crucial and a common border in literary criticism. As such, it is continuously disputed, violated, and redrawn. Kyōka himself spoke of the dangers of the inability to distinguish between reality and dreams, although he seemed at times to be confused about the boundary between the two. It is precisely this confusion that draws readers to his work and scholars to the task of reading his fiction against a hypothetically more veritable story of his life. Satisfied to note from a distance this borderland between two kingdoms of narrative—the supposedly imagined and the supposedly real—Kobayashi most likely chose not to elaborate for fear of being too clear about matters that are valuable for their ambiguity. Such is the risk of clarity.

Emphasizing the difference between an author's life and his works (or even the irrelevance of the former to the latter) was a tactic of the New Criticism. This desire to separate writer and text came in response to an older (modern) critical impulse to establish the authority of the author or to affirm the genius of artistic imagination. Eventually, this romantic emphasis on the writer was supplanted by the sophisticated readings that illuminated the endless complications of a given text, including the capacity of language to be disconnected from all else, even from itself. Affronted and humbled by the accomplishments of structuralist and post-structuralist critics, those who return to biography today do so with a heightened awareness of language, of politics, and of the ways in which the story of someone's life is somehow always inevitably and necessarily a fiction. In a way that is more than a simple denial of facts or a rejection of the possibility of such bits of truth, we have come to understand human life as a matter of make-believe, as a narrated residue of the will in action. The past cannot really be reconstituted. Nor can it be perfectly revealed or discovered. In the end, it can be imagined only as the aura of certain artifacts, or as the lasting effects of memory, or, at its highest, as the magic of one person's sensibility resonating with that of another even if—especially if?—the Other is dead.

Would we have been fond of Kyōka had we met in real life? This uncomfortable question sets biography apart from other forms of criticism. Certainly, we could have admired him, just as we can admire his writing. But would we have been required to feel more? What is to be gained by inventing more of a connection than this? In answer to the query of why we should venture beyond an understanding of texts, I can give one reason that is quite simple, though not easy to articulate. In the eyes of a literary biographer, an author such as Kyōka is compellingly foreign. Our fascination with him goes even beyond words written and deeds done. Kyōka's language can be learned, his texts mastered. We can carefully reimagine his life—call friends to testify, gather documents that damn and exalt. As scholars and students, we do all these things most readily. But beyond these motions toward accuracy, there lies similitude—the understandable sameness that is always utterly and profoundly foreign. To put it another way, the real subject of critical biography always lies beyond what is plainly known. It is neither mystery nor adulation—at least not in this age. It is, rather, a glancing away, an embarrassment of insight that creates a moment of centrifugal balance between the author and his reader. Only in these moments of looking away is there true understanding and something like sympathy.

In short, literary biography is a skillful form of disapproval. In few other ways can we espouse another's being with such familiarity, and in no other way can we be so bold about the shyness with which we admire and loath those who are in some way notable. It is not impossible to write at length about relationships that do not exist—a life unaccounted for by some text, a writing with no writer behind it, a bevy of signifiers dressed for a dance that will never take place. But because it would be, for all but the most sophisticated readers, a pointless thing to do, we assume, brazenly and crudely, that the connections between the real and the imagined are there to make clear,

to untranslate, to establish in reverse. We continue to make connections re-
flexively and immediately, wanting most of all to tell a compelling story. In
the end, that is what matters: a good story. That is what a reader wants to
read, and why a biographer wants to write. This desire is justified because
narrating the world is a compulsion that matters. To live, we need food,
shelter, and stories.

As we will see, the world of Kyōka's imagining was meant to be an anti-
dote to the reality he perceived. If "reality did not enter" unless it formed itself into beautiful language, we would still have to say that certain events in
his life and his regard for them had everything to do with the form and
function of his craft. The threatening presence of life is reflected in a clearly
defined and persistent narrative archetype that gives shape to his works. By
way of this paradigm, Kyōka successfully transformed a profound sense of
personal loss into redemption and reprieve. This privileged narrative, or
what I will call—probably too often for anyone's liking—the archetype or
meta-story, was nothing less than a translation of the real. It was constructed of a set of visual codes that he had received from his tradition.
These "linguistic images" were infused with a personal significance and
placed into a matrix of fixed relationships that changed surprisingly little
over time.

Adjusting Kobayashi's argument slightly, I will tell a story which shows
that the myth that gave direction and shape to Kyōka's literary creations was
not precisely everlasting. Although he relied upon it as the foundation of his
aesthetics from about the year 1900 to the end of his life in 1939, its effect
was uneven in two ways. First, its salutary powers were ephemeral, thus requiring its constant repetition: Kyōka doing his thing again and again and
again. Second, it finally failed him toward the end of his career. For a few
years prior to his death, Kyōka departed from the formula, with disastrous
results. Fortunately, he was able to resurrect the archetype in his final story,
"The Heartvine" ("Rukōshinsō," 1939), mentioned by Kobayashi.

This story is a masterpiece, but it is not without, as Kobayashi claims,
numerous connections to Kyōka's life. Without this work, the story of the
author's life would have a very different shape. Similarly, without this background of a longer narrative context, the story itself would not have as much
closure and, in this limited sense, as strong a meaning. Indeed, only by re-
covering the details of Kyōka's life can we fully appreciate why he would persist in writing "the truth made from lies." This tension between fact and fic-

tion is, I believe, what Kobayashi meant to express in speaking of the author's words as "the final mask of life's ephemerality, stained as they are with the trials of this floating world." Even the mask is marked with life. Its blemish is an essential part of its beauty.

In the end, it is hard to separate the writer from what is written, especially when our attempt to make sense of either is always an interpretive search for what must be imagined. The same can be said for the reader and the text. As its interpreters, we are wading in the very sea of signs that we wish to isolate and study, as if its fluidity could be uninfluenced by our presence. We proceed as if wading in a pool, trying to snatch up fallen petals from the surface. Around our legs, waves form, disturbing and deforming the target of our investigation. We reach out to gather. The pedals scatter. And so we make our mark upon that which is supposedly valuable for being marked by someone else.

In this neo-biographical age, we no longer claim that truth can be expressed without the mediation of signs or that meaning is possible without reference to historically formed patterns of creation and reception, always larger than any one person's ability to create true difference. Even the significance of those signs that we want most to agree upon—"god," "truth," "love"—are unknowable outside the particulars of lived experience. As readers, then, we are removed from what we seek with our own powers of sight and insight. The irony is that an awareness of the mediated nature of understanding might be the only way we can prepare ourselves to feel anything in an immediate way. Thus, at the crucial moment of understanding, the literary mind glances away. Sympathy knows what it sees by not seeing. We do not want flowers, but flowers in a mirror, a similitude of blossoms.

CHAPTER I

Contexts

❧

1873–1883

Kanazawa, Geography of Desire

The Asano River flows through the neighborhood where Izumi Kyōka (1873–1939) was born. Its waters roll quietly over rounded stones as it glides to its union with the sea a few miles away. The flow is steady, controlled by dams and aqueducts, and contained between banks of fitted granite stones that channel the water and leave only the narrowest of flood plains. Indeed, there is no shifting edge between river and city, no exposed space where itinerants gather in the summer to dance and perform. The usual no-man's-land of gravel bars and summer weeds has been severely reduced in this city where the uses of space are too obvious to allow much of a margin. Kanazawa, a castle town on the Japan Sea, was home to the Maeda clan, one of the wealthiest and most powerful families of the Tokugawa era. They developed the river and the neighborhoods through which it ran, training both through centuries of careful urban planning. The marks of social control are everywhere.

The Asano River and its environs appeared much the same in Kyōka's day as they do now. Kanazawa was one of a few major Japanese cities to escape the incendiary bombings of the final months of World War II. It was spared a death by fire because of its cultural importance, a special status and fortune it shares with the still more ancient city of Kyoto to the west and south. This comparison with Japan's ancient capital is not lost on the residents of Kyōka's hometown. Their respect for the glorious past of the Kaga domain, largest of all the non-Tokugawa fiefdoms, as well as their sensitivity to the quiet stories told by weathered tiles and old wood, has slowed the flood of ferroconcrete that has swept other parts of Japan since the Surrender. Largely preserved, the old neighborhoods of Kanazawa still crowd both banks of the Asano. Tile-roofed houses, shops, temples, and teahouses still follow the rise and fall of the embankment. Eave to eave, wall to wall, they stand together, accessed by narrow alleys that run straight for a few yards, turn, climb connecting flights of steps, descend others, then continue ahead.

Smaller alleys feed into larger streets, wide enough for cars and buses. The main throughway follows the original course of the Hokuriku Road, a centuries-old artery of commerce that connected Kanazawa with other centers of trade and administration. From the spot where this highway now crosses the Asano, the river's entry into the Japan Sea is within a few minutes' drive. And yet the slope of the stream is still steep enough to be obvious. The ribbon of water moves with surprising speed. Schools of dace (*ugui*) actively feed in shadowy pockets of water. Centuries ago, members of the ruling class angled for the trout-like *ayu* with long, exquisitely crafted bamboo poles. The Maeda encouraged fishing as a gentlemanly pursuit. They also encouraged the making of pottery and lacquerware, silk dying, the Noh theater, and a number of other artistic activities that would demonstrate to Edo that the Kaga domain was too absorbed in culture to think of mounting a serious political challenge to the Tokugawa regime.

Benefiting from this legacy of affluence and cultivation, Kanazawa is still an attractive city. The travel brochures exaggerate and distort its subtle graces. But there is some truth in advertisement. As they often state, the Asano River is a perfect place to stroll. Egrets stalk the shallows. The banks are shadowed by pine, willow, and cherry. And as every inquisitive tourist discovers, the Asano is, in fact, poetically a different water than the Sai, which runs parallel to the Asano through the southwest corner of the city. The Sai River is stronger and more turbulent. As such, it is associated with the poet Murō Saisei (1889–1962), another native son and one of many writers who figure prominently in any visitor's introduction to the city. Of the river, Saisei wrote:

> The beautiful Sai
> Flows through my town.
> On its dike where I sit,

Spring flowers blossom in spring,
Summer flowers in summer.[1]

Compared to the Sai, where salmon ply strong currents, the more delicate Asano is, at least in the local imagination, reminiscent of Izumi Kyōka. It is his river. As described in one popular magazine, its quietly gliding surface is "comforting" yet "ghastly."[2]

How can it be both? This odd pairing of adjectives provides a first context for this writer who called himself Kyōka—"Mirror's Flower." But to grasp the point, we must push further into the past. More than it does now, the Asano River once separated dissimilar worlds. On the south side of the Asano was the lattice-fronted, tile-roofed neighborhood whose narrow streets were home to the artisan class to which Izumi Seiji, Kyōka's father, belonged. They formed a domesticated space, more stable and civil than the world on the opposite side. That other territory, the north bank, was occupied by a complicated aggregate of peoples and institutions that the Maeda clan made a point of keeping on the periphery throughout the years of its rule. Historically, the land across the river had been the home of outcastes: the *eta* (tanners), *kawata* (leather workers), and *hinin* (beggars), who, according to religious strictures, were polluted because of their work with animals and other forms of unclean objects. The other bank was also where the poorer, unchartered merchants and artisans lived, especially along the Hokuriku Road and around the foot of Mt. Utatsu, which rises just beyond the Ōhashi, or Great Bridge, the nexus of Kyōka's childhood world.

By the final decades of the nineteenth century, the wooded heights of Utatsu invited a mix of the high and the low. Numerous temples and places of worship attracted parishioners, who in turn generated a market for straw sandals and raincoats, stick candy, and cups of tea. A flourishing commercial district sprang up along the roads that led to these places of worship, much like the approach to, say, the Kiyomizu Temple in Kyoto today. The north bank of the Asano even became a place for dalliance. The nearby Higashi no Kuruwa, or Eastern Brothel, added to the commercial and ebullient tone of the district. And, finally, beyond the temples and shops stretched the hinterland of lushly forested mountains and terraced valleys that Kyōka would evoke so magically as a space of loss and confusion, a sacred and threatening territory where the impossible becomes possible. Even in an age of "civilization and enlightenment," the stated agenda of the Meiji reformers, the mountains and their villages continued to be an inexhaustible watershed of folktales and legends from which Kyōka drew in Yeatsian fashion as he mixed past into present.

In short, the Asano is Kyōka's river because it suggests the parameters and vectors of the aesthetic that we hope to understand through this study of the author's life and writings. The flowing water naturally and narrowly separates a world of ordered domesticity from a world of erotic and religious mystery. Geographically speaking, the security of home was only a stone's throw from a contaminating yet holy world of pleasure, violence, and communion with nature. Water separates them and defines their difference. It is a barrier, but a barrier to be breached. Numerous bridges, these most candid structures of desire and convenience, overcome natural borders and allow movement from one world to the other. This crossing-over—this trespass into the world of the erotic, the dead, and the dispossessed—is what Kyōka's art is all about. The possibility of reunion with beloved ancestors dwelling on the other side is comforting. But because it is also a violation of the natural order and a breach of death's secrets, it is ghastly as well.

Father, Poverty, and an Image

A second context is provided by Kyōka's father. Izumi Seiji's house, in which Kyōka spent his childhood, no longer exists. The home had a mere six yards of frontage and was seventy-five square yards in area. A fire destroyed it in 1892, and only a granite monument and a wooden sign now mark its position near the main store of Morihachi, one of Kanazawa's many famous confectioners. The original address was 23 Banchi, Shimo-shinchō, Kanazawa City, Ishikawa Prefecture. Today, Shimo-shinchō, along with the riverbank geisha houses of Kazuemachi—the only ones on this, the more domesticated bank of the Asano—are included in Owari-chō. From the train station, it is only a few minutes by taxi.

Although this area was primarily an artisan neighborhood throughout the nineteenth century, it was located near the residences of the ruling class. Izumi Seiji was a carver of precious metals, an art that Maeda Toshitsune, third lord of the Kaga domain, had established in 1605 (Keichō 10), six years after the collapse of Toyotomi Hideyoshi's Board of Regents. Following the dissolution of this coalition, the Maeda, who had been allied with Hideyoshi since 1583, were successful in inducing many of the Kyoto- and Fushimi-based artisan families that had served Hideyoshi to relocate to the relative isolation of this snowbound province on Japan's northern coast. Along with weavers, dyers, lacquer artisans, carpenters, swordsmiths, painters, and ceramicists, metal crafters were also transplanted, bringing with them the elaborate Muromachi arts.

They flourished under the patronage of the Maeda clan, and the city became "renowned as a center of taste and fine craftsmanship, a reputation that the modern city maintains even today as the descendants of many of these same craftsmen preserve the family craft traditions."[3]

Because of its accomplishments, the city has also retained many aristocratic pretensions, making Kanazawa a place that Kyōka would ultimately come to dislike. To be the son of a Kanazawa artisan in the wake of the Meiji Restoration of 1868 was to have both pride in one's class and a certain amount of resentment toward the newly formed elite of late-modern (1868–1970) Japan.[4] Kyōka respected his father, whose shadow appears in stories such as "A Deaf Man's Single-mindedness" ("Tsunbo no isshin," 1895) and in the play *The Castle Tower* (*Tenshu monogatari*, 1917). Appearing in this play as the magic carpenter Tōroku, he has the power to make the blind see. A vignette set down by Kyōka's niece, Izumi Natsuki, presents a similarly lionized portrait.

One day, my grandfather was called to a wealthy man's home to repair the damaged eyes of a carved wooden bird. The story was that the very life of the figure depended on its eyes. Dressed in formal attire—a *haori* and *hakama*—he set out for the job with my father, Toyoharu, who carried his tools. The mansion was very large, and the figure of the bird was situated in a high place accessible only by ladder. Grandfather climbed up and, with a few deft taps of his chisel, recarved the bird's eyes. So it was that the bird came to life, or so I was told.[5]

An early photograph shows Kyōka, at age three, with his father (Fig. 1).

Despite, or perhaps because of, his reputation as one of the city's finest, Izumi Seiji found work hard to come by. Conditions were not favorable. The economic elite who had patronized craftsmen such as himself were weakened by the political upheaval of the Restoration. By the end of the nineteenth century, the fashioning of elaborate *sake* cups and hairpins was an art in decline, even though it enjoyed a brief revival during Izumi Seiji's lifetime. The lack of demand was exacerbated by Seiji's refusal to take just any job that came along. One Japanese scholar is of the opinion that the Izumi household was well off. His minority view is based on a scrap copied from Kyōka's mother's ledger that indicates she paid altogether too much for noodles to be truly poor.[6] Whatever the truth of this particular purchase, Kyōka would, in works such as "The Kunisada Prints" ("Kunisada egaku," 1910), choose to remember an impecunious and even poverty-stricken childhood. In this fictional return to his hometown, he described a struggling family forced to pawn a mother's cherished woodblock prints in order to pay for a son's textbooks. The pathetic force of

"The Kunisada Prints" reflects not only the author's unambiguous sympathies for those of limited means but also Japan's modern dilemma of having to relinquish the past in order to survive in the present.

To be sure, the intensity of Kyōka's empathy for the downtrodden owes much to his father's stubborn pride amid financial trouble. As a writer, Kyōka would align himself with *yin*—the poor, the female, the unempowered—in his antagonism for *yang*—the wealthy, the male, the empowered. Growing up in an artisan's home probably influenced Kyōka's traditionalism and singleness of purpose. Although he would eventually become financially solvent as a professional writer, he would not indulge in the mansion building of Tanizaki Jun'ichirō (1886–1965) or in the political fantasies of Mishima Yukio (1925–70). He was above all a steady craftsman of language, tending diligently to the work at hand. He followed the dictum that every writer pursue his own way, and that every drinker pay his own bill. As we will see, he was more than willing to be left alone in his pursuit of perfect craftsmanship, and his willingness to let others go their own way was not necessarily magnanimous.

His steady effort would produce some 300 stories, plays, essays, and travelogues. Along the way, his voice as a writer would undergo a number of significant modulations, allowing him to develop the idiosyncratic yet powerfully affecting worldview for which he is famous. Yet I will also argue that the bulk of his writing was largely a refinement, through repetition and variation, of a vision that came into focus as early as 1900 and, except for a brief hiatus, stayed with him with obsessive tenacity until his death in 1939. In light of such repetition, we might call Kyōka as much a practitioner of narrative craft as a destroyer of cliché. By this measure alone, perhaps he was not a typically modern Japanese novelist. Yet the artisan/artist dyad that has marked discussions of production in post-Meiji Japan is itself problematic, for it establishes a bias against the traditional and assumes a clear distinction between, for instance, the late-modern novel (*shōsetsu*) and early-modern (1600–1868) casual writings (*gesaku*). This distinction is not as straightforward as it might seem at first glance.

Indeed, Kyōka's life as writer challenges orthodox views on the inevitability of "modern literature" (*kindai bungaku*), the discovery of interiority, the emergence of the author as authority, and other accepted determinants of representational discourse. This is not to say that Kyōka was not modern. While conservative about his father's craftsmanship and even feudal in his subservient attitude toward his mentor Ozaki Kōyō (1868–1903), he was, at the same time, deeply committed to the modern project of self-expression and to the forging of a new language for fiction. For him, part of that expression happened to be unambiguously traditional. With his famous declaration, "How glad I am to owe nothing to Tolstoy!" Kyōka reveled in his resistance to the Europhilic mainstream, especially during the reign of naturalism. In an age as declaredly "progressive" as turn-of-the-century Japan, his decision to write in a highly figurative, lyrical manner meant spitting in the eye of Zola and kicking Dostoevsky in the shin.

In a concrete way, the poetic visuality of Kyōka's prose also owes much to his father. Izumi Seiji wanted young Kyōtarō (Kyōka's given name) to follow him in his trade as a metal craftsman, and he did what he could to guide his son's course. As an important first step, he provided Kyōka with sheets of tracing paper for the copying of sketchbook pictures—bamboo, orchids, and sparrows—standard images that would provide a template for his future work as a metal carver. Kyōka, who had already demonstrated a fascination with pictures, took to the tracing exercises with uncommon passion. Pleased to see him at work, his father checked what he was drawing, only to discover that his son was not replicating the well-ordered cosmos of sparrows and bamboo leaves but certain images he had found in his mother's personal library. According to his younger brother Toyoharu, Kyōka's favorite image to trace, one that he "reproduced again and again with the greatest fidelity," was "of a pathetic young woman, tied to a tree and beaten."[7]

Mother, Kusazōshi, Longing

Kyōka's life as a writer began with this act of tracing. Eventually the impulse to reaffirm the power of this and other images would lead him to produce verbal images that would reconfigure the world of his mother's illustrated texts. Although the intricate style of Kyōka's prose is reminiscent of Seiji's careful work, Kyōka's greater debt is to his mother, Nakata Suzu (1854–82). She provides a third context. Not only did she die young, leaving him to long for her his entire life, but she also allowed her son access to her library and thereby supplied him with the principal images for his literary imagination. Her library consisted mostly of *kusazōshi*, densely illustrated works of fiction that, because of their visual nature, were ostensibly written for women and children. These texts have an approximate analogue in the *gekiga* or more adult subgenres of contemporary *manga* (comic books)—often violent and monstrous and as much illustration as written text. Of his early exposure to them, Kyōka wrote,

My mother brought the books with her from Tokyo and kept them in a box made for storing dolls. Most of the collection was made up of *The Tale of Shiranui* (*Shiranui monogatari*), *The Eight Lives of Siddhartha, a Japanese Library* (*Shaka hassō, Yamato bunko*), and *Northern Snows, a Gorgeous Tale and Mirror of Our Times* (*Hokusetsu bidan jidai kagami*). She also had incomplete collections of other kusazōshi in ten or so volumes each. She took care of these books. But whenever I caught her looking the other way, they were mine! Not to read, though. I was only three or four at the time, and all I could do was lay the beautifully illustrated books out on the floor as if setting them out for a summer airing. This dashing samurai, that sad young woman. . . . As I kept looking at those pictures, I gradually became curious to know the stories behind them. I went to my mother, who was too busy with her sewing to answer my questions, and persisted until I finally got my way. Now that I look back on it, I must have been a nuisance. My poor mother. (28:653–54)[8]

As a writer in Tokyo, Kyōka would later make a point of collecting these and other works of kusazōshi, whose vivid images found an important place in his work. Just as their scenes of romance, mayhem, and transformation preceded the telling of the stories dwelling within, the foundations of the author's literary imagination, established by this process of *etoki* or explaining the pictures, required the visually oriented style of narration for which he became famous.

Kyōka's "poor mother" was the daughter of Nakata Toyoki, a Noh drummer of the Kadono school. Her grandfather, Nakata Mantarō, had been a Noh actor who performed under the direct patronage of the Maeda clan. Because of a long-held Tokugawa policy, the lords of Japan were required to maintain one residence in their own provincial castle towns and another in the capital. With the fall of the Tokugawa, the Maeda retreated from Edo to the relative safety of Kanazawa, leaving many of their associates behind to fend for themselves. Later, as Edo was being transformed into Tokyo, "the eastern capital," the Maeda felt sorry for the stranded and impoverished Nakata family and helped them relocate to Kanazawa.[9]

Kyōka would later write an imaginative re-creation of his mother's initial journey to Kanazawa. In "The Traveler's Cloak" ("Oizuru zōshi," 1898), he described "the beautiful Murasaki," a refugee from Edo, riding in a noble palanquin and accompanied by a number of family treasures: a Noh drum, a scroll of secret teachings, a mother-of-pearl screen, a pair of serving trays, and numerous volumes of kusazōshi. She is "murasaki," or purple, the color of royalty. Surrounded by these treasures, she resides in a properly worshipful context.

The exact date of Nakata Suzu's marriage to Izumi Seiji is unknown. But we think she was seventeen at the time. Her betrothal would have occurred in 1871, though her name does not appear on the Izumi family registry until the following year. Kyōka was born the year after that, on November 4, 1873, when his mother was nineteen. Her birth and rearing in Edo were appreciated by the Izumis. Izumi Natsuki remembered, "My great-grandmother, Kite, was extremely fond of her son's bride. Because Suzu was from Edo, she went to the trouble of searching for someone who knew how to set her daughter-in-law's coiffure properly. No one in Kanazawa was competent in the Edo style, but there was one woman who lived in a neighboring village. She had that woman called in."[10] Judging from this and other passages, the entire family shared Kyōka's worshipful view of his mother as a visitor from a more urbane place. Her being an *Edokko*, or child of Edo, by birth was important to the author, who would eventually leave Kanazawa for the capital, where he would make a career for himself. By going to Tokyo, was he not, in a sense, returning to his dead mother?

We frequently encounter shadows of Suzu in the stories and plays, but the details of her life largely escape us. After her marriage to Seiji, she lived long enough to bear four children. Kyōka was the oldest son. Taka, the oldest daughter, was born on August 3, 1877. Toyoharu, the second son, was born on January 31, 1880. And a second daughter, Yae, was born on December 3, 1882. Suzu died a few weeks after Yae's birth, on December 24, 1882, her life cut short at twenty-eight. Although puerperal fever is usually given as the explanation, the family records show that she died of smallpox.[11]

Kyōka was only nine at the time, and the loss of his mother haunted him throughout his lifetime. Perhaps in part, his writings flowed from the grief he felt. Setting words down on paper was one way to remember her—as a protector, as someone young and beautiful, as an alluring and even dangerous seductress. We will return to her importance again and again. But at this point it is enough to say that because she was remembered as an image of idealized womanhood, the boundaries of her identity were easily blurred with other constructions of female exemplars: Maya, mother of Śākyamuni; Kishibojin, the infanticidal mother who converted to Buddhism and mended her ways; the gallant sword-wielding daughter of Edo; Kannon, goddess of benevolence; and a number of other women whom he encountered in real life. This confusion of images suggests both the epistemological mode of Kyōka's worldview and the structure of his lyricism, based as they were upon a highly visual reconstruction of the past that served to soothe present fears by conflating many, even conflicting stereotypes into one untouchable figure. Layers of imagery are superimposed, so that we see one through the others.

One important key to understanding this quality of the remembered past, especially as Kyōka attempted to recover the halcyon days of his childhood prior to Nakata Suzu's death, is an essay entitled "Memories of Childhood" ("Osanai koro no kioku"). Here Kyōka explains a chance encounter with a woman who impressed him so profoundly that he was quite unable to forget her. He and his mother are riding in a vehicle, probably a boat, although it is not clear. A white light is pouring down all around them, as if reflected off water.

I am about five years old, still nursing from my mother's breasts. . . . I am sitting on her lap, fascinated by the movement of her lips as she talks with the people around us. . . .

Having drunken greedily from her breasts, I turn with innocent eyes to investigate the sounds that come to my ears and the strange sights that fill my eyes. Among those present is a beautiful young woman. My curiosity draws me to her, and I stare at this stranger without embarrassment or self-consciousness.

When I think back upon that day, I believe the woman must have been around seventeen years old, although I wouldn't have been able to tell at the time. She has a very pale complexion, and her eyebrows are two delicate arches. Her eyes, set off by double eyelids, are calm and clear. She has a long, oval face with well-defined features. Even now as I remember her, I believe she must have been a very beautiful woman. She is wearing a brightly patterned kimono, strange for a woman of seventeen. Why would she be wearing something so gaily colored? Maybe she is only twelve or thirteen, at the most fourteen or fifteen. At any rate, her brightly colored kimono leaves a strong impression. In autumn's weak light, the patterns dyed into the fabric of her sleeves seem to flicker like flames.

She is stunning, although her expression is sad. She seems preoccupied. Although the people around her are laughing and talking, she sits over in the corner, excluded from the group. She talks to no one. She stares out at the water and looks up at the sky, as if turning something over in her mind.

As I watch, a wave of inexpressible sorrow suddenly overcomes me. Why are the others shunning her? I couldn't understand it. Why doesn't someone talk to her?

I get off my mother's lap, walk straight ahead, and stand before this woman. I wait for her to speak to me. But she doesn't say a word. The older woman sitting next to her pats me on the head and even picks me up. I start crying and run back to my mother. Again in her arms, I keep glancing back. The young woman continues looking here and there, with the same dejected expression. What a thoroughly sad face! Eventually I fall asleep, and I do not know what happened after that.

For a long while I was unable to remember the incident. But then, when I was about twelve or thirteen, while I was playing with some friends outside on the same kind of fall evening, the scene came back to me.

Although I have never been able to determine what actually happened on that day, my memories of the light and the figure of that woman have presented themselves to me numerous times. Did I meet her in an earlier existence? Was it a dream I had as a young child? Was it a memory I had in connection with some event? I didn't know then, and I still don't know now. Perhaps it was a dream. Still, I feel as though I actually saw her. I believe the encounter actually happened because, even now, I can still clearly see that light and the way the woman looked, as if I were remembering something I had really seen.

Did I dream it? Did I experience it before I was born? Or did I really see it? If it is true that promises are made in the pre-existence and that karmic connections exist, then I feel as though I was born with some indestructible connection with that woman.

When I go for walks, I occasionally see someone with the same face or the same figure, and my heart begins to race. If I did see the woman, then I feel as though I'll someday see her again—perhaps in ten years, or maybe twenty. (29: 170–74)

As is usually the case, Kyōka remembered this mysterious woman in connection with his mother. Just as Nakata Suzu was his access to the fanciful world of kusazōshi, so was she his means to this unforgettable yet unidentified woman—beautiful, sad, and unwanted. We know that he actually did seek such woman, the geisha that he married. Ultimately, her image was conflated with that of his mother, and it became difficult for him to separate one from the other, protector from temptress. As a rule, Kyōka recalled all women according to aesthetic need, in much the same way as he apprehended and traced the pathetic young beauty, beaten and tied to a tree. There was beauty in the violence done to the one who suffered.

For obvious reasons, the image of his mother, this woman whom he deeply loved, is especially rarified. She does not exist outside poetry, not even in the autobiographical record. In the second of the two autochronologies that Kyōka wrote, we encounter the color purple (*murasaki*) again, in an elliptical account of her death.[12]

April 1880. I have mother explain the stories illustrated in her books of kusazōshi. I learn folklore and legends from the beautiful young women in my neighborhood. December, 1883. Mother. At twenty-nine.

June, 1884. I am taken by father to worship Maya. Along the path, flowers blossom in sympathy, and the lake reflects lavender woods. My longing for my dead mother grows deeper. (1:iii)

The temple alluded to here is the Kōzenji in Matto, where an icon of Maya still stands. It is a powerful image, draped in purple curtains, peering out on its beholders with glassy eyes set inside narrowly carved openings in its pale, smooth face. Writing in 1911, twenty-seven years after his trip to the temple, Kyōka described the visit in more detail. With the added delineation, the distinction between Maya and mother becomes more confused and ambiguous.

I fall to my knees. To my boyish eyes the statue seems to flow toward the ceiling. Maya's hair is a lustrously shining star. I look up. My devotion goes to her—her undulating brows and finely drawn lips, the dewy expression of her eyes. Her jeweled vestments are set off against the whiteness of her bosom as she calmly signals me to approach. Noble, gentle, awesome, wondrously beautiful, her figure is constantly before my eyes. (28: 476)

As we will see, Kyōka would become involved with several other women in his lifetime. Yet it is fair to say that the ones he loved most deeply reminded him of his mother.

The Japanese term for this emotional pattern is *hahagoi*. Mother (*haha*) longing (*koi*) is not uncommon in the literary imagination. Within the narrative tradition, statements of yearning are numerous. Works as early as the eleventh-century *Tale of Genji* establish the pattern. The great lover Hikaru Genji is irrepressibly attracted to women who remind him of his mother, especially Fujitsubo and Murasaki. Nearly a thousand years later, Tanizaki Jun'ichirō's "As I Crossed the Bridge of Dreams" ("Yume no ukihashi") describes a bewildered yet insistent Tadasu suckling his stepmother's breasts. A story like Kyōka's "Seishin's Nunnery" ("Seishin an," 1897), then, falls between these two poles, one ancient and one more recent. In Kyōka's case, his earliest textual access to this paradigm was probably Mantei Ōga's (1818–90) *The Eight Lives of Siddhartha, a Japanese Library*, one of the kusazōshi titles mentioned in his remembrance of his mother's library. Book 3, which Kyōka later purchased for his own private library, includes a scene in which young Siddhartha, while praying before a Buddhist altar, intuits that the woman for whom he is praying is his dead mother. Kyōka was too young to read the text, of course. But it is likely that he saw this image. Perhaps it was one of those he begged his mother to explain (see Fig. 2).

The Late Modern

Kyōka's personal clarification of such images did not come until many years later, not until he became more aware of what he wanted them to accomplish. But the foundation of his visually rich style was already being laid at this early, preliterate stage. Long before he could read and write, he was already absorbed in the decoding of a rhetorical tradition made available to him through pictorial images, especially those found in illustrated fiction. In fact, he became so profoundly affected by their power and method of signification that he later refused to rid himself of this influence despite the antifigural nature of the discourse that came to dominate Japan's late-modern culture. The trend toward increasingly sound-oriented forms of writing had begun as early as the seventeenth century with the publishing of *kanazōshi*, books that used the Japanese phonetic syllabary *hiragana* for the writing of a more colloquial, less classical idiom. Throughout the Tokugawa period, this strengthening phonocentric impulse was constantly contested by an opposing force. Some memorable instances of the pictocentric resistance were, for instance, the rejection of movable-type printing in the seventeenth century and the flourishing of illustrated books in the eighteenth. As the re-acceptance of the printing press and the rapid development of typographic culture in the late nineteenth century show, however, the gradual dominance of the phonocentric over the pictocentric was already reaching its peak by the time Kyōka began his career as a writer. This semiotic disposition to distance language from figurality, whether illustrations on a page or classical figures of speech, was, then, a fourth context within which Kyōka's works must be considered.[13]

While Kyōka was still a young boy reveling in images of "this dashing samurai" and "that sad young woman," the beginnings of a widespread literary reform that championed an increasingly un-illustrated literary mode were already under way in Tokyo. Generally speaking, the movement to modernize Japanese letters had three main concerns. The first was to reconfigure the sphere of the knowable, as both expanded and restricted by empirical science and other comprehensive ideological systems. As supported by the transcriptive (rather than originary) function of phonetic script and the Cartesian matrix of the typeset page, a higher (invisible) realm of thought took form around the notion that truth is systematic and universal. Thus, the typically conceited attitude of modernity as an improvement over the past led to exclusive, absolute systems rather than inclusive, relative ones. This result came about partly because the expressive function of language was no longer tied to the ambiguity (and figurality) of the material sign, which was held to be primitive. Supposedly unambiguous and comprehensive in nature, modern ideologies necessarily competed against each other for dominance, making one system of knowledge incompatible with others so that, for example, the nations and empires that coalesced around certain first principles of human nature came into conflict as they tried to invalidate each other. Just as modern Japan tried to find itself as a national entity within a threatening world of competing empires, so, too, did Japanese authors try to find themselves literarily within the same context of aggression.[14]

The second concern of the movement to modernize writing was to increase the accessibility and transmission of the knowledge being generated by these comprehensive ideological systems. Modern journalism and such democratizing initiatives as the People's Rights Movement required a simpler form of discourse, one closer to everyday speech. The use of phonetic glosses (*furigana*) to supply readings for Chinese characters (*kanji*) was one adjustment. The simplification and reduced use of *kanji* was another. The more extensive employment of the two Japanese syllabaries, *hiragana* and *katakana*, along with the attempt to transcribe the sounds of Japanese with an alphabetic script (*rōmaji*) were still others. Such adjustments in the semiotic field were made in order to establish a society of readers and to propagate a typographic culture in which the speedy dissemination of new information, whether in the form of the newspaper or the novel, could become available for mass consumption.

The wide scope of these two concerns forced a third. Stimulated by Cartesian perspectivalism and its concern for analysis, closure, and a renewed appreciation for the complexity of human character, Meiji writers attempted to formulate a rhetoric of plausibility. Much more was at stake than ever before because an expanded knowledge of the world outside Japan required solutions to human problems to be universal in their validity and general in their application. Thus, the historical moment of Kyōka's beginnings as a writer coincided with the rise of the author as authority. He (and occasionally she) was to be a towering figure who knew more about how the world worked than non-writers. He was to be one who could persuade the general reader of the truthfulness of his analysis, the one who could assume a stable and even omniscient stance while narrating the world. Both politically and artistically, the *sakka*, or maker, was to supplant the *gesakusha*, or scribbler, whose lack of authority had been ensured by what became an outdated Confucian disdain for "small talk" (*shō-*

setsu).[15] To engage the quotidian reality in the first decades of the twentieth century was to embark upon serious intellectual pursuit.

Given this conception of the author's function, Kyōka is usually seen as a minor figure who wrote surprisingly well. He has not been granted the stature of Natsume Sōseki (1867–1916), Mori Ōgai (1862–1922), or Shimazaki Tōson (1872–1943), because he does not fit as neatly as others into the conventional story of Japan's modernization—where *modern* and *Western* are conflated and Japan's progress is thought to be dramatically swift rather than the result of many centuries of steady development. Rather than attempt to find a respectable role for Kyōka in what has been the standard interpretation of Japan's modern period, we are better off searching for an alternative story in which he fits more naturally. In order to do this, however, we will have to expand the ways in which literary and artistic reform during the late-modern period is presented. Contrary to the tendency to locate a single main line of development—the dominance of naturalism, the centrality of the I-novel (*shishōsetsu*), the marginality of women and ethnic writers, and so forth—there are certainly other stories to be told here.

Because of the biographical focus of this work, the larger, theoretical issues will emerge from the details in the way that thoughts of meaning arise chaotically and unexpectedly from the movement of the body, even when circumscribed and guided by ideology—whether stared or mute, revealed or hidden. Certainly, an alternative theory of the modern that comes incidentally (and maybe even accidentally) from an examination of Kyōka's life tempts us to pursue many questions. For now, however, it is enough to say that the Meiji-period program to reform "modern Japanese literature" was an immensely ambitious undertaking that called not only for new, increasingly discursive and descriptive narrative patterns but also for, in the way of colonial prologue, a jettisoning of traditional iconography.

This is a crucial point for understanding Kyōka's work and its reception during his lifetime. Again, the dominant literary discourse in late-modern Japan was antifigural. It made no difference whether the offending figurality came in the form of classical figures of speech or lines drawn on the page. The new episteme of realism emphasized a mode of seeing that made both forms of figurality untenable as aspects of literature. It presupposed an invisible; thinking self and an accurately observable exterior, connected by the transparent tool of language, which, in its most advanced form, was nothing more than the phonetic transcription of thought. By the time Kyōka published his first story in 1892, the reform movement, coupled with the technology of movable type, had already all but destroyed the traditional symbiosis of word and image that had been the defining feature of the early-modern tradition. The lavish pictures of kusazōshi were funneled away from fiction and into the realm of nonfiction, where they served an emergent journalism with its heightened reportorial function. Illustration in the Japanese *shōsetsu* became limited to occasional pictures of centrally dramatic moments, as the newly streamlined and more transcriptive language of fiction tried to establish forms of narration in which description and psychological analysis seemed natural or, at least, naturalized.

How modern Japanese writers set about accomplishing this task is one of the most fruitful questions to ask of writing during Kyōka's era, for it immediately brings to our attention the many semiotic configurations by which meaning is established and understood. At a time when various rhetorical traditions were interacting intensely with each other, the resulting confusion generated a plethora of options, including photography and film. Yet it is also true that this multiplicity tends to be obscured by the perspective that attempts to locate a mainstream of literary realism that follows from an agenda established by Tsubouchi Shōyō's (1859–1935) essay "On the Essence of the Novel" ("Shōsetsu shinzui," 1885) and includes the naturalist movement and subsequent reactions to it.

To the extent that we exist in the wake of this critical tradition, it is difficult to stand outside any critique we might launch of Eurocentrism. Even those who have dared to place "modern Japanese literature" within quotation marks affirm the subject of critique by challenging its premises without providing a new discursive framework that would illuminate what the source of newness (or real departure from modern Western narrative patterns) was. Karatani Kōjin's influential and often brilliant *Origins of Modern Japanese Literature* (*Nihon kindai bungaku no kigen*), for instance, is a revisionist attempt to frame the modern that stays within familiar parameters of Western critical discourse. Although admirably clear in its application of phenomenological concepts—subject/object, interior/exterior, and so forth—its lack of rupture is made obvious by Fredric Jameson's preface to the work, in which he reads the Japanese example as a reflection and condensation of an essentially Western condition. The circularity of such a reading is obvious, following from a cataclysmic, linear view of Japanese history that is focused, once again, on the spread of Western influence.

Like Karatani's understanding of Meiji Japan, Jameson's could be strengthened by greater familiarity with the details of Edo culture, where earlier manifestations of modernity—the development of self-awareness, the discovery of landscape, the beginnings of perspectivalism, a shift toward phonocentric discourse, and so forth—are found.[16] As Karatani himself has argued, the great gulf that supposedly separates the Meiji period from the Edo period is an illusion, an aggressive erasure of the past that flows from modernity's conception of itself as an improvement and as a manifestation of progress. To be sure, maintaining distance from a feudal past was an endeavor shared by many of Kyōka's contemporaries. As many have noted, however, the practical problem with this break in time is that the erasure cannot last. Because the modern cannot really thrive without in some way heightening its traditional Other, sooner or later, the plausibility of progress is weakened, continuities are restored, and we come to a compelling reason for caring about an author like Kyōka, who was relegated to a place outside the mainstream yet was an artist of undeniable authenticity and accomplishment. Whether or not we are prepared to appreciate the eccentricity of his vision, we cannot help but wonder what *he* considered to be his own source of inspiration. To this end, a consideration of his life and works will, I hope, coalesce as one of many possible ways to ease the antipathy that has kept early modern (*kinsei*) and late modern (*kindai*) apart.

Kyōka is an important bridge not only to the past but also to the contemporary worlds of *manga*, or Japanese comics, and *anime*, or animation. During his own day, his writing would be criticized by the critic and playwright Osanai Kaoru (1881–1925) as "nothing but kusazōshi."[17] Undaunted by this criticism, Kyōka would hammer out his own compromise with the aggressively phonocentric agenda of the Enlightenment and its aftermath. As we will see, he would do this first by imbuing early-modern images with a personal, romantic intensity and second by seeking the banished visuality of the *gesaku* tradition in the body of language itself. Whereas the realists sought accuracy of description and plausibility of plot, Kyōka would, by *seeming* traditional in method and substance, anticipate the modern*ist* experiments of the neo-perceptionists, such as Yokomitsu Riichi (1898–1947) and Kawabata Yasunari (1899–1972). Like them, he would try to squeeze new poetry out of old words. For this reason, we will not be able to understand the real contribution of Kyōka's work unless we comprehend the material, graphic nature of language and the episteme of picture-centered writing as it continued to compromise a centuries-old trend toward realism and textual authority.[18]

CHAPTER 2

The Desire to Write

1883–1889

Loss, Childhood

The stability of Kyōka's childhood was shaken by loss—not only of his mother but also of his sisters. When Nakata Suzu died in 1883, both sisters were given away. The baby, Yae, was adopted by Miyazaki Sukijirō as his oldest daughter. He gave her a new birthdate of February 3, 1883. Taka, who was five, was transferred to the family registry of Kotake Yosuke, owner of a teahouse on the far bank of the Asano River, near Mt. Utatsu. The date of the transaction was March 29, 1886, though she probably left the Izumi household soon after the funeral.[1]

This draconian halving of family numbers seems to have been a matter of exigency. As mentioned above, Izumi Seiji was temperamental and a perfectionist, refusing to work unless conditions were exactly right. According to Kyōka's schoolmate Hosono Nobukazu, "Not much work came his way, and so the Izumis were very poor."[2] Izumi Seiji's transferal of Taka and Yae to other families may seem coldhearted, but it was hardly without precedent. Young girls were expendable, often sold or contracted out to men like Hosono who dealt in the pleasure trade. Boys, too, were sent away, although more often to become adopted heirs of the new families into which they were absorbed. Needless to say, the prospects of an adopted son were far more promising. Yae was fortunate enough to be sent to a home where she had caring parents. She made occasional visits to see her father and two brothers, who ate the sweet cakes her new mother had baked for them. But Taka, who grew up training to work as a geisha, would have an unfortunate life. She would plague Kyōka with her miseries, sorely testing his patience and pushing him to the end of his generosity.

Robbed of his sisters' company, young Kyōka witnessed his father's second marriage on December 27, 1884, about one year after his mother's death. He did not mention the occasion in either chronology. What we know about Seiji's second wife is largely hearsay, and none of it flattering. Her name was Saku, the daughter of Miyano Sasuke of Kanazawa-ku, Kanaya-machi 23 Banchi. Born in 1846, she was seven years older than Suzu. Kyōka's younger brother Toyoharu is said to have described her as "an outwardly gentle person, who caused no direct confrontations. But she seduced the younger brother and was finally kicked out."[3] Seiji erased her name from the Izumi family register a year after it was added.[4]

Kyōka, who remained silent on this topic, characterized himself as "weak-legged but of hearty appetite." Because of his mother's death, he was bereaved but not without female support. His paternal grandmother, Meboso Kite, assumed the role of principal caretaker and exerted a profound effect upon his development. Among other things, she inculcated in him a habit of extreme fastidiousness. She kept the two boys—Kyōtarō and Toyoharu—clean and well-fed, and their clothes starched and ironed. To protect them from harm, she made each a talisman, a necklace fashioned from their dead mother's hair ribbons. She was, as Kyōka would become, a devout Buddhist. A woman of great faith, she not only trusted in a dead mother's magic but also in Kyōka's ability to become a writer. At first, in a reflection of the Confucian bias against fiction, she resisted the idea of his becoming a professional writer. But eventually she encouraged him to leave Kanazawa in order to make a name for himself in Tokyo, even though his absence would be a burden for her and the family. She wished above all for Kyōka's success. No doubt, she had the same faith in Toyoharu, who also had artistic aspirations but did not reward her belief with equally impressive results. In a photograph, she appears as one dissolving into time (Fig. 3).

Besides Meboso Kite, other women helped fill the void left by Suzu's death. They were certainly no more influential than Kyōka's grandmother, although they are more often discussed. One was Kyōka's cousin, Meboso Teru. A few years younger than Kyōka, she lived nearby and often played at the Izumi residence. Her family owned a well-established business in Kanazawa. As they still do today, the Mebosos manufactured and sold needles, pins, and fishing hooks. Teru, who saw herself as a sort of guardian angel for Kyōka, was particularly helpful to the Izumi family after Seiji's sudden death in 1894. She provided moral support, and some say that she dissuaded Kyōka from committing suicide during the turbulent months that followed. Later, Kyōka would rely on Teru as his most dependable and valued friend in Kanazawa. As such, she was an important point of contact with a past that was not always pleasant for him to remember. Determined and noble, she was, in Kyōka's eyes, like the kusa-zōshi heroine Shiranui, a woman warrior and an archetype for the resourceful female who appears so frequently in his work. More specifically, she is the model for such characters as Okyō in "The Spider's Web" ("Sasagani," 1897) and Okō in *Women of Acquaintance* (*Yukari no onna*, 1919). For a photograph, see Fig. 4.

The second of these "women of acquaintance" was Yuasa Shige, daughter of a watchmaker whose shop in Shinchō was just a dash away from Izumi Seiji's residence. As a young boy, Kyōka fell in love with Shige. But then, at the age of sixteen, she was married to Fujitani Tomokichi, a descendant of Kitani Fujizaemon, a Kanazawa merchant of fabulous wealth. What was once the Fujitanis' walled estate is still situated on the banks of the Asano, not far from where Kyōka's modest home once stood. As Fujitani's second wife, Shige bore two children and was then divorced. Kyōka's image of her—a beautiful woman in her late twenties, exploited and unappreciated by men of wealth and power—would become another important nexus in his imagination. Specifically, she became the model for Ohide in *The Maki Cycle*—a series of short stories that includes "Book One" ("Ichi no maki"), "Book Two" ("Ni no maki"), up to the final installment, "The Book of Oaths" ("Chikai no maki," 1896–97). She is also the inspiration for Oyuki in *Teriha Kyōgen*, and Oyō in *Women of Acquaintance*. Her photograph reveals the sort of person we might find in Kaburagi Kiyokata's illustrations of Kyōka's stories (Fig. 5). As was the case with other women, Kyōka superimposed her image over that of his mother, thus obscuring the boundaries of love and incest in order to allow for the fullest possible sublimation of sexual desire.

No wonder, then, that Shige herself denied her role as a model for Kyōka's creations. She claimed to be unaware of his literary depictions of her. At the same time, she was more than willing to name yet another beautiful young woman who was a sixth model for Kyōka's lifelong attempt to construct a feminine ideal. Her name was Francina Porter, and she was a missionary from Tennessee.

Red and White

Kyōka studied English with Francina Porter for three and a half years, from 1884 to 1887. The earlier of the two chronologies mentions her, under the year 1884, when Kyōka was eleven years old. His mother had been dead for approximately one year.

> I enter Kanazawa Upper Primary School. Within one year, I transfer to the Hokuriku Eiwa Gakkō [an English-Japanese school], run by Americans and affiliated with the United Church. Although I get a perfect score on the entrance examination, I present a problem since I am still small enough to ride upon the palms of the corpulent ones who taught there. Granted special permission, I matriculate. My classmates are all about twenty years old. One is already married and has his own family.
>
> Headmaster Porter is a tall man with a red beard. His wife and the daughter are in charge of instruction. The daughter, eighteen or nineteen years old, is extremely neat in appearance. Schoolmaster Winn is plump and has black hair. (29: 717–18)

There are many errors in this account. Not only did Kyōka miscalculate the woman's age by about five years—Francina was twenty-five at the time; he got it right in "Book Five" ("Go no maki")—but he also misrepresented her relationship to the headmaster, who was Miss Porter's brother rather than her father.[5]

Born in Riceville, Tennessee, in 1859, Francina Porter arrived in Kanazawa with her older brother Z. B. Porter and S. K. Cummings, who would marry Z. B. the following year, on November 3, 1883. The three of them came to Kanazawa to teach English and to spread Presbyterianism in an area of Japan where proselytizing had begun only five years earlier (through the efforts of the plump, dark-haired Thomas Winn). Francina, "very young, very beautiful, gentle and good,"[6] is reported to have arrived in Kanazawa thinking that she "had come to the end of the world."[7] As Kyōka would later rephrase the emotion in "A Chronicle of a Famous Princess" ("Meienki," 1900), "She sacrificed herself for her faith, crossing the seven seas to come to Japan and to this obscure part of the country" (5: 411–12). Francina came, in fact, to Kyōka's very neighborhood in Shimo-shinchō. He probably met her soon thereafter. Early the next year, the Porters moved their school a few blocks away, to Tono-machi. By the fall of 1884, Kyōka had quit the school he had been attending,

Yosei Elementary in Higashi no Baba, and was given, as he says, special permission to enroll in the Eiwa Gakkō.

It is impossible to know why Kyōka transferred from Yosei Elementary, where he had been enrolled since April 1880, to the Porters' newly established school. The move might have had something to do with his success as a young student. Since he was doing exceptionally well, he was allowed to sit at the back of the room, as was then the custom. But because of his acute nearsightedness, the farther back he sat, the harder it was for him to see the blackboard. Rather than say anything about this handicap, he tried to compensate by memorizing every word his teachers spoke, thus further enhancing his reputation as a good student. According to Yuasa Shige, Kyōka's natural gift for learning English won both Miss Porter's favor and the persecution of his classmates. The more Kyōka was mistreated, the more openly Miss Porter showed her affection.[8]

There were two more likely reasons for changing schools, however. One was poverty. Because the Porters' school served larger evangelical ends, they encouraged education for everyone by charging nothing. Izumi Seiji, struggling to come up with tuition of any sort, had at least this motivation to send his son to the English school. And then there was Kyōka's obvious fascination with this pale, angelic woman who had suddenly appeared to brighten his death-saddened world. In a city where foreigners still required the protection of bodyguards whenever they walked in the streets, she must have been a bold and unforgettable presence. He was most likely drawn to her for reasons other than any particulars of Christian soteriology, although, as we will see, the possible influence of a Christian sense of blood sacrifice on Kyōka's romantic formulation is considerable. We can imagine that he pursued her because she, like many women he loved, reminded him of his dead mother. She was a woman beyond his grasp, both physically and intellectually.

Fictional reconstructions of Francina Porter appeared in three works: the previously mentioned Maki cycle of stories, "A Chronicle of a Beautiful Princess" ("Meienki," 1900), and "A Throw of the Dice" ("Machi sugoroku," 1917). I mention them here, out of chronological order, to emphasize Kyōka's sense of loss and to point out how this emotion fueled the melding of various identities that represented a flat rejection of the integrity of human, inner character that was emerging in the writings of many of his contemporaries. In the first of these formulations, Kyōka discounted but did not deny Miss Porter's exotic qualities: "When one talks about Westerners, one probably thinks of frizzy hair, coarse as hemp, someone tall with a pointed nose and eyes as round as chestnuts. . . . But when she smiles, it's as if a beautiful Buddha has come to earth to bestow his grace" (2: 431). Indeed, the character called Lyrica in "Chronicle of a Beautiful Princess" is, very consistently, all these things once again. She is tall. She has big eyes and a large nose (see Fig. 6). Despite her foreign features, however, she is noble and beautiful. In the end, most physical characteristics simply did not seem to matter, for the qualities developed in a sustained fashion in all three works are precisely those that tie this woman from Tennessee to the author's remembered image of Nakata Suzu.

Here in the concluding scene of the Maki cycle, the character that has been identified as Milliard suddenly becomes "mother": "As I gazed upon her profile sunken into the pillow—so pitiful, precious, beautiful, noble, a pure rose mallow petal vanishing away in the smoke of burning incense—I felt as if I could see the face of my dead mother. 'Mother!' I cried out, and collapsed at the foot of Milliard's bed, clinging to her breast, sobbing like a child" (2: 482).

In this curious passage, Milliard becomes perfectly replaceable with the narrator's mother. Kyōka even claimed to have another woman in mind when he wrote this scene: Higuchi Ichiyō (1872–96), the famous woman novelist. The images of three women overlap to establish an ideal. Admittedly, each possesses definite, distinguishing characteristics. Yet they are important only to the extent that they share the one quality that qualifies them all as signifiers of an ideal. Young and fair, Francina Porter—presented as Milliard, as Lyrica, and as Benten in "A Throw of the Dice"—is attractive to Kyōka because she is white. Being a white woman (or perhaps we should say being white and a woman), she is pure in an untainted manner. But she is also a confusing being because, while suggesting cleanliness and a lack of defilement, white is also the seductive surface that invites, by virtue of its beauty, the contrast of blood. It is also the color of a corpse and of Japan's death candles. Kyōka's women, associated with the world of the steadily flowing waters of the Asano River, are transcendent yet vulnerable. Both white *and* red, they, like the river, are comforting yet ghastly.

What such women clearly are *not* are characters in the familiar, late-modern, sense of the word. Rather than possessing psychologically differentiated, individual identities, they are more accurately understood as permutations of certain types, which often have unmistakable precedents in "traditional" figures. In his desire to create a feminine ideal, Kyōka would end up giving a personal and even romantic spin to the well-worn *onryō* (vengeful spirit) trope of Edo-period texts. He made his ghosts creatures of an unassailably higher realm, however. They are beings who are victimized not because of political intrigue but because of their irresistible beauty and goodness. Lyrica is "of a beauty quite beyond the human" (5: 417). By the time of Francina's 1917 transformation in "A Throw of the Dice," the apotheosis is complete. She is remembered into this story as Benten, the Japanese goddess of beauty, love, and the arts. Her existence is fully symbolic, stripped of its unessential particulars—among them her foreignness. "Yes, it's strange to be calling a Western woman 'Benten.' But the way she looked, there by the stone wall at the Bishamon Shrine. . . . She jumped on her horse and rode off as though riding upon the clouds. What's more, her horse was white" (17: 140).

As was the case with Meboso Teru and Yuasa Shige, Kyōka's apotheosis of Francina Porter was prefigured by the trauma of losing his mother and sisters. The friendship of these young women seemed to help Kyōka gain emotional equilibrium, although his placement of the beautiful just beyond reach was a necessary torture. It was a reluctant admission of a taboo, since the construction of the ideally feminine was not free of sexual desire even though the ideal was, in part, maternal. To be sure, without lust (as an interplay between desire and guilt), Kyōka's reconstruction of his dead mother would never have attained such religious intensity. The escalating degree of this passion for union explains why, for instance, we encounter other permutations that are overtly worshipful. Besides Benten he frequently mentions Maya, the mother of Śākyamuni; the benevolent Kannon; and Kishibo, the child-killing mother turned guardian of children. In Kyōka's mind these images came together in a sublime confusion.

This melding of the base and the ethereal manifests itself variously: a worshipping of women, a denial of female sexuality, a sadistic and bloody sacrificing of women to make them better than death. It is also a condemnation of the ugliness and depravity of men and, frequently, a complicated and troubled erotic compulsion that can neither be satisfied nor denied. No wonder, then, that Satomi Ton, one of Kyōka's closest friends, was utterly confused about Kyōka's true feelings toward women. "Did he love women or did he hate them? Someone please tell me which! I offer my own confusion as a key to unlock the puzzle of this man Izumi Kyōka."[9]

No doubt, the image of the beaten woman that Kyōka meticulously and obsessively traced led him to balance the womanly whiteness of purity and beauty with various hues of violence. The difficulty for the reader arises when violence (or its possibility) is presented as both good and bad, as both necessary and regrettable. In this passage from "Book Six," the whiteness of Francina Porter is dressed and naturalized by the crepe garment she wears. In this case, red is covertly violent.

I could see a flash of crimson in the flickering lantern light. There she was before me, a graceful figure dressed in nothing but a scarlet crepe undergarment. It was tied loosely beneath her bosom. Her sash trailed down. Her hand was bared, pure white and carrying the candle, her arm showing through her unsown sleeve like snow, white and radiant against the scarlet, as if on fire. I was struck by the unearthly beauty of that slender figure. I stood speechless, staring.

The crimson figure turned away and hid her face in her sleeve, tilting her head as if to peer at me, standing very still. Perhaps she was amused by the expression of surprise on my face. I heard a stifled peal of laughter and, more quickly than an extinguishing breath upon a flame, she set the candle down, turned, and fled into the interior of the house. It was her I saw, the beautiful foreign one. (2: 451–52)

Whether a thin trickle of blood trailing from the point of decapitation or a tastefully worn crimson undergarment, the *iro*, or hue, of violence and sexuality—red and crimson—are complementary to white. The tie is deeply rooted in the Japanese tradition, finding its physical locus in the erotic nape of a woman's neck. Whether exposed in the act of love or in bowing, the pale skin there signals an offering, a vulnerability. Aware of both his sympathy for the suffering of women and his need for it, Kyōka himself would come to the belief that the possibility of violence begets erotic attraction. It would take many years of iteration and exploration before he understood the matching of these colors well enough to write something sufficiently subtle to draw the reader to this vivid perversity. But ultimately he would succeed, showing us the ways in which decadence can become a form of insight.

The Power of English

It would be tempting, for purely narrative purposes, to cast Kyōka as a maverick, an anti-modern writer in a modern age. As an adult, he himself attempted to cultivate just such an image. We know, however, that as a boy he was far from resistant to the cultural field of phonocentric writing that was inexorably overtaking Japanese letters. As mentioned above, he was an eager student of English, the *lingua franca* of the late-modern world, an alphabetic and therefore more rational writing system than the more graphically oriented Japanese. Shige reported that as soon as school was over, Kyōka went home and gave English lessons to her older brother and to a few others. "Everybody called him

Taikō-san."[10] Taikō, a nickname for the sixteenth-century hegemon Toyotomi Hideyoshi, hardly seems appropriate for a weak-legged boy. Yet the sobriquet is apt because it suggests someone who is capable, and, beyond this, shares Hideyoshi's penchant for things foreign.

Kyōka's course of study under Francina Porter began with the popular *Willson's First Reader*, an illustrated primer that made the most of short declarative sentences and easy questions. Chapter 1 appropriately begins with an introduction to the alphabet: A is for ape and ant: "The ape and the ant. The ape has hands. The ant has legs. Can the ant run?"[11] In the illustration accompanying these four short sentences, both creatures share a setting of grass and rocks. The ape stands with knuckles scraping the ground, looking over one shoulder. The ant occupies the foreground. The lesson seems simple, yet many Japanese students had trouble discerning the connection between text and illustration. For one thing, the ape and ant are placed much too far apart for what the English seems to be saying. In Japanese, having a hand, *te o motsu* (as in "the ape has hands") signified *holding* a hand rather than *possessing* one. Thus, the ape should be holding (*motsu*) the ant's hand, and the ant should be grabbing the ape's leg, both creatures engaged in a tussle rather than regarding each other from a distance.

Kyōka may have had a good enough feel for foreign words to be spared this confusion about "The ape has hands." But either at this point or another in the textbook, he could not have helped but notice the differences between the language he knew and the one he was acquiring. In this particular case, the gap was bridged by creating a neologism such as *shoyū suru*, to have, to possess. But other problems were harder to solve. Influenced by English and by translations of Western literature that began to appear in the last few decades of the nineteenth century, the written Japanese language was gaining not only a vast, new vocabulary but also an increasingly discursive and descriptive force. In a few years, Kyōka would join other Meiji writers in fashioning his own version of the new forms of language that would make the birth of literature (*bungaku*) possible. Inspired by the study of English and other Western languages, the movement to reform language along alphabetic lines was too all encompassing to allow Kyōka to escape it.

Under Francina Porter's guidance, Kyōka mastered bat and boy, cow and cat. We can imagine his difficulty in getting past the D lesson: "See the big dog with the ring on his neck! What a good face he has! He is not a bad dog. He is kind and good." The thrust of this passage must have been wasted on Kyōka, who is said to have witnessed a man get killed by a dog in the streets of Kanazawa and was fearful of them all his life. He would try to depict a canine, "kind and good," in his first published work, *Crowned Yazaemon* (*Kanmuri Yazaemon*, 1892), a work possibly influenced by Takizawa Bakin's (1767–1848) highly metaphorical *Tales of the Canine Eight* (*Nanso satomi hakkenden*, 1814–42). But he would never overcome his personal dread of these animals. As an older man, he would carry a cane with him on walks. He considered having a maid or even his wife walk with him for protection and was ready to sacrifice them to an attacking animal. But this strategy was socially awkward, since being seen too often in public with one's wife or with a maid was gauche. Thus, the cane.

Dogs were only one item in a long list of natural objects and phenomena toward which Kyōka demonstrated extraordinary fear. Thunder, mice, bacteria, were others. Kyōka's phobias were fears in the dual senses of both horror and reverence. His emotional precariousness was reinforced by an ambivalent wish both to deny and to affirm the supernatural powers that he sensed all around him, whether saving or damning. Were this feeling more one-dimensional—simply terror or simply awe—no mystery would have emerged. There would be no tension. And he would be just another gothic mind or just another inspirational writer. The conflicted nature of his vision, however, guaranteed that the symbols of his imagination would have complication and depth, that elegance would include the grotesque, and that the beautiful would also be ugly. Ultimately, his sincere and unmediated response to nature would generate the powerful lyrical force of his writing. At this point, of course, he was still far from a fullness of these emotions. In the years ahead, horror and reverence would, like his prose style, develop sophistication.

To return to English, the rigorous curriculum of the day led to *Parley's Universal History, On the Basis of Geography*. Its author, Peter Parley, was Samuel Griswole Goodrich, who was said to be none other than Nathaniel Hawthorne (1804–64).[12] A standard of English pedagogy until the Taishō period (1912–25), the work presents 718 pages of fairly complicated and clearly written prose, the mastery of which, according to the mid-twentieth-century Japanese scholar Yanagida Izumi, qualified one to teach English at the middle-school level. In need of money, Kyōka would later try to teach English, though only for a brief period.[13]

To some extent, the acquisition of English must also have also required a mastery of concepts. This massive reader was one among many competing attempts to set the nations of the modern world in proper order. Fukuzawa

Yūkichi's *The Nations of the World* (*Sekai kunizukushi*, 1869) and the even more overtly racist *Mitchell's New School Geography* (Philadelphia, 1872) were among the more notable. A source of linguistic, racial, and political paradigms, *Parley's* gave Kyōka bits of information about all that mattered in a certain world perspective. It was a view that, for better or worse, the Japanese took seriously. They could not have but noticed that Asia was mentioned only briefly. "Adam and Eve were created in Asia, and were placed in the garden of Eden, not far from the river Euphrates. This river is in the western part of Asia, and is about six thousand miles in an easterly direction from New York and Boston."

Within Asia lie the isles of Japan. In Chapter 36 we read:

Japan is an extensive empire, containing twenty-six millions of inhabitants. These live to the east of China, upon several islands, of which Niphon is the largest. The people live crowded together in large and well-kept cities, and resemble the Chinese in their religion, manners, and customs, and the American Indians in their personal appearance.

The Japanese seem to wish, too, to know something of the history of the nations from which they have so long lived apart. For every now and then, the publishers of this little book which you are now studying, receive an order from far off Japan for two, four, six hundred copies of *Parley's Universal History*.

It is hard to say how proficient Kyōka became. In speaking with his widow in 1943, Yanagida Izumi learned that throughout their years of marriage Suzu never once saw her husband read an English book. But Yanagida, who claims to have perceived a glint of uncommon intelligence in Kyōka's eyes, was skeptical of the author's claim to have forgotten all his English. (Given the political climate in 1943, it would not have been expedient to profess a foreign involvement.) If he could get through Parley's after only three years of English instruction, Yanagida considered, he must have been proficient. This became an issue in the first place because Yanagida felt, without being able to supply any proof, that Kyōka's early writing was influenced significantly by English.[14]

This is far from an unreasonable claim. At a time when the language of narrative was being refashioned to accommodate Western modes of constructing reality, practically everyone's style felt the pull of foreign languages, especially written English. The tendency during the Meiji period for Japanese to write sentences with an obvious subject and predicate was, for instance, one of many significant responses to this influence. Nishi Amane's (1829–97) proposal that Japanese be written with an alphabetic script was another phonocentric reaction.[15] Mori Arinori (1847–89), another leader of the Enlightenment, went so far as to advocate that Japanese be replaced by English.

The commercial power of the English-speaking race which now rules the world drives our people into some knowledge of their commercial ways and habits. . . . Under the circumstances, our meagre language, which can never be of any use outside our islands, is doomed to yield to the domination of the English tongue. . . . Our intelligent race, eager in the pursuit of knowledge, cannot depend upon a weak and uncertain medium of communication in its endeavor to grasp the principal truths from the precious treasury of Western science and art and religion. The laws of state can never be preserved in the language of Japan. All reasons suggest its disuse.[16]

Far from abandoning Japanese, Kyōka would seek to "revive the *renga*-like leaps of association and the imagistic splendor of the Japanese language that modern Japanese literature had forgotten" and to "raise the Japanese idiom to an extravagant level, to its highest potential."[17] He would do this, however, against the background of proposals such as Mori's, fashioning a new language for fiction in response to the more abstract powers of English. Every author responded in a unique way. Kyōka's most intriguing reaction was described by Teraki Teihō, Kyōka's principal biographer. According to Teraki, many of Kyōka's stories developed through a chain reaction of associations set off by a single word, which he jotted down in his notebooks. Oddly enough, the word that triggered the chain was often from a Western language. It is as if Kyōka consciously sought to reverse the phonocentrism of alphabetic systems by creating elaborate visions and imaginative figures from the stark abstractions of the English alphabet. In the West, an awareness of the origin of the letter A as a picture of an ox's head had all but disappeared. In Kyōka's writing, the graphic life of words would be emphasized.

An Awakening

For all his success as a student of English, Kyōka's most important lesson at the Porters' school came incidentally. At the Eiwa Gakkō he discovered another form of writing that helped widen his literary horizons beyond those provided by his mother's kusazōshi and the "serious" books that he was reading at the time, such as *The Fall of Osaka Castle* (*Namba senki*), *The Three Kingdoms* (*San-kokushi*), and *The Water Margin* (*Suikōden*).[18] The newspaper (*shinbun*) was one of the new shapes of Meiji discourse. As a venue for the publication of fiction, it had a profound influence on the development of literary culture.

The Porters' school subscribed to *The Postal News* (*Yūbin hōchi shinbun*), which Kyōka claims to have read greedily. The Japanese newspaper evolved from kusazōshi, the one subgenre of *gesaku* that survived the transition from early to late modern most handily, no doubt because of its visual flexibility. Then, as now, newspapers were an important vehicle for the publishing of prose and poetry. Through *The Postal News*, Kyōka discovered Morita Shiken (1861–97), whose translations of Western literature were highly acclaimed and whose influence on Kyōka's early development would be considerable. He read Shiken's rendering of "The Golden Ass" ("Kinroba"), which began running on January 18, 1887, and possibly his version of Jules Verne's "Michael Strogoff" ("Mekura shisha"), which appeared from September 16 of the same year, four months after Kyōka left the Porters' school.

It is likely that over the next few years Kyōka remained a faithful reader of Shiken's work. Tezuka Masayuki argues that from Shiken's free and very readable translations of Victor Hugo—"Choses vues" ("Zuiken roku," 1888), "Detective Hubert" ("Tantei Yūberu," 1889), "Claude Gueux" ("Kuraudō," 1890), and "Dernier jour d'un condamné Claude Gueux" ("Shikei mae no rokujikan," 1896)—Kyōka learned not only useful patterns of prosody but also a more Western sense of social justice.[19] The "Shiken style," known in more formal parlance as the "detailed style" (*shūmitsu buntai*), might best be described as a colloquial form of Chinese read in Japanese word order (as in *kanbun kuzushi*). Because of its persistent sinitic element, it was not so different from the language of Takizawa Bakin's reading books (*yomihon*) or that of translated colloquial Chinese novels such as the tremendously popular *Water Margin* (*Shui-hu chuan*). Like these other more traditional styles—a mixing of the elegant with the colloquial (*gazoku setchū*), and a melding of Japanese and Chinese (*wakan konkō*)—Shiken's language was yet another hybridized idiom, a linguistic compromise both troubled and enriched by the cultural mixing brought on by the Enlightenment. Kyōka was well acquainted with all three styles and would eventually produce something like them in his earliest publications.[20]

Kyōka left the Porters' School in May 1887 to take the entrance examinations for the Kanazawa Senmon Gakkō, a high-school-level institution that would later become the present-day Kanazawa University. He later joked about his lack of motivation. "My wish to matriculate came from an interest in the school's uniforms—black hooded overcoats with a crimson lining and gold buttons" (29: 718). The flippant tone belies the school's importance to him and ameliorates a disappointment. "I received a perfect score on the English part of the exam. While I was taking the mathematics test, a neighborhood friend, who was older and already a student at the school, felt sorry enough for me to toss a test paper in from outside the examination room. It didn't get to me, though, and I failed" (29: 718).

This account from the earlier chronology is admirably honest. The relevant passage from the later one is less candid. "I withdraw from the Eiwa Gakkō in May 1887. While preparing for entrance into the Senmon Gakkō (later the Fourth High School), I receive a serious injury while playing samurai games with some rascals in the neighborhood. Because of this, I change my mind and begin attending a private English/math boarding school" (1: 4). These two very different explanations for never donning the black-hooded coats of the Senmon Gakkō might have neutralized each other were it not for Tokuda Shūsei's (1871–1943) account, which confirms the former. Shūsei, a Kanazawa native, would later follow Kyōka to Tokyo with the hope of apprenticing himself to the same mentor. Because of shared origins and his lifelong affiliation with Kyōka, his perspective is particularly valuable to our concerns. Of these early years, he wrote, "Kyōka had been going to the mission school and could read English fluently. I secretly admired him. But the next day we were tested on other topics such as physics and mineralogy. I finished and handed in my exam. As I was about to leave through the rear exit, I noticed Kyōka sitting on the very back row. It seemed he hadn't prepared like the rest of us and was having difficulties. As it turned out, he didn't get in."[21]

A New School and More Reading

The private boarding school that Kyōka entered was run by the grandson of Izumi Seiji's colleague, Mizuno Genroku. Perhaps because of this connection, he was able to secure a place there. Kyōka later described how his distractions grew more intense.

The school was strict, and so I had difficulty trying to get away from the dormitory. Whenever I did manage to sneak away, I'd borrow books from the lending library, first one volume at a time . . . eventually getting up to five or six volumes a night. I read everything I could get my hands on—all the new things that were coming out, and also the older books that were being reprinted in movable type. I don't remember all the titles, but there was one book that I really came to resent with all my being. It was written in the style of *The Fall of Osaka Castle*. The schoolmaster discovered it in my room and confiscated it. Borrowing fees weren't so expensive back then, but the replacement cost of the book was thirty-five *sen*.

My God! Thirty-five *sen*! How could I pay such a fine when my resources were practically nil? In order to raise the money, I was forced to sell two volumes of a reader that my elementary teacher had given me as a prize. Thus began evil. After that I sold four more books. You might say I murdered the Five Classics to keep my study of popular fiction alive and well. (28: 656–57)

After his discovery and punishment, it became increasingly difficult for Kyōka to satisfy his compulsion to read. Yet he did manage to get to the book lenders through various ploys such as spilling his lamp oil in the garden pond and going out to purchase more, and even the loincloth-up-the-sleeve trick. "I would undo my loincloth and hide it in the sleeve of my kimono . . . so, if I got caught, I could say that I was going out to wash it in the creek next to the school. I could say I was too embarrassed to say anything" (28: 657).

Recreational reading at the boarding school continued to be a secret affair, as it had been at home, where reading in closets had contributed to "a ferocious nearsightedness." As the desire to read more and more books became overwhelming, however, the process was forced to become more public. Employing elaborate strategies, Kyōka continued his amusements while still in the classroom.

I'd spread the book out on my desk, then place . . . the *New National First Reader* or *Outlines of World History* above it. Off to the side I'd open a dictionary. Whenever I heard someone coming I'd quickly turn the dictionary over and cover whatever it was that I was reading. This worked fine for thin books, but thick ones posed problems. For these I would make a pile of textbooks on one side, and rest my dictionary against it at an angle. Then even the thick ones could be concealed. (28: 657)

For the adolescent Kyōka, the enjoyment of literature seems to have been a sybaritic obsession. "When it got dark every evening, I would feel the infatuation even more strongly. I'd embrace my books. I would sleep with them, dreaming of the secret liaisons made possible through stories. I would encounter ladies and daughters, whose lives were being ruined by obstinate stewards and jealous husbands" (28: 657). Indulging in the sort of illicit union that only reading could afford, Kyōka saw himself as closer to and better for the women in his books than their real men. This surreptitious element reflects, once again, a Confucian bias against fiction that still prevailed despite the arrival from the West of more sympathetic attitudes toward imaginative writing. As it had been for the *gesakusha*, so it would be for Kyōka. Fiction would be a subversive amusement. As a reflection of late-modern attitudes, however, even amusement would become serious business.

Ozaki Kōyō and the Writer's Passion

Kyōka left his school the next year, in 1888, and went to Toyama, where he was hired by a friend to teach English in a private school. Because Toyama was closer to Tokyo than Kanazawa, the town was that much more affected by the new technologies that had already transformed life in the capital. While Kanazawa still lay in darkness, Toyama was brightened by gas lighting. "When the sun went down, the lamplighters came out. Wearing stylish navy-blue knickers and holding their footstools in one hand, they would call out as they lit the street lamps one by one. Hearing them coming, Kyōka abandoned his students and ran out into the street to gaze in rapture at the lights."[22]

These days of independence lasted only a short while. After six months, Kyōka gave up teaching and returned to Kanazawa, where he lived at home with his father, his grandmother, and his younger brother. Out of school and unemployed, he spent his days reading. Shūsei spotted him at the Tanada, a bookstore in nearby Minami-chō. He was wearing wire-rimmed glasses and browsing near the store front. It was here, in April 1889, that he discovered a book that would change his life: Ozaki Kōyō's (1867–1903) *Confessions of Love* (*Ninin bikuni iro zange*, 1889). Kyōka was fascinated by this account of two nuns who meet by chance and, upon exchanging life stories, discover they have forsaken the world on account of the same man. Kyōka marked the momentous occasion in the first chronology: "April 1889 (Meiji 25). I read Kōyō-sensei's *Confessions of Love* at my friend's apartment. It was the height of spring. The color of plum blossoms was at my window. From next door came the sound of a weaver's shuttle. Unforgettable" (29: 718).

Apparently, he was far from alone in his enthusiasm for this book. Tayama Katai (1871–1930), who would later exasperate Kyōka with his naturalist agenda, praised Kōyō's *Confessions*. It had the power "to bewitch the young men of the time, making us think that even we could write such a story!"[23] After two decades of enthusiastic borrowing from the West, Japan's newly emergent reading audience was prepared by a reactionary shift in the 1890's to perceive Kōyō's less than cutting-edge book as, to use Katai's words, "immediate and fresh." In fact, Kōyō himself had mixed feelings about the new, antifigural idiom being produced by followers of the *genbun itchi* movement, which sought the melding of colloquial and literary language. Having demonstrated his own interest in the movement, he came to find Yamada Bimyō's (1868–1910) self-important dedication to language reform offensive. And yet, Kōyō could hardly have helped being *nouvelle* himself, regardless of what he wrote. So much about the writing of fiction was changing.

In the preface to *Confessions*, Kōyō notes his intention to try something new.

As for style, I thought over the different possibilities. Bored by the usual compromise between literary and colloquial, irritated by the melding of colloquial and written language (*genbun itchi*), I have in the end created a new, individual style. It is not for me to judge whether my prose is a phoenix or a barnyard fowl, a tiger or a cat. Although I cannot claim any credit for this creation, I would be grateful if, before passing judgment, the reader considered the tremendous price the author has had to pay.[24]

Kyōka's positive reaction to *Confessions* makes sense in at least a superficial way: both writers proved to be noted stylists, deeply concerned with the texture of language. So compelled was Kōyō to get every detail right that he virtually rewrote *Confessions* after it was in proofs. When Kōyō's publisher urged him to be more moderate about corrections, Kōyō is said to have replied, "If this book fails, you lose money. And I? I lose my life."[25] Elegant and sentimental, a mixture of classical language (for the narrative parts) and more colloquial language (for the dialogues), *Confessions* was considered retrograde by the most progressive. That is to say, Kōyō came to slow rather than promote the reforming impulses of Futabatei Shimei (1864–1909) and Bimyō, who were committed to the development and use of plain, transparent language for all parts of the modern novel, whether dialogue or narrative.

The critical reception of *Confessions* was mixed. In contrast to those who were opposed, critics such as Ishihara Ningetsu (1865–1926) preferred this step backward. He praised Kōyō and helped establish him as one of the two leading writers of the day, along with Kōda Rohan (1867–1947).

This work is a masterpiece that rises well above the field of recent writing. Of what worth is [Shimei's] *The Drifting Cloud* when compared to Kōyō's *Confessions*? . . . Each word excites a tear, and the entire work is filled with tragedy and pathos. . . . We recognize this work as a masterpiece and cannot refrain from reading it again and again. We marvel at how it describes many and varied kinds of love. The author has successfully depicted the love in pathos and the pathos in love.[26]

Ningetsu's review helps us locate Kyōka's position. Beyond its well-turned sentences, the more powerful attraction of *Confessions* for Kyōka was how it made love a problem. Kyōka had no way of knowing, of course, that this would be the most dreamily romantic of all Kōyō's works, and that it was, therefore, less than representative of the man he would soon be seeking out. Far more spiritually akin to Kyōka was the poet and critic Kitamura Tōkoku (1868–94). Like Tōkoku, Kyōka would delve into the problems of love and marriage with uncommon intensity, eventually venturing where Kōyō could not follow. But even this predilection, too, was yet unknown to him.

What Kyōka *did* know with complete surety was that he wanted to become a writer. With Kōyō on his mind, he sought a brief respite from the regularity of his routine in Kanazawa by spending a brief period with his mother's sister-in-law, who after the death of her husband had remarried and now lived in Tatsunoguchi, a small resort town in the mountains south and west of the city. Here he encountered Kōyō's work again, this time quite by accident. The contents of a package that had been shipped to his relatives were wrapped in a discarded copy of *The Yomiuri News*, which happened to be running Kōyō's story "Summer Decline" ("Natsu yase," 1890). Kyōka was moved by this story of a woman who uncomplainingly adopts her husband's illegitimate daughter, even though she herself is the child of her husband's master. Of the encounter he wrote, "My desire to write gradually grows stronger. I try writing a piece called "Hachimoji," or something like that. I follow with two or three other stories. I pen a letter to Kōyō but get no reply" (29: 718–19).

CHAPTER 3

Master and Apprentice

~

1890–1892

A Year of Wandering

When Kyōka announced his desire to be a novelist and to go to Tokyo to seek out Ozaki Kōyō, "the great writer who lived in the East," he met strong opposition (28: 461). Kyōka later recalled the reasons why both Izumi Seiji and Meboso Kite resisted.

To become a novelist was quite a decision on my part, especially when you consider how very differently people in those days thought about novels. In the eyes of all my relatives and family friends . . . my wish to become a writer made even less sense than if I were to decide to become an actor today. Even the priest at our family temple was surprised. Somehow what the young men in the neighborhood were doing—shaving their eyebrows and staging plays in rented halls, dipping into their own pockets to promote themselves—was still more acceptable than what I wanted to do. Trying to make a living as a writer seemed like an absurd idea. After all, even the reading of novels was thought to be decadent. (28: 827)

Recalling the days just prior to his departure for Tokyo, Kyōka wrote: "I can still remember walking in front of the Gongen Dō, one of those lonely places in the woods next to the Kanazawa Castle. I was thinking of writing, dreaming of Tokyo, wondering about Kōyō, lost in my dream of somehow being able to meet him" (28: 827). The invitation to leave for Tokyo came from a student who had formerly rented a room on the Izumis' second floor and was now living in the capital. After receiving additional assurances of financial support from a business acquaintance, Hayakawa Sentarō, Seiji finally decided to let his son go. On November 28, 1890, with the blessings of his family, Kyōka left Kanazawa with Mizuno Genroku's wife and Yamao Kōro, one of Seiji's fellow metal craftsmen.[1] The three set off for Tsuruga by *rikisha* since rail service had not yet been extended as far as Kanazawa. They stayed the first night in Maruoka and arrived in Tsuruga the next evening. The Tōkaidō Line, which connected Shinbashi in Tokyo with Kobe, brought them as far as Shizuoka on the third day. Again, they stayed the night, then proceeded to Tokyo, still seven and a half hours away. They arrived at Shinbashi Station at 4:00 in the afternoon. The date was November 31. The trip from Kanazawa had taken four days.

Kyōka later remembered that when he reached the front portico of the station, his courage was immediately stolen away by the broad streets, the bustle of the crowds, and the size of the buildings. Mizuno's wife encouraged him to stay the night at their home, suggesting that perhaps a night's rest might restore his resolve to pay Kōyō a visit as originally planned. Riding together in a horse-drawn trolley, they proceeded to Kanda Yamamoto-chō, where Kyōka stayed the night. He left the Mizunos' the next day, on December 1, 1890.

He did not go to see Kōyō. Instead, he sought out Fukuyama, presumably the young man who had rented a room in the Izumis' house while attending the Kanazawa Senmon Gakkō. Fukuyama was a medical student. He lived in a three-story apartment building in Yushima 1–chōme Onnazaka shimo, and his welcome to Kyōka still stood. In the month that Kyōka lived in Onnazaka, Fukuyama introduced him to a number of urban refinements: *oden* (a sort of stew), which was sold in streetside stalls; beef (one of the new foods of the Enlightenment); *mugitoro* (boiled barley topped with a white slurry of ground mountain root, *yamaimo*); cards; vaudeville; the brothels of Yoshiwara; and, alas, the pawnshops.

Kyōka was destitute. Hayakawa's offer of financial support did not materialize, and Kyōka was dependent on the generosity of Fukuyama, whose financial situation was no better than his own. Kyōka soon learned that his host had not paid the rent for nine months. Neither had he taken care of his kerosene bill, a reality that Kyōka understood when the vendor did not replenish Fukuyama's barrel when he came by. In order to ward off the winter cold, Kyōka was forced to spend his own money on heating oil. As the end of December approached, Fukuyama disappeared.

Suddenly, Kyōka was alone in Tokyo. He knew no one and had nowhere to turn. One of Fukuyama's friends, a man named Mitake, came to his rescue. He introduced Kyōka to a fellow worker, Iguchi, who was living in a temple complex in Azabu's Imai-chō. Kyōka stayed with Iguchi for the next three months and then roomed for a short while with one of Fukuyama's cousins, a politico named Morikawa. This move took him across town to Asakusa. In May, Kyōka rejoined Fukuyama. His friend had found new housing in nearby Kanda but no new wealth. "Without money for tobacco, we smoke seaweed" (29: 720).

In June, they moved together to Hongō. But then came the inevitable split, and Kyōka left Tokyo for the nearby city of Kamakura, where he lived with another medical student, whose name is not known. Kyōka's new partner rented a room at the Myōchō Temple and had no more success than Fukuyama in paying the rent. In fact, as Fukuyama had done, he also fled, leaving Kyōka hostage at the temple grounds. "Whenever I go out for a walk, the priest, who is afraid I am going to run away without paying him, follows me. Penniless, I burn dried leaves and inhale the smoke. Going hungry is one thing, but going without tobacco is quite another" (29: 721).

Sometime during the first week or so of September, the medical student sent money to the temple. Freed from debt, Kyōka immediately joined him in Tokyo, where they shared a room in Hongō's Tatsuoka District. They spent their time reading novels and going to hear women balladeers chanting tales until their alliance ended for the second time toward the middle of the month. Kyōka next found lodging in a townhouse in Asakusa's Tawara-machi (Tsumagoizaka shimo) district with a number of failed medical students, all of them older and some of them married. With all other means exhausted, it was his fate to depend on the charity of others. "All I have is the single unlined kimono I have been wearing all summer. Begging off my cousin [Meboso Teru] in Kanazawa, I am sent a five-*yen* money order. She has pawned her coral hairpin in order to raise the money. But when I think of all my debts, and of all the things I need to buy, I . . . tear it up" (29: 721).

Kyōka never dwelled at length on the details of what happened during this extended period of wandering, although obviously it was a difficult time. There is some speculation that, while living in Yushima, Kyōka was hired as a house sitter and may have been forced to have sex with other men. But there is no evidence to support this claim. We can safely say, however, that his poverty deepened Kyōka's sense of humanity and strengthened his identification with the poor. In fact, the early works are notable for their youthful sense of outrage and for their contempt for the Meiji *nouveau riche*, whom Kyōka saw as a self-interested class who flaunted their wealth through charity while leading the people to death on the battlefield and to means of livelihood they would never have chosen for themselves. This anger would cool and mellow. By at least midway through Kyōka's career, poverty would become one of many lyrical forces available for artistic orchestration.

"Osen and Sōkichi" ("Baishoku kamonanban," 1920), one of the most graceful short stories from the author's mature period, is a beautifully crafted remembrance of this earlier time of hardship. Its male protagonist, Hata Sōkichi, an impoverished young man who later becomes well-to-do and influential, is clearly a shadow of the author.

Sōkichi had come up to Tokyo without any definite plans and without any money to pay for an education. Since he had nowhere to call his own, he joined up with a gang of vagabond day laborers who helped him manage to stay alive.

These were people who, through indolence and dissipation, had been forgotten by the world—failed medical students, some of them well along in years, even some with wives; half-baked politicians; businessmen of the lowest order; charlatans; and even a few who were seriously trying to become policemen. (12: 245)

In the story, Sōkichi is saved by a beautiful mother / lover figure, Kyōka's typical heroine. Such women find a place in this squalid urban scene because the city evoked memories of Nakata Suzu. In Tokyo, which was his dead mother's hometown, Kyōka felt close to her. The first month after his arrival in Shinbashi, while staying at Fukuyama's dilapidated quarters, he met a young woman of fifteen or sixteen whose manner was arresting. "I am amazed at the beauty of her everyday speech. It makes me remember the sound of my mother's voice, which I heard until the age of nine. One night a fire suddenly breaks out, and this woman asks me, '*Choito, doko deshō ne.*' [Oh, I wonder where it could be.] The way she says '*choito*' [Oh] moves me deeply" (29: 719). Both the confusion and the comfort began with this resemblance. With this discovery of a temporary replacement for his mother, Kyōka's literary career began to assume its first vague outlines.

As winter approached, Kyōka was advised by a friend from Kanazawa, Matsui Tomotoki, "to return home and quietly plan his next attempt."[2] He seriously considered retreat, but his luck suddenly changed. He learned that one of the medical students with whom he was living had rented a room from

Kōyō's uncle, a man named Araki Shuntarō. Kyōka pressed for a letter of introduction, and this "slightest of connections" proved to be all he needed. Early on the morning of November 19, 1891, nearly a year after he first arrived in Tokyo, Kyōka set out from Asakusa for Ushigome, armed with the letter and just enough courage to bring himself to meet the man who would help launch his career and even at one point help save his life.

Subtle Communications

Kyōka remembered his visit to Kōyō's home in Ushigome in this way:

I looked up at the roofed gate and the doorplate hanging there—Tokyo, Ushigome District, Yokodera-machi. I saw the name Ozaki and knew I had come to the right house. For years I had dreamed of being here, but now I couldn't bring myself to do what I had come for. I backed away. I turned into a side street where I lingered beside a row of cryptomeria. When I realized I couldn't stand there forever, I straightened my collar, entered the gate, and walked twenty or thirty steps to a front door. I quietly opened it and, standing at the entrance, rudely made my presence known. No answer came, but I heard the sound of footsteps coming from inside. An elderly woman appeared. I asked for Ozaki-sensei, "I would like to meet him, if I may."

"Just a moment," she said, then disappeared.

Eventually I was taken to an eight-mat room just off the entrance. I was sitting there . . . looking up at a work of calligraphy by Ichiroku—"Melding the Elegant and the Common" (*gazoku setchū*)—when the woman came in with an ashtray. "Would you care to smoke? The Master's still sleeping." She smiled.

I remember the day—a mild morning in late autumn. The sky above the treetops was cloudless. The heavens were swept clear by a refreshing breeze. It was November 19, 1891, 8:30 in the morning. (28: 460)

The woman was Kōyō's grandmother Sen, who soon disappears from Kyōka's account of this fateful meeting with Kōyō. The author's young bride, Kiku, whom Kyōka mistook for Kōyō's older sister, led him up a spiral staircase to where Kōyō waited. "He was sitting behind his desk with a fancy-looking brazier placed on the floor by his knee. He was twenty-three or -four years old. His hair was cropped short, and in his splash-patterned jacket he looked manly and dignified. Struck by his presence, I lowered my head. To think that this was the person who had written the *Confessions*" (28: 460–61).

Kyōka later felt the need to apologize for this account of their initial encounter, "My First Meeting with Kōyō-sensei" ("Hajimete Kōyō-sensei ni mamieshi toki"). "I sent this to a friend at the time of the incident described.

The present version has not been reworked, and so I must ask the reader to pardon its childishness" (28: 462). The passage does suffer from overpoliteness, but its obsequious tone probably captures Kyōka's adoration for Kōyō at the time. "Childishness" points not only to his struggle with language but also to his self-deprecating status within a patrimonial (*oyabun/kobun*) relationship that began with this first encounter and was passionately and strictly maintained by both men. To many writers at the time, such hierarchical relationships were an unwanted carryover from the unenlightened past. In Kyōka's case, however, the loyalty was not feigned. At eighteen years of age, Kyōka was profoundly struck by Ozaki Kōyō, who was already famous at twenty-four. So awed was he that he found himself quite incapable of expressing "the desire I had held in my heart for many years." Fortunately for Kyōka, Kōyō was able—heart to heart— to guess his intent.

I told him of my needy circumstances, that I was thinking of returning to Kanazawa but wanted at least to be able to meet him before I left. Then something knotted in my chest, and I looked down at the floor. What happened next was like a dream. "You've been bitten by the writing bug, too, have you?" he laughed. "All right. If I can arrange something, I'll take you on. We're short of space here, but there's an apartment building nearby where you can work. Whenever I need you to do something, I'll call you here. Anyway, leave it to me. Come back tomorrow, and I'll let you know whether I've decided to have you stay here in my house or at the apartment."[3]

According to Kyōka, their rapport was immediate. It was as if they had known each other, even though "those who write novels are very different from normal people, and everything, even the shape of the house, seemed strange."[4]

As instructed, Kyōka returned the next morning to hear the good news. Kōyō wanted him to live at his home. He could take the small room just off the entrance. A clothes chest and a few other things were cleared out to make space, and Kyōka set up his desk that afternoon. After almost a year of wandering, he suddenly found himself not only freed from indigence but also occupying a position as the student of one of Japan's most influential writers.

A few days later, on the twenty-fifth, he broke a long silence and wrote to his father about his success. The letter, it seems, doubles as a report to the dead.

Greetings.

As always, I must apologize for such a long silence. Father, I have neglected to keep you informed of past events and by doing so have certainly caused you no end of irritation, even though you have been so understanding. Now I entreat you to welcome a repentant Kyōtarō, your new son, and to forgive his habitual neglect of filial piety.

I trust that you have recently heard the news from Fukuyama. At last your humble servant has fulfilled his dream of many years' standing. From the twentieth of this month, I have been in the keeping of Ozaki Kōyō–sensei. My circumstances have truly changed for the better, and my future is full of hope. As you know, my intention to become a novelist has been firm—from the beginning and forever more. A novel is not a cheap and vulgar thing. . . . I will do nothing to disgrace my mother's grave, nor will signing my work as "the oldest son of Izumi Seiji" bring you any embarrassment. Above all, please understand this.

Accordingly, I ask that you pay no attention to what you might have been hearing from those around you. Have nothing to do with those who criticize Fukuyama and Morikawa. Rather, quickly distance yourself from anyone who would sing the praises of Hayakawa. The words of your son are far more reliable than the voices of ten speaking together. . . .

When Master Kōyō invited me to live with him . . . he still didn't know my name or age. Although this might not be necessary, since I met Kōyō for the first time only on the nineteenth . . . I was wondering if you could write him a letter. I am sure that he would appreciate something written in your honorable hand.

In times of difficulty and danger, I have called out to my dead mother for help. And so I ask that you and Toyoharu take some flowers to mother's grave on my behalf. . . .

A while ago, my aunt in Tatsunoguchi agreed to loan me five yen. No doubt, you've heard about this money from Fukuyama. I would ask that you please see to this matter as quickly as possible. In anticipation of receiving this amount, I have procured an advance of three yen from Hayakawa. Please give my warmest regards to Nakabayashi-sama, who sent a truly wonderful letter. Please take care of yourselves in this cold season. Your humble servant will mind to all matters of health and will soon be unfurling the banner of "Kyōtarō, the Nearsighted."

All respects, Kyōtarō.[5]

Kyōka distinguished clearly between friends and foes. He acknowledged his debt to Fukuyama and to Fukuyama's cousin Morikawa, who, contrary to rumors circulating in Kanazawa, were not leading him down a path of dissipation. Though penniless, the two had been of far greater assistance than the entrepreneur Hayakawa Sentarō, who, having gone against his word to Seiji, finally proffered the three-yen advance. Perhaps Kyōka's disdain for the wealthy was intensified by his experience with this man; for Hayakawa, the temporary loan was probably only a courtesy extended to the son of a business associate, but for Kyōka, the gesture was inadequate.

Other friends mentioned in the letter are Nakabayashi, about whom we know nothing, and Kyōka's aunt in Tatsunoguchi, with whom Kyōka was staying when he read "Summer Decline." The most important people to Kyōka are his brother Toyoharu, his father, his aging grandmother, and his deceased mother, who is called by her posthumous name, Tōgakuin-sama. Though dead, her spirit had come to his aid in times of difficulty and danger. Only through her love was he able to realize his long-held dream of establishing himself as Kōyō's protégé. As if to repay her love, he would make his name among respectable practitioners of fiction by writing novels for a steadily growing audience of Meiji-period readers. As a storyteller, he would do for others what his mother had once done for him.

But even Kyōka's mother is merely an angel in this chain of being. As much as family mattered, it was Kōyō and no one else who had given him a future. Kyōka's thinking is clear on this point, and his devotion to his mentor seems to have been as intense as his feelings for family. As we will see, a profound sense of indebtedness to Kōyō stayed with him throughout his life. Long after Kōyō's death, Kyōka would start each day by setting a fresh cup of tea before a scroll of his mentor's calligraphy. Immediately after performing his duties to his family before the Buddhist altar, he would honor his teacher.

Apprenticeship and Mirror's Flower

The Ozakis' house was destroyed by American bombers in 1945, along with most of Tokyo. Since the garden still remains, however, we know exactly where the house once stood, and our knowledge of its interior is helped by a floor plan that still exists. On the ground level were five rooms—two-, three-, six-, and eight-mats in size, plus a four-and-a-half-mat annex. On the second floor, where Kōyō and his wife slept and where the Master also did his writing, were two rooms, one six-mat room and one eight-mat. Kyōka's assigned quarters was the two-mat room on the ground level, next to the front door and on the shadowy west side of the house. He would live there until February 1895.

Kyōka's primary task was to learn to write a publishable story. His peripheral duties were many, however, and included answering the door and receiving guests, accompanying Kōyō on outings, watching the house when everyone else was out, chopping wood, serving as a messenger, and copying and mailing manuscripts. These tasks were a normal part of discipleship, and Kyōka accepted them uncomplainingly. Kōyō would have liked him to take dictation as well, but he soon learned that Kyōka's knowledge of written Japanese was insufficient to the task. In the autobiographical *Of the Mountains and Sea* (*Sankai hyōbanki*, 1929), Kyōka described a scene in which Kōyō suddenly descended the stairs, came into Kyōka's room, and ordered him to take dictation. Intimidated by the request, Kyōka somehow managed to get all the Chinese characters right in the story. But in actuality he failed miserably, ignorant of the proper characters for the words that Kōyō spoke.

Kyōka was a nonentity from the provinces. In contrast, the short-tempered yet generous Kōyō perfectly embodied the Edokko urbanity that Kyōka wished to acquire. To him, Kōyō was an expert on taste as well as a master of letters. Without his assistance, he would not attain the same level of sophistication. Neither would he be able to find publishers for his work. As a pair, they were incongruous yet, perhaps for this reason, well-matched. Kyōka was timid and narrowly focused. Kōyō was bold and had wide-ranging interests. His photograph captures this easy confidence (Fig. 7). As a student, Kyōka was willing to be scolded. As a teacher, Kōyō, famous for the colorful and often witty lash of his tongue, was ready to scold. If Kyōka needed him, Kōyō also seems to have needed Kyōka.

Some faulted both for their participation in the traditional system of training that the novelist, playwright, and critic Masamune Hakuchō (1879–1962) characterized as a thinly disguised form of tyranny, an old-fashioned subjugation of the individual will that interfered with self-cultivation and, therefore, art. Although the hierarchical orientation of Japanese society was, at least ostensibly, being challenged by notions of individual will and self-definition, Kyōka, who had grown up in an artisan's home in which apprenticeship had been an important part of training, had a practiced feel for discipline and self-denial. He had no desire to follow his father as a craftsman of precious metals, but he did know the importance of mentorship. Without Kōyō's support he would not realize his goals, and it seems he willingly did whatever was necessary to keep his relationship with Kōyō alive and meaningful. When, for instance, Kōyō, Iwaya Sazanami (1870–1933), and the members of the inner group began their drunken roughhousing at Kōyō's home, the frail Kyōka was not excused from the *sumo* competition. And when Kōyō decided to go kite flying on New Year's day, Kyōka had to run with the kite as Kōyō, standing on the rooftop of his house, held the string. "The string would get tangled in the trees in the garden, or the kite's tail would wrap itself around the gravestone of the Daishin Temple next door. When the kite didn't take to the air right away, Master Kōyō would lose his temper and shout out, 'Push that gravestone over, you clumsy fool!'" (28: 837).

Contributing to group solidarity, Kōyō also bathed at the public bathhouse with his disciples. On such occasions, the privilege of washing the teacher's back was reserved for Kyōka. The hazards of wrestling and kite flying aside, this last service was to Kyōka's mind a privilege. Kōyō eventually had a large number of students, but only Kyōka was worthy to wash his back on their joint visits to the public baths. From an opportunistic perspective, the intimacy of being washed by his protégé must have made Kōyō more attentive to the manuscripts that Kyōka began taking up the spiral staircase for correction. Indeed, the early manuscripts show that Kōyō went over Kyōka's work with remarkable thoroughness. One manuscript from this period, "Two-headed Snake" ("Ryōtōja"), published in 1898 as "The Snake Eaters" ("Hebi kui"), bleeds red with Kōyō's numerous corrections and suggestions. Kōyō was highly critical, from beginning to end. But his final comment could not have been more kind and encouraging. "Your idea is extraordinary. Your writing is like that of an experienced hand. You are a small snake that already shows the spirit of a dragon. I have read many stories in my time, but never one such as this. Are you a pearl in the palm of my hand? You should feel proud of what you've done."[6]

Although few writings survive from this early period, Kyōka's pen name does. Even before they met, Kyōka had written a story to show Kōyō. Upon reading its title, "Flowers in a Mirror, the Moon on the Water" ("Kyōka suigetsu"), Kōyō immediately saw a fitting name for his new student. The title is a phrase borrowed from Chinese poetics, *Ching-hua shui-yueh* (鏡花水月) a metaphor for an ephemeral beauty that forever escapes our grasp. We can appreciate the reflected image of a flower in a mirror or the shape of the moon on the water, but we can touch neither flower nor moon. Their beauty is beyond, a simulacrum. In a slightly different form, the metaphor appears as *ching-chung hua-ying* (鏡中花影), the image of flowers seen in a mirror. Kōyō's selection of this particular image for Kyōka's pen name was perspicacious. His student's literary career would be a lifelong search for a rarified beauty and an ephemeral love made more attractive by reason of its being impossible to fulfill.

Other Students

The disciplined and passionate relationship Kyōka had with Kōyō was very nearly the last example of its kind among Japanese writers. Natsume Sōseki, too, had many adoring followers, but their ties to him were more obviously grounded in commonly held intellectual and artistic interests than on the moral bedrock of duty and reciprocity. If Sōseki's Thursday Society was, in this sense, more collegial and Kōyō's mentorship more familial, both institutions were nevertheless alike in serving the purpose of helping young writers. The business of literature was burgeoning once again, as it had in eighteenth-century Edo. And although the expanding scope and variety of publishing were making the process of getting into print easier, the relationship between writers and publishers was still limited and personal. Especially in the sphere of literary publication, it was practically impossible for an unknown writer without connections to find someone willing to publish his work.

Kyōka was thus hardly alone in his wish to gain Kōyō's full support. Sometime before the beginning of the new year, another young man came calling. Kyōka greeted him at the door and showed him in. The visitor introduced himself as Kosugi Tamezō (1865–1952) and announced that he had brought a writing sample that he would like Kōyō to see. Kyōka had no way of knowing that Kosugi had already visited Mori Ōgai, who, upon reading the story, had encouraged Kosugi to "look for another profession."[7] Kōyō received the visitor in his upstairs study and, upon learning of his plans to become a novelist, read over the satirical piece Kosugi had brought. After seeing the visitor off, Kōyō confided in Kyōka that Kosugi would never realize his ambitions. Undaunted by even this second rejection, Kosugi would eventually find a mentor in Saitō Ryokuu (1867–1904). Writing under the name of Kosugi Tengai, he would eventually gain a reputation as an interpreter of Emile Zola's (1840–1902) work to the Japanese. With the publishing of "New Year Apparel" ("Hatsusugata," 1900), he would establish himself as a leading figure in the naturalist movement.

A few months later, in February 1892, Kyōka greeted another aspiring novelist at Kōyō's door. This was Oguri Isoo (1875–1926), who, unlike Kosugi, was expected. Kōyō had already agreed in October 1891 to take Oguri on as a student and was waiting for him to return from his hometown near Nagoya. Oguri had returned home in order to convince his parents to let him pursue a career as a writer rather than force upon him what he envisioned would be a dreary career in the family business. Impressed with the talent that Oguri showed in his story "Flowing Water" ("Mizu no nagare," 1891), Kōyō had selected it for publication in his newly formed literary journal, *A Thousand Lavenders, Ten Thousand Crimsons* (*Senshi bankō*).

Oguri Fūyō, as he came to be called, was two years younger than Kyōka, but in some ways more practiced as a writer. Without question, he was more naturally Kōyō's student than Kyōka was or ever would be. Fūyō had effectively copied Kōyō's style in "Flowing Water" and thus invited the many comparisons made between them.[8] Kyōka and Fūyō eventually became Kōyō's two most prominent students and were rivals in this sense. But it was Fūyō, not Kyōka, who later came to be known as "Kōyō II." Kyōka, who was more profoundly a romantic than his teacher, was resistant to Kōyō's influence in some ways. To Tokuda Shūsei, who later joined the group, Kyōka's art was essentially incompatible with their teacher's. According to Shūsei, Kyōka treated Kōyō with respect only because he did not want to be considered a traitor to his teacher's cause.[9] Kōyō's "cause" was the realistic depiction of common manners and a probing of the problem of love. To this end, Kōyō sought inspiration first from Ihara Saikaku (1642–92) and then from Emile Zola. Kyōka clearly had no interest in either of these two authors.

No one was more keenly aware of this apparent tension in Kyōka's regard for Kōyō than Shūsei, who was the next young aspirant to visit Kōyō's home in Ushigome. Shūsei had hesitated to vie for Kōyō's attention, since he had learned, from the owner of the bookstore in Kanazawa, that the frail, myopic Izumi Kyōtarō had somehow managed to align himself with one of the most powerful literary figures in the country. Joining with someone from the same provincial town seemed a bad idea, but Shūsei's admiration of Kōyō's "elegant style" prevailed. He visited Kōyō's residence with a friend, Kiryū Yūyū, sometime toward the end of March 1892.

Shūsei's autobiographical novel *Pursuing the Light* (*Hikari o otte*) mentions the visit. Shūsei speaks through the protagonist Hiroshi.

Izumi came to the door. . . . He was dressed in a patterned kimono that made him look very urbane. The underseams of his sleeves were coming unraveled. He smiled as he greeted us, "The Master's not in at the moment—"

"When will he be back?" Hiroshi asked, standing in front of the door.

"He goes out a lot, whenever he gets the urge."

The two of them had little recourse but to leave with their manuscripts still tucked away in their sleeves. It seemed to Hiroshi that they were getting snubbed, but it was possible that Kōyō really was out.[10]

It would have been proper for Shūsei to keep visiting until Kōyō finally agreed to see him, but he was apparently ambivalent about Kyōka even at this point and was loathe to go back. In another account he wrote: "The Master was not at home when Yūyū and I visited his home in Yokodera in Ushigome. Had Izumi not been there at the door, I might have gone again."[11] Rather than take the chance of embarrassing himself once again, Shūsei sent his manuscript to the Ozaki home with a cover letter. Kōyō read it and sent it back with a few discouraging words. "While a persimmon is still unripe, even a crow finds it forbidding."[12] Shūsei tore up the letter. Spurned by Kōyō, he and Yūyū sought employment at the editorial office of the Hakubunkan, which was fast becoming one of most influential publishing houses in Tokyo. The interview went poorly, however, and, still searching for some sort of employment, he next visited the famous translator and critic Tsubouchi Shōyō for possible tutelage. Shūsei was more sharply focused on getting published than on becoming Kōyō's or anyone's student—either Ōgai or Shōyō would do just as well. But unlike Kyōka's first trip to the capital, his did not end successfully. Both he and Yūyū were already showing the first symptoms of a smallpox infection at this point. Without the support that would enable them to remain in Tokyo, Yūyū returned to Kanazawa, and Shūsei went to the home of his older brother in Osaka to recuperate. Shūsei would try again in a few years.

In the meantime, Kyōka devotedly followed the regimen that Kōyō set before him. It was not an easy life—Kōyō was temperamental, at times even cruel. But Kyōka would later defend his teacher.

Sensei had a sharp tongue. If you weren't used to his scoldings, you'd probably think he was being overly harsh. But the truth is that once Sensei committed himself to a student, he did everything in his power to help that person succeed. If, after working with someone, he could see the person wasn't going to make it as a writer or if he was veering off course, then he'd do what he could to set that person up in a shop selling baked yams or boiled hodgepodge or doing whatever he could to make a living. And if that student happened to be supporting a family and was having a hard time making ends meet, Sensei would do what he could to make sure that no one, including that person's parents, went hungry.

Because of his paternalistic attitude toward us, Sensei felt as though he had to carefully oversee everything we did and to reprimand us whenever necessary. . . . The sharpness of his tongue and the difficulty of his training required you to have a worshipful feeling about things like cutting firewood and drawing well water. Without a heartfelt commitment, you just couldn't endure. In other words, rather than sitting around and talking about writing, you had to roll up your sleeves and write. Unless you were willing to put something down on paper and then learn what you could from the corrections that Sensei wrote in red ink, you'd fail or go off on some tangent. That's why those who thought of studying with Kōyō as merely a way to get ahead, or those who came for only a short while at their own convenience, or those who wanted to get published or to start making money from their writing as quickly as possible, couldn't endure the scolding or the evil eye.

This applied to more than just writing. Whenever I was thoughtless about anything I did, Kōyō-sensei would yell at me. The saving grace was that the reprimand would be for that particular offense only. Sensei never dwelled on the past. Even if he had, just minutes before, knocked someone down with his glare, he would descend from his study on the second floor and say to the person still cowering in the corner, "Come on. Let's go take a bath." He would take that person along as if he hadn't been yelling at him just a minute before. That's why, no matter what you did wrong, he never made you feel like you had to walk on eggs. (28: 835–36)

No names of students are mentioned in this apology, but Kyōka's criticisms of the opportunists among Kōyō's disciples are probably directed at Tokuda Shū-sei, among others.

Secrets

There were two peaks in Kōyō's career, and Kyōka reached him at the first of these. Having made a name for himself with *Confessions* and been given a sala-ried position with the *Yomiuri News*, Kōyō now wanted to tease the reading public by withholding his name from it. In collusion with Wada Tokutarō of the Shun'yōdō publishing house, he agreed to publish a story without signing his name to it. Shun'yōdō would sponsor a contest and give prizes to those who correctly guessed the author. The enterprise was devious in a way, since the work that Kōyō produced for the contest was an adaptation of Moliere's *L'avare* (*Aware*). The educated reader, however, would know that working from West-ern models was something that Kōyō often did (and encouraged his students to do), since it allowed him to concentrate on issues of style.

Kyōka was asked to copy the final manuscript for this secret work and so became privy to the secret. Not even the printers and editors at Shun'yōdō knew the true author of "Beggars Can't be Choosers" ("Natsu no kosode"). While puffing on a Richmond cigar, Kōyō underscored to Kyōka the honor of being an accomplice. "There are only three people in Japan who know about this" (1: v). Taken into his teacher's confidence, Kyōka was granted a word-by-word examination of Kōyō's style as he wrote out the clear copy. While he doubtless considered his participation something of an honor—"I received Kōyō's trust as his prodigy" (1: iv)—he was soon secretly imbibing the style of another famous writer, Mori Ōgai.

Kyōka dated the appearance of "Beggars" to June 1892, but it actually ap-peared in September. Sometime in July, quite likely while still in the midst of copying Kōyō's manuscript, Kyōka used his allowance to purchase a copy of

Bubbles on the Water (*Minawa shū*), a selection from Ōgai's early writings and translations. Kyōka read it secretly, not wanting Kōyō to know how enchanted he was by its powerful beauty. The influence of this book on Kyōka's early style is difficult to determine, but it has been argued that Kyōka owed much to Ōgai and his familiarity with various strains of European romanticism. The emphasis placed by such interpretations on writers such as Ōgai and Shiken may be an attempt to recognize the obvious differences between Kyōka's style and that of his mentor, or to think of Kyōka's achievement as something new rather than copied. But the truth is that Kyōka, like anyone writing during this transitional period, was both new and old in his own way. It is possible to make an argument for different and even conflicting critical agendas.

Many Kyōka scholars, as well as writers like Nagai Kafū (1879–1959), Tanizaki, and others of the two generations that followed Kyōka, have preferred to formulate the author's indebtedness to Kōyō in terms of the old and, even, antimodern. Muramatsu Sadataka writes:

> We can sense Kyōka's own brand of romanticism in his so-called conceptual novels and in his descriptions of the mysterious world of ghosts and spirits, yet the essential form of his novels came to him through the Ken'yūsha methods he acquired from Kōyō. In a word, that method consisted in the faithfully realistic depiction of manners as they are based on sentiments expressed in Edo-period literature, as especially found in the rhetoric of the *ninjōbon* [romances of the gay quarters] and kusazōshi of the Bunka-Bunsei periods [1804–29].[13]

In other words, Kyōka, like Kōyō himself, would learn how to be current by recycling the past. Perhaps it was in this common regard for tradition, a typically modern awareness of what might be lost as "progress" occurs, that they were best matched as teacher and student. Still, even if they shared the sentiment of the ninjōbon writer Tamenaga Shunsui (1790–1843), as Kafū saw it, we know that Kōyō never read kusazōshi extensively, and that, as already mentioned, Kyōka, unlike Kōyō, never cared for Saikaku. In short, they sought different things in tradition. For Kyōka, the famous haikai poet and *ukiyozōshi* (prose tales of the floating world) writer was irrelevant to his concerns. Saikaku did not believe in ghosts. But then, neither did Kōyō.

An Unfortunate Debut

To Kōyō's credit, such differences did not stand in the way of his role as a mentor. He not only read his students' work promptly and carefully, but also sought opportunities for them to publish. In April, Kōyō traveled with a few other Ken'yūsha writers to Iwaya Sazanami's (1870–1933) new home in the Kansai area. This group, "Friends of the Inkstone," had coalesced in 1885 with the publication of the magazine *Rubbishheap Library* (*Garakuta bunko*). It dominated the literary world for a season, until the naturalist movement supplanted it. Sazanami had recently been made the literary editor of the *Kyoto Rising Sun* (*Kyōtō hinode shinbun*) and had plans to showcase Ken'yūsha writers in that paper. When Sazanami asked Kōyō to recommend a writer for serialization in the paper, Kōyō proffered Kyōka's name as the appropriate candidate.[14] Upon returning to Tokyo, Kōyō's *omiyage* (souvenir) to Kyōka was the announcement that his time had finally come to publish.

The first installment of Kyōka's *Crowned Yazaemon* (*Kanmuri Yazaemon*) appeared on October 1, 1892. Far from being the great success Kyōka had hoped, the novella was so poorly received that Sazanami immediately took in over twenty letters from disappointed readers, all asking that the story be discontinued. Sazanami implored Kōyō to "change to another writer if possible and to come up with some way to release the present one." But Kōyō refused to comply on the grounds that such an action would be a crushing blow to his student.[15] Protected from any knowledge of the poor reception of his work in Kyoto (Sazanami claimed to be losing readers by the day), Kyōka had the satisfaction of seeing his manuscript printed in full. The final installment appeared on November 18. Two epilogues were published in December.

It is not hard to imagine the dissatisfaction that *Rising Sun* readers had with Kyōka's first publication. Even for a story of its kind, *Yazaemon* offers little new in the way of theme, its plot is difficult to follow, its characters are numerous and weakly developed, and its scenes often seem to lack any obvious connection with one another. Kyōka's inexperience as a young writer explains many of these shortcomings, but the fragmented and highly imagistic nature of the work is also characteristic of the narrative tradition from which *Yazaemon* developed. More specifically, the associative, visual qualities of the prose have a well-established origin in what is called the *shōhon jitate* of the kusazōshi tradition. Just as this subcategory of illustrated fiction presupposes a kabuki source upon which it elaborates, Kyōka's *Yazaemon* similarly plays off an established work— Takeda Kōrai's *The Pine of Kanmuri, the Storm at Mado Village* (*Kanmuri no matsu Mado no arashi*), a kusazōshi in two bound volumes of three books apiece that first appeared in the fall of 1885.[16] This parent work is a straightforward, heavily illustrated reporting of a peasant uprising that took place in Kanagawa prefecture in 1883. It begins by illuminating the avarice of the landlord Matsugi Chōemon, who through deceit has stolen land from the peasants of his village. The peasants' appeal to a higher authority succeeds, only to be overturned by Matsugi's legal advisers. The desperate peasants plan and then successfully carry out a vendetta, led by Kanmuri Yazaemon, who is often cited as their leader although the only real development of his personality is through an aside, which shows his son's reaction to a report of his father's participation in the rebellion.

Kōrai's commitment to the facts was unwavering. As a representative example of the newly emergent Meiji reportage, his account also mentions how the newspapers of the time eagerly took up the story and how the public's sympathy for the rebels influenced the Kanagawa peasants' eventual exoneration. From other documents we know that, in fact, the Kanagawa uprising (*ikki*) was a newsworthy event and that it became the material not only for Kōrai's kusazōshi but also for the raconteur Matsubayashi Hakuchi's oral account, which was taken down and published as *A Fire and Sword Showdown at Mado Village* (*Mado mura yakiuchi sōdō*) by Imamura Jirō in October 1898, six years after the initial publication of Kyōka's story. From the existence of this and other versions, we can assume that interest in the event was sustained. If the details of the rebellion were already common currency at the time of Kyōka's writing, he would have been justified in expecting the reader to fill at least some of the many narrative gaps in *Yazaemon*.

Kyōka was probably attracted to the dramatic potential of Kōrai's account, as well as to its strong indictment of class oppression.[17] But to this rather straightforward incident of class struggle are added various human entanglements that remind us more of the bizarre, rococo patterns of Bunka/Bunsei-period drama than the more factually oriented kusazōshi of the mid- and late Meiji era, of which *The Pine of Kanmuri, the Storm at Mado Village* is an example. Tangled *à la* the works of the kabuki playwright Tsuruya Namboku (1755–1829), the threads connecting the principal characters in Kyōka's story tie themselves into a melodramatic knot. Kanmuri Yazaemon's sister Onami is the wife of Shinjurō, whose daughter Kohagi is forced to marry Ishimura Jirozō, the son of Ishimura Gohei. Gohei is the main villain of the story and is finally killed by Yazaemon, but only after Kohagi's failed attempt to assassinate Iwanaga, the lecherous lord of the province who colludes with Gohei in his oppression of the peasants. Kohagi's marriage to Gohei's son is actually part of Iwanaga's long-term plan to acquire her for himself. Knowing this, Kohagi takes a sword to her bridal bed. Her murderous intentions are found out, however, with the result that her father, Okino Shinjurō, is incarcerated and her mother, Onami, is tortured to death.

The death of this woman is the turning point of this story. It persuades her brother, the reluctant Yazaemon, to fight. As the new leader of the rebellion, Yazaemon replaces Unosuke, who, in an additional complication of the original story, is Kohagi's real beloved and also the illegitimate son of the evil Lord Iwanaga, who raped Unosuke's mother. Unosuke's father, Togama Rihei, is no less unfortunate, for he is falsely accused by Gohei of bribing Iwanaga. A scapegoat for Gohei's own crimes, Rihei is thrown into jail and executed. Knowing this past misdeed, Yazaemon delivers Iwanaga to Unosuke, who has the pleasure of killing Iwanaga, his biological father, at the story's climax.

Crowned Yazaemon tries to work as a narrative by establishing a genealogy of conflict. In articulating definitions of both class and self, its method of establishing the identity of characters is decidedly more external than internal, more a matter of clothes than of psychology. Kyōka advances the plot (again, in kabuki-like fashion) through the changing of garments and by way of the confusion and exploitation of identities that dressing and undressing represent. Kohagi poses as a bride, but conceals a sword beneath her kimono. Onami dresses like a peasant woman and frolics with the jail guards in order to deliver a blade to her husband so that he can commit suicide. Unosuke and Denji, another partner in the rebellion, travel about in disguise. Unosuke dresses up like a young prostitute in order to get into Iwanaga's residence. And Iwanaga, lured by the beauty of his own bastard son, demands that she (who is actually a he) sleep with him or else be forced to dance naked before his guests.

For Kyōka, costume was an acceptable way of defining character, not only here but in the works that follow. Yazaemon's surname Kanmuri, for instance, means "cap" and refers to his family's onetime noble status, which, as much as shrewdness and physical prowess, validates his position as the hero of the story. Kyōka tries neither to see through nor to undermine this formal, attributive system of mask and garb. Despite the supposed birth of interiority in the late-modern Japanese novel, for Kyōka the development of character remains largely a matter of surfaces—one costume replacing another, and one character having several different identities. Kyōka's world is still one of frozen lyrical moments that depend upon the meaningfulness of superficiality. It is a series of the essentializing *mie*, or frozen dramatic moments, that break the flow of action into static bits. As a world of unrounded portraits and life in outline, *Crowned*

Yazaemon shows a late-modern society populated by early-modern images that are not, we should remember, unlike the ones he traced from his mother's books as a child.

In short, Kyōka was being true to a well-established Japanese narrative tradition by making emotion spatial. The whole sweep of activity surrounding the peasant rebellion—the maneuvering by Iwanaga and Ishimura, on the one side, and that of Denji, Unosuke, and Yazaemon on the other—is summarized by a series of visual distillations that come at the work's conclusion. After the vendetta is accomplished, for instance, Kyōka gives his readers pictures of the injured and the whole.

Kohagi and Utaji were wounded. But their wounds were not deep. We can hope for their full and lasting recovery. And should fortune allow death to be turned away, then let Kohagi become Unosuke's wife; and let Utaji, a woman not to be despised, be the obvious choice for Unosuke's favorite mistress. What could be a more appropriate pose for a *sharebon* illustration than the three of them smiling at each other, wishing a thousand autumns of happiness to Mashira no Denji? Or perhaps it would be better to have them die, just as they are. Or more wonderful yet, to have the two women vie for his love. (1: 141)

Two similar portraits follow. After the rebellion, Unosuke and the other rebels are tried and pardoned. As they travel back to their village, throngs press forward to see them.

In the lead comes a man with a swarthy complexion, a gaunt face, a prominent nose, thick dark eyebrows, his hair grown out and shining like lacquer, and in his hand a long sword. All eyes follow him and everyone says, "That is Mashira no Denji."
In the middle of the line is a young woman of great beauty. She has clearly defined features, jet black hair trailing down her back, her bangs swaying in the breeze, locks brushing her cheeks. The long sleeves of her brightly patterned kimono are tied and thrown up over her shoulders. Actually she is not a woman, but a handsome young man, still dressed in woman's clothing from the night before. His appearance draws the crowd's attention. The way he looks down at the ground is charming and coy. What a lovely sight! His feet move gracefully, his slender waist sways as he walks. With one glance, all the women are captivated by his charm. Those standing along the road look at each other and say, "There goes Ryōzen Unosuke." (1: 142)

The play between these two different types of visual moments is analogous to the dynamics established between the *mie* and the narrative flow of a kabuki play, which provides a context for that frozen moment. Whereas the former is static and lyrical, the latter is concerned with process and connection. A *kusa-*

zōshi such as *The Pine of Kanmuri, the Storm at Mado Village* preserves this duality with its mixture of illustration and text: the pictures mark eventful points of emotion, and the words serve to connect one scene to the next. In the words-only *Yazaemon*, in which these two realms of signs have been separated by the phonocentric forces of the post-Enlightenment, the author had to rely on language to fulfill both lyrical and narrative functions. Kyōka was clearly uncomfortable using language to replace the lost world of illustration, however. Because of their syntactic and denotational powers, written words are often more effective than figures for the portrayal of those causal connections that are the concern of the psychological novel. Yet the employment of this discursive power depends upon the perceived need to understand and express the tiniest particulars of human motivation. Kyōka's choice of topic and the manner in which he presents character tell us that, if anything, he was not drawn to such explanation.

In other words, if the trend in modern Japanese letters was for language to wean itself from illustration in order to develop this potential to describe and to distance itself from formulaic explanations of cause and effect—such as praising the good and condemning evil (*kanzen chōaku*)—Kyōka nevertheless tried to find himself as a late-modern novelist in a visually static and, in this sense, anachronistic way. Here, in his first published work, it is obvious that he, like the author of the kusazōshi text from which he was working, had the kabuki stage in mind as he tried to approximate and exploit a formula of events that could develop over time. What is also amply clear is that as Kyōka strived for at least some degree of dramatic fluidity, time was both friend and foe. He was thwarted rather than empowered by the narrowing of viewpoint that authoritative narration requires. Note how in the following passage he tried to achieve some semblance of order by adding notes to the reader.

The curtain falls, and now as the author I must say a few words. Please try to imagine that the things said, the changes in time, and the order of events all belong to the same night, from the beginning of Chapter 29 until Onami's seclusion in the mountains of the next chapter. The time when Kanmuri leans upon the stone Jizō and smiles is exactly the same time as when Ishimura agonizes upon hearing his constable's report. If the reader would be so kind as to read my story in this manner, it would do no harm to your understanding, and it would greatly help the writer. (1: 98)

Where is omniscience? Being here rather than there or, rather, not being able to be at all places at once seems to be made an obvious narrative problem in *Crowned Yazaemon*. Although the system of omniscient narration has gener-

ally been employed to deal with this problem, Kyōka's early reading and cultural background did not prepare him to take such a radical and absurdly em-
powering notion too seriously. Perspectivalism fails to address the possibility
that the thing seen is as important as the seer, for instance, or that other centers
of "omniscience" would produce only difference. Consequently, Kyōka's close
and vivid perception of the actions of one of his characters can only mean that
he loses track of the others. Given the visual, imagistic nature of Kyōka's writing, therefore, the author tends to obscure the "larger picture" for the reader
rather than create one. For Kyōka, the largeness of life will be dealt with mythi-
cally, circumscribed by obvious constructions of personal belief rather than by
transparent systems of rationally achieved validation, as, for instance, supposedly occurs when the world is described objectively.

To return to the original point, Kyōka's inability to find a suitable
time/space schema for this kusazōshi-turned-novel is certainly one reason why
Crowned Yazaemon is a difficult story. In order to compensate for the all-
important discursive transitions that his visual style has pre-empted, he felt
compelled to offer instructions on how to read the work. Typical examples of
such directions are "The words of an old woman to be read from the middle of
the preceding chapter"; "This scene follows from the end of the previous chapter"; "This follows from the donjon scene, the stage swirls (*butai mawaru*)."
Needless to say, these types of transitions do not satisfy those who expect to
encounter a logical, plausible, and internally generated flow of events. Where
is the inevitability expressed by plot? These parenthetical traffic signs, so revealing of Kyōka's initial difficulty with constructing plots, will eventually disappear as he gains more experience. But the deeper reasons for this sort of
fragmentation will linger. In short, Kyōka will improve as a writer by first mas-
tering the rationale of a words-only plot. He will then go on to make his stories
conform to a more visual kind of logic, one supported more energetically by the
particulars of myth than by the universal laws of science. Stated in another way,
Kyōka's long-term response to the problem of narrative structure will not be an
improved temporal ordering so much as a more confident style of spatial ordering. Rather than affirm the modern development toward the extended,
linear forms that had been gradually forming in Japan since Ejima Kiseki
(1666?–1736) and Ihara Saikaku, he will begin experimenting with alternative
devices—especially multiple narrators, internal narration, and flashbacks—in
order to allow his stories to suggest themselves piece by piece. He will resist the

totalizing force of perspective by modifying early-modern picture-centeredness so that it becomes increasingly symbolic.

Fire and Return

Kyōka's eventful first year of discipleship ended in misfortune. On November 1, seventeen days before the final installment of *Crowned Yazaemon* was published, Kyōka received word that a fire had destroyed his father's home in Kanazawa. The flames sprang up in neighboring Hashiba-chō and spread toward the Izumis' home, burning a total of eighty-one houses. Kite, Seiji, and Toyoharu found refuge with the Meboso family in Yokoyasue-chō.

With Kōyō's permission, Kyōka hurried back to his family in Kanazawa. He stayed until the middle of December and returned to Tokyo in the middle of a heavy storm. In a postcard, dated December 15 and posted from Kasuga Pass, he wrote of the dangers of his return trip: "Today, at the risk of losing our lives we crossed the pass at Kasuga. . . . It is hardly possible to express in writing the travails of this trip." The general purport of this communication from Tsuruga was not the danger of travel, however, but that the trip was costing more than he had anticipated. Kyōka, still far from being self-supporting, asked his father, whose home had just been destroyed, to send more money.

CHAPTER 4

Crisis

∽

1893–1894

A Detective Story in Red and White

On February 28, 1893, Kyōka began his next project, a first and last attempt at detective fiction. As with *Crowned Yazaemon*, the piece was written at Kōyō's bidding. Sales of serious literature (*jun bungaku*) had been flagging, overshadowed by the recent successes of more popular writers such as Kuroiwa Ruikō (1862–1920), who, writing for an expanding urban readership, threw his net widely and reaped the economic rewards. Following the lead of the many newspapers that carried the strongly plotted detective stories of Ruikō and the historical novels of Murakami Namiroku (1865–1944), Shun'yōdō went after the popular market by publishing its own series of detective fiction. Kōyō was asked to help with this project, and many of his students became involved.

Kyōka's contribution to the detective novel craze, "The Living Doll" ("Iki ningyō"), is significant because the work suggests that he could have written more linear, plot-oriented stories had he wished. The story is confidently straightforward. Although far less devoted to problem solving than the ratiocinational pieces of Edgar Allan Poe, it is nevertheless a story that contains a puzzle and requires a rational search for answers. The questions that supply the momentum begin when twenty-two-year-old Honma Jisaburō, gasping for breath, collapses at the front door of a hospital. Kurase Taisuke, a famous detective and the hero of the story, finds a photograph in the stricken man's possession. It is of a beautiful woman who, Kurase intuits, is an important clue to solving the crime at hand. Actually, Kurase has more than this to go on since the man lives just long enough to relate the particulars of his crisis. He has been wandering for over three years, trying to convince someone to believe his story: in the Kamakura mansion where he was raised as an orphan, his stepuncle Akagi Tokuzō has poisoned his aunt and is now forcing his two female cousins, Shizue and Fuji, to relinquish their inheritance to him. In answer to the man's plea that someone help them, Kurase promises to rescue the young women from a life of horror.

This trope of the wicked stepparent is a late-modern, capitalist twist on the early-modern succession dispute (*oie sōdō*), especially as it is found in the kusa-zōshi tradition (where the succession of the wrong person to a powerful figure sets off a bloody conflict). Assuming a central role in this formula story, Detective Kurase is a type rather than an individual—an invincible doer of good with a flare for makeup and disguise. By any standard, he is impressively unbelievable. But, then, even Kyōka's better-developed heroes will similarly tend toward types, a disappointing tendency for anyone reading for what E. M. Forster famously called rounded characterization.

The persistence of Kyōka's archetypal characters can be understood variously: as the author's own lack of self-awareness, as a technical flaw, as a retention of an outdated narrative practice. Yet perhaps the most fruitful way to consider this paucity of delineation is to think of it as a critique of the expectation of personality that defines the modern tradition generally. What is a well-developed character, and why should we be interested in encountering one? Certainly, the modern requirement of individuality follows from a confusion about human nature: the more disagreement, the more important a concept such as personality becomes in accounting for the lack of consensus and for the possibility of meaning. In the case of late-modern Japan, social disorientation and reorientation were, like the invention of race and culture, a foregone conclusion of *bunmei kaika* or "the beginning of civilization." Japan's having to tread the waters of imperialism necessarily forced the issue of who is human and who is not. Whereas a writer like Sōseki allowed the trauma of social change to lead him to articulate the assumptions implicit in the discovery and propagation of the modern ego, Kyōka was more content to let the confusion stand. His lyricism worked with bigger pieces—images, symbols, large patterns of conflict and resolution—rather than the finely delineated distinctions of psychology and "truth." His own art focused upon icons—the tortured young woman, the worshipful mother—that were valuable to him precisely because they did not change and were therefore constantly available for either affirmation or denial.

At the time he wrote "The Living Doll," it is obvious that Kyōka was not yet aware of the eventual meaning of such icons of (non-)personality. But, as the narrative unfolded, this contemplation of a doll significantly advanced his thinking on the issue. As the story's title indicates, the doll is central to this world of pistols, knives, and secret passageways. Located in a strangely bare room deep within the sprawling, dilapidated Akagi mansion, it has enough life (*iki*) to become the point of everyone's reference. To the tortured Shizue, who finally gets rescued, it resembles and stands in place of her poisoned mother. To the murderously greedy Tokuzō, it is a monument to his lust, an icon before which he finally kills himself in frustration. And to the clever Kurase, who prevails at the story's end, it is a giver of gratitude, the source of his worth as a detective and as a man who can make and keep promises.

In this way, the doll is open to many interpretations. It can be various things to so many people because it is essentially an empty sign, a ready vessel for ascribed meanings. It is confused and complicated, a modern ego in this substantive sense. Structurally the doll is multivalent and lacks the discursive power to generate a psychological context that would allow it to show will and perception, that would allow it to have interiority. As an early prototype of Kyōka's archetypal woman, it is highly inclusive—woman as mother, woman as savior, woman as an object of lust, woman as bestower of manhood. Yet its lack of "real life" is suggested by an episode of ventriloquism. Hiding behind a double wall, Shizue pretends to be the doll speaking and condemns Tokuzō's selling of her sister Fuji to the lecherous Takata Dahei: "Fiend of the pit! Have you forgotten Heaven's judgment? The marriage will never be!"

The doll is also wounded in Shizue's stead. In a rage, Tokuzō tries to stab the haggard but beautiful Shizue. But because Kurase has secretly switched her with the doll (a move made possible because both are hidden beneath a covering), his knife cuts into wood instead of flesh. Still more mother than lover, the doll bears only a slight mark on her left shoulder. It has a body that is white, but a wound that is not red. Although Kyōka spared this mother figure by making her wooden, he would later insist that such a woman can be truly beautiful only if she is made flesh and her blood is shed. This deflecting of violence from the image of the beautiful young woman to that of the mother is the tentative beginning of a melding process that will join these two images of the feminine so that Kyōka's archetypal woman can emerge.

In contrast, the sisters Shizue and Fuji are beautifully human. As a result, they must suffer terribly. The aesthetic of red and white, already a factor in *Crowned Yazaemon*, requires their frequent torture.

How cruel! Fuji gasps for breath. Her face, once flushed, now becomes pale as she succumbs to the agony of torture. "Please! Kill me!"—hers is the death wish of a virgin. Knowing that his plan will be foiled if he kills her now, Tokuzō, as if losing heart in the midst of battle, rubs his arms and rests his whip. . . . Without the strength to stand, she collapses and faints. (1: 188)

This declaration marks an important moment in Kyōka's development as a writer. Here for the first time, he presents in words the image of the young beauty, tied and beaten, that so captured his fascination as a child. White legs flashing against crimson undergarments, white skin marked with red wounds, a rag of white silk bearing a message written in blood—with these other presentations of red and white Kyōka entangles the beautiful with the erotic. As we shall see, he would even dare to paint maternity in the same seductive shades.

Sickness and Return

Shun'yōdō published a total of twenty-six volumes in its detective fiction series. Kyōka's "Living Doll" came out on May 3, 1893, as volume 11. Writing to his younger brother about his contribution to the effort, Kyōka distanced himself from the work slightly. "I began writing 'The Living Doll' on February 28, and was able to get it published. For this I should like to visit mother's temple and offer thanks. The story was something I quickly threw together. I'm embarrassed to receive your praise."[1] Perhaps this is modesty. If nothing else, the story surely meant something to him as his second publication. Later, Kyōka would send a copy to his father in Kanazawa as proof of his growing success. Toyoharu, who had also begun to consider a career as a writer, liked what he read.

Another early publication was "The Gold Watch" ("Kindokei"), an adventure story written after the fashion of Morita Shiken's translations of European fiction. It appeared in the June 28, 1893, issue of Hakubunkan's magazine *Juvenile Literature* (*Shōnen bungaku*), and was paired with Kōyō's "Gallant Black Youths" ("Kyōkokuji"), a story about young black men rioting in Jamaica against the cruelty of the English. Kyōka's is similarly contemptuous of the white man. In this instance, the object of hatred is an expatriate named Arthur

Hagen, a scheming fellow who, in order to get his snake-infested grass clipped, posts a notice near his summer home in Kamakura: "Last evening I was walking in this area and lost a gold watch. I will give a reward of one hundred yen to anyone who returns it."

The Japanese villagers, who will do anything for money, swarm over the ground in great numbers. They cut the grass in their search for the watch and the reward that will last half a lifetime. Luckily for them, Saburō, child wonder, overhears Hagen conversing (in English) with his beautiful Japanese wife about the "Japanese fools" he has duped. Saburō's hatred for Hagen leads him to enlist the services of a pickpocket, who promptly pilfers the golden watch and delivers it to him. In the final scene, he and his sidekick Daisuke pay Hagen a visit, bringing him the missing article and demanding the promised reward. From his window the contemptuous Hagen looks out over many Japanese youths, all waiting to kill him if he does not deliver. Realizing he has been outsmarted, he gives the one hundred yen to Saburō, who yells out to the crowd that he will share his fortune with them all.

"Gold Watch," like Kōyō's "Gallant Black Youths," belongs to Japan's 1890s, a period of nationalist reaction that followed two decades of enthusiastic borrowing from the West. As for Kyōka's specific place within this context, his apotheosis of Francina Porter counterbalances what seems to be the total rejection of Arthur Hagen. Indeed, both sides of the issue are complicated by how Kyōka attributes positive and negative value. Francina is good (and female) to the extent that she becomes Japanese; Hagen is despicable (and male) because his privilege allows him to retain his distance as a foreigner. The symbolism of the watch connects the work with the world of the Enlightenment. Along with the bustle and top hat, gold pocket watches were an indispensable accessory of late-modern fashion. In Kyōka's story, the gold watch functions as an indictment of the Japanese ruling class, which was enthusiastically engaged in cultural cross-dressing. In sum, "The Gold Watch" is as much about class as it is about race.

In terms of personality, Kyōka shared fewer qualities with either Hagen or the remarkable Saburō, son of a Meiji nobleman, than he did with the pickpocket who colludes with Saburō. In a later conversation with Tobari Chikufū (1873–1955), Kyōka heard a story about a pickpocket that became the stimulus for *A Woman's Pedigree* (*Onna keizu*, 1907). The appearance of pickpockets in these and other stories led some to wonder if he had become acquainted with, and even sympathetic to, such down-and-outs during his year of wandering in

Tokyo and Kamakura.[2] He would use the figure of the pickpocket again in such works as "Shrine of Wonder" ("Tae no miya," 1895) and "Black Lily" ("Kuro yuri," 1899). As Kyōka continued to speak for the downtrodden, he displayed both resentment and admiration for the powerful. What more immediate way than thievery to share wealth?

Just two months after publication of "The Gold Watch," Kyōka returned a second time to Kanazawa. He was suffering from beriberi and returned to recuperate. In Kanazawa, he stayed with the Mebosos in Yokoyasue-chō. The Izumi residence had been rebuilt, but he did not stay there, probably because his father was also ill. It was not a happy time. Kōyō wept for his ailing student and told him that he planned to pay him a visit. Kyōka anxiously waited. In a letter dated September 13, Kōyō wrote, "I have finished negotiations with the *Citizen's Friend (Kokumin no tomo)* about contributing to their magazine. By the twenty-fifth of this month I would like to have a twenty-four or -five page manuscript completed. My plans to go hunting around the sixteenth have not been finalized." Kōyō's trip to western Japan was actually set back about a month. On October 5, he wrote again, saying that he would leave around the thirteenth, in time to see the Nagahama Festival, then "start out for Maibara around the sixteenth. My schedule after that is undecided. Maybe I'll contact you from Fukui."

But Kōyō's next communication was not a call from Fukui. Rather, it was a letter from Iwaya Sazanami's home in Kyoto.

I left Tokyo on the eleventh and reached Maibara Station at 2:00 A.M. on the twelfth. The connection north to Tsuruga wasn't going to arrive until the next morning, so I changed my mind and came straight to Kyoto. Until today we've been rained in.

> How depressing,
> A local song from next door—
> The autumn rain.
> I'll be heading your way for sure on about the twentieth.[3]

Kōyō never made it to Kanazawa. Feeling stronger and wanting desperately to go back to Tokyo, Kyōka set out for Kyoto around October 15. He met Kōyō there and borrowed enough for the train fare back to the capital. Aware of his imposition on his grandmother's family and of his inability to help his father, who was bedridden and could not work, he expressed his desire to go back to Tokyo. Driven to desperate measures, Kite sent Toyoharu, then thirteen years old, across the river to Mt. Utatsu, where he visited the teahouse of

Kotake Yosuke, the man who had adopted Taka. He explained their situation and asked that his sister be sent home for a short while. Kotake consented. Taka returned, and Kyōka, thinking he could be of more help to his family if he were working toward his goal of becoming a famous writer, left for Tokyo.

More Sorrows

His return might have seemed like a flight to some, but it was not necessarily false pride on Kyōka's part. He was, in fact, becoming a writer, filling Kōyō's orders for new work and getting paid for what he did. His plan depended on his family's being able to do without him for the time being, but this wish was dashed only a few months later. On January 9, 1894, as the city was getting ready to return to full activity after the New Year's holiday, Kyōka received the worst news possible. His father had died.

Kyōka rushed back to Kanazawa to take care of funeral arrangements. Kōyō wrote to him soon after.

I learned with sadness that your father's recovery was unsuccessful and that he has passed away. I can imagine the grief you must feel because you weren't with him at his final moment. Since life is fleeting, we should resign ourselves to the truth that each person's days are numbered. Your duty to your father now will be to make a name for yourself, to make your family prosper, and to revere your ancestors. No funeral, however glorious, could do more than this. Study with all diligence. Insufficient though it is, I will provide some assistance.[4]

For Kyōka, there was no escaping Kanazawa and all that a return to the provinces meant. Cut off from the city, he was certain that his life as a writer had been brought to an early end. With the full weight of family responsibility falling upon him, he despaired. His grandmother was over seventy years old. Toyoharu, a teenager, was still far from independent. Certainly, he could not take them back with him to Kōyō's house. And if he remained in a place as isolated and conservative as Kanazawa, how could he possibly further his career? Sooner or later, even his connection with Kōyō would not be enough to guarantee the future publication of his work.

To fight against the possibility of failure, Kyōka wrote feverishly. As he had done while living at the Ozakis, he continued to send his manuscripts to Kōyō for his mentor's approval. Not surprisingly, death and poverty were his themes. "A Deaf Man's Single-mindedness" ("Tsunbo no isshin," 1885), for instance, echoes Kōyō's rumination that the days of one's life are numbered.[5] This idea is bravely demonstrated by a metal craftsman, most surely modeled after Kyōka's recently deceased father, who lives only for the purpose of doing the best work he can. Tragically, he succumbs to cancer just before completing the commission he has been waiting for all his life: the designing and crafting of a turtle (a symbol of longevity) that will be splendid enough to be the capstone of his career.

He was a carver of precious metals, known for his skill at carving. Throughout the prefecture people knew him as "The Single-minded Deaf One." Only a few knew his real name. He was fifty-two years old. Having been a goldsmith from a young age, he could manipulate 365 different carving tools with great finesse, never letting them veer from their intended course.

His intentions were pure. His deeds were correct. He was a convert to the Nichiren sect, and his manner of speaking was peculiar. In disposition, he did not get along easily with others. He was immune to flattery, foolish, stubborn, sometimes even crazed.

When making a silver hairpin that would take most people half a day, he would spend three days of painstaking planning and execution, never giving a thought to his family's poverty. (1: 641–42)

This depiction of the deaf craftsman generally agrees with what is known of Seiji—a skilled artisan, a man absorbed in his work, a perfectionist. As described by Kyōka, his principal concern was to please himself artistically so that he might please others as well. As we are beginning to see, this was an attitude that Kyōka inherited from his father.

The emotional focus of the story is not this craftsman, however, but Fujii, a doctor and the first-person narrator. Through this character, Kyōka expressed emotions of guilt and the urge to confront suffering with still more suffering. He borrowed the authority of the medical profession (as he would do frequently from this point on) to create a persona capable of helping the father figure. Of course, the greater purpose of creating such a character was to show Fujii's inability to help. Expressing the pain he himself was no doubt feeling, Kyōka set up a scenario in which the old man's life becomes endangered just when the doctor is away on a visit to his hometown. In other words, the act of returning home has exactly the opposite value that it had in Kyōka's case: he returned to Kanazawa in order to deal with a crisis. This reversal might be read as a form of self-justification on the author's part. As Kōyō surmised in his letter, Kyōka's absence from his father's deathbed was a source of tremendous grief. His anguish suffuses every word of this powerful though not widely read story. This quest for respite led him to discover an important part of the narrative archetype that would eventually give shape to his artistic career generally: life's hardships were best made tolerable by the compensation offered through the suffering of a young and beautiful woman. In the most vivid and dramatic scene of "A Deaf Man's Single-mindedness," Fujii discovers a woman lying on a bridge at night. It is snowing and bitterly cold. He goes to her. He finds she is none other than the old man's daughter Okoma, another woman encoded with red (clothes) and white (snow).

> "What are you doing here?"
> She didn't answer.
> "You'll die if you stay here." I tried to add a tone of encouragement to my voice.
> "I . . . I . . ." Her voice became choked with tears. At last she was able to say, "I hate you for saving me." She cried and fell against the bridge railing.
> "But why?"
> Okoma swallowed her tears. "There's no hope for my father. He's going to die. I wanted to help him get better by trading my life for his. If only he could live long enough to finish his work." (1: 649)

Kyōka himself would come to depend on this notion of a woman's willingness to sacrifice herself so that art (and men) could continue. Beyond all limits of reason, this ideal of a woman's sacrifice would become a perfect and constant guide.

Suicide

Upon completing "A Deaf Man's Single-mindedness," Kyōka immediately began another contemplation of death, this one even more gloomy and terrible. In "The Night Bell Tolls" ("Shōsei yahanroku"), a young man, Teshima Ryō-suke, wanders late at night in Kanazawa's famous Kenrokuen Park. As he broods over his poverty and utter worthlessness, his mood is interrupted by a young woman, also desperately unhappy, who leaves the park and heads straight for the Kanazawa Castle moat. Her name is Yoshikura Sachi. She is a renowned seamstress, persecuted for having embroidered a handkerchief with an erotic scene (commissioned by an English missionary). Her attempt to kill herself is thwarted once, but at the story's conclusion, we learn from the protagonist that her death cannot be prevented. She commits suicide by throwing herself into the black water that would have taken Teshima's life had she not startled him.

Even more so than "A Deaf Man's Single-mindedness," this story expresses Kyōka's despair. Three of four main characters commit suicide, and the remaining survivor vows to murder one of the story's few minor characters, even at the price of losing his own life. In these pages, we find no hope. For the reader, there is only resignation, grief, and death. Kōyō was the first to know this. As with the other Kanazawa writings, Kyōka sent the manuscript to Tokyo. Upon reading it, Kōyō was so alarmed by its morbidity that he immediately wrote what has come to be his most oft-quoted letter to Kyōka.

I changed the title of your manuscript "Until the Dawn" to "The Night Bell Tolls." . . . It seems that your character Teshima is abnormal in his emotions. His morbid fascination betrays a mental illness.

It occurred to me that the creation of such a character might come from similar emotions in the writer. Indeed, today as I read your letter I could sense that because of your poverty of courage, your heart is like wind-blown hemp. Because your life is difficult, you have been enticed by the allure of death, like a poppy frightened by the demons of the moat. Your heart is as weak as a reed. What does it matter that your poverty is miserable? When you came into this world, you weren't surrounded by walls of carved wood and curtains of brocade.

To be born amid crumbling walls in a ramshackle house, to chew bread and drink water, is this not heaven? Enjoy that heaven! A great poet is one whose soul is like a diamond. Fire cannot burn it, water cannot drown it, no sword can pierce it, no cudgel can smash it. How much less, then, can it be damaged by hunger for a bowl of rice!

Because the time has not yet come for the diamond of your mind to give its light, heaven has sent you the sands of hardship and the whetstone of privation to polish that gem. After polishing yourself for several more years, your light will shine with an indestructible brilliance that will reach the ends of the earth. . . .

Your mind is a diamond! And a diamond is the most precious jewel under heaven!

If you possess the most precious jewel under heaven, are you not, then, of all men, the most wealthy?

Why aren't you, the wealthiest man under heaven, seeking the elixir of immortality? Spread beauty, and master joy!

I haven't yet had time to read your manuscript, "The Poverty Club." I've found a children's publication that may take it. I'll send it back to you after I've polished it to my satisfaction.

I, too, have had a lot of expenses recently, but I'm lending you three yen, which I'm sending by separate mail. Don't give up. Don't slacken the pace. Work hard. And grow up, as quickly as you can.

May 9. Kōyō[6]

Kōyō was justified in writing with such urgency. Kyōka later admitted he had been contemplating suicide seriously (28: 680). Other documents suggest that, as "The Night Bell Tolls" vaguely intimates, Kyōka went to the Kanazawa Castle moat to end his life but was caught up short by the death of another. The moat was a famous spot for suicides. In 1894 alone, nine people killed themselves there, including a woman who seems to have been the model not only for Yoshikura Sachi but for Hatsuji of "The Heartvine," Kyōka's last story. An article from Kanazawa's *Northern Reporter* (*Hokkoku Shinbun*), dated April 16, 1894, gives the following account.

Suicide at the Castle Moat

Yesterday at about ten in the morning, a body was discovered floating in the Kanazawa Castle moat. It was immediately reported to the West Kanazawa Police Headquarters, and . . . the corpse was retrieved and an autopsy performed. Pathologists determined that the woman was eighteen or nineteen years old. Although her address and name are unknown, from appearances she was either a prostitute or a serving girl at an eating establishment. To avoid unbecoming exposure, she had tied the skirts of her kimono to her legs with string. According to regulations, the corpse was buried in a temporary grave on Mt. Utatsu.

A follow-up article appeared in the same newspaper:

Young Beauty Throws Herself in Moat, Family Background

The young beauty who threw herself into the Kanazawa Castle moat was Yuki (nineteen years old), daughter of Yoshimura Matsutarō, resident of Yokoyasue-chō 84 Banchi. She was employed as a head worker at a local sewing factory, and was noted for her skillful work. . . . Recently, she was ordered by her employer to fill an order for a customer. She worked diligently to produce the work, but her employer found it unacceptable. . . . Yuki, usually reserved in all she did, felt compelled to do the work over again. Her employer did not care for the results of this second attempt either. . . . On the night of the fourteenth, she left her home, saying she was going to pray at the Kaji Hachiman Shrine, and killed herself.[7]

We do not know if Kyōka actually witnessed this woman's suicide. Even if he only enacted the scene in his mind, the death of this beautiful girl must have seemed like a divine intervention. Not only would its shock have helped postpone his own death, but it would also have given tremendous authority to the developing vectors of his literary imagination. A second, slightly different version of what transpired on that fateful night comes to us from Meboso Teru's son, Kanbara Enkō. According to his account, Teru awoke to discover the door open and Kyōka's bed empty. She told her son that she immediately ran out into the night and made her way to the castle moat, where she found Kyōka about to jump. "Had I not run after him, we would have lost him."[8]

In either case, whether it was Yoshimura Yuki or Meboso Teru, or both, who played the role of saving angel, the event gave the image of the woman savior then developing in Kyōka's mind enough power to counterbalance the ubiquitous threat of water, which was another principal image of the myth forming in his mental landscape. At this point, he was still years away from finding the larger narrative form into which such images would fit. But, having discovered an important part of the larger story here, he could begin to search for the proper structure that would allow him to save himself from destruction.

Rebounding from Sorrow

This season of tribulation had an end. Despite her son's death, Meboso Kite urged Kyōka to return to Tokyo and to rededicate himself to his work. He left Kanazawa with the understanding that he would temporarily leave his grandmother and Toyoharu there and that he would send back whatever money he earned from his writing. He was on the verge of independence. Once established, he would move to his own house and have the two of them join him in Tokyo. With this plan in mind, he made his way back to the Ozakis in September 1894, just one month before the publication of what some have considered to be his "first important work."[9]

Kōyō mentions an early draft of Noble Blood, Heroic Blood (Giketsu kyōketsu, 1894) in a letter addressed to Kanazawa; so we know that Kyōka wrote the work—along with "A Deaf Man's Single-mindedness" and "The Night Bell Tolls"—during his stay there.[10] In this instance, the protagonist is a woman, a sideshow performer named Taki no Shiraito (or Mizushima Tomo), who became (as the play based on this story grew increasingly popular) one of the best-known female literary characters of the Meiji period. On the one hand, Shiraito is reminiscent of the poisonous female characters (dokufu) popular fifteen years earlier, women like Torioi Omatsu, Hara Okinu, and Takahashi Oden whose murderous activities piqued the salacious imaginations of numerous journalists and their readers. Shiraito is a murderer, sentenced to death for killing a rich man and his wife for money. Yet she is far more sympathetic than poisonous.

Although she has murdered, she has acted out of love, resorting to violence for a reason that Kyōka would defend time and time again: if the price of a woman's life is the success of a young man, it is one worth paying.

Murakoshi Kin'ya rises from his status as a lowly carriage driver to "a digni-fied gentleman" because of Shiraito's sacrifice. She encounters him one summer evening as he sleeps on the Tenjin Bridge, which spans the Asano River, the very nexus of Kyōka's literary landscape. Gazing at his face, she recognizes him as the gallant young man who, responding to her challenge, raced his horse-drawn carriage against a man-powered rickshaw and, when the carriage broke down under the strain, brought her alone into town on his galloping horse. She learns that he has lost his job, probably because of her, and has come to Kana-zawa to look for work. In this age of opportunity and success (risshin shusse), his real desire is to get an education, although he is penniless and has little hope of fulfilling his dream. Able to perceive his real worth, she volunteers to pay for his education and to support his widowed mother, for whom he has been responsi-ble. In describing Kin'ya's shocked reaction to this sudden and unexpected fortune, Kyōka finds a way to perfect the all-important figure of the woman savior: "The coachman's placid soul was now moved to the point of leaping. More taken aback than surprised, more terrified than taken aback, his face changed color as he stared at this beautiful sorceress. . . . With a face as beauti-ful as a flower, her waist gently curving as a willow tree, was she a fox? a ghost? a witch? a voluptuous monster?" (1: 446–47).

Now the way is clear. The imaginative landscape after "The Night Bell Tolls" gives way to something more redemptive and, at the same time, more powerfully erotic and monstrous. Water imagery becomes increasingly sinister and acts as a border between the real and the ideal that has to be trespassed if salvation is to be gained. At the same time, the benevolent woman becomes a figure to be wor-shiped since the dangers for the trespasser are increased. This dramatic need forces the author to fashion a new type of ambiguity. What was more plainly described in the earliest writings becomes increasingly metaphoric, so that Kyōka can proceed a step further in his search for aesthetic salvation by setting up and then annihilating the clear distinction between loss and presence. Indeed, he will need to progress beyond the metaphoric, to a point where the border between tenor and vehicle itself no longer holds. That is to say, his need for reunion with the Absent will compel him to progress beyond an ontology that requires the metaphysical to be above the physical, the invisible to be more powerful than the visible, and absence to be more mysterious than presence. As we will discover, Kyōka's women will actually become the metaphoric beings that they at first *seem* to be. To their admiring men, they will become ghosts and sorceresses, beautiful and terrible, alluring and fearsome. Reaffirming the proto-psychological discourse of such woodblock-print artists as Hokusai and Kunisada, their images will exist prior to discursive analysis, as a monstrous reality.

The self-sacrificing, devoted, and gallant Taki no Shiraito is doomed because, as a savior figure, she must bear more pain than those whom she saves. Here, then, is the tension in Kyōka's logic of love, in this mythical solution that gives his works their deep, unresolvable mystery. If, for instance, Shiraito's shedding the blood of another for a good cause is somehow noble and heroic, the spilling of her blood is not. Consequently, Murakoshi, who becomes a lawyer and then a judge, is forced by his social position to be the one who, at the story's conclusion, has to sentence her to death. Even more intensely than was the case with Detective Kurase in "The Living Doll," Murakoshi is trapped by his success. Reflecting an ancient trope of the Japanese narrative tradition, he is torn between his duty to the public world and his private emotions. He loves her as she has loved him; yet because he is male and therefore more inextricably rooted in the mundane world of social responsibility, he cannot let her crime go unpunished even though that crime was committed for his sake.

This public/private dilemma can be understood as a turn-of-the-century version of the earlier obligation/emotion (*giri/ninjō*) conflict that was central to the work of early-modern playwrights. The Meiji-period evolution of a new public discourse based on paternalistic ideologies of national identity and imperialistic expansion clarified Kyōka's Edo-esque posture toward authority and social obligation. Like the authors of the well-known samurai play *A Treasury of Forty-seven Loyal Retainers* (*Chūshingura*), Kyōka did not make the choices easy for his male characters. Although bound and propped up by Meiji-period ideas of manhood, they are nevertheless sympathetic to (and aware of their dependence upon) a profound yet muted feminine discourse of resistance. By heightening the disastrous consequences of his heroes' choices, Kyōka expressed his discomfort with the male success ethic of *risshin shusse* or triumph at all costs. Murakoshi eventually kills himself because of his betrayal of Shiraito. The spilling of his own blood is an atonement, the only sacrifice that could be as noble and heroic as hers. But for Kyōka, even this suicidal heroism does not justify intolerable social structures.

In this and many stories to follow, duty will continue to triumph over emotion. It has been suggested that this pattern expresses Kyōka's "exaggerated respect for authority."[11] But, as we are beginning to see, the author's regard for power of *any sort* was extreme. Kyōka was, above all, a fearful man. The manifestations of this emotion—both in the positive sense of reverence or respect and in the negative sense of terror—are exaggerated, dramatically necessary, and innumerable. Accordingly, his respect went far beyond a simple esteem for figures of authority. It includes, for instance, such pairs as a horror of water and the worship of women, a dread of disease and an admiration of doctors, a loathing for the grotesquerie of shrimp and an appreciation for the comfort of well-cooked noodles, a repulsion toward the cannibalistic Kishibo and an adoration of the peace-giving Kannon, an impatience with language used clumsily and a sense of wonder for the power of words used well.

Teraki Teihō recounted several anecdotes to establish the extreme sensitivity that helped make Kyōka both a puzzling man and a powerful writer.

Sensei was very devout. Whenever he'd pass by a Shinto shrine or a Buddhist temple, he'd fall to the ground in worship. This happened more than a few times. He'd be walking along with someone and suddenly get down on the ground, much to the surprise of his partner. Truly fastidious and overwrought, he'd suddenly squat, touch the ground, then stand back up, and keep walking. He quit the habit as he grew older, but for many years, whenever something was bothering him, he'd lower himself to the street in order to rid himself of a disagreeable emotion.

When he was young, living with his younger brother, Sensei would suddenly turn to Toyoharu and call out in a loud voice, "Hey!"

Toyoharu would nod and say, "You're all right."

Again Kyōka would repeat, "Hey!"

"You're all right," Toyoharu would say again.

"Hey!"

"You're all right."

This question and answer would repeat itself ten times or so. Finally, feeling some degree of comfort, Sensei would lapse into silence again. Once, when Sensei wasn't around, I asked his brother about this habit. He told me that whenever something unpleasant or disagreeable or inauspicious clouded his brother's mind, he would suddenly yell out, "Hey!" And then he would have to reply "You're all right"—back and forth, until Sensei was satisfied.

Of course, Sensei didn't force others to do this with him. Since they were young boys, he had been in the habit of relying on his brother's help in dealing with his anxieties. I once witnessed such an exchange. Toyoharu was already grown and old enough to think the habit inane. Nonetheless, he respected his older brother, and to Sensei's loud "Hey!" he could not help but to respond with a lifeless "You're all right."[12]

Like shouting out "Hey," the process of putting words on paper was similarly cathartic and ritualistic. Both are inquiries into the nature of disease and the possibility of healing. Both are concerned with threat and its possible amelioration. Despite the incessant melodrama and gothic excess of Kyōka's work, it has the power to affect us because we can sense that it truly affected him. Sincerity alone cannot make great art. Yet it is certain that without this sort of genuineness, Kyōka's work would not have the power to lead us to the familiarity of strange places. We would not bother to follow where he would lead; neither would we feel the aura of that emotional territory in which we find ourselves.

Kyōka's fear recognized and required authority. This is not to say, however, that all figures of power were equally respectable. If he was worshipful of the emperor (whom he revered as a sort of personal god rather than as the ruler of a homogenized, atomized, and ever-growing public sphere), he vehemently opposed Japan's militaristic campaigns of expansion. Indeed, he was wary and often openly critical of bureaucratic and elected powers. Truly respected were more localized foci of energy: a mountain, a river, a tree, a mother, a lover. Although Kyōka was unquestionably modern in his hopeful regard for the possibilities of the self, he was less enthusiastic about the institution of the nation that concurrently arose to frame and control the powers of the individual. If anything, Kyōka possessed the self-absorption of the truly devout, confirming only those forces—medical, financial, or spiritual—that confirmed his own sense of self. He carefully protected his own interests, whatever the costs to others. As we shall see, he would not allow even his mentor to impinge upon his private needs as a lover.

Comings and Goings

Kōyō practically rewrote *Noble Blood, Heroic Blood*, guiding Kyōka's hand with regard to word choice, punctuation, names of characters, matters of plausibility, plot, and even the name of the piece, which was originally "The Blind Judge" ("Mekura hanji"), inspired by Morita Shiken's translation ("Mekura shisha") of Jules Verne's "Michael Strogoff."[13] So similar was the style of *Noble Blood* to Kōyō's writing that many readers thought Kōyō had written it. This confusion was furthered by the way Kyōka had signed his name—"Mr. So and So"—a common way to confirm that the writing of fiction was often, especially for young writers, a communal effort even in an age of the increasingly authoritative author. Indeed, it was a Ken'yūsha convention for both student and mentor to sign a manuscript together—written by Kyōka, revised by Kōyō—if and when an easily identifiable name was given at all.

Serialized as a newspaper novel, published as a book, then quickly adapted as a play by Nemoto Ryōha and Hiraoka Ryūkō, *Noble Blood, Heroic Blood* became widely known to the public as Kōyō's work.[14] Insiders, of course, knew differently. Having recovered from smallpox, Tokuda Shūsei was working for a newspaper managed by the People's Rights Party in Nagaoka, Niigata prefecture, when it came to his attention that some of the younger people in the company were excitedly reading a novel then being serialized in the *Yomiuri News*. Upon reading a few lines, he immediately knew that it had to be Kyōka's writing. The piece was far from his own idea of what a novel should be. Yet the success of someone from his own hometown fanned the embers of rivalry. In January 1895 he returned to Tokyo. With an introduction from one of Ōgai's relatives, he secured a job at Hakubunkan Publishers. This house was doing exceptionally well with its publication of two magazines—*Literary Club* (*Bungei kurabu*) and *Children's World* (*Shōnen sekai*)—and with its massive reprinting (in movable type and largely without illustrations) of the Edo-period classics. This was the tremendously influential *Imperial Library* (*Teikoku bunko*), still an important reference for early-modern texts. Shūsei's goal was to try once more to gain entry into the literary world, and in this effort he was encouraged to hear that Kyōka often visited the office where he was working.

Kyōka came there to consult with Ōhashi Otowa, a member of the Ken'yūsha group and the son-in-law of Hakubunkan's owner, Ōhashi Shintarō. Otowa, who had taken his wife's name and thus became the heir to the Ōhashi fortune, was an extremely influential member of the *bundan* (the very self-conscious circle of writers, publishers, and critics whose careers were built upon each other's work). He was editor of *Literary Club* and chief editor of the *Imperial Library* series. In the attempt to enhance the reputation of the Hakubunkan, he had already identified two rising stars in the literary firmament—Kyōka and Higuchi Ichiyō—and was doing what he could to support their development. He not only offered Kyōka a much needed job, assisting with the compilation of the *Family Encyclopedia* (*Nichiyō hyakkasho*), but room and board as well.[15] In February 1895, shortly following the publication of *Noble Blood, Heroic Blood*,

Kyōka ended his period of live-in apprenticeship at the Ozakis' and moved into the Ōhashis' home in Koishikawa Tozaki-chō.

Shūsei remembered Kyōka's frequent visits to Otowa's office. Kyōka's appearance had changed since his days in Kanazawa: "His complexion had lost some of its boyish blush, and the roundness of his face was gone. He was neat in appearance, possessing a charm and urbane refinement that was something more than run-of-the-mill. He was small and agile."[16] Kyōka, who also remembered Shūsei, came up to his desk near the front door of the editors' office, filling his pipe with tobacco and wearing a smile on his face. Shūsei's fictionalized version is as follows:

"They still talk about you at Sensei's house in Yokodera. 'What happened to those two?'"

"Is that right?" Hitoshi remembered how he had made such a fool of himself four years earlier.

"Why don't you visit again? Kōyō hasn't forgotten about you."

"Maybe I should."[17]

Shūsei did not act immediately on Kyōka's advice. He waited a few days, then wrote a letter to Kōyō to test the waters. Shūsei was now more cautious, more mature. He had already been rejected once, and writing ahead was consistent with Shūsei's way of doing things. As Shūsei himself described his fictional alter ego, "He was the sort who preferred writing letters over paying someone a visit. He got tongue-tied when in the company of others. Writing, on the other hand, allowed him to say things more freely. Afterwards, he realized the difficulty of writing letters and stopped altogether."[18]

Feeling badly about snubbing Shūsei the first time, Kōyō made sure to meet Shūsei when he came calling the second time. Kōyō invited Shūsei to attend a poetry party at Sazanami's home shortly thereafter, and he also handed him a five-yen note in payment for an adaptation of an American story he had done for Sazanami. This was the first money that Shūsei received for anything he had written, and it signified his acceptance as one of Kōyō's students. In the years ahead, he would prove to be one of the most accomplished writers of the group. With the coming shift within the *bundan* toward more realistic writing, his influence would eventually surpass Kyōka's.

As Kōyō's reputation continued to grow, the numbers of his students kept increasing. Yanagawa Shun'yō (1877–1918) had become a live-in disciple in 1893 and had been sharing duties at the front door with Kyōka. Oguri Fūyō, a student since 1892, immediately filled the vacancy created by Kyōka's removal to the Ōhashis. He and Shun'yō had less tolerance for the rigors of life at the Ozakis and began to complain. There were too many visitors to care for, and Kōyō's children, now crawling about the house and making a nuisance of themselves, were keeping them from their work. In the way of welcome to Shūsei, they made a proposition. The three of them would share the duties at the front door. But they would rent a flat nearby and offer private tutorials to bring in income. Shūsei thanked them for wanting to include him, but he rejected the offer outright. Shun'yō and Fūyō went ahead with their plan without him, and Shūsei later joined them in December 1896. Living at the Ohashis', Kyōka was on the verge of becoming famous.

CHAPTER 5

First Successes

~

1895–1896

Social Order and the Absurd

Kyōka's desire to establish himself financially was intensified by the need to send money to Kanazawa to support Kite and Toyoharu. Sensing his impatience, Kōyō himself had arranged for him to move to the Ōhashi residence and even held a celebration to mark the occasion. Kōyō and a number of the members of his ever-growing circle met at the Meishinkan in Kagurazaka for a Western meal. Kyōka used a knife and fork for the first time, but disliked the food that was set before him, the guest of honor. He would eventually develop a taste for Western cigarettes and movies, but this encounter with red meat was not at all satisfying. Many years later, on his doctor's orders, he would force himself to eat small portions, but only because his body was wasting away in its final decline. Although the celebration was an honor, Kyōka noted, "There is still no *sake*" (1: vi).

After Kyōka's departure from the Ozaki residence in 1895, Kōyō had to find someone else to wash his back. They were in each other's company less frequently, but their well-established relationship of mentor and apprentice continued without interruption. Kyōka's success as a writer was still far from guaranteed. His earlier pieces had shown promise, but he was still months away from the work that would finally establish him as a new talent.

Even before leaving the Ozaki residence, he had come up with an idea for the story. Not surprisingly, he decided upon a setting before he formulated a plot—space preceding time in the formation of his work. The place would be a watery one, a deadly one. He chose a spot called Cows' Abyss (Ushi ga fuchi), not far from Ushigome. Kōyō gave him time off from his responsibilities to allow him to reconnoiter the area. He strolled through the willow trees near the English Embassy, took in the details, had lunch at a noodle shop in Kōjimachi 3 Chōme, all the while putting the pieces of the story together in his mind. By the time he returned to the Ozakis', the plot was becoming clear. After a few more minutes of sitting alone in his small room off the entrance, everything came together.[1]

He tested the rough outlines of the story on Shun'yō, who did not seem much impressed with what eventually became the famous "The Night Patrol" ("Yakō junsa"). But Shun'yō's tastes, even though he and Kyōka were both under Kōyō's tutelage, ran in different directions. A native of Tokyo, Shun'yō was four years younger than Kyōka. Like both Kyōka and Kōyō, he had lost his mother at an early age and had grown up in straitened conditions. After attending an English school, he joined Kōyō's coterie at the age of twenty-six, and, along with Kyōka, Fūyō, and Shūsei, became known in an apt metaphor as one of the "Four Devas," the four guardian gods who share a center but face in different directions. They were connected not through any shared aesthetic principles but through their personal ties with Kōyō, and it was Kōyō's empathy as a teacher that allowed them to play to their different strengths. Given Kyōka's humble arrogance regarding his own talent, Shun'yō's lack of excitement becomes even more understandable.

Kyōka was disappointed but undaunted. If Shun'yō did not like "The Night Patrol," Otowa did. He encouraged Kyōka to develop the idea during those spare moments when he was not involved with the *Family Encyclopedia*. Eventually, Otowa saw to it that the piece got published in *Literary Club*, the magazine he was then editing. Compared to *Noble Blood, Heroic Blood*, this work more clearly bears the stamp of Kyōka's mind, but the critics largely misunderstood the story when it appeared on April 20, 1895.[2]

A short story in six brief parts, "The Night Patrol" concentrates on the conflict between private and public, introduced as a minor theme in "The Living Doll." Kyōka painted a decidedly unflattering portrait of a policeman, Hatta Yoshinobu, who stupidly throws himself into a moat (a place of terror already familiar to us from "The Night Bell Tolls"). The act is futile, because Hatta sacrifices his life to save the one man who stands between himself and his lover. Even more to the point, he cannot swim. His dive into the water is motivated by an uncompromising sense of responsibility that leads him to absurd extremes of behavior. Hatta is nothing if not committed—to his job, to his community—but this dedication is misguided and cruel. As he makes his rounds on the night of his death, he berates an impoverished rickshaw man for having torn trousers. Later, he forces a homeless mother and child who are sleeping in a public place to leave. Kyōka's portrayal of such actions suggests that Hatta is nothing short of monstrous in his zealousness and lack of compassion. By mentioning that others praise Hatta's death as an act of Confucian benevolence, Kyōka extended his argument to imply that late-modern Japanese society in general was similarly outrageous in its insistence on public duty. The gist of the story is that Meiji Japan is obsessed with maintaining order but coldly unconcerned about matters of the heart.

In this formulation lies a point we must not miss. A vigorous cultural critique is implicit in Kyōka's formative experiments with the supernatural. The inhuman Hatta represents a borderline soon to be crossed, as the "monstrous" ceases to be simply a metaphoric state. If Kyōka's apotheosis of women led him toward the exaggerated and unreal, his denigration of the vulgar similarly enticed him toward the obviously nonhuman. The memorable consequence of this predilection to exaggerate is that Kyōka's romantic valorization of the imagination and his distortionist critique of the mundane will eventually create a world in which normal people and realistic situations occur as a depleted middle ground: realism as relief rather than rule. The monstrous realize their plastic potential as Kyōka, beginning with an indulgence in pure melodrama, essentialized and exaggerated his characters until his stories became variations on a personal myth and his characters turned into demons and wraiths.

This tie between formulaic expression and Kyōka's heightened sense of the fantastic invites exploration. Seki Ryōichi, for example, suggests a linkage between the "night travel" (yakō) of "Yakō junsa" and the yagyō of the famous eighteenth-century illustrated guide to monsters, Hyakkiyagyō. (The characters for the two words—yakō and yagyō—are the same, although pronounced differently.)[3] In Seki's interpretation, Hatta is the monster that, like his Edo-period counterparts, emerges at night to roam the frosty streets, keeping a controlling eye on the dehumanized Meiji landscape. Hatta is a monster of the sort to which Kyōka would later refer in his essay "My Attitude" ("Yo no taido," July 1908). Writing to deflect the criticism of Fūyō and others who deemed the world of monsters (*bakemono*) a thing of the past, he was forced to express this fascination metaphorically. He situated the issue in a modern literal/figurative discourse that his colleagues could understand, although he himself rejected the binarism, since "figurative" was for him all too narrowly defined by realism. Monsters, he argued, do not belong solely to the mountains; they cannot simply be dismissed as cultural products of the unenlightened past. Rather, they are still an appropriate aspect of the civilized urban landscape; so much so, that Kyōka preferred to make them materialize "in the middle of the city, within the sound of streetcar bells." Monstrosity was an emotional and personal matter. Thus the famous dictum: "Monsters are the embodiment of my emotion" (28: 697).

Given the wide-ranging epistemic shift toward realism that made "modern Japanese literature" possible, we should not be surprised to see that much criticism of Kyōka has focused on the unnatural quality of his characters and events. Although formulaic in the way the narrative's central conflict is established and developed, "The Night Patrol" saves itself as a work of art by exploring conventional morality in ways that seem intentionally absurd and unreal. Hatta's heroism, for one thing, makes no sense, because (as his girlfriend Okō reminds him) he cannot swim well enough to save himself or anyone else. He knowingly sacrifices all, "both life and love," for no apparent reason other than his extreme idealism. Kyōka must have calculated that most readers would have difficulty sympathizing with such a man. Hatta has none of the tragic desperation of a thwarted lover. He is simply duty-bound in an absurd and inhuman way. Lacking true ability, he can hardly be called noble.

And yet the premise of the story is that Meiji society could see a man like Hatta as a hero, and thus stands condemned. This judgment of his society is Kyōka's not very subtle point: "With his life, he had also cast away his love. Afterwards, it was generally felt that Hatta was a benevolent man. But was this really benevolence? How can we praise a man who so thoroughly carried out his duties to the point of being coldhearted and cruel, chastising the old rickshaw man who deserved his pardon, berating the woman and child whom he should have pitied?" (1: 715). In sum, the society that Kyōka criticized was unable to value anything but his public, formal function. The private aspect of Hatta's life is utterly crushed by the public one, just as the poor rickshaw man's reason for living is taken away by the government, which conscripts his only son.

As already mentioned, in pitting public against private, Kyōka was following an example established by early-modern dramatists and scribblers. But "The

Night Patrol" orchestrates the tension in a way that is infinitely more devastating than that found even in the puppet plays of Chikamatsu Monzaemon (1653–1724). Unlike Chikamatsu, Kyōka allowed no possibility of rebirth or of lovers reuniting in their next lives. Where the tenets of a Buddhist afterlife once provided hope for star-crossed lovers, this vision is now eclipsed by the rationalism and paternal authoritarianism of the Meiji state. Okō watches Hatta die. There is nothing double about his death, except perhaps the way he dies with Okō's uncle, a man equally one-dimensional and inhuman. Having secretly been in love with Okō's mother, the uncle is dedicated to making his niece's life miserable. He endeavors to deny her marriage to Hatta, whom he ridicules as nothing but an eight-yen-per-month wage earner. In his warning to her, "When I die, you die," we read only the lack of love's fulfillment, whether in death or in life. This is no longer the early-modern age of double suicide, but the late-modern era of murder-suicide.

Critical Response and Literary Categories

Kyōka was disappointed by initial reactions to "The Night Patrol." A fellow boarder at the Ōhashi residence read it while Kyōka waited for his comments. Kyōka watched him turn the pages and carefully scrutinized his face for any signs of expression. As far as he could tell, there were none. The piece clearly left his friend unaffected. Nevertheless, as he himself read the printed version of his story over and over again, he could scarcely believe that he was the genius who had written it. Shun'yō looked over the copy he had received in the mail and sent it back with the brief note "Read your story." As it turned out, Kyōka's inflated expectations caused only disappointment. Forty-five days after publication, he had settled into "a fit of depression" (28: 676). Luckily, on the seventy-eighth day after "The Night Patrol" appeared (Kyōka counted the days), he received an astonishing report.

I happened to run into Ōhashi Otowa's wife in the hall, and she asked me, "Aren't you the one who wrote 'The Night Patrol,' you know, that story in the recent issue of *Literary Club*?" I felt awkward about claiming credit and gave only a vague answer. Then she said, "You know, I just went over to Ichiyō's house to run an errand. She said she really enjoyed your story. She was saying it was the best thing she'd read in a long time. She had nothing but praise for it."

I felt as if I were dreaming. I was enthralled. It was the first time for me to be praised, flattery or not. Ah, so this is what it feels like for a man to be flattered by a woman. . . .

Shortly thereafter, a detailed review appeared in *Literature for Today's Youth* (*Seinen bun*). It was written by Taoka Reiun, to whom I feel greatly indebted. (28: 676–77)

The first praise was especially welcome because it came from Higuchi Ichiyō, whom Kyōka had met through his connection with Otowa's office at Hakubunkan. She was an obviously gifted writer herself. Having recently broken off with her patron Kusaka Yoshitaka, she was also as destitute as Kyōka. For both these reasons, she had become one of Otowa's personal concerns. Sharing a similar status, Kyōka's regard for her was collegial and possibly romantic.[4] As a fellow writer, he considered her his "good rival."

As for Taoka Reiun (1870–1912), the review to which Kyōka is most likely referring appeared in *Literature for Today's Youth* on May 10, 1895. Its enthusiastic praise—"we can anticipate that Izumi Kyōka will advance without hesitation to the realm of the masters"—did much to establish Kyōka's reputation.[5] Yet there is good reason to believe that Reiun did not write the review. The one he did produce was equally fervent, if less detailed. It appeared somewhat later, on July 10, in the same journal. "The truth is that Kyōka has gotten where he is today through Kōyō's effective guidance and protection. Kyōka is truly gifted. . . . He has flown from the nest of outmoded thought and has broken new ground for the novel. . . . If Kyōka continues in his efforts, he may very well surpass Kōyō and Rohan."[6]

The critics were impressed with the freshness of Kyōka's latest effort. Both *Literary World* (*Bungakkai*)[7] and *Imperial Literature* (*Teikoku bungaku*)[8] praised "The Night Patrol" for its "pathos" and "seriousness" and for its ability to say something profound. Originality, seriousness, and depth were the critical order of the day as Japan's writers sought a new persona in the relatively higher status of the Western author. In this transition from *gesakusha* to *sakka*—from scribbler to creator—both the extinction and the birth of genres became inevitable. Since new forms required new labels, Shimamura Hōgetsu (1871–1918) felt compelled in his review in *Yomiuri News*, on August 26, 1895, to give Kyōka's experiment an appropriate name. As a member of the Tsubouchi Shōyō's reform-minded Waseda school, he called "The Night Patrol" a "conceptual novel" (*kan'nen shōsetsu*), a term that eventually established a new category for Japanese literary historians.

Hōgetsu's reputation as a critic was strengthened by the survival of this neologism. He defined the term to mean "a demonstration of a certain type of concept (*kannen*) regarding present social conditions."[9] *Kannen shōsetsu* were, in other words, stories that problematized social ideals. In the end, this subgenre of the modern Japanese novel was short-lived and only vaguely defined. As such, it was like other terms put forward at the time—the "tragic novel" (*hisan shōsetsu*) and the "profound novel" (*shinkoku shōsetsu*), and so forth. These new labels were intended to give order to a second, more fully developed phase of Meiji-period realism. Their proliferation suggests the robust energy with which the role and status of a new type of narrative (and therefore a new method of establishing meaning) was being negotiated.

Kawakami Bizan (1869–1908), another early member of the Ken'yūsha, also wrote ideological novels. By considering them, we can better grasp Hōgetsu's reading of Kyōka. "The Secretary" ("Shokikan," 1895), for instance, is a story of a businessman who sacrifices his daughter's purity to further his scandalous relationship with corrupt government bureaucrats. In a similar manner, "Front and Back" ("Ura omote," 1895) describes a reputable gentleman, known for his charity and virtuous conduct, who breaks into the home of his daughter's lover in order to steal a handbox. He is discovered and finally commits suicide after entrusting his daughter to her lover.

What Bizan's stories have in common with Kyōka's "The Night Patrol" is an interest in concretely demonstrating a particular notion about the nature of contemporary society: for example, the absurdity of conventional mores, as in Kyōka's work; the corrupt nature of capitalism and bureaucracy, as demonstrated in "The Secretary"; or the hypocrisy of a society that forces a conscientious man to degrade himself to the level of a culprit, as explored in "Front and Back." Kyōka had no clearly articulated political agenda in mind when he wrote "The Night Patrol," and he cannot easily be called an ideologue. No alternative system of social value would emerge from his mind. Yet the public sphere impinged enough upon his private life to help him clarify an essentially populist stance toward "government, money, and violence."[10]

For one thing, the war with China was on, disabusing Japan of its moral innocence as a world victim and giving it instead a vision of a future as an imperialist power. At this moment of national victory, Kyōka was desperately poor, saddled by his father's death with the responsibility of supporting a family. He was not irresponsible. Yet if he were going to save his grandmother and brother, he would do it *his* way. Struggling though self-assured, his bitter determination can be felt in a polemical essay entitled "Love and Matrimony" ("Ai to kon'i"), which appeared in *The Sun* (*Taiyō*) on May 5, 1895. Awkwardly phrased, repeti-

tive, and rambling, the piece attempts to make three points: that love is unquestionably desirable; that marriage kills love; and that women have the most
to lose because of the other two truths. To Kyōka's mind, love (*ai*) is "free" and
"oblivious to social hierarchy." Love should be self-fulfilling rather than self-
denying. Yet Japanese society does not allow this to be so. "Double suicide,
elopement, and disinheritance are similarly the fruits of love. We might exalt,
celebrate, and congratulate the persons involved. But from our society's point
of view, all such acts are lamentable" (28: 242).

Prevailing social structures required love to be channeled into marriage. But,
Kyōka argued, marriage has little to do with emotion. If anything, matrimony
only extinguishes one's feelings and thus ruins the lives of those who fulfill its
onerous obligations.

In short, marriage is a cruel and vindictive legal institution that has been created to
restrict and oppress love and to steal away one's freedom.

From old it has been said that beautiful women are unhappy. But this is only because society makes them unhappy. If we had no marriage, how many beautiful women
would become miserable? All the terrible aspects of love—conflict, deceit, despair,
suicide, illness, and so on—result from the institution of marriage. (28: 243)

Reflecting the militarism of the day, Kyōka's polemics could not help but draw
comparisons between marriage and war. Matrimony, for instance, finds a perfect analogue in conscription. Death is painful, yet men still gladly give up their
lives to die on the battlefield. Women, knowing that marriage will consume
them, still enter into its deadly promise.

Of course, Kyōka was not the first to question the institution of marriage in
the late-modern era. The romantic poet and critic Kitamura Tōkoku had done
so three years earlier in the essay "The Pessimist-Poet and Womanhood" ("En-
sei shika to josei," 1892). If anything, Kitamura's critique was even more woeful
than Kyōka's, its point of view constricted to that of the (male) poet, a being by
definition too sensitive and "pessimistic" to thrive in matrimony.

The pessimist is a man who cannot comply with the rules of society and refuses to
consider society his home. (*I love not the world, nor does the world me.*) He cannot be
restrained by the accepted standards established by rulers and compasses. (*My pleasure
is not that of the world, etc.*) In a word, he lacks the qualifications to organize a society in
this world of dust, which he reviles as a place of foulness. Therefore, the state of matrimony, which he enters with so much hope and imagination, is like an enemy territory
into which he ventures.[11]

Although Kyōka disclaimed adherence to any particular ideology, he shared with Kitamura a belief in love's supernal nature, a conviction of the individual's importance, and a dread of the mundane and the crass. In maintaining that a society's interests are clearly not the individual's, Kyōka's agenda is actually more romantic than democratic: men and women are fully differentiated when they are fulfilled as lovers rather than as citizens. Kyōka's feminism, if we can call it that, was powered by an amatory and even anarchic impulse that, whatever its ideological shortcomings, was appreciated by a great many female readers and critics.

The lesbian novelist Yoshiya Nobuko (1896–1973) expressed an opinion often heard from Kyōka's readers, female or male.

I believe that of all the writers working today the strongest feminist [*feminisuto*] among them is Izumi Kyōka. No other writer writes about women so frequently. The warm sympathy he extends to them, his gentle praise, his sense of appreciation, and the strength of his passionate love for them are infinitely greater than the concern of politicians who champion women's participation in government. Many of his works are praises of beautiful, noble women who shine in both body and spirit, and his understanding and observation of them is utterly thorough. . . . I know of no other writer who is as inspired in his depiction of women.[12]

To be sure, Kyōka's critique of Meiji society ought to garner more sympathy than Tōkoku's, if only because, in absolute numbers, there are more unhappy women than pessimistic poets. As Kyōka put it:

In most cases, society is unable to deal with private matters. A woman must endure hardship, she must cry, suffer, and, in the worst of circumstances, die for the sake of her parents, her children, her husband, her friends and relatives, her servants, her town, her village, and her household. Unable to gain for herself the status of an independent physical self, she is manipulated by others, criticized, and controlled. In the name of love, the concept of a freely operating self gets turned into the selfless, supposedly another name for perfected love. Consequently, for the sake of such love, no matter how bitter or difficult the trials that others bring to her, a woman contently, even joyfully, receives them. Unhappiness, misery, and long suffering are nothing but words of complaint that we who have a sense of our own selves level toward society. How can there be joy and sorrow if the self is extinguished by love? (28: 242)

In this way, Kyōka learned to speak for the oppressed. Fortunately for him, the downtrodden and marginalized found and appreciated shadows of themselves in his stories, although it is also clear that Kyōka was exploiting their suffering for his own artistic purposes.

Love and Surgery

Having at last captured some recognition as a writer, Kyōka moved out of the Ōhashi residence and established himself in nearby Ōtsuka-chō, then on the outskirts of Tokyo. In May 1896, he welcomed his grandmother and younger brother, whose reunion was described much later in the autobiographical *Plum Blossom* (*Usu kōbai*, 1937), written just two years before Kyōka's death. Itoshichi is the name he chose for himself.

When rickshaw men approach Ōtsuka, lying on the outskirts of the city, they unfailingly declare that the neighborhood lies outside Tokyo proper and press for an increase in fare. In a small, three-mat room just off the main road where the oxcart drivers pass, Itoshichi trembles as he writes of his grandmother's plight—how she finally received the long-awaited call to come to the capital but was unable to sleep on the train because of the wretched circumstances of her grandson, the would-be novelist—a mountain of worry towering over her gray head. Upon her arrival, she made a makeshift Buddhist altar by setting a rat-eaten basket in the alcove where the Buddhist altar should be; on top of it she displayed the memorial tablets of their family's deceased ancestors. The offering candle that was lighted this morning was frugally extinguished a third of the way down. Out on the veranda, where there was a splash of sunlight, she patched his worn stockings. (24: 534)

As if given new strength by his grandmother's presence, Kyōka scored another success only one month after her arrival. Having broached his radical ideas about matrimony in the essay "Love and Matrimony," he next chose to demonstrate these notions in a short story entitled "The Surgery Room" ("Gekashitsu," 1895). As in "The Night Patrol," the possibilities of melodrama are once again pushed well into the realm of the absurd.

The surgery room itself was bathed in a luminescence so radiant that I could count the particles of dust in the air. It stood somehow apart, stark and inviolate. And there in the center of the room lay the Countess Kifune, focus of concern for both those outside the room and those inside, who were closely observing her. Wrapped in a spotless white hospital gown, she lay on the operating table as if a corpse, her face drained of color, her nose pointed upward, her chin narrow and frail, and her arms and legs too fragile to bear even the weight of fine silk. Her teeth were slightly visible between pale lips, her eyes tightly closed, and her eyebrows drawn with worry. Her loosely bound hair fell lightly across her pillow and spilled down on the operating table.

At the sight of this noble, elegant, and beautiful woman, now ailing and feeble, I felt a chill spread through my body. (2: 13–14)

Present at the Countess's surgery are members of Japan's new aristocracy and several of their servants; a famous surgeon named Takamine (Towering Peak) and an attending physician; a few nurses; and the narrator, who is an artist and the doctor's friend. Once again, eros, beauty, and death are encoded in red and white as we witness the operation unfold through the narrator's eyes. If the Countess's pallor reminds us of Poe's marblelike heroines, it is because Kyōka, too, is sadistic enough to appreciate the death of a beautiful woman. And yet the dissimilarities between Poe's and Kyōka's heroines are pronounced: Kyōka's archetypal woman eventually becomes a counterforce to death. This role is not yet apparent, though. In the early works, death pulls inexorably. It is liquid and red, and always more bloody (and more frankly sexual) than it was for Poe.

Lying on the operating table, Countess Kifune is doomed. Despite the pleadings of nurses and family, she refuses anesthesia because she is afraid the medication will make her reveal the secret she has been hiding deep in her heart. She finally relents, not to the anesthetic but to the knife.

The Countess crossed her arms and grabbed her own shoulders. Takamine, now transformed into a sacred, all-powerful being, spoke to her in a solemn voice, as if taking an oath. "Madame, I take all responsibility. Allow me to proceed with the surgery."

"Yes," she answered with a single word, her ashen cheeks suddenly flushing crimson. The Countess gazed directly at Takamine, oblivious to the knife now poised over her naked breast.

A red winter plum fallen to the snow, the smooth trickle of blood flowed down her chest and soaked into her white gown. The Countess's cheeks returned to their pallid hue, but her composure seemed complete.

It had come to this. Takamine worked with superhuman speed, not wasting a single movement. None of us in the room, from the servant to the attending physician, had a moment to utter a word. As her chest was cut open, some trembled, some covered their eyes, some turned away, some stared at the floor. I was gripped with a cold chill.

In the space of a few seconds Takamine brought the surgery to its critical juncture as the scalpel found the bone. At this point the Countess, who had been unable to turn over in bed for these past twenty days, released a deep "Ah" from her throat. Suddenly she sat up and firmly grasped the doctor's right arm with both hands.

"Are you in pain?" he asked.

"No. Because it's you. You!"

The Countess slumped back. Her eyes stared upward and fixed themselves upon the famous surgeon's face in one last ghastly, cold gaze. "But you couldn't have known."

At this instant, she grabbed the scalpel in Takamine's hand and plunged it into her body, just below her breast. Takamine, his face ashen, stammered, "I haven't forgotten!"

His voice, his breath, his handsome figure.

A smile of innocent joy came to the Countess's face. She released Takamine's hand and fell back on her pillow as the color faded from her lips. At that moment the two of them were absolutely alone, oblivious to earth and heaven and the existence of another soul. (2: 23–24)

At this point, we do not know what it is exactly that Takamine has not forgotten or why the Countess is willing to sacrifice herself at his hands. The answer is given in the second half of the story, which takes us back nine years.

The narrator and Takamine, now only a medical student, are strolling in the Koishikawa Botanical Gardens in Tokyo. As they climb a verdant hill covered with azaleas in bloom, "a beautiful red color," they meet three striking young women, walking in the opposite direction, carrying parasols and accompanied by coachmen in stovepipe hats—all trappings of late-modern power. Takamine's eyes meet those of the "stunning" woman who is walking in the middle; and this single glance enables them to fall in love with each other and, later, to die for each other.

For the next nine years, until the incident at the hospital, Takamine never said a word about her, not even to me. Given his age and position in society, he could have married well. Yet he never did. If anything, he became even stricter in matters of personal conduct than he had been in his student days. But I have already said enough. Although their graves are in different places—one in the hills of Aoyama, one downtown in Yanaka—the Countess and Takamine died together, one after the other, on the same day.

Religious thinkers of the world, I pose this question to you. Should these two lovers be found guilty and denied entrance into heaven? (2: 28)

Ending with a question and the posing of a problematic *kannen*, "The Surgery Room" resembles "The Night Patrol" in both form and critical tone.

To readers of the day, Kyōka's critique of Meiji society was new and forceful. One critic for *Imperial Literature* wrote:

Izumi Kyōka is an up-and-coming writer. Yesterday he was one of Kōyō's nameless students. Today he is clearly one of our best new talents. He is in touch with the latest thought from modern Europe, and his prose possesses a certain liveliness that is not easy to come by. . . . Kyōka understands life's regrets; he knows that these regrets should not be suppressed by the beaten path of morality; and he comprehends that the violent waves rushing within the human heart are likely to drown out reason.[13]

The "latest thought from modern Europe" is Victor Hugo's. Hugo's stature in France as a spokesman for the people impressed Japanese writers struggling to cast off the Confucian bias against fiction. This is not to say that the critical function of imaginative writing was new or that there were no other sources for Kyōka's critical disposition. In fact, there were many springs for this acidic water. One is the very identity of the *gesakusha* as a marginal and, therefore, critically disposed artist. Kyōka certainly absorbed some of this force from his extensive reading of Edo-period texts. In a similar way, Kyōka's artisan background placed him near the margin in Kanazawa, affording him a perspective on the rulers and the rules that was disparaging and even resentful. Yet a third, which accounts for the greater part of Kyōka's indignation, is the matter of aesthetics. As Akutagawa Ryūnosuke (1892–1927) would put it so elegantly, Kyōka's sense of social justice was buttressed by a "morality grounded in poetic justice."[14] For Kyōka, as for Tōkoku, it was poetically right to stand against the Meiji patriarchy, to rail against the institution of marriage and the falseness of political and bureaucratic power.

When placing this piece in the sweep of Kyōka's early works, we get a sense that this aesthetic foundation of Kyōka's critical spirit was largely lost on his audience. For one thing, in the year 1895, the world of Japanese fiction was in tumult. Realism and romanticism were sprouting like branches from the same tree; given the unsettled and experimental nature of the rhetorical field at this time, it was no wonder that intellectuals like Reiun and Hōgetsu chose to see Kyōka's work as ideologically rigorous. Despite the unnaturalness and implausibility of "The Surgery Room," they read Kyōka's story as proto-naturalist and saw it as penetrating the surface of things to grasp the principles by which modern society worked. In fact, he had no such objectives in mind. If Kyōka's "conceptual novels" led to certain concepts, they were less the fundamental principles of a nascent social science and more obviously the first steps toward establishing the poles of a deeply personal mythology.

The major elements of the myth are present in these two stories, ready to be developed in ways that will continue throughout Kyōka's career as a gothic writer. Beyond the encoding of red and white, there is deadly water. There is woman as sacrifice, unfortunate in beauty. There is the tyranny of brute masculinity. And, most important, there is the hapless male protagonist, Kyōka's latest and most romantically enabling discovery. Ennobled, tempted, and crazed by a bottomless whirlpool of desire, these men would dance with taboo in the many works to follow. As we shall see, only the dependence of the male, the weak and needy hero, would allow beauty, love, and salvation to become fully possible.

Turning from Success

By the end of the year, Kyōka had made a name for himself. He must have realized, however, that his newly won status came to him largely through a misreading of his work—that he had been caught by a spotlight on his way to another place on stage. Rather than dwell in this light, and despite critical expectations for more of the same "stories about ideas," he bravely departed from the formula. If he had the integrity to continue deepening and perfecting his artistic vision regardless of the market, it is partly because he had much encouragement to move in such a direction. Stimulus came from a familiar source. In January 1895, Ichiyō had begun publishing her remarkable *Growing Up (Takekurabe)*. By January 1896, all seven installments had appeared in *Literary World*, the principal publication of the romantic movement in Japan, and a revised edition of the entire story appeared in a single issue of *Literature Club* in April 1896. This masterfully written story about children and their painful passage into the world of adult responsibility and sexuality established Ichiyō as one of the great writers of the day. Mori Ōgai, who had said little about Kyōka's work, lavished praise on Higuchi Ichiyō.

At the risk of being mocked as an Ichiyō worshiper, I do not hesitate to bestow upon her the title of "poet." . . . This author has captured the "local color" of Daionji-mae so effectively that one might say it has ceased to exist apart from *Growing Up*. Having done this without leaving a trace of the effort involved, she must truly be called a woman of rare ability.[15]

Another prominent writer to praise Ichiyō was Kōda Rohan. He might have had "The Surgery Room" in mind when he wrote the following review.

The works of this author, Ichiyō, are never inconsequential, but the present work is especially notable, both for the beauty of its style and for the profundity of its themes. Some phrases do have a slightly familiar ring, and you can find flaws with the writing. But the skill of the whole dazzles the eyes and intoxicates the mind, leaving us at a loss for words. . . . One can appreciate the dense texture of her prose by observing how not one word can be omitted. Surely, this is an example of "Take away one part and you destroy the sense of the whole." For those many critics and novelists who seem to think that a novel does not merit serious attention unless it puts a knife to someone's throat, strips away the skin, and digs out the internal organs, I suggest they swallow a dose of her language. They should take five or six words at a time, as a miracle-working anti-dote, guaranteed to improve their literary technique.[16]

In the end, it is difficult to determine whether Kyōka benefited from Ichiyō's brilliant example. For one thing, he had already started with a young hero story before Ichiyō finished her work and before these reviews appeared. He called it "Maidenhair" ("Bake ichō"). Like Ichiyō's work, it also appeared in Otowa's *Literary Club*, in February 1896, two months before Ōgai's famous critique of Ichiyō.

As Reiun noted in his May 10, 1896, review of this story, "Maidenhair" marked a significant advance for Kyōka. His writing is noticeably more mature and confident. Although he was still addressing social problems in the style of the conceptual novel, he was finding himself in the process, discovering something that seems both more familiar to him and, given the increasingly realistic literary context in which he had to write, weirder to others. "Maidenhair" continues to explore the possibilities of monstrosity as social critique, allowing Kyōka to advance one step beyond the absurdity of "The Night Patrol" and "The Surgery Room" to something even wilder and more extraordinary. Here he clearly ventured into the realm of the *bakemono*, as in "Bake ichō." The female protagonist Otei is just such a "monster," the sort of unfortunate woman Kyōka had in mind when he wrote "Love and Matrimony." She is trapped in an arranged marriage forced upon her by exigency at age fourteen. Now twenty-one, she has lost her child and realizes she wishes her husband dead. It is a maddening situation that ultimately leads to murder and insanity.

We receive most of the story as an extended confession, a one-sided dialogue between Otei and the largely sympathetic sixteen-year-old Yoshinosuke. He rents a room on the second floor of her house and represents a glimmer of romantic hope for Otei. To him she delivers what for us is already a predictable speech on the evils of marriage.

"Oh, but Yos-san. What a ridiculous thing the world is. After exchanging a few cups of wine, you're suddenly somebody's husband or wife. What a strange arrangement. Your body becomes a man's property, and no matter what he says, you have to do it. If you don't? Then you're sulky. Then you don't know 'a woman's place.' Then you're immediately the subject of everyone's gossip. . . .

"Protect chastity. Obey your husband. Those are the rules, I suppose. But doesn't it make you wonder who made up the rules in the first place?

"And once the wedding's over and you turn out to be 'flawed,' then the marriage is dissolved, and it's always an embarrassment to the woman. With no freedom over her own body, why should a woman have to spend her lifetime with someone she hates, when her life with that man is worse than death? What kind of sense does that make?

"I know marriage wasn't a revelation from God or from the Buddha. And if it's something that someone made up, then, since we're all human, having a lover shouldn't be wrong, and running off with someone else should be understandable. You should be able to say what you think, and people should be able to accept it. If that was how things really were, then it would be the virgins and the virtuous wives who get booted out." (2: 304–5)

Despite the forceful simplicity that Kyōka tried to give this passage, he did not make Otei simply a mouthpiece for women's rights. Her stand against matrimony is easily identifiable, yet her particular situation is complicated by the compromise she has made with the prevailing social system. When her husband contracts tuberculosis, she prays for his recovery. When he probes for her motives, she answers all too honestly that she wants him to live only because she fears the loss of financial support. Not only this, but she refuses to divorce him and to run off with Yoshinosuke (as he prods her to do), since what others think does, in fact, matter. She is compromised, thoroughly and painfully. Exploiting her feelings of guilt and expediency, he demands that she kill him. Unable to control her rage, she obliges, maddened by the lack of other possibilities.

The world, having pushed Otei to this point, is nevertheless able to judge her with some measure of sympathy. She is not executed but allowed to live out the remainder of her days in a sort of living hell. She huddles in a dark room, avoiding any light that might reveal her ghastliness. Ghostlike, she changes her hairdo back to the premarital maidenhair (*ichō*) style, and this we understand to be a false and pitiful attempt to play the role of temptress. Hers is a pathetic swank, a decrepit *iki* (chic), a hideous makeup. Things do not end as she would have liked. But her monstrous transfiguration actually appeals to Yoshinosuke, not because she has become more attractive in her ghoulish state but because she reminds him even more now of his dead sister. In the final analysis, "Maidenhair" seems to be yet another remembrance of the dead.

In setting out the pathetic aspects of *iki*, Kyōka tied an aesthetic knot that would not unravel throughout the remainder of his career as a novelist. This is why the infrequently discussed "Maidenhair" is important to understanding what is to come. Here the attraction of feminine beauty begs the question of sexual desire while inflaming Kyōka's own yearning for his deceased mother. At the same time, it deepens his obsessive belief that women are essentially beings of suffering. This story is unusual in its dearth of water imagery, but even without the constant peril of water, the threat of disease, death, and insanity still reverberates in the background as a steady chord against which the melody of the plot situates itself. As a balance to these dark forces, the "character" of the ideally feminine will require an impossible list of necessary characteristics: style, power, beauty, allure, calm, long suffering. Working steadily toward a way to reconcile these antinomies, Kyōka learned by writing this piece that the only way he could proceed with his construction of the archetypal feminine was to deconstruct the masculine image through a process of regression. As already suggested by the development of figures like Policeman Hatta, Doctor Takamine, and the "naive but not simpleminded" Yoshinosuke, Kyōka would find a suitable mode of male sexuality by (almost) always making his male protagonists younger than the women they love.

CHAPTER 6

Pursuing a Vision

1896

Ichiyō's Death and the Masculine Regression

Perhaps his dual life as a physician and a writer made Ōgai particularly disposed to dislike "Maidenhair." His criticism of Kyōka was harsh. "We look forward to reading poetry but regret having unexpectedly been made to read an article on medical jurisprudence."[1] To Ōgai, Kyōka could not compare with Ichiyō, who, having won the recognition of all, was now dying of tuberculosis. She first became aware of her disease in April 1896, while working on her contribution to the *Family Encyclopedia*. Otowa had commissioned her to write the volume on *Daily Correspondence*, which Kyōka would have edited. Although it is impossible to know how close she and Kyōka grew through their business dealings, it is safe to say they had a number of opportunities to meet each other. Only two letters survive from Kyōka's correspondence with her. One is dated May 6, 1896, and begins with the wish that she were a man rather than a woman: "Greetings. As it is especially difficult for me to proceed, knowing that my reader is a woman, I have written this letter as though to a friend of my own sex. I hope you will consider it in this light."

The matters taken up in the body of this letter are largely inconsequential. Ichiyō had apparently asked Kyōka to inquire of Kiryū Yūyū about housing for

one of her friends. Yūyū, as mentioned above, had come to Tokyo from Kanazawa with Shūsei and may not have necessarily been on the best of terms with
Kyōka. At the time of this letter, he was enrolled in the law department at the
Imperial University. According to Kyōka, Yūyū was angered by the request: if
the person in question had enough money to pay tuition, couldn't he also pay
for housing? Kyōka's ostensible purpose in writing was to ask Ichiyō for the
name of the person in need. The transaction, perhaps, was simply an excuse.
Learning the name would have changed little.

The letter closes with another thought on gender, which clarifies the intention of the opening lines.

> Could you do me the honor of a short visit? . . . I would go to you but I hesitate since
> I still remember the last time. It seems that I am not at ease among women, and this is
> why I am always thinking how much better it would be if you, Higuchi-san, were a
> man. I don't know if saying this sort of thing pleases you or not. But I hope you will
> take it in the best possible light. At any rate, I hope to see you soon.
>
> > May 6
> > From Izumi Kyōtarō
> > To Onatsu-sama[2]

We do not know if Kyōka's interest was returned in any way, although the
curious silence of Ichiyō's famous diary on the topic of Izumi Kyōka has led to
much speculation. Perhaps she simply had nothing to say about this young man
who preferred to think of her as a man. Or it may be that portions of the diary
were erased and that she did write about him but later regretted it. One Japanese scholar accounts for the silence in an even less probable way: *Kyōka* had
parts of Ichiyō's diary erased.[3]

There is little in the way of new information to add to this puzzle. However,
Kyōka's later description of Ichiyō in *The Plum Blossom* differs considerably
from her public image. Having established his own persona as a writer, Kyōka
seemed (even in his final years) to be struggling against the image of this woman
who had surpassed him in the eyes of almost everyone who mattered.

> Most people hold this image of Ichiyō in their minds. She is seated before a small
> writing table, brush in hand, properly composed as she writes away. But how realistic
> is this picture? . . . It was a dreary day during the rainy season when Itoshichi visited.
> There was a latticed door, and beyond it a dark, narrow hallway. Her house was situ-
> ated in the shadows of the Hongō heights. There were rooms on both sides, and from
> the still murkier darkness of what appeared to be the sitting room on the left came the
> sound of bare feet. Her coiffure was coming apart in places, her face had a sallow hue.

In this fictional account, Ichiyō is half-dressed when she comes out to greet the protagonist, Tsujimachi Itoshichi.

"Sorry. . . . It's such a gloomy day. I was just drinking wine out of a mug. That's our little secret, if you don't mind."

So this was the proper Higuchi Ichiyō? More like decadent, the way she tied her sash in front of Itoshichi. But perhaps such behavior can only be expected of a kind-hearted older sister who kept young gallants in her company as she wrote of courtesans killing themselves for love. (24: 476–77)

There are obvious problems in relying upon this fictional work as a source of information for the early years. In fairness to Higuchi Ichiyō, we should note that *The Plum Blossom* contains a number of personal jabs at different members of the Bungakkai school. Perhaps this description should be considered simply another one of these blows (even though her affiliation with this group, regardless of the romantic quality of her work, was in fact quite loose). Affiliations aside, the passage is clearly not meant to make one of the best-known female writers since Murasaki Shikibu look good, even with the final qualification. On another occasion, Kyōka was forthcoming about his respect for her. "I knew that, given the right conditions, it would be possible for me to write the sort of the things that Kōyō and Rohan were writing. But I knew I would never be able to write anything like Ichiyō's *Growing Up*. When I read it, I found it so surprising that my head started to spin."[4]

Perhaps it is enough to say that Ichiyō's influence as a writer upon the twenty-three-year-old Kyōka was considerable. The most remarkable aspect of *Growing Up*, at least as noted in Ōgai's review of the work in *Literary World*, was its portrayal of children. "Ichiyō has brazenly made children the protagonists of stories that are to be read by adults. Whether such writing existed or not in the distant past is something I cannot say, but I can state with confidence that this is the first of its kind in the world of contemporary letters."[5] Encouraged by Ichiyō's success, Kyōka himself wrote a series of stories in which the youth and inexperience of the male protagonist is not simply a convenience of plot but close to the center of his concern. Doubtless, he would have taken this path even without the appearance of *Growing Up*. But with the precedent of Ichiyō's work, the powerful desires of youth were that much easier to explore.

The first of this series of "weak-male" stories appeared in May, at about the time Kyōka was seeing Ichiyō about her manuscript for Hakubunkan. Entitled simply "Book One," it forms the first installment of a seven-part work—*The Maki Cycle*—completed in January 1897. Uesugi Shinji, the hero throughout, is an echo of Kyōka as a youngster. Shinji, who lost his mother at age eleven, is only fourteen when the story begins. The confusions of adolescence lend themselves well to the many powerful and conflicting passions that are incubated in an environment of nurturing and death, the bivalent yet ambiguous sanctuary of Kyōka's fictive drama.

This narrative also marks the beginning of a long line of grave-visiting stories that sustained Kyōka's access to the dead until the end of his life. Indeed, "The Heartvine," his final story, is one such work. As we shall see, it is the culmination of the author's remembrance of the deceased and of the many proxies who made his life bearable through their sacrifice. Populating this string of narratives from "Book One" to "The Heartvine," Kyōka's women share the principal function of favoring and saving the male protagonist. In this series of closely related stories, Shinji, who has trespassed the space of death and loss, is helped by one mysterious woman who introduces him to another. This second woman, Ohide, modeled after Yuasa Shige, competes for his love against the competition of a third, who is based on the figure of Miss Porter. This third woman, who reminds Shinji of his mother even though she is Caucasian, is, by Kyōka's admission, reminiscent of the dying Higuchi Ichiyō. In the Maki cycle, then, the images of no less than five women coalesce in the eyes of the young male protagonist.

Entitled "The Book of Oaths," the series's final story describes the consumptive and dying Milliard asking Shinji to promise the impossible: to forgive Tominoichi, his rival, and to forget Ohide, whom he also loves although she has become the married property of a wealthy Kanazawa merchant. In the final deathbed scene, we find an extraordinary confusion of Milliard (modeled after Kyōka's English teacher), Shinji's mother (who is a shadow of Kyōka's real mother), and Ichiyō.

As I gazed upon her profile, buried there in her pillow—so pitiful, so precious, so beautiful and noble, like the blameless petal of a rose mallow, rising away like the curls of incense smoke—I felt as though I was looking at the face of my dead mother there before me! "Mother!" I cried out and collapsed at Milliard's side. Clinging to her breast, I sobbed like a child. (2: 482–83)

Although Ichiyō is not explicitly named in this story, in a 1928 publication of the novel in Shun'yōdō's *Meiji and Taishō Masterworks* (*Meiji Taishō bungaku zenshū*), Kyōka confessed that he had drawn Milliard's deathbed from a visit to Ichiyō shortly before her death.

Again and again, the sound of the wind whirling in the sky. What will this winter wind do to her who lies ill? "Milliard. Milliard." I am sure I saw her eyes open. Again and again, the winter wind in the darkening night. It was the night I visited Higuchi Ichiyō, whose consumption had suddenly taken a turn for the worse. As I write this, the raging winter gale howls. What will the storm do to Ichiyō, who lies ill? Laugh at my childish thoughts if you must! How could I hold back my feelings of regret for the one I considered my good rival?[6]

Kyōka probably visited Ichiyō shortly before her death, while he was working on the final scene of the story. As the concluding segment of this series of connected narratives, "The Book of Oaths" appeared in the New Year's (1897) edition of *Literary Club*. Kyōka's "good rival" had died of tuberculosis on November 23, 1896, a few weeks earlier.

Kyōka's admiration of and romantic attraction for Ichiyō, his exotic fascination with the American woman Miss Francina Porter, his warm regard for his childhood friend Shige, and his yearning for his deceased mother are all brought to bear in the creation of this female archetype, a woman who is clearly no one in particular and everyone at once. The common qualities of these women include kindness, a greater age than the protagonist, and, certainly, physical beauty. Similarly, all are oppressed by circumstances, whether death, illness, bad marriages, or the haunting presence of someone like Tominoichi, a blind man, whose inauspicious and polluting presence requires the magic of spiritual cleansing. The figure of the beautiful, dying woman is Kyōka's abode of superimposed surfaces; in effect, these surfaces are the author's denial of the particularities of psychologically constructed character. He had no fascination with depth and roundness, no desire to copy those such as Sōseki who attempted to create a discourse of individuality. If Kyōka was typically modern in his loneliness, his remedy was not the creation of an interiority that could be called a self. To reinforce a point already introduced, his solution was, rather, a recasting of a medieval cosmos, a ritualistic positioning of uncontested visual signs, a proto-psychological discourse of yet-to-be rationalized metaphor and monstrosity.

Of course, current literary trends denied the efficacy of Kyōka's surfaces, even though Taoka Reiun, in a July 10, 1896, review in *Literature for Today's Youth* praised the work for its strong characterizations of Shinji, Tominoichi, Milliard, and Ohide. At this juncture in the development of the modern ego, even such one-dimensionality of character must have seemed full and "real" to readers. But as the discourse of representation among the literary elite spread and continued to grow in sophistication, Kyōka's characters were becoming no less superficial. His was not an inward search for the honest truth of the "I" but, rather, a worshipful quest for an external Other that reigned beyond the boundaries of factuality. His characters were not analytical but emotionally charged surfaces superimposed upon ancient archetypes as transmitted through the Japanese oral tradition and made textual with words and pictures.

As mentioned above, these images of women are also layered with those of the beneficent Kannon, the gallant Shiranui and other woman warriors of the *kusazōshi* tradition, and even with prototypes of the ancient shamaness or *miko*. In one ancient prototype, women, naturally blessed with abundant spiritual powers, gave their strength to men, usually brothers, who could not survive without them.[7] As constituted in "The Book of Oaths," the sexually attractive older woman (Miss Porter), a lost love (Shige), a dead mother (Suzu), and the dying woman of power (Ichiyō) together form the archetypal heroine, a figure essentially higher in status than men, who are both dependent on her and frightfully aware of her tremendous powers. As Mishima Yukio put it, the yearning for such a figure is the obsessive "drama hidden in the deepest recesses of Kyōka's self," "the story of a sensitive and handsome young man and an endlessly beautiful, endlessly compassionate, yet endlessly frightening older woman."[8]

Teriha Kyōgen

Kyōka gradually began to make more friends outside the narrow and often tension-ridden circle of Kōyō's apprentices. From Ōtsuka, it was a short distance to the residence of Yoshida Kenryū, an acquaintance from Kanazawa who had graduated from the distinguished Third School in Kyoto and was now a student at the even more prestigious First School (or Tokyo Imperial University). It was through Yoshida that Kyōka met Sasakawa Rinpū (1870–1949), who would become one of his two closest lifelong confidants.[9] Sasakawa, who later distinguished himself as a haiku poet and an expert on Edo-period art, lived next door to Yoshida in the same Hongō dormitory. Kyōka and Rinpū discovered a common interest in Jippensha Ikku's (1765–1831) *Shank's Mare* (*Tōkaidō dōchū hizakurige*) and took their sobriquets from it. Just as the bumbling adventures of Ikku's two indomitable heroes had attracted wide interest during the previous era, the friendship between Sasakawa and Kyōka came to be famous among Tokyo artists. Older by three years, Sasakawa became Yaji. Kyōka was Kita.

Kyōka would later reconstruct a scene of his visits to the Hongō dormitory in the story *Worship at Yushima* (*Yushima mōde*, 1899). A new refreshment, *kōcha* (black tea) served with sugar, was the beverage of choice among Imperial University students, attesting to their enlightened status. Offering tea to the protagonist, Sasakawa is portrayed as a serious student of history. He is an acquaintance of another character, modeled after Yanagita Kunio (1875–1962). This college friend happens to be passing by and calls up to their window. Yanagita, who eventually became Japan's most prominent folklorist, shared with Kyōka a fascination for the traditions that were rapidly being abandoned in their country's rush to gain the acceptance of Western institutions. Indeed, all three—Sasakawa, Yanagita, and Kyōka—seemed more than willing to be caught looking backward in a decidedly forward-looking age. If this antiquarian gaze kept Kyōka tied to the graphically rich texts of the Edo tradition, it would also lead him (along with Yanagita) to that other repository of the past: oral tales preserved among those living in the countryside.

For Kyōka, rural Japan would come to have a special importance. His need to construct the regressive male required a nostalgic regard for the space of his hometown on the Sea of Japan, since the dependent male required childhood and childhood required the places that had formed it: the narrow alleys of his neighborhood along the Asano River, the ribbon of water that was the river itself, and the mysterious world of mountains, temples, and villages of the nonhuman that lay beyond its far bank. Kyōka's continuing search for an archetype that would allow him to address the sense of loss and impoverishment that so profoundly plagued him required the overwhelmingly strong impressions of youth—perhaps the most insightful and direct encounters with reality that come our way.

Kyōka's next major work, *Teriha Kyōgen*, published serially in the *Yomiuri News* from November 14 to December 24, 1896, is another story about a young man. Mitsugi, a typical *bishōnen* or handsome youth, is the protagonist. Echoing Kyōka's personal bereavement, Mitsugi has lost both parents. He is living in Kanazawa with his aunt, who, being more interested in her own amusement than in Mitsugi's welfare, is the antithesis of Kyōka's nurturing female. Consequently, his emotional needs must be met by other women who live in his neighborhood. They pity him. In particular, Oyuki, who lives across the way from her stepmother, treats him like a younger brother. Like Ohide of the previous story, Oyuki is also modeled after Yuasa Shige, one of the girls whom

Kyōka remembered in his second autochronology: "I heard many legends and tales from the beautiful young girls in my neighborhood" (1: iii). Not surprisingly, Shige's memory is invoked within the context of local legends.

Together, teller and listener alike place the damp and inwardly focused world of Kanazawa not in the distant historical past but in a realm of twilight and mystery. For Kyōka, Kanazawa and the mountainous hinterland surrounding it steadily became an alternative to the more urban world of the late-modern, the civilized, and the masculine. Kyōka would insist on access to both worlds, bringing his discovery of each to bear on how he configured the other. Although Kyōka had escaped from Kanazawa, his imagination still needed the possibilities it presented. Tokyo was the world of change, of Westernization, of power, of a liberating and nonprovincial milieu; Kanazawa was the locus of the essentially native, the eternal yet marginal, and the stiffly provincial. No longer his actual home, the countryside increasingly became for him an imaginative space of magic. The dynamics of entering and leaving this world became the overriding narrative mechanism in his work.

Into Mitsugi's neighborhood of shadowy, narrow streets comes a troupe of performers. Female dancers and singers, they set up a tent and begin their mesmerizing performances. Glad to get Mitsugi out of the house, the aunt encourages her nephew's fascination with them. Kochika, the troupe's leading dancer, falls in love with Mitsugi, who is equally enchanted with her. They are not, however, equals in the relationship. She is the more aggressive. Planting a blood-red kiss upon his cheek, she makes him fear that his bodily fluids are being sucked by a *nobusuma*, a huge bloodsucking bat that can supposedly live for a century. The link between women and flying creatures had long been established iconographically within the kusazōshi tradition. Kyōka would play with this image of flight and aggression before finally settling on an image more unambiguously powerful in its saving function. But more important than its latent powers of salvation is the bat's function to extend the concerns of love, as a sort of blood-dripping flight, to its farthest points of reverberation within a distant and romantic hinterland of eternal yearning.

Mitsugi continues to see Kochika every night despite his love for Oyuki and despite the taunts of the neighborhood bully Kunimaro, who challenges him to "Get away from the whore." Kunimaro's animosity eventually leads to a tussle, in which Kochika, who tries to hold Mitsugi back, becomes injured. Her injury is understandable only when we remember her position as a savior: she needs to demonstrate superiority by suffering more than the one she saves. Such is the plight of Oyuki, as well, who becomes more attractive to Mitsugi the more he learns of her unhappiness.

Eventually Mitsugi is forced to choose between the two women. When Kochika walks him home after his fight with Kunimaro, they discover that his aunt is being arrested for gambling. Without a guardian, Mitsugi's painful decision is hastened. Does he move in with Oyuki or join Kochika? His decision to become a member of the *kyōgen* troupe and to align himself with Kochika takes him away from Kanazawa and Oyuki. When he returns with the actors eight years later, his hometown seems completely changed, drained of the magic it had for him as a young boy.

If one story of late-modern Japan is of growth and development, another is of loss and nostalgia. Eventually both will merge in a fascist aesthetics of lyrical imperialism, foreshadowed here by Mitsugi's smoldering rage upon learning of Oyuki's misery. Having pleaded for sentimental reasons to spare the maple tree that stood between her and Mitsugi's house, Oyuki unwittingly contributes to the decline of her household. When a great flood uproots this emblem of her love for Mitsugi, it damages her family's house and allows the raging Asano River to wash their entire fortune to sea. Impoverished, Oyuki has been forced to marry for money. Her husband, Mankichi, is abusive, another brute like Kunimaro. Her unremitting unhappiness causes Mitsugi to despair.

The narrative logic is simple. Oyuki's life is miserable because of her love for Mitsugi. Realizing this, he searches for a way to save her. For Kyōka's weak male, however, the only way to solve such a problem is by sacrificing (other) women. Although the plan is not his, he asks Kochika to seduce Mankichi and give Oyuki an excuse to divorce him and free herself from the hell of matrimony.

> "So you'll do it?" Mitsugi asked Kochika.
> "I suppose I have to."
> "They tell me he's a real bastard!"
> "Just another bumpkin, I'm sure."
> "What's wrong? Is something wrong?"
> "Just look at me," she laughed. "I've become the great deceiver."
> "Great. Then Yuki's saved."
> Kochika's face became pale. "Mitsugi, forgive me for saying this, but I don't think it's a good thing you're asking me to do."
> Mitsugi didn't answer.

"It's not a good thing, Mitsugi."

What was he feeling? His heart was pounding.

"Mitsugi, I make my living on the stage. But since we met, I've been careful about who I see. I knew that if people talked about me behind my back it would be hard on you. So I've protected my reputation." Kochika moved closer to Mitsugi and held his hand. "Of course, there's no reason why you should know this. And there's no way I can really be your sister. Suppose I could. Even a sister can become the subject of rumors. I didn't want anyone to come between us, but it's been hard on me. I'm not saying this to make you feel like you owe me something. I don't expect anything. I'm not complaining either. I just need to know, Mitsugi. Are you saying that as long as you get to see the Hiraoka girl again, you don't care about what happens to me? Do you care about me at all?" (2: 627–28)

Mitsugi realizes how insensitive he has been to Kochika. As they continue to talk in the garden, a cat with a white dove in its mouth walks by. This carnivore obviously represents Mankichi, one of the crass, moneyed men of the world; the white dove with its wing spotted with blood just as obviously represents Kochika, who must sacrifice herself in order to save Oyuki and to provide emotional comfort for Mitsugi. As Kochika raises her hand to scare the cat away, a bolt of pain races through her elbow, expressing her identification with the killed bird.

Kyōka does not develop this dramatic tension. Rather, he chooses to diffuse it with images that turn time into space. He widens the geographic particularity of Kanazawa so that it becomes a place of past sentiment, a center for a much larger connotative field. As readers, we are thus connected with an even larger tradition and iconography, and loss becomes enormous. With this aim, Kyōka made the nostalgic force of this climactic scene between lovers even more evident. In the final section of *Teriha Kyōgen*, Mitsugi, in an act appropriate to a weak male, confronts a choice. Will it be Kochika or Oyuki? Unable to make such a decision, he leaves at night to begin a new life. Climbing a pine-covered mountain, he discovers a hall where the lines of the famous Noh play *Matsukaze* are being chanted. And it is with this allusion to parting lovers that the story ends.

The ending is not without problems. To be sure, Mitsugi and Kochika's final conversation explains their predicament in terms of conventional standards of morality. But the story does not achieve closure in a way that confirms these mores. Mitsugi leaves Kochika while bearing the burden of Oyuki's suffering; he is alone, wandering in between. Things must end this way because he is in a state of transition in which dualities are broken down into infinitely more complicated patterns than the laws of conventional morality can explain. What we are also reading here is Kyōka's fascination with twilight, the bewitching hour, *au ma ga toki*, traditionally held to be that moment during the day when visitors from the other world—hostile or benign—appear. For Kyōka, twilight is a state between good and evil, where one thing turns into the other, where the love of one's mother becomes complicated with Eros, where resolve becomes indecision.[10] Only in such ambiguity is resolution possible, because the sexuality of Kyōka's hero is similarly complicated.

Given the lack of clarity this situation creates, we can understand why some readers felt that Mitsugi's choice to be alone did not make much sense. Ten years later, Kyōka explained the ending to one of his fans.

I am writing in response to your inquiry about the final chapter of *Teriha Kyōgen*. Let me assure you that your question follows not from your shortcomings as a reader but from mine as a writer. As far as Mitsugi is concerned, nothing would make him happier than being with Kochika day and night. He realizes, however, that it is not within his power to save Oyuki, who had shown him great love when he was a child. He is neither able to help her, nor able to bear the thought of living happily with Kochika. And so, in place of saving Oyuki, he leaves Kochika and wanders aimlessly. His desire is to be as dejected and as pained as she.[11]

Mitsugi's final action is meaningless except as atonement. His masochism is essentially the attitude of a weakling who punishes himself in the hope of erasing an unfortunate reality.[12] That reality is, in the end, a state in which one is deprived of love, forced to live with a profound sense of isolation. He is cut off from parents, from his past, from the possibility of love, even from his hometown. He searches for maternal protection but is lured away by the power of mystery (as embodied in artistic practice). His relationship with Kochika does not go beyond the need to protect and to be protected. Thus, we understand his return to loneliness at the story's end. It is an attempt to avoid confrontation with *real* sexuality. His hesitation is a form of narcissism, in which the beauty of women and of art (as symbolized by the bat) are allowed only within a world of childhood. This explains why Mitsugi tries to keep his distance when Kochika makes her sexuality felt. By choosing Kochika in the first place, he rejects Oyuki, who cannot be his mother's replacement; yet he comes to yearn for Oyuki because her suffering makes her more and more powerful as an erotic symbol. In short, it is Oyuki's ability to suffer and thereby occupy Mitsugi's thoughts that leads him to reject Kochika. Ultimately, he is led to neither woman, only to his own narcissistic meditation on their meaning to him.[13]

The Chaste Planet

The growing success of Kōyō's many pupils began to raise questions about Kōyō's own future as a writer. In answer to the criticism that he was spending too much time on his students, Kōyō wrote and published *Passions and Griefs* (*Tajō takon*), a story of an ordinary man's inner struggles with the death of his wife. This novel, which appeared serially in the *Yomiuri News* from February to December 1896, dwells at length upon the protagonist's sorrows as he yearns for his deceased partner. He refuses to remarry, despite the urgings of others. When he finally begins to respond to the ministrations of a friend's wife, he is accused of being sexually interested in her. A falling out occurs, and the novel ends as the protagonist decorates his room with both a painting of his wife and a photograph of his friend's spouse. The tentativeness of the conclusions of Kōyō's *Passions and Griefs* and Kyōka's *Teriha Kyōgen* are surprisingly alike: the men in both stories long for two women at the same time, while being unable to be with either one. For contemporary readers, the similarity must have been impossible to miss, since these two endings were published concurrently in the same newspaper. Because of its similarity to Kyōka's story, Kōyō's new work only made him more vulnerable to the criticism that he was mentoring too much and writing too little.

Along with Fūyō's "Bedtime Cosmetics" ("Ne oshiroi"), a story about an incestuous relationship that was printed by the *Literary Club* in September but was banned by the authorities, these works by the writers in Kōyō's circle represent a common way of conceptualizing sexuality. It is a method that defines the Meiji-period protagonist generally. Beyond being dependent on the female, the male protagonists these three portray are either literally or metaphorically adolescent. They are not yet fully experienced with the disappointments of sexual involvement, which were made relevant by a gradually spreading discourse on romantic love that, by raising expectations, also increased the possibility of disillusionment and even despair.

The naturalist movement would seek a different solution to the possibility of a new kind of relationship between men and women by underscoring its carnality. Already at this point, Kyōka was able to escape this brutish disillusionment, since the reification of women resulting from his desire to resurrect his dead mother was utterly aesthetic. Exceeding commonly encountered levels of indulgence, his men are thoroughly young—more childish than adolescent in their dependence on women. Noguchi Takehiko clarifies Kyōka's position by comparing it with that of Tanizaki Jun'ichirō, another male writer obsessed with defining female sexuality as a combination of mystery and comfort.

Tanizaki Jun'ichirō also sought from women a sort of transcendental salvation. Accepting the corporeality of their everyday existence, Tanizaki's men are constantly lowering themselves in a masochistic way in order to position women on a higher "other ground." Kyōka had little need to do this, however. Thus, the usual resistance felt by writers trying to elevate the female to such levels did not exist for Kyōka. Not that Kyōka's women have no reality; for they do. But the women about whom Kyōka found fit to write were not actually existing entities to be described but, rather, ideals that needed to be presented. Perhaps no other quality best distinguishes them than their "otherworldliness." Thus we understand their mystery and bewitching nature. To Kyōka, who believed wholeheartedly in the existence of spirits, women were, above all, visitors from the other universe.[14]

If Kyōka's writings are peopled with such untouchable women, his personal world was not exactly a chaste planet. Both Kōyō and his students were in the habit of visiting the brothels. Out of deference to their teacher, who preferred Yoshiwara, Kyōka and his colleagues frequented Fukagawa and other districts. Kyōka's participation in such excursions is confirmed by Shun'yō.[15] Still unsubstantiated are claims that during his year of living dangerously, previous to becoming Kōyō's live-in student, Kyōka had been hired as a housesitter for a short period and was forced to have sex with the woman of the house.[16] The original source of this rumor is apparently Yanagida Izumi, who is said by some to have misunderstood what he was hearing from Kyōka's wife after the author had passed away.[17]

Whatever the truth of Kyōka's year of wandering, in his work we encounter none of the sexual rawness of, for instance, Iwano Hōmei's (1873–1920) novels or Ishikawa Takuboku's (1886–1912) *A Diary in Roman Script* (*Rōmaji nikki*). If, as Masao Miyoshi puts it, the Western novel is essentially appropriating in its urge to discover and conquer the Other, Kyōka's stories are not novelistic in the same sense. In them, discovery is solipsistic, and the relationship between protagonist and his context fundamentally passive.[18] The sexual appropriation of either male or female is always suggested but rarely accomplished. Kyōka chose eroticism over sex, establishing an equilibrium that is not so much a balance as a standoff, a lyrical vein of sexuality deposited within formations of good and evil, an "other world" in which the forbidden and the sacred are inextricably and beautifully linked. Entrance into this space is dramatic, clearly a trespass and unquestionably erotic. Yet it is also a temptation granted only to Kyōka's neutered and appropriately mythic males.

In "Mino Valley" ("Minodani"), published in *Boy's World* (*Shōnen sekai*) in July of the same year, the hitherto vague outlines of the Kyōka myth begin to emerge with increasing clarity. This lucidity is, without doubt, made possible only by the abilities of the imagination to exaggerate, as if an emphasizing of the essentials takes over as the author's principal artistic mode. In this story, Kyōka wrote of a young boy who follows a firefly into forbidden territory. Rather than be destroyed (which would be the sure fate of an adult male), he is embraced by a goddess who saves him. In "Of a Dragon in the Deep" ("Ryūtandan," 1896), published in *Literary Club* in November, he continued to indulge this obsession with the neutered male.

"Of a Dragon in the Deep" further amplifies the pattern of trespass, making graphically explicit the knot that binds erotic taboo to social oppression. In the earlier stories, that union was made understandable within the conventional discourse of moral "concepts," ideas sufficiently clear to be understandable to critics such as Hōgetsu and Reiun. But from this point on, Kyōka's dance with taboo becomes hysterically antagonistic and even antisocial. Not coincidentally, his prose sheds its debt to Shiken's sinocentrism in order to affirm a tradition older than translations of Victor Hugo could supply. Perhaps his encounter with the antiquarian Sasakawa and the budding ethnologist Yanagita helped open his mind to the repositories of traditional madness and obsession that begin to give his subsequent writings their tremendous power. Here, in this work, his progress toward a discourse of monstrosity reached a higher level: Kyōka became a writer of that incarnation of deep, formalistic social critique that (in a modern framing of the phenomenon) is sometimes called "fantasy."[19]

Chisato, the protagonist of "A Dragon in the Deep," is, above all, a trespasser. He violates the rules and is thereby drawn into forbidden places. Despite ample warning, he plays by himself, with neither supervision nor friends. He wanders into the mountains, where he is bitten by a poisonous insect and, in violation of propriety, befriends a group of outcaste children. "The people living in these small houses were called 'outsiders' (*katai*). Their customs differed slightly from ours. Even though their parents might be well off, they dressed poorly, most of the time they went barefoot.... My friends warned me never to play with them" (3: 9).

But he does befriend them. And their game of hide-and-seek leads him deeper into forbidden territory. Both the children of the far bank and the game they play belong to the other world, and the protagonist's involvement in this amusement allows his trespass into the world of death and mystery. The Meiji Enlightenment notwithstanding, in Kanazawa and elsewhere it was commonly believed that people who disappeared and then reappeared after several days were "hidden by the gods" (*kami kakushi*). Such is the fate of Kyōka's protagonist. In order to make this belief central to the story, Kyōka establishes the time as twilight, when such kidnappings were most likely.[20] The game provides, in fact, the very structure of this story: only by being discovered by a goblin (the "it" of hide-and-seek) can one eventually return to normal society.[21]

This structure of winning-by-losing forms a critique of its opposite paradigm: unambiguous success and failure, or the spirit of modernization and the Meiji-period success ethic as encapsulated in *risshin shusse*. Seen this way, Chisato's journey into the forbidden can be interpreted as a departure from the late-modern present (*kindai*) into the time before literature, a rejection of an improved, more phonocentric and discursive semiotic field in favor of a recasting of the decrepit past. To place the movement in a personal context, it is a journey that Kyōka had to take, since the erotic recovery of his deceased mother was becoming inextricably linked with the crumbling pictocentric tradition, which was no longer available except through the fading tokens of early-modern culture.

After losing himself in the mountains, Chisato encounters a woman, the dragon of this tale, who is "in every way like a treasured court doll." With well-defined eyebrows, clear eyes, a prominent nose, and scarlet lips, she is like an elder sister, a temptress who is also a not-precisely-maternal mother.

She put her hand on my shoulder and pulled me to her, filling my mouth with the precious jewel of her nipple. Locks of her disheveled hair fell down, over the frost-white collar of her kimono. How unlike my sister, who always turned me away when I asked for her breasts.

Whenever my hand began to explore beneath my sister's kimono, she would scold me. It had been three years since my mother passed away, but I hadn't forgotten the savor of her bosom. This woman's were not like those. The gems of her breasts were as delicate as the thinly falling snow, melting instantly upon my tongue, overflowing and cooling my mouth. (3: 20)

She is, in other words, a woman of another world, a frightening being who, nevertheless, gives unimaginable comfort. Later, when all the parameters of the

archetype had become clear, Kyōka would re-create her as the famous heroine
of *The Holy Man of Mt. Kōya* (*Kōya hijiri*, 1900). But here her development is
partial and fleeting. Darkness falls, and the ghostly world outside the protected
sanctum displays its horror in full.

> "I have company tonight," she called out sharply. "That's enough!"
> Gradually, the night grew calm.
> "Don't be afraid," she said. "It's nothing but a mouse."
> Still, I quivered. The cries that I detected within the commotion still echoed in my
> ears. The beautiful woman got halfway out of bed, reached over, and produced a dagger
> from a lacquered box. She placed it, still sheathed, near her body. "Don't be afraid—let
> them come," she said bravely. "Now, rest." (3: 20–21)

She sleeps peacefully, but Chisato is kept awake by her beauty. In his confusion, he tries to analyze her loveliness.

> Was I dreaming? I tried to calm myself, gazing at the arm she had lent me for a pillow,
> supple, lifeless, lying across the quilt.
> The other hand had fallen upon her chest, her graceful white fingers spread, resting
> lightly upon the dagger with its hilt clasp of brilliant gold and its shiny lacquered scab-
> bard. She lay face up, lips parted as if to speak. Her eyes were closed, as if she were
> smiling, and her long black hair flowed down on her pillow. Yes, I could have sworn
> that this woman, even the hand resting upon the dagger, was the very image of my
> mother as she lay dead! Haunted by the fear that this woman, too, might die, I reached
> for the blade. I pulled it toward me, and the scabbard loosened. There was a flash of
> silver and then—what have I done!—a tide of blood began to flow. My God! I pressed
> down with both fists, trying to staunch the wound. Try as I might, the issue continued
> unabated, almost gushing, turning the white of her gown a bloody red.
> As the beautiful woman lay there, still as a marble statue, the tide of blood flowed
> down from her belly and soon covered the entire bottom half of her body. And yet, I
> could see that there was not so much as a single drop of blood on my own hand as they
> pressed down upon her wound. Held before the lamplight, my fingers glowed red, but
> not with the blood of another. How strange, I thought, touching my hand again to the
> wound, inspecting my palm again to see that the blood had not stained it. Directing my
> gaze back to her, I realized that her nightgown had come open. Seen through her silken
> undergarment, I saw the color red, covering her skin.
> Losing my senses, I cried out, "Mother! Mother!" I called to her. I pushed her away.
> I pulled her toward me. But all to no avail. Tears came to my eyes. I cried and cried
> until I fell asleep. (3:22–23)

As in "The Book of Oaths," the connection between the beautiful woman and
Kyōka's mother is perfectly clear, although here the image of an older sister is

also superimposed. Chisato will be reunited with his sister, but only after having embraced this woman who is sister, mother, and temptress.

The encoding of red and white in "Of a Dragon in the Deep" connects itself,
through the image of blood flowing over pale skin, to a realm of folklore that
resonates in eerie harmony with Kyōka's private symbolism of these colors.
Blood is polluting, and yet the author resists the admission of defilement. This
is an uncleanliness that leaves no stains. Chisato's hands are undefiled because
his knowledge of the woman is not carnal but sublime, purified not only by
what many critics have identified as a romantic fire but also by folk tradition.
Red was thought to have magical powers of purification and protection.
Women divers used a red sash, for instance, to ward off the many dangers of
the ocean. But to the extent that red is also associated with blood and, therefore, with pollution, Kyōka's aesthetically driven negotiation of these conflicting
values is necessarily twisted. In the end, we must conclude that such an ambiguous understanding of defilement is inclusive to the point of being forced,
a pure perversion, as it were.

This explains why Chisato's accidental murder of the woman turns out to
be a dream, that particular mental state that conveniently fades into forgetful-
ness and, therefore, holds inner vision apart from reason. If the possibility of
dreaming is a simplification, the introduction of an actual dream established yet
another border with which Kyōka was learning to play in a complicated way.
When Chisato awakes, he is being carried back to his home. His re-entry into
the world of the civilized is painful. He is bound, declared possessed, stoned,
rejected by friends, and finally exorcised. Only his sister comprehends what he
has experienced and protects him as the Buddhist priests chant and a tremendous storm approaches.

I felt uneasy, my sense of doom great. But I could find no place to hide. Wanting to
disappear, I clung to my sister's shoulders and pressed my face into her bosom. She
pulled her kimono open, thrust my head deep beneath her breasts, and shielded my
back with her sleeves. I rejoiced, thinking that this must be just how the child
Siddhartha was once held. My emotions settled. I felt purified. My heart grew peaceful
and calm. Eventually the priests ended their chanting, its thunder rolling off into the
distance. My sister relaxed her hold on me. I slipped my head out and, still trembling,
looked up at her. She was as beautiful as ever. But how gaunt her face had become! The
storm had returned, making it unthinkable to leave. Waiting out the rain, which continued until morning, my sister and I spent the entire night together. (3: 31–32)

Before the end of this story, Kyōka added three more important parameters to the female image. One is a passing reference to the ambiguous Kishibojin, the Buddhist deity (Hariti), a murderer and devourer of others' children who becomes converted and worshiped as a guardian of children. The second is Maya, the mother of Siddhartha. And the third is the Far Eastern trope of the woman as dragon, thus explaining the title of this story. In each case the reader perceives the female figure as a being of the other world, which is consistent with the geographical truth of Kyōka's mother, whose grave lay on the far side of the Asano River, the setting for this story. Her being on the other side of a watery barrier is an important structural element of the author's narratives, since this god/demon figure is accessible only to those willing to pass through the dangers of water.

The abundance of water imagery follows from this requirement. We encounter it in many forms: the beckoning waterfall, the mirror water of the stone basin in which Chisato sees his transformed face, the deep pool in which the naked dragon woman appears to him for the first time, the great marsh pond on which he is ferried back to the human world, the rainstorm that pounds the temple where Chisato is being exorcised, and the bottomless lake that suddenly forms at the story's conclusion. In the end, the forbidden space of Chisato's trespass becomes nothing but water, a fitting place for the dead. If we can trust the influential philological studies of Orikuchi Shinobu (1887–1953), such associations with death were formed anciently, as in the Japanese concept of the bottom of the sea as the home of the dead.[22] A sensitive reader of traditional iconography, Kyōka used such ancient reverberations to express his own private mythology. From this point on, he used legend liberally, returning to the figure of the dragon/demon in two of his most famous works, *The Holy Man of Mt. Kōya* and the play *Demon Pond* (*Yashagaike*, 1913).

His turn away from what his critics had appreciated in the conceptual novels was nearly complete by this point. It was, as Kyōka must certainly have anticipated, a highly unpopular move. Reviews in the literary column of *The Sun* expressed confusion. His readers were not accustomed to this sort of imaginative freedom. "Is this piece a fairy-tale for children? No, it is far too difficult to be called that. Should we then consider it a strange, idealistic work that attempts to capture a classical age? No, it is too womanish and fanciful. . . . It seems that Kyōka has taken a wrong turn."[23] Similarly, the literary critic for *Tangled Tales* (*Shigarami zōshi*) had difficulty understanding Kyōka's attempt to achieve a new synthesis of the oral and the figurative. "This is an unsuccessful attempt to write a legend. Oral tales have an interesting simplicity. On the other hand, Kyōka's piece is too nonsensical to be a short story because the author has added frills and decorations of various sorts. As for the characters, their speech is detailed and too modern-sounding for the story to be a legend."[24]

Falling between stools, "Of a Dragon in the Deep" was dismissed as an attempt to create an original style that failed. Kyōka's experiments with young protagonists had gone far beyond anything Ichiyō would have considered. For many readers, such extremes represented a dangerous retrenchment.

Once concerned with the serious and tragic, Kyōka's short, poetic pieces sought out and brought to life the dark tides of human destiny. His ideas used to be simple, his rhetoric admirably clear. Consequently, he was able to place himself one step ahead of his competition. A young writer should aim for maturity in the pursuit of his various interests, but Kyōka has failed to do this. He should try to sharpen his skills of observation, to read, and to gain more experience. He is still young. Why, then, has he gone backward in order to learn such foolishness? Why has he thrown away his simple, refreshing perspective? What compels him to give up concise, straightforward writing?[25]

As we look back on the entire span of Kyōka's work, the answer to these questions are obvious. But at the time it was not easy for his contemporaries to grasp how new Kyōka's writing was becoming by being so strangely old-fashioned. To them, his resistance to realism seemed old, or at least retrograde in a foolish, antiquarian way.

Positive appreciations came in limited number. One was a simple but important observation published in *Woman's World* (*Jogaku zasshi*). It recognized the emergence of an aspect of Kyōka's writing for which he would soon become famous. "His handling of goblins is notable."[26]

Fig. 1 Izumi Kyōka, age 3, with his father, Izumi Seiji, 1876

Fig. 2 Siddhartha's instinctive praying to the image of his dead mother moves his "substitute mothers" to tears; from Book 3 of Mantei Ōga's *The Eight Lives of Siddhartha, a Japanese Library.* Kyōka viewed images such as this in his mother's library.

Fig. 3 Meboso Kite, Kyōka's
paternal grandmother. As had his
mother's death, her passing away in
1905 left him profoundly shaken.

Fig. 4 Meboso Teru,
Kyōka's cousin. After
the death of his mother,
Kyōka relied on Teru.
One account puts her
at the Kanazawa Castle
moat just as Kyōka was
about to commit suicide.
Did she save his life? Or
was it the seamstress
Yoshimura Yuki?

Fig. 5 Yuasa Shige, one of Kyōka's childhood loves. She married a wealthy Kanazawa merchant but was mistreated by him and eventually divorced. She became a model for the beautiful, suffering woman, a common figure in Kyōka's writings.

Fig. 6 Francina Porter, Kyōka's English teacher. He fell in love with her whiteness, then turned her Japanese.

Fig. 7 Ozaki Kōyō, Kyōka's mentor, a true Child of Edo.
Kyōka worshipped him. But perhaps he also hated him, as
Katsumoto Seiichirō claimed.

Fig. 8 Izumi Toyoharu (Shatei) (*left*) and Izumi Kyōka (*right*), ca. 1897. Both were members of Ozaki Kōyō's group, but Toyoharu never attained the success of his brother. Although close during their childhoods, they became estranged in later life.

Fig. 9 Images from Mantei Ōga's *The Eight Lives of Siddhartha, a Japanese Library*. (*top*) An eight-winged creature plucks a drowning man from a river (from Book 33); (*left*) a bird/woman savior figure (from Book 16). Kyōka's "Bird of Many Colors" and other works show the influence of kusazōshi texts such as these.

Fig. 10 Itō Suzu. Eight years younger than Kyōka, Suzu was seventeen when they first met in 1899. Kōyō disapproved of her and threatened to break with Kyōka if he did not leave her.

Fig. 11 Kyōka at his home in Tokyo, Ushigome, Minami Enoki-chō, 1900.
Here he wrote *The Holy Man of Mt. Kōya*.

Fig. 12 The archetype in visual form. A young man dreams of deliverance and is united with his mother. Water threatens but also makes this trespass into the realm of the dead possible. From Mantei Ōga's *The Eight Lives of Siddartha, a Japanese Library*, Book 13.

Fig. 13 Kyōka (*left*) with his grandmother Kite (*center*) and his brother Toyoharu (*right*) at the Kagura house. Around this time, Suzu moved in and was paid to leave by the ailing Kōyō.

Fig. 14 Kyōka in his early thirties, ca. 1903. By this point, Kōyō had died and Suzu was living with Kyōka.

Fig. 15 Suzu at the Banchō house, 1925. Age 44.

Fig. 16 At the Kōyōkan, 1925. *From left*: Komura Settai, Okada Saburōsuke, Minakami Takitarō, Kyōka, Akutagawa Ryūnosuke, Kubota Mantarō, Hamano Eiji, Satomi Ton.

Fig. 17 (*right*) Kyōka at his writing desk, ca. 1928

Fig. 18 (*below*) Picking wild bracken at the Shūzen Temple in Izu. Kyōka is the first figure on the left, and Suzu third from the left.

Fig. 19 Kyōka in 1937, two years before his death. Photograph by
Kimura Ihei.

Fig. 20 At Tanizaki Junichiro's daughter's wedding, 1939. Kyōko and Suzu flank the bridal couple in the center of the front row. The Tanizakis are on the right end of the front row. Satō Haruo and his wife, Chiyo (Tanizaki's first wife and the mother of the bride), are second and third from the left in the middle row.

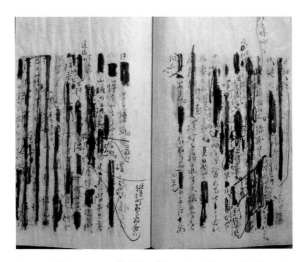

Fig. 21 Manuscript of "The Heartvine," 1939. Evident in this labored manuscript is the difficulty that the dying Kyōka experienced in his final attempt to complete the archetype.

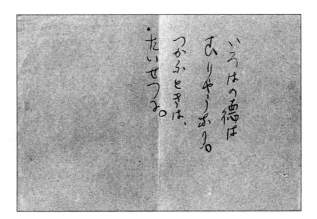

Fig. 22 A paper found in Kyōka's writing desk after his death. "The power of letters (*iroha*) is immeasurable. Use them with care."

CHAPTER SEVEN

Embraces

~

1897–1899

The Gold Demon

Keeping ahead of Kyōka's small successes, Kōyō launched his next major work, *The Gold Demon* (*Konjiki yasha*), on New Year's Day, 1897. Serialized in the *Yomiuri News*, this novel about a young man, Hazama Kan'ichi, who loses his beloved to a wealthier man and is permanently embittered by the loss, soon gained a wide audience. Indeed, *The Gold Demon* proved to be Kōyō's signature work. Its themes of greed and wealth's corrupting power were judiciously chosen for the times. Japan had recently emerged victorious from its first modern war, and many celebrated the victory over China as a measure of Japan's new power and prosperity as a nation. Kōyō, whose sympathies lay with those who did not prosper in the new society, was eager to express his disgust for the unbridled rush for wealth and power that the new militarism seemed to encourage. Because of its melodramatic strength and its critique of those who gain at the expense of others, *The Gold Demon* was the perfectly topical newspaper novel.

Beyond these thematic qualities, the book's success can also be attributed to Kōyō's image as a national artist. He was one of the few writers who could seemingly respond to the needs of an entire nation. The intimate relationship he had cultivated with his readers had raised expectations and, therefore, the potential for disappointment. Far from disappointing his fans, however, the book won for Kōyō a status shared only with, perhaps, Kōda Rohan. *The Gold Demon* captured for Kōyō an enormous following that Kyōka, who had written against the war effort in works such as "A Dispatch from Kaijō" ("Kaijō hatsuden," 1879) and against poverty in stories like "The Poverty Club" ("Hinmin kurabu," 1895), would never enjoy in his lifetime.[1]

In contrast to his mentor, Kyōka was becoming increasingly preoccupied with private matters and was steadily developing a highly personal, even eccentric, voice. In his search for an authorial persona, he did not reach out to the public as Kōyō did. And yet the issues of the day—greed and the disparity of wealth that Japan's economic development had brought—did help his cause in a small way. By the end of the year, "The Poverty Club," which had originally appeared two years earlier in the *Hokkaido Daily News*, was republished (in part) and given a new title: "The Charity Association" ("Jizenkai"). Like *The Gold Demon*, this exposé of the venality and hypocrisy of the Meiji upper crust spoke directly to the perception that the rich were getting wealthier at the expense of the poor and that the blessed rain of modernity was falling only in scattered showers. "You're always talking about acts of charity," the heroine, Otan, says, indicting the ladies of high-society Tokyo, "but the truth is that you treat us like beggars" (2: 87). With unmistakable venom, Otan points out that the rich care only about being seen at the charitable functions held each year in the Rokurokukan, an obvious allusion to the Italianate Rokumeikan, or Deer Cry Pavilion, which served as the cultural center of the new Europhilic elite.

Kyōka, who had never attended one of these functions himself, worked from Matsubara Iwagorō's *Darkest Tokyo* (*Saiankoku no Tokyo*, 1893), a study of Tokyo's impoverished underclass. Like the people in Matsubara's work, Kyōka was similarly a bumpkin "come up" from the countryside. Having personally experienced the cruelty of the city, he was moved to discover that many of the capital's destitute, as illuminated by Matsubara's investigations, were recent arrivals from Kanazawa and its environs.[2] He himself had been saved from a life of wandering only by the kindness of Kōyō and others. By writing about the hypocrisy of charitable functions, he was playing the role of one of Kōyō's come-to-the-city heroes, a provincial man who in one of Kōyō's minor stories visits a charitable bazaar and is astounded by the exorbitant prices paid and then donated to various worthy causes.

Perhaps this critique of privilege suggests the bedrock of Kyōka's devotion to his teacher, and the real meaning of poverty. Both he and Kōyō had similarly impecunious backgrounds in the artisan class, although Kōyō had become an urbane *tsū* or connoisseur, and Kyōka was fast becoming one. In this sense, Kyōka's debt to his mentor was multiple. Without Kōyō, Kyōka would have had neither the means of bettering his financial situation nor access to the quickly vanishing culture of Edo that the images in his mother's library had taught him to appreciate. At a time when the mentor-disciple relationship was being castigated as backward and feudal, Kōyō served as a model for Kyōka to follow, and, despite the differences in their writing styles, Kyōka's relationship with his sophisticated and even flamboyant mentor was something he never took for granted.

As pointed out above, Kyōka's devotion to Kōyō was well known among the members of the *bundan*. In the more egalitarian times of the late-Meiji period, Kyōka's dedication had come to seem obsequious both to those within and to those without Kōyō's circle. The apprenticeship system practiced by Kōyō and Kyōka was being supplanted by other forms of social organization, such as the numerous groups that formed around coterie magazines, by schools that coalesced around ideological tenets, or by more loosely formed groups such as the Thursday Club (Mokuyōkai) over which Sōseki presided, not as parent but as colleague. While recognizing the virtue of loyalty, Shūsei found Kyōka's attentiveness an irritating attempt to monopolize Kōyō's attention.[3] He and Kyōka felt very differently about their indebtedness to their teacher. Whereas, for example, he and Fūyō used the title *sensei* (master) in addressing others of the *bundan*, Kyōka refused to call anyone but Kōyō *sensei*, even so prominent a figure as Ōgai.[4] And while others laughed in Kōyō's presence, Kyōka did not.[5]

Locked securely into this master-disciple relationship, Kyōka was discovering that the greatest difficulty was not breaking from Confucian order but remaining true to his mentor despite his own growing success. He had already been used to denigrate his master by the poet and novelist Miyazaki Koshoshi (1864–1922), one of Kōyō's avowed enemies. As Miyazaki put it: "Kōyō has no poetic imagination. He corrects Kyōka's manuscripts and signs his own name to them. He has fooled the eyes and ears of all. And that is why Kyōka has been forced to flee, leaving Kōyō to continue as a mere 'sketch writer.'"[6] Kyōka had moved out—that much was true—but the departure could hardly be called flight. If anything, Miyazaki's criticism of Kōyō had the effect of strengthening the bond between the two writers. Shūsei later reflected that the criticism aimed at Kōyō "made Kyōka all the more considerate toward his teacher, so that in the long run his feelings of respect evolved into a form of worship."[7]

That Kyōka was worshipful of Kōyō is beyond question, but devotion is not so easily understood. Beyond whatever feelings of indebtedness Kyōka might have felt, the practical dangers of outstripping one's teacher were real. He had published enough work to establish himself as one of the most promising young writers in Japan, but at the age of twenty-five he could hardly afford to lose Kōyō's backing despite what was becoming more and more obvious to the critics of the day: the two did not share the same aesthetics. This became especially clear when they touched upon similar themes. The more plausible narrative lines of *The Gold Demon* stand in stark contrast to the grotesque and tortuous lyricism of the "Poverty Club."

Shūsei even suggested that Kyōka's art was utterly incompatible with Kōyō's and that Kyōka was solicitousness toward his teacher because "he didn't want to become a traitor."[8] If this is true, we can imagine that the enthusiastic reception of Kōyō's *Gold Demon* must have been a relief to Kyōka, who had every reason to want his master to remain a prominent figure. This is not to suggest, of course, that Kyōka was persuaded to veer from his own path. While Kōyō pursued the vengeful capitalist machinations of the jilted Hazama Kan'ichi, Kyōka steadily sought to add more detail to the archetype he was developing. He would pursue his private vision by pushing the search for the weak male still further into the realm of the fantastic and the episteme of the monstrous.

Kyōka's place within this group of young writers that formed around Kōyō was further complicated by the presence of his younger brother Toyoharu. Upon coming to Tokyo, Toyoharu seriously considered a military career; but when it became clear that he would not be able to pursue this path because of his nearsightedness, he turned to writing and eventually became one of Kōyō's students. He took his older brother's place in the small room just off the entrance of Kōyō's house and lived there as an apprentice and servant for three or four years. As he had done for Kyōka, Kōyō also gave Toyoharu a pen name. He was known as Shatei (斜汀), "Slanting Shoreline," a pun on the word for "live-in disciple" (洒亭) and also a homonym with "my younger brother" (舎弟). Perhaps this slightly humorous and even degrading *nom de plume* reflected Kōyō's lack of confidence in Toyoharu's abilities from the very start. A charming and even flamboyant man, Shatei is posed with Kyōka in a photograph taken around this time (see Fig. 8). He never distinguished himself as a writer. Forever being compared unfavorably with his brother, he suffered embarrassment and eventually allowed their relationship to become distant and even antagonistic. He did become close to Kyōō, however, especially during the last years of his mentor's life. He edited all six volumes of Kyōō's collected works.[9]

Moving Ahead, Looking Back

Kyōka's next major success was a short story entitled "A Bird of Many Colors" ("Kechō," 1897). It was featured in the first number of the *New Wave Monthly* (*Shinchō gekkan*), a magazine that ran only from April 1897 to May 1898 but was successful during its short life in attracting the contributions of many prominent writers. Started by Gotō Chūgai (1866–1938), the *New Wave* briefly rivaled Hakubunkan's *Literary Club* and Shun'yōdō's *New Fiction* (*Shin shōsetsu*). Kyōka, now sufficiently well known to be publishing steadily in all the major magazines, thought highly enough of Chūgai and his attempt to rally the literary forces of the day to give *New Wave* special mention in one of the autochronologies.

Much was at stake with this story. Kyōka had experimented with colloquial narrators before, but now he broke cleanly from classical Japanese to write dialogues, narrative passages, and descriptions in the vernacular. The use of colloquial language for fictional narrative was already a well-established trend by this point in time and had been earlier practiced by other members of the Ken'yūsha: first Yamada Bimyō, who had left the group in 1889 to become one of its most aggressive rivals, and later Kyōō, who wrote *Passions and Griefs* in what is called the *de aru* style but reverted to the more ornate rhetoric of the classical tradition in *The Gold Demon*. Even though the practice was still not universal at this point, the movement away from the more figurative diction of classical Japanese was gaining strength in the late-modern shift toward a more phonocentric semiotic field.

Kyōka could not help being engulfed within this shift, especially since changes in printing technology, combined with the will to employ new narrative methods, ended the close intermingling of text and illustration characteristic of so much early- and mid-nineteenth-century fiction. After centuries of being carved from wood blocks, the literary page was now printed with movable type. Illustrations, which came to be done on separate plates rather than inscribed on the same surface as the text, were no longer so intimately tied to the scenes of a story, as in kusazōshi. *Ehon* (picture books) and works of Edo-period fiction continued to be printed from wooden blocks in the traditional manner until about the turn of the century, but the new practice of literature (*bungaku*), which chose to take European realism as its model, became largely a words-only venture.[10]

The general movement toward a more representational discourse had far-reaching ramifications, including (in its most radical purity) a corrosion and even rejection of all forms of traditional iconography. Figures of speech imbedded within classical literary language were jettisoned in favor of a more transparent, descriptive idiom. Stock characters were replaced by psychologically differentiated individuals. Narrative formulas gave way to the linear plausibility of process and discovery. The visual element (*grapheme*) of the written script was contested in various language reforms, such as the simplification of Chinese characters (*kanji*) and the use of romanized script (*rōmaji*). And, once again, the traditional symbiosis between illustration and text was supplanted by the typeset page. This last point had special consequences for Kyōka, whose earliest encounters with writing were based on his childhood exposure to the picture books in his mother's library. His adjustment to the loss of illustration was less accommodating than that of his contemporaries, for here in "A Bird of Many Colors" he restored the outlawed images of the late Edo period at the very moment he switched to the new vernacular idiom of *genbun itchi*.

For reasons that lie at the center of Kyōka's aesthetic, it was impossible for him to accept the obvious political and artistic consequences of this movement away from illustration and figurative language. In the political arena, the use of vernacular (and therefore more easily readable) Japanese was championed by democratic reformers who, in pressing for "freedom and the rights of the people" (*jiyū minken*), wanted to include more people in the political process.[11] Although the debate focused on the language of political tracts and newspapers, it eventually encompassed the nature of fiction and poetry as well. In fact, the place of written narrative in this push for higher levels of literacy and increased political involvement had always been obvious. Not only had the *shōsetsu* undergone an important incarnation during the 1880s and 1890s as the *seiji shōsetsu* (political novels that served to disseminate democratic ideas), but it had largely come to be published at that confluence of "large" (i.e., political) and "small" (i.e., entertaining) types of information which eventually came to be called the *shinbun* (or newspaper).

Kyōka's work had always had much to say about such topics as the suffering of the underclass, the war with China, the venality of the new aristocracy, and so forth. But Akutagawa's observation about the poetic (rather than political) roots of this populism is clearly borne out here, for Kyōka's regard for the *gen-bun itchi* movement proved to be as ambivalent as his attitude toward the wider notion of *bunmei kaika* (civilization and enlightenment) under which language reform came to be subsumed. Whereas Yamada Bimyō adhered to the use of the vernacular as an unquestionable improvement over a less civilized past, Kyōka rejected this aspect of implied modernity in order to embrace the iconographic richness of traditional texts. This happened, once again, even as he negotiated the new author-reader relationship by adopting the *de aru* level of formality. The language of "A Bird of Many Colors" did lower the narrator's position vis-à-vis the reader's. Yet it is also true that while being more linguistically simple, it is also more visually rich. Freed from past figures of speech, Kyōka developed the new narrative language toward, rather than away from, new modes of figurality. He went beyond Kōyō's trick of fashioning new metaphors from old. He did nothing less than establish a rhetoric of metamorphosis: as vehicles meld with tenors, the representative function of words collapses so that the opaque, metaphoric nature of language comes to deny not only the transparent transcription of the real but also the stale, sinocentric categories of aesthetic diction that the late-modern writers were trying to supplant.

More clearly than ever before, "A Bird of Many Colors" reveals the ontological consequences of the author's developing vision. The story's hero, Ren'ya, sitting in a shack with his mother on a rainy day, gazes out at a rain-soaked world in which people are wild boars, a fisherman standing on the dike holding an umbrella is a champignon, a boy dressed in red is a tiger finch, and a girl in blue is a Japanese white eye warbler. From the perspective of this boy, who admittedly "doesn't know anything," the objects he sees are consistently not what they seem. In short, the denial of realism is the very issue expressed. This was a topic posed in the much earlier "Night Patrol," but here metaphorical expression becomes unequivocally magical, more modern*ist* in perspective than modern, as if Kyōka was leapfrogging from the early modern to the postmodern without settling into an intermediate phenomenological position.

What Ren'ya sees is intended not to be a delusion but, rather, a vague sort of insight. In comparison, the boy's teacher at school is not perceptive enough to know, as Ren'ya and his mother do, that "people, cats, dogs, and bears are all beasts" (3: 119). The teacher's vision is limited because she is too civilized. That is to say, she is compromised by the prevailing structures of late-modern authority and is unable to see past them. She argues that human beings are not a part of the world but above it, clearly at the top of the evolutionary heap, separated from the earth they dominate. In her assertion of authority, supported by Japan's historical moment as the almost-colonized colonial power of East Asia, she allies herself with civilization and in particular with one aspect of the hegemonic modern agenda. She is nothing less than an evangelist of social Darwinism as it applies even to poetics. She assumes a position of social privilege that Kyōka, who sought to remember and to reify the suffering of his mother, chose to reject. If he gives to his female characters a certain authority, the source of that power is the marginal world of the riverbank rather than the new red-brick structures of Meiji Japan.

If anything, Kyōka made this teacher's role as a foil too obvious. She is totally out of place in this narrative. Diffuse and rambling, not much more than a string of visual associations, "A Bird of Many Colors" is a narration of things seen from Ren'ya's admittedly limited (though poetically correct) perspective. The boy views the bridge. He sees the river. He notices a passerby. He sees everything and everyone *as metaphor*, as something more than objective observation might reveal. Tied to each object of sight are associations so grand that they can only be suggested. And it is in this process of suggestion that the narrative develops, one thing leading to another. As he takes in the scenery of this rainy day, the first-person narrator sees a monkey tied up near the bridge. It reminds him of how it came to be there, and this memory leads us eventually to the end of the story.

Ren'ya recalls how he and his mother first met the animal and its trainer as they were returning from a visit to a temple on Mt. Utatsu. They found the trainer in tears, lamenting his fate as a human being. "Madame, how I wish I were a beast. You and I, we are all born of beasts, cousins to the monkey. Yet everyone throws food to my animal while I don't even get a look" (3: 133). In other words, the monkey (who is noticed) is luckier than his trainer (who struggles unnoticed). Precisely because he is invisible, he has insight. He has suffered enough of life's trials to grasp the totalizing view that the boy's mother espouses: people are no better than the beasts and the plants with which they share the planet. To maintain that they are anything more is arrogance. In Akutagawa's formulation of the Kyōkaean aesthetic, the Darwinian view is wrong mostly because it is ugly. In Kyōka's mind, the ascent of humanity is a movement in the wrong direction. Like the authoritative status of the author, it offers only the negative effect of preventing our access to the earth, to the dead, and to love.

This anti-science or primitivism represents Kyōka's reaction to the epistemic shift that the *genbun itchi* movement was imposing upon the writers of the period. As the call for civilization became associated with positivism, an increasingly realistic rhetorical field, built upon the premise of the subject/object split, began to put tremendous pressure on writers like Kyōka. Lamenting the dismissal of Japan's past, he found himself in the unpopular position of using the new language for old purposes. In its wealth of imagery, "A Bird of Many Colors" could not be more obvious in its rejection of realistic assumptions. It stands as Kyōka's declaration of independence from the modern iconophobia that would have made his (or anyone else's) vision of salvation impossible. Kyōka understood that the semiotics of salvation required icons as well as descriptions, incontestable objects that are ontologically higher than a universally atomized reality. For him, the end of writing could be served only if the affirmation of self could be accomplished through a romantic glorification of the Other, not by dismantling it through analysis and history. By writing this piece, Kyōka placed himself on a path that would eventually lead him to become the most talented idolater in late-modern Japan. To his mind, landscape existed as a description of belief rather than of what the late-modern manifestation of the self viewed as being objectively exterior and Other. Seeking myth, he was not interested in revealing what was "there" by virtue of its place within a universal, absolute, and rational system of perspectival value.

The monkey trainer finally abandons his animal, tying it up by the bridge, where it lives within the young boy's view. Ren'ya's rainy-day observation of it is not a sketch but a memory—not a distant exterior that confirms an interior, but a pre-psychological projection of interiority onto an exterior object. The monkey, as image, is a link to many other visual emblems, all conjoined through the nonlinear narrative mechanism of the flashback that was quickly becoming one of Kyōka's favorite devices. We learn that the boy went out one day to play with the monkey, fell into the river, and would have drowned had it not been for a beautiful bird/angel figure with five-colored wings that swooped down from the sky and plucked him from the water. Having established this salutary image, the remainder of the story becomes a simple inquiry as to what or who this winged creature might be.

Ren'ya searches but does not find. He comes to suspect that the bird is his mother. He so closely associates this bird/angel with the dangers of the river that he decides to fall into the water once again to see if his mother will save him a second time. It is, as it were, a planned accident, a dangerously childish (and utterly effective) way to force the issue of his own salvation. Fraught with paradox, the well-conceived crisis of "A Bird of Many Colors" is emblematic of what was becoming Kyōka's standard narrative procedure. He discovered the formula here and went on to repeat it incessantly. What he found is that only by entering the dangerous waters of death is the truth of love known.

The story concludes strangely, with a faith that highlights doubt: "The sky is clearing, and the rocks on the bank are slippery. Mother says to stay away, but I'm going to bump right into that monkey and fall into the river again. I know she'll pull me out. But, then again, maybe—No, I'll be fine. My mother is here. My mother was here" (3: 149). By this change in verb tense—from present to past—we are to understand that the bird is the boy's mother, who is both present and absent. She is with the boy, present in his mind. Yet in reality she is a part of the past and, therefore, no longer with him. Because of this gap between ideal and real, she will become available to him if and only if he throws himself into the rushing water.[12] Again, the well-designed result of the planned mistake is reunion with her. Still, her presence is dead because it is a present that is always past. The quality of Kyōka's faith and his reasons for writing require this bending and folding of time. Because his mother was here, she will be here again. Having lived, she will again be present—in the water, in the stories that have now revealed to the author this imaginative process that makes her available to his mind.

In a pure sense, this is not really a discovery, since she is found only in order to be found again and again. Neither is it exactly an interpretation that admits of other readings, for the perspective is narrowed and fixed by emotional need, just as the boy's need for his mother is beyond speculation. By extension, the value of the things seen by Kyōka's weak hero—water, beasts, mother—are not to be questioned. Such mythic elements do not encourage other readings (which are, nevertheless, impossible to resist). Their value for Kyōka is given, fixed by a profound sense of loss and by his worshipful attempt to revere such images as privileged foci of being. Thus, even when using the new language of *genbun itchi*, he has not found a transparent medium. Neither has he discovered a describable modern landscape. If anything, it is more easily a medieval one that invites the eyes to fix upon the stasis connecting the seer with some deeper truth beyond what is objectively available to the imagination.

In this way, Kyōka refashioned jettisoned rocks into jewels. Not only did he defy the late-modern process of new discovery—the possessive locating of consumable personality and nameable space—but he consciously borrowed his images from the highly illustrated texts of the vilified gesaku tradition. To be specific, Kyōka very likely borrowed the image of the winged bird/angel from *The Eight Lives of Siddhartha, a Japanese Library,* a prominent text in his mother's library. In Book 33 of this lengthy kusazōshi, a man falls into a river and is saved by an "eight-winged creature with a human face," who plucks him from the water and returns him to dry ground. Admittedly, its face is not that of a beautiful young lady, as described in Kyōka's story. Still, we can find just such comely angels in Books 11 and 16 of the same text (see Fig. 9).[13]

A comparison of the word images of Kyōka's work and the figural images found in the books in his kusazōshi collection leads us to wonder if Kyōka wrote his stories while leafing through these texts. What we can safely say is that the images of his childhood reading continued to direct the flow of his imagination. We know that he collected volumes from *The Eight Lives of Siddhartha, The Tale of Shiranui, The False Murasaki, the Rustic Genji,* and *A Praiseworthy Tale of the North (Hokusetsu bidan jidai kagami)* for his library. Collecting these illustrated texts was, in fact, one of his greatest amusements. Often in the company of the artist Hirezaki Eihō (1881–1910), who eventually became an illustrator of Kyōka's work, he would walk about the city purchasing kusazōshi from used book stores and from homes that looked as though they might house neglected collections of such works.[14] Like his writing, his gathering of these books was an act of remembrance.

Once again, bringing the past into the present was an urgent task. Because he desired the visual presence of his dead mother and the morbid world of gentle reprieve that she inhabited, Kyōka rejected the progressive agenda of realistic narrative, just as he rejected history, for its positioning of reality into the completed past. The will to resurrect the past as a still-completing present is expressed here as "My mother is here. My mother was here." But because of the turn that printing technology had taken since the Enlightenment, the sense of presence so easily accomplished by the materiality of two-dimensional kusazōshi images required the compensatory flair of figurative language that was quickly becoming Kyōka's stock in trade. Working within the phonocentric environment of late-modern Japan, he did his best to retrieve the past through a twist of language that would result in one of most distinctive literary styles in all of Japanese literature. Surely, the deeply poetic nature of Kyōka's prose finds a source in this crisis of language. Caught in a historical trend in which the texture of the Japanese language was thinning, Kyōka was forced to find the outlawed figurality of the pre-modern tradition in the very body of language itself. In doing so, he began swimming against the current of literary fashion.

Many could not understand his aesthetics as anything but a misguided return to the goblins of the past. One critic even wrote that he feared Kyōka had lost his senses.

The way the mother teaches her child about human behavior through comparisons with the birds and beasts is stupid. And for the child to repeat such nonsense to his teacher is a joke. This sort of thing might be converted into an Aesop's fable to good effect, but this attempt to have us weep over man's inhumanity to man asks far too much of the reader. In going from "Maidenhair" to "A Bird of Many Colors," Kyōka himself has gone through some strange sort of transformation. One wonders what kind of creature he will eventually become. One can only hope Kyōka comes to his senses and rejoins the world of human beings before it is too late.[15]

On the other hand, Taoka Reiun, who had earlier praised Kyōka for his conceptual novels, was one of the few who anticipated the beginnings of what would become Kyōka's inimitable accomplishment. "The writer's poetic nature flows from the tip of his brush. We find no trace of vulgarism. Rather than falling back on the usual tricks of less talented writers, he has broken new ground in the direction of fantasy. Both style and content are far-reaching."[16] Like the most powerful artists of the early-modern period—painters such as Kunisada and Hokusai, and writers such as Santō Kyōden (1761–1816) and Takizawa Bakin (1767–1848)—Kyōka, in staying close to pictocentric roots, had discovered both word and world as *bakemono*, the "thingness" of percept *and* concept. Although not often enough stated, these earlier artists were also modern, similarly engaged in an attempt to discover the human will through metaphor—whether distortion by line or by letter. Possibly because the discourse on modernity has been dominated by a phonocentric bias, the monstrous origins of psychology have been all but forgotten. Nevertheless, we will not achieve a satisfactory understanding of modernity until we widen the terms of the debate to consider how a discourse of visual excess ultimately frames modern consciousness (and its explication) by problematizing the imagination, thereby making the awareness of awareness a possible, if not a compelling, obsession.

Adult Distractions

Closely following the narrative scheme established in "Of a Dragon in the Deep" and "A Bird of Many Colors," "Seishin's Nunnery" ("Seishin an," 1897) and "In Nightingale Hollow" ("Ōkakei," 1898) similarly establish a magical, hostile world seen through youthful eyes. After this point, Kyōka's works about boys begin to taper off. Kyōka ceased to give the pattern his full attention, not because it had lost relevance to his continuing search for salvation but because it had fulfilled its role of establishing a solid foundation for what was to follow. The trope endured in a slightly modulated form. Heroes continue to be dependent upon the salutary powers of women. If not exactly boys, they are emotionally young, and usually a few years younger or otherwise less experienced than the women they desire. This unequal relationship between men and women becomes an essential component of a narrative paradigm that is now only two years away from full development.

The Kyōkaean hero now awakens to, and is even tortured by, the attractiveness of the female body. Having established the protecting figures of mother and older sister, Kyōka complicated this nurturing aspect of the feminine ideal by introducing, and even stressing, an erotic potential. Woman as mother becomes woman as lover, not in a way that precludes either possibility but through an overlapping of the maternal and the sexual so that both coexist. From this point, there is a change of emphasis in his heroines rather than a turn to a new project altogether.

Perhaps we should not be surprised that this subtle though important development coincided with changes in the author's personal affairs. Publishing regularly and earning money for his work, Kyōka, now age 25, began to pay for the company of women. As noted above, by 1898 he was making infrequent trips to the brothels with Kōyō's other students. Along with his fellow writers, he learned not only sexual indulgence but how to drink as well. Often, the two were made to coincide, as in the New Year's party held for Ken'yūsha writers and their associates in 1899.

Present at this affair were such notables as Kōyō, Yamada Bimyō, Iwaya Sazanami, Kawakami Bizan, Hirotsu Ryūrō (1861–1928), and Emi Suiin (1869–1934). But the person who captured Kyōka's attention was one of the geisha who had come to entertain them. She was seventeen years old, eight years younger than Kyōka. Her professional name was Momotarō, but her given name was Suzu, the same as his mother's! The attraction was immediate. As a young woman carefully trained in the seductive ways of old Edo, this woman would become Kyōka's mother's replacement, an incarnation of his need for both another mother and a lover. An early photo shows her as she might have looked when Kyōka met her (see Fig. 10).

Of Itō Suzu's (1881–1950) background, we know very little. Her mother, the daughter of a Kyoto merchant, fell in love with a *rōnin*, or masterless samurai, from the Tosa domain. They had one child together before he died shortly thereafter. Without the means to support herself or the child, Suzu's mother became a professional entertainer. She eventually became the mistress of one of her patrons, a businessman who supported her financially until his business failed and he sold his stepdaughter, Suzu, to one of the Yoshiwara houses in Tokyo. He disappeared shortly thereafter, and Suzu, who was then only six, never saw him again. We have no details of her mother's fate.

As a young apprentice in Yoshiwara, Itō Suzu received the usual training. She learned Kiyomoto-school *jōruri* (storytelling to the accompaniment of a shamisen) and various styles of dance appropriate for performance in the *zashiki*, or sitting room. She began entertaining when she was fourteen or fifteen. As the "embodiment of art," she was not distinguished, however. Apparently she was "quiet and not overly charming."[17] By the time Kyōka met her, she had already moved from her original situation to an establishment in Kagurazaka, not far from where Kyōka was living.[18] It was this move that enabled their meeting. Kōyō's lover, Oen, was also a Kagurazaka geisha. She and Suzu had come together to the party as members of a group hired for the celebration.

Oen was accomplished in ways that Momotarō was not. Talented and promising, Oen had been adopted by the owners of the Sagamiya, a Kagurazaka establishment. While she entertained Kōyō and the other leaders of the Ken'yūsha, the "quiet" Suzu spent the evening with Kyōka, who was himself also playing a supporting role. It was just as well. Kyōka did not have the economic power to support anyone more accomplished. That he had the power to support anyone at all was precisely the point that put him at odds with his mentor. Their difference of opinion on the topic of Itō Suzu nearly ruined his career.

From the start, Kōyō objected to Kyōka's serious involvement. The precise reasons have been left unstated, although a contemplation of them forms the core of Kyōka's most famous play, *A Woman's Pedigree* (*Onna keizu*, 1907). We will examine this important work when we consider Kyōka's career as a playwright. For now it is enough to say that one possible reason for Kōyō's objection might be that, in addition to a career, he also planned to provide his most promising student a wife as well. As a matter of principle, Kōyō should have had nothing against Kyōka's seeing a geisha. Marrying one was another matter, however. On this point, Kyōka could not have misunderstood his mentor's disapproval, since Kōyō had spoken to the very issue just two years earlier. A roundtable discussion organized by Chūgai, Kōyō, and three of the Four Devas—Kyōka, Shun'yō, and Fūyō—had publicly addressed the topic of love. "When a man buys a prostitute, he's not cheating on his wife. It's a kind of play (*share*), a slightly evil sort of amusement."[19] This was Kōyō's stated position. Tossing the matter back and forth among them, the five came to a vague consensus. The kind of woman to love (and marry) is one with a good education. That is to say, she must be able to write letters and read a newspaper (not simple matters in the Japanese context). In addition, she must also have mastered home economics. Kōyō, who did not feel that his own marriage was being threatened by his extramarital involvements, established a contrast that Kyōka would later reject: love is for marriage; geisha for play.[20] As it turned out, Oen did in fact love Kōyō deeply, a point neither he nor his wife denied.

Quite likely, Kōyō's disdain for Suzu was rooted in his own desire for respectability as well. Like Kyōka's father, Kōyō's was a craftsman, a well-known carver of ivory. Like Izumi Seiji, Kōyō's father was also a perfectionist, selective about which jobs he took. Unlike Seiji, however, Ozaki Sōzō was not above hustling for money. He took a second job working in the brothels as a professional jester. The bright red jacket he wore was a source of tremendous embarrassment to Kōyō. Ashamed of his father, Kōyō kept this family connection with the gay quarters a secret. His rejection of a geisha for his prize student's wife, then, makes sense in this regard.

Kyōka obviously viewed disgrace more positively. If beauty is born of suffering, then it flourishes under oppression. For this reason, Kyōka favored the geisha of Tokyo to those of the Kansai region to the west. In Tokyo, he argued, it was considered disgraceful to be a geisha, whereas in the ancient capital of Kyoto this was less true. Thus, a sense of charm developed in the east as a reaction to this stigma, whereas the Kansai geisha, at least in Kyōka's eyes, tended to become proud and even arrogant. According to Kyōka, Tokyo geisha had backbone (*iji*) and pluck (*hari*), qualities invariably found in the author's ill-fated heroines. Despite Kōyō's opposition, then, not only was a Tokyo geisha the perfect model for his literary creations, but, to the extent that Kyōka saw his mother as an Edo native and as a woman who had been made beautiful by suffering, someone like Itō Suzu, a struggling geisha of limited ability, could well be the one for whom he had been searching.[21] Kōyō, guided as he was by his own need to be respectable, to be able to speak to a whole nation of readers with novels such as *The Gold Demon*, could not understand Kyōka's attraction to Suzu. Despite the closeness of mentor and protégé, Kōyō did not fathom the real depths of Kyōka's compulsion to be reunited with his dead mother. Even if he might have understood Kyōka's passion for Suzu, the profundity of his disciple's need to make her his wife apparently escaped Kōyō, leading them to confrontation.

Whatever Kyōka's involvement with the gay quarters, there were limits to his liberality and to his sympathy for geisha and other downtrodden members of society. For instance, his relationship with Taka, his older sister, reveals the extent to which his image of the demimonde was idealized. Taka probably began working in the *zashiki* from the age of fourteen or so. The details of her life after leaving the Izumi household are difficult to reconstruct, but Muramatsu Sadataka surmises that while working at her stepfather's establishment, the Umemoto, she fell in love with a customer and fled her erotic bondage.[22] When this passion cooled, she was left without financial backing. Unable to go back to Kotake Yosuke, she became a geisha again and worked in the smaller towns surrounding Kanazawa. She eventually contracted a disease that left one hand and one arm paralyzed. Upon raising enough money to buy her out of contract, Kyōka sent Toyoharu back to Kanazawa to find her.

Toyoharu rescued their sister from prostitution, but this hardly ended Kyōka's problems with her. Taka insisted on relocating to the capital. Accompanied by Meboso Teru, she even traveled to Tokyo to make her case. But Kyōka rejected her requests and sent her back to Kanazawa. He promised her a monthly stipend of five yen if she would remain there, and he arranged for her to rent a room in a house adjoining the Mebosos' hook factory in Kanazawa. Having just met and fallen in love with Suzu and now writing the first of his thirty or so stories about geisha, he needed, for his own apotheosis of such women, to keep his sister out of sight. She was unhappy in Kanazawa, and when she threatened to come to Tokyo a second time, Kyōka sent a strongly worded letter.

I heard from Toyoharu that you want to come to Tokyo, and when I read your letter, I was taken aback.

Our father and mother are buried there in Kanazawa, and for you to say that you have grown tired of provincial life is impudent and utterly outrageous. Because you think that way, you've been drifting from one place to the next, never settling down. Because of you we've had to impose upon the hospitality of our grandmother's family, the Mebosos. Now is the time to show restraint. As for your living in Tokyo, let me tell you in no uncertain terms that this is absolutely not the right time for you to come.

If you dare to go against my will, I will cut off the monthly allowance I have been sending you. Reflect carefully upon the fact that you were originally adopted into the Umemoto house, where you spent your childhood. If you refuse to follow my directions, I will tell the Meboso family to have nothing more to do with you. Then you will have to fend for yourself. If, however, you come to your senses and wholeheartedly comply with my wishes, I will continue your monthly allowance as before.

Once you realize how selfish you have been, ask Meboso Hachirōbei or even his daughter to write a letter of apology for you.

March 1
To Taka
From Kyōtarō[23]

As it turned out, Taka did not go to Tokyo. She eventually married a man from the Mebosos' neighborhood named Sogawa Yasanjirō. They moved to Takaoka, where they lived for seven years. She bore two children and died of dysentery in 1908. Kyōka did not attend her funeral. His sister was not noble enough in suffering to fit Kyōka's image of the geisha (or the ideal woman, for that matter). He fulfilled his duty as the head of the family by keeping her alive, but he cut her off emotionally. It seems she was beyond the pale of an "ethics based on aesthetic principles."

Worship at Yushima

What can be said of Kyōka can be said of most late-modern Japanese writers. The lives of prostitutes were of great interest to them because such women were an important prototype for the construction of selfhood—the so-called *kindaiteki jiga*, or modern ego—that so many authors sought. Given a new name and a new standardized language to speak, trapped in a situation from which they cannot easily escape, aware of their lives because of the boundaries (metaphoric and literal) that circumscribe them, the geisha and her sense of identity were givens to be appropriated by Japan's authors. No doubt, they saw the harlot's sexual captivity as a paradigm for selfhood, especially from their positions within a colonial world where survival went to the fittest. For most, this preoccupation was something of a theft—the female being made into the seen object so the male can become a seeing subject.[24] But in Kyōka's case, this harlot writing, or pornography (*pornē graphien*), feels less like the modern discovery of interiority and more like a recasting of an old trope.

As in the early-modern tradition, love cannot easily be fulfilled in Kyōka's world. Here the well-established premise that lovers must face death in order to overcome the censure of a rigidly class-structured society is still very much in place. Occasionally, as in *Nihonbashi* (1914), heroines struggle against each other. But in Kyōka's aesthetic formula, they usually stand together on the side of good, contending against the crassness of wealthy men who have the means but not the sensitivity to commune with the beaten, and therefore spiritually higher, female soul.

Kyōka's indebtedness to the early-modern tradition could not be more obvious than in his first story about geisha, *Worship at Yushima* (*Yushima mōde*, 1899). Kozuki Azusa, an intelligent but impoverished young man, marries Countess Tamatsukasa Ryōko, whose family undertakes to finance his education as their part of the matrimonial agreement. Their ties to one another are primarily financial in nature and, therefore, emotionally weak. In fact, Azusa does not really love his wife. Through a series of chance meetings, he comes to know and eventually falls in love with Chōkichi, a young geisha who is herself just learning her place in the world. Unbeknown to him, she becomes pregnant with his child and has an abortion. For reasons of propriety, he is finally forced to break with her, leaving them both miserable. Chōkichi loses her mind, crushed by Azusa's abandonment of her and by the guilt she feels for having killed their baby. They can live neither with nor without each other. At the story's conclusion, their bodies are discovered on the riverbank, where they have committed double suicide.

When reading this narrative, Chikamatsu Monzaemon and the early-modern tradition readily come to mind. There are many ties between this story and previous formulations: the way in which obligation (*giri*) collides with emotion (*ninjō*), the double suicide at the riverbank, the use of fetishes and other such narrative tricks to further the plot and reveal character. Despite the obvious pull of tradition on this work, however, *Worship at Yushima* was enthusiastically received by many contemporary critics as an excellent example of the new (realistic) writing. "Since its publication, *Worship at Yushima* has received a warm welcome. We hear Kyōka's name constantly being praised. There are critics who commend him for the great progress he has made, grateful that he has mended his ways and has gotten back on the right path."[25] As always, the exact nature of the "right path" is hard to determine—as obvious to the critics of the day as it remains enigmatic to us now—but certainly Kyōka's treatment of adultery, insanity, and suicide was adult fare and, therefore, more acceptable than the more imaginatively eccentric boy stories from which he was turning. We can also guess that the theme of a woman's gradual decline into madness, a favorite theme of late-modern Japanese literature, appealed greatly to the reviewers.

Writing in 1923, Masamune Hakuchō reflected back on this work's reception and remembered that Tsubouchi Shōyō, the very father of the "right path," had nothing but praise for the work.[26] According to Tayama Katai, in his study *The Modern Novel* (*Kindai no shōsetsu*, 1923), Gotō Chūgai (like Shōyō) similarly held up *Worship at Yushima* as a model of Japanese realism. But Katai, who never liked Kyōka's work, used the advantages of hindsight to add: "But you could hardly call Kyōka's work realistic. Gradually it became clear that the source of his romanticism was the old kusazōshi texts of the Edo period."[27]

Katai is right. And his discounting of "the old kusazōshi texts" is important to remember when we consider the reasons for Kyōka's eventual banishment to the margins of the *bundan*. If we discount the larger issues of the developing representational discourse—the fashioning of a transparent language, the adoption of Cartesian perspective, and so forth—Kyōka's use of stark details might be seen as a technique of the emerging realistic style. In truth, however, the appearance of these details about the lives of kept women was not driven by the new epistemology. More likely, it was a response to Suzu, a real geisha, and an expression of the author's devotion to her. Kyōka, who wrote and published *Worship at Yushima* during the first year of his romance with Suzu, now had an informant who could introduce him to the details of a world structured so perfectly like the fiction he wanted to create with words: a prison of colored silks and careful fragrances, an alluring illusion, a presentation of destitution's comeliness, the romanticism of the captured and the rebellious, the untouchable blossoms in a mirror. If *Worship at Yushima* seemed realistic to some, it was probably because the beauty of suffering was less a fiction than other things. That is to say, Kyōka's geisha stories seemed less fantastic and melodramatic than the more legend-based works because this cruel and alluringly distorted world actually existed in the gay quarters.

Kyōka's "geisha stories" and "monster stories" are often commingled, since they derive from the same impulse to picture the sad glamour of the captured. The telling difference between them might simply be that the distortions of life in the brothels were already a cliché by the nineteenth century, whereas the mental and economic sufferings of "normal people" were just becoming topics of narration. Opinion is divided as to which type represents Kyōka at his best—a domestic play such as *A Woman's Pedigree*, which became a mainstay of the "new wave" (*shinpa*) theater, or a novella such as *The Holy Man of Mt. Kōya*, which has become his signature work. Given the virtues of both, the author's greatest contribution to the corpus of Japanese writings seems to be the latter, which is more originally traditional and thus less easily confused with the traditionally original impulse that Shōyō found here to be realistic.

Quite unoriginal is the love triangle and the choice Azusa must make between two women. In a way already familiar to us, Kyōka used the formula to contrast the harlot's beauty with that of the refined, upper-class woman that Azusa has married. The Countess has been educated in France, and her accessibility to Europe is an unambiguous sign of late-modern wealth and privilege. As attractive as this might make her, she is nevertheless unfeeling and sexually unavailable to Azusa, who is tempted by extramarital liaisons. While some of his friends urge him to choose practicality and stay with his wife, Tatsuta Wakakichi, who is based on the figure of Yanagita Kunio, articulates the Kyōkaean argument (and Azusa's deepest feelings) that, though lacking a formal education, Chōkichi is in no way inferior to the Countess. Azusa should be true to his feelings for her regardless of the financial and social consequences.

Tatsuta explains:

While the Countess was off in France eating bread and reading the Bible, Chōkichi was being sent outdoors on snowy mornings to practice the flute. She would shiver in the cold, but her trainer would tell her that her suffering would help strengthen her wind. They would feed her nothing for breakfast, and nearly every morning while she practiced, she'd faint for want of breath. They'd throw water in her face to revive her, and she'd be given two frozen riceballs, as hard as rocks. Once inside, it was time to practice the shamisen. And then it was time to be scolded by her dance teacher. Chōkichi's body was always covered with cuts and bruises. At night, she would walk through the street to the parlors where she was to entertain. The older geisha would knock her down. If she fell face up, they'd slap her, saying it was unbecoming. How can that be fair? Aren't we all similarly born of flesh and blood? Yet one woman receives respect from the bearded gentlemen riding in their horse-drawn carriages, while another has to entertain those same horse bones with her music and dance. Our friend Azusa is torn between the two women, but I say to him, "Leave your wife and save Chōkichi!" (5: 248)

The reader may wish Chōkichi herself had delivered the details of her suffering. This litany, a critique of the cruelty of the gay quarters, would have had more force coming from her. Nevertheless, the point remains that without Suzu, Kyōka would not have gained as detailed a knowledge of the geisha's world as he did. Throughout his career, Kyōka carried a notebook and was an assiduous note taker. He asked many questions, especially about geisha and actresses, about their attire and lifestyle. But his extensive knowledge of kimono accessories, coiffures, and even the emotional patterns of the brothels are in large part Suzu's contribution to his work. Kyōka was able to write Suzu's suffering into Chōkichi's portrait. At the same time, he was able to include her in the archetypal female as she finds a place in the ritual script of his life.

Tatsuta's advice speaks to Azusa's heart. But, being one of Kyōka's creations, he is a hesitant man. The considerable tension in the story is established, then, in intersecting vectors: Chōkichi's salvation comes a bit more slowly than the steady deterioration of her mental state. Abandoned by Azusa, tortured by guilt, and tormented by the cruel manipulations of Genjirō—an unwanted suitor who represents the crassness of the male world—the innocent Chōkichi loses her mind before Azusa makes his decision to choose her rather than the Countess.

Timing is everything. Things have progressed so far that the only solution available to them is death. "Chōkichi was lying face up, Azusa's cheek touching hers. When they had jumped to their deaths, they were holding each other in their arms, but their dead bodies had been drawn apart by the current of the great river" (5: 379). In this chilling picture of double suicide, the Sumida River gradually pulls two corpses apart, carting their flesh away to the sea, where it will be swallowed up in the press of change and impermanence that have always been central elements of Japanese aesthetics.

If the allusion to Chikamatsu's lovers is powerful, it is because the morbid connotations of water imagery are well established within the tradition, traceable in classical texts as far back as the *Records of Antiquities* (*Kojiki*, 712) and more recently reinforced by kusazōshi illustrations. The deaths of Azusa and Chōkichi are complicated and amplified, however, by the positive connotations of water imagery highlighted by the story's title. *Worship at Yushima* refers to Azusa's chance meeting with Chōkichi at a temple in the Yushima district of Tokyo. For Azusa, the area has endless appeal. It reminds him of his mother, who lived in Tokyo during her childhood. He comes to worship at the temple but forgets to bring the few coins he needs in order to perform the ritual ablution that is part of the ceremony. Chōkichi, who happens to be standing behind him, pays his "water money," and he is able to commune once again with his dead mother.

The import of this encounter is clear. By way of this sacred water, Azusa meets both his mother and Chōkichi, who will later be her replacement. Water is thus also cleansing and enabling, and Chōkichi's proximity to it, as the young

woman tending the well, alludes to ancient formulations of water's erotic powers, as found, for instance, in the poems of the *Man'yōshū* (3439).

Suzugane no	She tends the well
Hayuma umaya no	Where ring the bells tied fast
Tsutsumi i no	to quick-leg'd horses,
Mizu no tamae na	I can't but think of drinking
Imo ga tadate yo	From the bare hand of that maiden.

The tie between Azusa's mother and Chōkichi is, then, both erotic and morbid.
As a strong confirmation of eros and death, Kyōka's water imagery is now
developed well enough for its full expression in the narrative archetype that is
on the verge of formulation.

   Worship at Yushima is perhaps not entirely a success, not much more sophisticated than the generic novels of manners (*fūzoku shōsetsu*) that present the
details of the gay quarters with little or no creative energy.[28] But, despite the
obviously formulaic structure of the piece, we find here a truly remarkable
facility with language. With this story, Kyōka seems to have reached another
level of accomplishment, displaying his quickly developing talent as a stylist.
The shifts from voice to voice demonstrate an unmistakable boldness and confidence. In mixing realism with the fantastic, this piece anticipates the even
more competent and memorable "Order Book" ("Chūmonchō," 1901).

   What these two stories—*Worship at Yushima* and "The Order Book"—have
in common is the manner in which the narrative meanders down the line that
divides the usual from the uncanny. Zigzagging down this ontological border,
such stories never allow the "real" to be taken for granted. It is when reality is
being undercut that Kyōka did his best writing. By toying with (but not flatly
dismissing) the concerns of realism, he succeeded in establishing a fictive world
that is both profoundly disturbing and truly absorbing. With works such as "A
Bird of Many Colors" and *Worship at Yushima*, he had already made significant
progress toward his mature style; but before he finally arrived at that point, he
had to set down, once and for all, the archetype as it was developing in his
mind. Everything came together in *The Holy Man of Mt. Kōya*.

CHAPTER 8

The Archetype

1900

The Archetype Defined

In the fall of 1899, Kyōka moved from Ōtsuka to Enoki-chō in Ushigome.[1] A photograph shows the young author sitting on the veranda, looking out over the backyard (see Fig. 11). The neighborhood was thick with nettle trees, and Kyōka's small two-story home, shaded and dark in midsummer, was "wild and lonely." On the first floor were two 6-mat rooms: one for Meboso Kite, the other for Toyoharu. On the second floor, another 6-mat room served as Kyōka's study and as a retreat for Kōyō when there were guests in his own home and he needed a place to work.[2] In this dark space, decorated with verses that Kōyō, Fūyō, Shun'yō, and others wrote on the walls during their frequent parties, Kyōka brought order to the various images that he had been developing over the years.

In essence, they form the following narrative. A young (or otherwise sexually hesitant) male passes through a watery barrier. Water (in its various manifestations) connotes death but is, at the same time, an ambivalent sign of birth and possibility. It establishes limits and, therefore, makes possible the high drama of trespass. The protagonist, driven by intense desire to heal an emotional loss, moves from the normative world of the day-to-day into a space of the sacred and the dead. There he encounters an alluring yet nurturing woman, who is always in some way a manifestation of the author's mother. With her, he experiences both horror and fascination. Her extraordinary powers allow him to survive this encounter, even though she herself is part of the danger. Returning to his normal state, he learns something about his own nature and about the deeper meaning of love.

The general contours of *The Holy Man of Mt. Kōya* (*Kōya hijiri*, 1900) coincide closely with this archetype. Seeking to save a lost soul, a wandering monk crosses a flooded road and enters into a mountain wilderness. He eventually meets a woman who lives there. Both seductive and maternal, she bathes and feeds him, while tenderly caring for her idiot husband. Frightened yet comforted by her powers, he spends a horrifying night in her mountain cottage. He is tempted but remains true to his life of self-denial as a monk in training. The next morning, he leaves but stops to gaze at the rushing currents of a waterfall, which entice him to go back to her. Just as he is about to forsake his life as a monk, he meets an old man who tells him the truth about the woman: she has supernatural powers and turns the men with whom she sleeps into beasts. He realizes he has narrowly escaped the same fate. Feeling as though he has been given a second chance to live, he flees, having learned something about his own sexual nature and about the meaning of love.

The correspondence is rarely as clear in other works, and this largely explains why *The Holy Man of Mt. Kōya* is Kyōka's most readable and best-known story. In essence a clarification of the archetype, it is an important key to the vast and often maddeningly difficult expanse of writing that both precedes and follows. The early stories build up to it, and the later ones owe much to it. Certainly, there are variations and exceptions. Yet when considering the entire sweep of Kyōka's career, it is obvious that this mythic frame was the ground of meaning for his life as an artist. Once established, he revisited it with religious regularity. He forsook its power toward the end of his life, but returned to it with even greater appreciation during his final months.

The prototypical nature of *The Holy Man of Mt. Kōya* becomes clear if we notice the way in which Kyōka expresses the mendicant's changing emotional status through the use of water imagery.[3] Water figures importantly in every part of the story. Its connotations are those we have considered in earlier works: death, metamorphosis, violence, eroticism. They link this story to the kusazōshi of the author's childhood reading and to an ancient iconography. Here, however, these various possibilities are made largely thematic; that is, the powerful connotative force of water is carefully controlled by the need to tell a carefully structured story. The water imagery in *The Holy Man of Mt. Kōya* supports rather than dominates the narrative line. It fulfills an ordering function and is given a clearly defined place within the archetype. Only in one passage is water allowed to depart significantly from its discursive role, for reasons that are crucial to the continued development of Kyōka's work.

In the story's outermost frame, water first appears in the crystalline form of snow. A winter storm envelops the priest and his young friend as they search for and find a place to stay the night. Structurally speaking, the blanketing storm is important. Without the presence of some form of water, the story cannot happen. It is as simple as that. Once the narration has begun, water quickly reappears in a slightly more suggestive way, pointing toward the danger that lies ahead.

As I waited, I noticed an inviting brook running in front of the stool on which I had taken a seat. I was about to scoop up a handful of water from a bucket nearby when something occurred to me.

Disease spreads quickly in the summer months, and I had just seen powdered lime sprinkled over the ground at the village called Tsuji.

"Excuse me," I called to the girl in the teahouse. I felt a bit awkward asking, but forced myself to inquire. "Is this water from your well?"

"It's from the river," she said.

Her answer alarmed me. "Down the mountain I saw signs of an epidemic," I said. "I was just wondering if this brook comes from over by Tsuji."

"No, it doesn't," she replied simply, as though I had nothing to worry about. (5: 580)

As is the case with the woman it surrounds, water both sustains and threatens life. We are already familiar with the ambiguity. For narrative purposes, Kyōka uses these conflicting values to reinforce the reader's mounting anticipation of whether the priest will be able to survive the danger and the temptation that is to come. Water's connection with the heroine is hidden at this point, however, and is only gradually revealed. In this way, water contributes to the narrative, which steadily and carefully develops the image in a way that piques the reader's interest.

The road forked at that point. One of the two paths was extremely steep and headed directly up the mountain. It was overgrown with grass on both sides and wound around a huge cypress tree four, maybe even five spans around, then disappeared behind a number of jutting boulders that were piled one on top of another. My guess was that this wasn't the road to take. The wide, gently sloping one that had brought me this far was, no doubt, the main road, and if I just stayed on it for another five miles or so, it would surely take me into the mountains and eventually to the pass.

> But what was this? The cypress I mentioned arched like a rainbow over the deserted road, extending into the endless sky above the rice paddies. The earth had crumbled away from its base, exposing an impressive tangle of countless eel-like roots; and from there a stream of water gushed out and flowed over the ground, right down the middle of the road that I had decided to take, flooding the entire area before me.
>
> It was a wonder the water hadn't made a lake of the rice paddies. Thundering like rapids, the torrent formed a river that stretched for more than two hundred yards, bordered on the far side by a grove. I was glad to see a line of rocks that crossed the water like a row of stepping stones. Apparently, someone had gone through a lot of trouble to put them there. (5: 583)

While hesitating before the rushing water, the mendicant sees a young farmer jumping from rock to rock. From this man, he learns that the flooded road is indeed the main one, and that the grass-covered trail is the old road, now dangerously overgrown and virtually impassable. Water is a barrier that blocks the way. But it is also a bridge to a more mysterious world. Prompted by his conscience, the monk decides to brave the water in order to save a medicine peddler who has mistakenly taken the wrong path. Water thus defines the borders of this other world and helps us anticipate his eventual union with the woman who presides there. But, again, the image is also concealed by the story so that its full force is saved for the appropriately lyrical moment. The articulation of the image, in other words, is suspended for the sake of coherence and structural completeness. Although we see the crossroads now, it is not until the end of the story that we understand that this was the site of a great flood that obliterated the woman's home village. The rushing water killed her father and sealed her fate as the woman who would reign over this forbidding and dangerous mountain territory.

What immediately follows is an account of the mendicant's passage into this other world. Searching for the wayward peddler, he enters a dark forest and encounters snakes, birds, a rushing wind (which is actually the roar of a waterfall), and, worst of all, mountain leeches that fall "like slender black strands of rain" from the trees. Driven nearly insane with fear and discomfort, the mendicant thinks not only of his own lonely demise but of the earth's as well.

These terrifying mountain leeches had been gathering there since the age of the gods, lying in wait for passersby. After decades and centuries of drinking untold quantities of human blood, they will have had their fill and disgorge every ounce! Then the earth will melt. One by one, the mountains will turn into vast, muddy swamps of blood. And at the same time, all these enormous trees, large enough to black out even the midday sun, will break into small pieces that will then turn into even more leeches. Yes. That's exactly what will happen! (5: 594–95)

This journey through leech hell, bloody and damp, is the mendicant's rite of passage. Only upon emerging from the forest and crossing yet another stream does he encounter the alluring young woman. She lives by a rushing river with an idiot, who turns out to be her husband. With this juxtaposition of water and woman, Kyōka tried to sublimate water's danger by first associating it with the woman's hospitable nature. Carefully leading the reader, he did not give the connection away but formed it gradually until the overlap became obvious. The woman welcomes the mendicant and takes him down to the river. She is to wash the evening's portion of rice. He is to bathe. Attracted by her kindness, he is acutely aware of the dangers but soon finds himself in a compromising situation nevertheless.

The stream gradually grew narrower, each bend bathed in moonlight so its water gleamed like plates of silver armor. Closer to where we stood, its waves fluttered white like a shuttle being taken up at the loom.

"What a beautiful stream."

"It is. This river begins at a waterfall. People who travel through these mountains say they can hear a sound like the wind blowing. I don't suppose you heard something along the way?"

I had indeed, just before I entered the leech-filled forest. "You mean that wasn't the wind in the trees?"

"That's what everyone thinks. But if you take a side road from where you were and go about seven miles, you come to a large waterfall. People say it's the largest in Japan. Not even one in ten has ever made it that far, though. The road is steep. So, as I was saying, this river flows down from there.

"There was a horrible flood about thirteen years ago," she continued. "Even these high places were covered with water, and the village in the foothills was swept away— mountains, houses, everything was leveled. There used to be twenty homes here at Kaminohora. But now they're gone. This stream was created then. See those boulders up there? The flood deposited them."

Before I realized it, the woman had finished washing the rice. As she stood and arched her back, I caught a glimpse of the outlines of her breasts, showing at the loosened collar of her kimono. She gazed dreamily at the mountain, her lips pressed together. I could see a mass of moonlit rocks that the flood had deposited halfway up the mountainside.

"Even now just thinking about it frightens me," I said as I stooped over and began washing my arms.

It was then that she said, "If you insist on such good manners, your robes will get wet. That's not going to feel very good. Why not take them off? I'll scrub your back for you."

"I wouldn't—" (5: 610)

The woman has her way with the mendicant since this is her world and her river. And it is at this compromising moment that Kyōka brings the three most important images of the story together for the first time—water, woman, and man. From this point, the narrative becomes largely a decoding of these images, so that their fullest meaning can be revealed at the story's conclusion, where every relevant moment of the river's story is set out for the reader's benefit. Meanwhile, the mendicant, still far from grasping the danger of his situation, is standing in the moonlit water beneath the imposing flood-carried boulders. He is increasingly tempted by the woman's charm. As Kyōka weaves images of water and woman together, the story moves ahead, and the relationship between woman and water gradually becomes obvious.

She poured water over my body and stroked my shoulders, back, sides, and buttocks. You would think the cold river water would chill me to the bone, but it didn't. True, it was a hot time of the year, but even so. Perhaps it was because my blood was aroused. Or maybe it was the warmth of her hand. Anyway, the water felt perfect on my skin! Of course, they say that water of good quality is always soothing.

But what an indescribable feeling! I wasn't sleepy, but I began to feel drowsy. And as the pain from my wounds ebbed away, I gradually lost my senses, as if the woman's body, so close to mine, had enveloped me in the petals of its blossom.

She seemed too delicate for someone living in the mountains. Even in the capital you don't see many women as beautiful. As she rubbed my back, I could hear her trying to stifle the sounds of her breathing. I knew I should ask her to stop, but I became lost in the bliss of the moment. (5: 612)

Water and woman are inseparable. After washing the mendicant, the woman disrobes.

She raised one hand to hold back her hair, and wiped under her arm with the other. As she stood and wrung out the towel with both hands, her snowy skin looked as if it had been purified by this miracle-working water. The flowing perspiration of such a woman could only be light crimson in color, the shade of mountain flowers.

She began combing her hair. "I'm really being a tomboy. What if I fell into the river? What would the people downstream think?"

"That you were a white peach blossom." I said what came to my mind. Our eyes met.

She smiled, as if pleased by my words. (5:614–15)

The mendicant, freshly bathed, gradually comes to discover her darker powers. Out from the woods flies a bat. Next comes a monkey, which tries to feel one of her breasts. Although the monk does not yet realize it, these creatures are her former sexual partners, whom she has changed into various beasts. She scolds them and sends them away. Unlike the mendicant, they are fully sexual and, therefore, doomed to be subsidiary characters, according to Kyōka's archetype.

She was gentle yet strong, lighthearted yet not without a degree of firmness. She had a friendly disposition but her dignity was unshakable, and her confident manner gave me the impression that she was a woman who could handle any situation. Nothing good could come of getting in her way if she were angry. I knew that if I were unfortunate enough to get on her wrong side, I would be as helpless as a monkey fallen from its tree. With fear and trembling, I timidly kept my distance. (5: 617)

As described here, the heroine of *The Holy Man of Mt. Kōya* is nothing less than Kyōka's image of the ideal woman—a composite of the spirited Edokko, the alluring geisha, the nurturing Maya/mother, the cannibalistic Kishibo, and the benevolent Kannon. Drained of personality, she is an iconic distillation. Water complements, envelops, and cleanses her. It penetrates this image of Kyōka's woman. But the integrity of this visual sign is not compromised at this juncture because the mendicant is still in control of his passion, and the writer is still in control of his imagery. The two images are, in other words, still separate, not fully integrated. But this distinction will break down at precisely that moment when Kyōka's reading of them shifts from this discursive mode to a more intensely emotional, visual one.

The mendicant returns to the woman's home, where her idiot husband is waiting. He feels rejuvenated by the water, which, she tells him, "is good for everything." Despite his feelings of relief, however, his fear builds as she continues to display her stronger side. She pacifies a bucking, whinnying horse that (although the mendicant does not yet realize it) is none other than the medicine peddler, now turned into a beast. As night closes in and as numerous creatures stir noisily about, the world of the small mountain cottage becomes "a hellish scene from the Realm of Suffering Beasts," not just because of the animals stirring about outside but also because of what is happening in the next room.

I held my breath. From the room where the woman and the idiot were sleeping came a moan and then the sound of someone drawing a long breath. It was the woman, overcome by a nightmare.

"We have a guest tonight," she cried out.

A few seconds passed before she spoke again, this time in a clear, sharp voice. "I said we have a guest."

I could hear the woman tossing in bed, and then a very quiet voice, "We have a guest." Then followed more tossing.

The beasts outside stirred and the entire cottage began to shake back and forth. Frightened out of my senses, I began reciting a *dharani*.

> *He who dares resist the heavens*
> *And vainly tries to block truth's route,*
> *May his head be split in seven*
> *Like the young arjaka sprout!*
> *His sin is worse than parricide,*
> *His crushing doom without relief,*
> *His scales and measures telling lies*
> *Like Devadatta, we despise*
> *Offenders of belief!*

I chanted the sacred words with heart and soul. And suddenly the whirlwind twisting in the trees blew away to the south and everything became still. From the couple's bed came not a sound. (5: 635–36)

The next morning, the mendicant departs. He has been tempted but not compromised. Still, he cannot forget the woman and the sounds of her love-making, nor does he forget his true feelings of sympathy for her and the way she so impressively cared for her idiot husband. He contemplates forsaking his vows in order to spend the rest of his life "in the river with her, unclothed, she breathing on my back, and I wrapped in the delicate fragrance of petals."

He follows the river as far as the Man-and-Wife Falls. Gazing at the curtain of water, divided into two parts by a huge stone projection, the mendicant finally begins to comprehend the full import of his temptation.

A large jagged rock, like the gaping mouth of a black killer shark, stuck out from the cliff, dividing in two the quickly flowing stream that rushed down upon it. The water thundered and fell about fifteen yards, where it reformed, white against dark green, then flowed straight as an arrow toward the village downstream. The branch of the waterfall on the far side of the rock was about six feet wide and fell in an undisturbed ribbon. The one closest to me was narrower, about three feet across, caressing and entangling the huge shark rock in the middle. As it tumbled, the water shattered into a thousand jewels, breaking over a number of hidden rocks.

The smaller stream was trying to leap over the rock and cling to the larger one, but the jutting stone separated them cleanly, preventing even a single drop from making it to the other side. The waterfall, thrown about and tormented, was weary and gaunt, its sound like sobbing or someone's anguished cries. This was the sad yet gentle Wife.

The Husband, by contrast, fell powerfully, pulverizing the rocks below and penetrating the earth. It pained me to see the two fall separately, divided by that rock. The brokenhearted Wife was like a beautiful woman clinging to a man, sobbing and trembling. As I watched from the safety of the bank, I started to shake and my flesh began to dance. When I remembered how I had bathed with the woman in the headwaters of this stream, my imagination pictured her inside the falling water, now being swept under, now rising again, her skin disintegrating and scattering like flower petals amid a thousand unruly streams of water. I gasped at the sight, and immediately she was whole again—the same face, body, breasts, arms, and legs, rising and sinking, suddenly dismembered, then appearing again. Unable to bear the sight, I felt myself plunging headlong into the fall and taking the water into my embrace. Returning to my senses, I heard the earthshaking roar of the Husband, calling to the mountain spirits and roaring on its way. With such strength, why wasn't he trying to rescue her? I would save her! No matter what the cost.

But then I thought that it would be better to go back to the cottage than to kill myself in the waterfall. My base desires had brought me to this, to this point of indecision. As long as I could see her face and hear her voice, what did it matter if she and her idiot husband shared a bed? At least it would be better than enduring endless austerities and living out my days as a monk.

I made up my mind to go back to her, but just as I stepped back from the rock, someone tapped me on the shoulder. (5: 639–40)

The violent aspect of these images becomes obvious only now. The mendicant, ready to kill himself, thinks of embracing the waterfall called Wife. But he is mistaken to think that returning to the woman is better than committing suicide. Woman is water; water is death; therefore, woman is death. His confusion is, on a semiotic level, a confusion of images, made possible because Kyōka has now reached his most profound and passionate level of image reading, the point at which the integrity of each visual sign no longer holds. What has been gradually brought together and thematically developed in a narrative way now violently merges for a brief moment as the story is interrupted by the lyrical moment it has worked to establish. In an energetic fusion of imagery, the woman is dismembered, torn apart. She is blended with water, mixed with blossoms, made into a similitude.

This scene provided Kyōka with a solution that would serve him well in the years to come. Standing out from the rest of the story because of its lyrical force, his use of imagery in this particular description of woman and water indicated what for him would be the limitations of narration. The shift from discursive to lyrical mode foreshadowed the future relationship between himself and language and between language and the archetype it was meant to convey. This temporary shift in the function of imagery within *The Holy Man* antici- pates the more fragmented pieces of the middle and late periods, in which Kyōka's images are much less carefully laid out for the reader. Here, this lyrical explosion of water imagery appropriately coincides with the mendicant's point of greatest vulnerability, since, for Kyōka, greater drama presupposes a height- ened sense of visuality. Having given in to his desires, the mendicant is totally compromised and mistaken. He is on the wrong path. Yet only because of this trespass is he ready to learn the truth of just how far he has strayed. His under- standing of love deepens upon realizing how close he has come to death or to being transformed into a beast.

Fortunately for this character, Kyōka chose not to indulge further in the powers of the image. Rather, he reverted to the previous mode of discursive narration. Another structural prop, a second messenger, delivers an explanation that will cool this impassioned moment of vision. An old man, whom he had met the day before at the woman's house, happens to be on his way back to the woman's cottage after having traded the medicine-peddler-made-horse for a large, shiny carp that the woman will eat for dinner. With the fish dangling from his rope, this fellow tells the mendicant all he could ever wish to know about her.

The woman, he says, once lived in the village down at the crossroads, thir- teen years ago, before a great flood destroyed it. Her father was the village doc- tor, capable of "scraping open a boil but little more." And the idiot, now the woman's husband, was a patient who lost the use of a leg due to the doctor's incompetence. During the idiot's long period of illness and recuperation, he grew attached to the woman; when the time came for him to go home, he in- sisted that she be the one to take him back up the mountain. This explains why she happened to be at his home when a torrential storm struck and the swollen river obliterated both the village at the crossroads and the one upstream. She and the boy survived, as did the old man. But all others perished.

Here again is a familiar pattern. Like many of Kyōka's heroines, the woman of *The Holy Man of Mt. Kōya* has passed through death. She has suffered and is, therefore, an appropriate temptress—capable of providing motherly care yet also able to deliver the touch of death or mutation.

"She was born with a lustful nature, and she likes young men best of all. I wouldn't be surprised if she said something sweet to you. But even if her words were sincere, as soon as she gets tired of you, a tail will sprout, your ears will wiggle, your legs will grow longer, and suddenly you'll be changed into something else." (5: 648–49)

Her accomplice is water. Although once merged with the waterfall in the mendicant's vision of her, her connection with water is brought back to a more discursive plane with the old man's explanation.

"And the river that carved out these mountains? Since the flood, it's become a strange and mysterious stream that both seduces men and restores her beauty. Even a witch pays a price for casting spells. Her hair gets tangled. Her skin becomes pale. She turns haggard and thin. But then she bathes in the river and is restored to the way she was. That's how her youthful beauty gets replenished." (5: 648)

Realizing how close he has come to being turned into a beast, the mendicant takes up his staff and runs away from the woman as fast as he can. Having been spared by his faith and by her appreciation of the purity of his heart, he lives to tell his story. On a snowy night many years later, he relates his experience to another young man, who also learns something important about the nature of desire and love. In the story's final scene, falling snow and enveloping clouds shroud the priest, who now seems blessed by water's dangers. *The Holy Man of Mt. Kōya* ends, then, when the relationships of water, woman, and man are fully explained. While water's associative powers are carefully suppressed in deference to the "moral of the story," on another level the lucid style of this piece results from the near-perfect conformity of its structure to that of the archetype itself.

Bakemono, Fear, and "The White Witch's Tale"

The Holy Man of Mt. Kōya is one of Kyōka's most accessible stories. Its Noh-like structure—a simple passage from the real world to the other world and then back again—is a paradigm for what some have argued to be the essential structure of the *monogatari*, as in Urashima's travel to the sea and back again.[4] Certainly, this is an eminently readable framework for whatever interpretation or emphasis a critic may wish to make. To some, *The Holy Man of Mt. Kōya* is a symbolist work and a masterpiece of the romantic persuasion.[5] To others it is a reiteration of the East Asian flood myth,[6] a work of fantasy,[7] a critique of modernism and industrialism,[8] an anachronistic affirmation of a traditional

Japan then being erased by its transition to modernity,[9] a repository of folklore and legend,[10] an attempt to rediscover abandoned matrilineal roots,[11] a return to the womb,[12] and so on.

Despite its prominence in critical studies of Kyōka's work, which began to appear around 1933, the story was not well received when it first appeared. The rise of a new group of writers, such as Kunikida Doppo (1871–1908) and To-kutomi Rōka (1868–1927), no doubt diverted attention from those associated with the Ken'yūsha school, whose goal of playfulness in writing was disdained as the conception of literature's role grew increasingly serious.[13] The Ken'yūsha writers themselves were becoming more serious. One critic, writing in April 1900, found Kyōka's new work "a moral tale for gullible children, nothing but a ghost story about crossing the Amo Pass."[14] Like the protagonist of his story, Kyōka was said once again to have taken the wrong path.

Kyōka was not swayed by such criticism. If anything, with *The Holy Man of Mt. Kōya* he boldly declared the ghostly foundations of his artistic vision and his indifference to the predictable comments of critics. By searching for and finally locating the archetype, he officially announced his freedom from the need to discover the late-modern realities being brought into focus by a more positivistic mode of representation. His passions now placed him not within the more discursive discourse of the articulate but within a mode of thought and description that best found expression in the impressionistic points and planes of visual signs. In the end, it was this formalistic, mythic approach to writing that brought him fame as a stylist. Freed by the archetype to concentrate on the act of writing at the level of word and image, he was able to recover the suppressed figurative wealth of the early-modern narrative tradition in the body of language itself.

Mishima Yukio later described his accomplishment:

Kyōka was a genius. He rose above his time and made a god of his individuality. Using a dangerously playful style of Japanese, he cultivated a garden of peonies that steadily blossomed amid the anemic desert of modern Japanese literature. His accomplishment did not arise from a sense of intellectual superiority or from any sort of aristocratic pretense; neither did it come from a contempt for the masses nor from some aesthetic theory. Bound always to ordinary sentiment, he was a pioneer of language—who raised the Japanese idiom to an extravagant level, to its highest potential. Using the narrative methods of popular historical stories (*kōdan*) and of human-nature stories (*ninjō banashi*), he drew from a vocabulary as rich as the sea to craft sentences of lasting stone and to pioneer barehandedly the deep forest of Japanese mysticism and symbolism.

His style, which revived the *renga*-like leaps of association and the imagistic splendor of the Japanese language that modern Japanese literature had forgotten, was not the result of an intellectually contrived anachronism. He himself became a mirror of the artist's timeless spirit. Fervently believing both in words and in spirits, he ranks with E. T. A. Hoffmann in the pureness of his romanticism.[15]

In other words, Kyōka discovered that words themselves are *bakemono*—deformed and deforming locations of sight mingling with sound. Routed by the phonocentric biases of the new realism, the banned visuality of nineteenth-century Japan had fled into the body of language, to the cave of Amaterasu, where it waited to be rediscovered and enticed into the light. In the word-as-image, the forgotten "imagistic splendor" of Japanese needed to be found and released upon the land.

Of this process, Mishima was right to say that Kyōka's embrace of visual language was not "an intellectually contrived anachronism." If anything, it was a consequence of a sincere emotional need, a result of Kyōka's fear—once again, both in the sense of horror and reverence. Because his regard for language anticipates the modernist concerns of the neo-perceptionists (*shinkankaku-ha*) and even post-structuralism, Kyōka might be considered ahead of his time. On the other hand, he, like William Butler Yeats and other thoughtful modern writers, was admittedly retrograde in his enthusiasm for folklore, superstition, and legend—the stuff of which a story like *The Holy Man of Mt. Kōya* is so obviously made.

Kyōka was not the only one in Japan to react to modernity in this way. Although the pragmatism and positivism of the age attempted to clear the air of ghosts, the new rationalism had the effect of stimulating interest in the supernatural, whether in the form of Kyōka's attempts to reinstitute the archetypes of legend, of Orikuchi Shinobu's study of myth and ancient song, or of Yanagita Kunio's explorations of folklore.[16] To the extent that critics continue to discuss Kyōka's work as fantasy (*gensō*), however, we can see how the tenets of realism have come to influence the critical reception of his work. Although this is not the place to pursue the issue fully, to call this story fantastic is to make an important distinction between a freer mode of the imagination and a more systematic one. Certainly, there is no questioning the utility of this distinction. Yet the entire point of Kyōka's work is lost if we block ourselves from understanding the seriousness of the author's relationship to the archetype and to the metamorphic beings who move about within it as "characters." If Kyōka stated that "monsters are the concretization of my emotion," the same can be said of his words. They, too, are both *a* matter of emotion and *the* matter of emotion. They, too, are *bakemono*, a congealing of emotional reality that Kyōka took seriously.

Stories of transformation are not new, either within the larger narrative tradition or within Kyōka's works. Beyond the emerging monstrosity of exaggerated figures such as Hatta Yoshinobu in "Night Patrol" and Otei in "Maidenhair," we can find precedents for this figure of the woman in the mountains in works such as "Mino Valley" (1896), "Of a Dragon in the Deep" (1896), and "Seishin's Nunnery" (1897). More precisely to the point is evidence that Kyōka wrote a preliminary version of *The Holy Man of Mt. Kōya* several years earlier. This is significant because it indicates that many works of his earlier career, including the conceptual novels, were conceived either after or while the author first struggled to write this early "ghost story," which eventually became his rosetta stone.[17]

The manuscript was not discovered until 1956. Approximately twenty-three regular manuscript pages in length (400 characters per page), it was stored in the childhood home of Meboso Kite. It bears no inscription, but, judging from the handwriting, there is little doubt that Kyōka wrote it. Entitled "The White Witch's Tale" ("Shirakijo monogatari"), it is a first-person account of an attractive young man's encounter with the uncanny. The narrator travels through the mountains, in this case from Tsuruga to Takefu, over the Kasuga Pass. Despite warnings of the dangers ahead, he feels compelled to wander where few dare, eventually encountering, as in *The Holy Man of Mt. Kōya*, both a horse and an old woman. She has "a face like jewels and skin like snow." She is, as her name suggests, pale in complexion. But her eyelids are painted crimson, thus establishing the ubiquitous color scheme of red and white. She snuggles seductively against the young man's knees. But the story breaks off just as the carefully prepared seduction is about to begin.

We do not know why Kyōka did not finish the story. One possibility is that he did not know what to do with it. That is to say, the truncated eroticism suggests both a technical and a spiritual inability, a building of interest without the possibility of fulfillment. Kyōka's early solutions to this impasse are melodramatic, even cataclysmic, tending toward torture on the one hand and worship on the other. What he could not do here but learned to do in the waterfall scene of *The Holy Man of Mt. Kōya* was to aestheticize the erotic violence that arose from his complicated regard for female comfort. He learned to do this by exploiting the ambiguity of the image, these multivalent signs that would allow tenderness to meld with violence, distance with passion, horror with aggression. The mendicant, thoroughly tempted to go back to the woman, does not take her into his arms, but *sees* the woman in the turbulent water, being pulled apart like a blossom.

Written at least five years later than the truncated "White Witch's Tale," this play of imagery showed Kyōka the appropriate relationship between language and the archetype. It inspired him to forge an appropriate idiom that would allow him to continue exploring what it was that he wanted (and desperately needed) to write, despite the risks involved. This lyrical moment of poetic confusion, framed within a context of narrative clarity, encouraged him to write himself into being, to pursue his own very private (and in this sense, modern) vision by employing words in unprecedented ways. Taking form within the phonocentric tendencies of antifigural late-modern culture, Kyōka's life as a writer would distinguish itself as a rebellious affirmation of mythical visions such as those found in Mantei Ōga's *The Eight Lives of Siddhartha, a Japanese Library*.[18] In Book 13, the young Śākyamuni longs for his mother, Maya. This scene establishes a paradigm for Kyōka's search for lost beauty, for the inexhaustible similitude of love. It establishes, by the non-present presence of the living and heavenly mother, a beauty that is both an arousal and a cessation, source and end, life and death, womb and vagina (see Fig. 12).

If *The Holy Man of Mt. Kōya* is the textual key to the archetype, this figure from Ōga's work is the visual paradigm. The image contains what Kyōka most wanted to see: woman, man, and water, the principal images of the archetype situated in prototypical relation to each other. Having dozed off to the lapping of waves, the sleeping prince yearns for his dead mother. Water delivers like the cloud upon which she descends, and threatens like the waves that reach and claw. Responding to his earnest desires, the benevolent Kannon, who represents salvation, grants the desired vision. Maya appears with *him*, the dreamer as a child, as he once was when she was still alive. Seeing himself, he is both dreamer and dreamed, delivered from the horrors of loneliness, but only temporarily, until that moment when the tide rises up to touch his foot, and he awakes to be filled with the desire to dream again.

CHAPTER 9

Language, Love, Death

1901–1903

Mono and "The Order Book"

Despite the lukewarm reception accorded *The Holy Man of Mt. Kōya*, not all members of the critical establishment felt Kyōka had gone astray. One writer for *Imperial Literature* compared him with Li Ho (style name: Ch'ang-chi; 791–817), a T'ang poet whom Kyōka had come to know through Sasakawa Rinpū. According to this critic, both Kyōka and Li Ho were kindred spirits, sharing the same "demonic language" (*kigo*). For this reason, neither artist should cultivate connections with the world of realism.

You mustn't let the world's opinions about your work make you forget where your real talent lies. This is a matter of grave importance. Why deny your strengths? I say: Make that which is dark all the more dark, and what is horrible all the more *horrible!* Employ the evil spirits of the mountains and forests, and bring together all that is *horrible* under heaven! Display your talent for all to see. Why should you feel obliged to write in a realistic vein? You were not made for writing social critiques or romances. That would be a mistake.

When you made your debut with "The Surgery Room," already at that point you displayed your true colors. Having grown tired of realistic novels, my eyes were taken aback by your demonic language, and I welcomed the change. But you have not been understood in your attempt to display the true focus of your concern, and many have had difficulties understanding your work. They've led you astray. They've corrupted you. In their confusion, they're still trying to lead you astray. This is why they ignore works like *Teriha Kyōgen* or "Black Lily" and praise *Worship at Yushima* as your masterpiece, a work that is obviously far from the center of your main interest. Is this not a tragedy? Is this not a lamentable development?[1]

This review, which appeared in July 1900, marks an important moment in Kyōka's critical reception. It expands a point made earlier, in February of the same year, by the same critic, who took exception to a critique in *The Sun* (and many other places) praising *Worship at Yushima* as Kyōka's best work to date. Against that opinion, the July review argued at length that even in the present age of science, there are matters that escape explanation by the learned. By aligning themselves with the new rationalism, the latest generation of novelists are self-important, arrogant, and base. Placed in the company of Li Ho (and Edgar Allan Poe), Kyōka supposedly represents an important counterpoint to the growing influence of the realists.

Although Kyōka himself avoided taking a position in the increasingly heated debate over what became the most prominent literary movement of the late-Meiji period, in many reviews to follow he was made to represent what ultimately came to be the minority opinion. The ongoing discussion of various mimetic theories of representation, especially naturalism, spilled over into the newspapers and became a focal point for the Meiji bundan. As a mainstream coalesced around issues of accuracy, honesty, and truth, Kyōka's reputation suffered. Despite his professed indifference, Kyōka's fate was tied to these larger trends. As naturalism became major, Kyōka became minor.

Whatever the effects of this marginalization, Kyōka certainly did not rely upon critics to point the way. The general direction of his career had long been established, and, having just received brilliant clarification in *The Holy Man of Mt. Kōya*, his artistic vision was more lucid than ever before. A comparison of *Worship at Yushima* with Kyōka's second attempt to write about the gay quarters reveals how intent he became, in further exploring his obsession, with the geisha as a supernatural figure and manifestation of the archetypal woman. Published in April 1901, "The Order Book" ("Chūmonchō") gives us Kyōka's mature style for the first time. Fragmented, elliptical, allusive, colloquial, temporally complex, and highly visual, the difficult style and structure of "The Order Book" builds with unmistakable confidence on the already discarded clarity of *Mt. Kōya*. Readability suffers as both the discursive force of allegory and the descriptive impulse of late-modern mimesis are weakened by the emergence of language in its physical splendor. As much as this is a story about the vengeance of a beautiful woman, it is more pointedly the author's contemplation of a few images—razor, mirror, snow, plum blossoms—and their significance as signifiers of death, salvation, threatening Eros, and blood.

When we sort out the story's many starts and stops, we discover two narrative lines embedded within a wealth of imagery and dialogue. They are, in the end, not only simple but, within the context of a wider oral tradition, also familiar. On the nineteenth of every month, a razor disappears from the shop of Gosuke, a knife sharpener. On November 19, the day when the events of the story unfold, Gosuke is sharpening a razor for a young geisha named Owaka who lives and works nearby. Braving the cold weather, Gosuke's friend Sakubei, a mirror polisher, pays a visit. While Gosuke sharpens the razor, Sakubei tells him a story about the mirror, an important family heirloom, that he has just finished polishing. It was a special request and had to be finished by the nineteenth, since the mirror was to be a gift from a certain woman to her favorite nephew. Sakubei finished the job, for which he was paid generously. To celebrate, he has come to Gosuke's, where they will drink together.

Sakubei narrates the story within the story. It focuses on a woman named Onui, a daughter of a samurai family forced into indigence by the collapse of the Tokugawa shogunate. She became a Yoshiwara geisha and fell in love with Matsushima Chikara, a young samurai from Chōshū who, as a member of the Meiji military elite, is an enemy of her family. Sensing he has lost interest in her, Onui plans their double suicide. In a moment reminiscent of the famous "Hair Combing" scene of the kabuki play *Fuwa*, she stands behind her lover, this time not with a comb in hand but a razor. At this moment of vulnerability, he holds a mirror in his hand and, seeing his mother's face superimposed upon Onui's visage, is overwhelmed with emotion. Incensed that he should yearn for his mother rather than think of her, Onui strikes with the razor. She misses his throat, and the blade hits the mirror, which he has brought to his chest. As she draws her hand back, she cuts her own throat. Knowing that her beloved will live on to be loved by other women, she dies, filled with regret and anger.

The night deepens, and Sakubei and Gosuke steadily become intoxicated. They do not realize that Onui's vengeful spirit lingers. That very night, after Owaka's newly sharpened razor mysteriously disappears from Gosuke's shop, the dead Onui lures Wakiya Kinnosuke, the young nephew of Matsushima Chikara and the intended recipient of the mirror that Sakubei has just finished polishing, to the brothels. Knowing its protective powers, his aunt wants Kinnosuke to receive the heirloom as soon as possible, before he is tempted to visit places of ill-repute, as his uncle once did. Concerned that her nephew might make the same mistake, she sees to it that someone delivers the mirror to him on the night of the nineteenth, while he is attending his farewell party.

He is going to Germany to study, and his friends have gathered to wish him well. Rather than accept the gift then and there, however, he has the mirror delivered to his home. He returns to the company of his friends and drinks without reserve. Later that evening, he ends up at Yoshiwara after a series of *jinrikisha* rides through the snowy night. Trudging through the snowstorm, its gathering strength a measure of the story's increasing dramatic intensity, he meets a woman, Onui's ghost, who asks him to deliver something for her. Thus, he finds his way to the House of the Scarlet Plum, where he meets Owaka and her colleague Osugi. He explains why he has come and talks of the confusing and foreboding circumstances by which he has arrived. When he reaches for the object he is to deliver, however, he discovers that it is missing. Since it is late and still snowing heavily, Kinnosuke is persuaded to stay the night. It is then that the beautiful young Owaka, now possessed by Onui's spirit, takes the razor from Kinnosuke's coat pocket and slashes him. Gosuke and Sakubei, who are drunk and have fallen asleep, see the murder in their dreams. Startled, they rush over to the house, but it is too late. Kinnosuke is dead, and Owaka has killed herself. They see that in sympathy for her suffering, Kinnosuke used his last bit of strength to write above Owaka's signature on her death note the words "Kinnosuke's wife." He has made her his partner in death because he recognizes the beauty of her pathos. Stunned by the horror of Kinnosuke's brief and fatal encounter with Owaka, Sakubei and Gosuke have no recourse but to congratulate the dead lovers.

Masamune Hakuchō's review of "The Order Book" was not favorable.

It seems the author's sympathy for the heroine is less intense than even Sakubei's. Neither is there much depth to Kyōka's feelings for Kinnosuke, who suffers such a strange and unexpected fate. Indeed, the writer's main interest seems to focus on the razor and the mirror. Accordingly, the relationship between Owaka and Onui does not follow from who they are as people but is based on the coincidence that the razor was sharpened on the nineteenth of the month. Neither can we discover in Kinnosuke's nature nor in his background the reasons for his tragedy, other than the coincidence that he did not have in his possession the protecting mirror and that he was led to his death by Onui's ghost.[2]

Hakuchō is typically late-modern in his assumptions that literary characters are people, that the events of a story ought to flow plausibly from a natural history of the characters, and that the author's focus (as indicated by his "sympathy") ought to be on the creation of character rather than on objects. Post-structuralism has challenged the validity of such notions, placing into question that which was once held to be certain and true. Yet the prevailing expectations of the day were not sympathetic to what Kyōka was trying to accomplish. In the final analysis, Hakuchō has done us the favor of emphasizing Kyōka's indifference to what was for him the already irrelevant issue of characterization. In truth, Kyōka's interest actually *was* focused on razor and mirror, white snow and red blossoms. If these inanimate images are as important as the people who develop in connection with them—Gosuke, Sakubei, Onui, Owaka, Matsushima Chikara, Kinnosuke—it is because they share a place in the same ontological stratum, heightened (or perhaps flattened?) to the same status as language—nothing more yet also nothing less. Like words, they are a reproducible system of referential signs that can be themselves only by pretending—through metaphor and metonymy—to be something else.

Kyōka's own comments about "The Order Book" confirm Hakuchō's indictment of the novelist's utterly poetic intent.

In describing Owaka's residence, for the season of the blossoming plum trees, lightly falling snow is perfect. And for unrequited love, what could be better than the deep snow in which we lose our way? Writing this scene, I suffered through the night. But when morning came, my courage swelled because of the heavily falling snow outside. Struggling within that freezing cascade of white, I wrote Chapter 14—"The Snowbound Gate."

In the title of the story, "The Order Book," I wrote the wrong character for "order" and received Kōyō's wrath.[3]

Kyōka drew attention to "The Snowbound Gate" for good reason. His description of the snowstorm, anticipated in Chapters 12 and 13—"Something white? Taboo! Taboo!"—vividly marks the beginning of the denouement. The reader's interest, having dawdled on the circuitously narrated events of missing razors and protecting mirrors, is now focused on the present drama of red and white. Enveloped in the cold whiteness of the night storm, Kinnosuke makes his drunken and ill-fated arrival at the House of the Scarlet Plum. Here is the famous passage:

From the early evening hours, the lightly falling snow started to cling to the joints of the wooden fences, the edges of the rain doors, and the eaves of the houses. In the streets beyond the fence, it touched the cheeks of those passing by. It clung to their hair, and to the brims of their hats. What once came down with a rustle, eventually lost its voice, no longer falling from the sky but filling it with white—the tops of the trees, the crests of the tile roofs, the paving stones below, and the boards over the gutters. Around anything that emitted light—the flame in the tobacconist's shop, the lanterns of the street vendors and rickshaw men—the flakes gathered like tatters of cotton, or fire-stealing bugs of purest white, beating their wings against the brightness. By nine or ten, the weaving traces of traffic on the street were gradually erased to two footprints here and three there. Eventually, you could see only the slightest indentions on the ground, the indistinct traces of wheel tracks trailing off in the distance.

The voices of those on the street had long since died away. Lingering at the crossroads, a policeman, his shoulders covered with snow, shook his overcoat and made its black pleats appear once again. He withdrew to the shelter of an overhanging eave, a few doors just this side of the knife sharpener's shop. The road before him, running from Mishima Shrine, past the Daion Temple, and all the way to Tamachi, was covered with white.

Occasionally the wind would gust. It dipped down to shave the ground and caressed the surface of the snow as if with a scoop, obliterating the paths where people walk, leveling everything while erasing the color of night. In an instant, the wind swept over the outer fence and blew hard against the sides of the buildings. Then it skimmed the eaves and moaned in the treetops. For a short time the sky cleared, and the wind howled even more loudly. Then the blizzard gave way to something less threatening, as the snow continued to fall silently and quietly upon the city.

Since this was the season of plum blossoms, the snow should have been more fleeting than frost beneath the morning sun. But there was something odd about this storm that had come so forcefully upon the city, at this time of night, at this time of year. What evil power had launched such a grinding assault?

Flowing from the rooftops splashed with bluish lantern light, reaching into a sky faintly brightened by the Yoshiwara's electric streetlights, the piercing sounds of women's laughter and the intermittent notes of a shamisen mixed perversely upon the Tamachi district of Tokyo. Blending with the sky, as if taking advantage of the earth's new whiteness, the voices of the women hung like the whispers of specters. How ghostly (*monosugoi*)!

Midnight passed. Now, just after one in the morning, when the wind and snow had reached the height of violence, someone came quietly calling at Owaka's residence, on the corner where the plum trees were blossoming. (6: 612–13)

In Kyōka's understanding of the image, snow is another manifestation of water. As such, it carries the same connotations of danger while being both more erotic and more deadly in its whiteness. Opaque and transparent, pure and polluted, supporting and engulfing, reflective and penetrable, insoluble and diffusible, hard and soft, solid and fluid—the wide range of water's physical qualities are exploited according to the season and dramatic need. Certainly, water's ubiquitous and mutable characteristics make it particularly apt as a metaphor for the elemental horrors of metamorphosis itself, an emotion well explored by the tradition within which "The Order Book" can be placed. To reiterate an earlier point, in the pages of the illustrated fiction found in Kyōka's library, the presence of water imagery invariably signals either violence or metamorphosis.

The historical situation of Kyōka's reaffirmation of this particular pedigree of imagery, however, forces us to go beyond the particular limits of each element of the archetype. In the context of Japan's second stage of modernity, propelled as it was by phonocentric forces, the author was pressed to advance the classical iconography to that point where images blend and merge, where language becomes entirely opaque and unmistakably revealing of its metaphoric nature. The melding of women's voices and snow in the passage above, for instance, emphasizes not only the ontologically mutable nature of the snow image but, beyond this, the mechanism by which the linkage between the various topoi of the Kyōkaean myth could come together. Needless to say, it was a method that violated the laws of plausibility that the naturalists would soon be advancing with great success.

The point of heresy is suggested by the exclamation "*Monosugoi!*" in the passage above, a comment made by the narrator about the similarity between specters and beautiful women. The term *monosugoi* has today lost much of its force, for *mono* has now been largely reduced to the status of an adverbial heightener for *sugoi*, which in contemporary speech usually means something like "impressive" or "extraordinary." Here, however, Kyōka obviously intended to express something more than this. His wish was to convey something anciently modern. *Mono* thus retains its sense of thingness, of materiality. Yet this corporeality is thoroughly mutable, a tangible quality that is rendered as "thing," "monster," "language." Widely signifying the sensible and the semiotic, it is a noun among nouns—animate and inanimate, person and non-person, modified by and modifying. *Sugoi* is "ghastly," "weird," "eery," "terrible," "terrific," "dreadful," "frightening," "horrible," "awesome." When framed in the context of Kyōka's place at the turn of the twentieth century, *mono* is the lyrical counterpoint to the more descriptive and discursive powers of narration. Taken together, the author's "lyrical narrative" can be understood as *monogatari* or the "telling" (*kataru*) of "thing-ness" (*mono*) in which language endeavors to expose its own metaphoric expansion.[4]

This desire to explain is driven by a narrative compulsion that quickly becomes a denial of *mono*. Paradoxically, it is made possible *because of* the need for language to be monstrous, to meet the requirement of being itself by being other. The reliable sign is reliably mutable. It claims to be intelligible by pursuing the creation of difference. Flowing from its source as *mono*, Kyōka's language is alive because its spirit is made valid by the author's belief in it. Its power derives from his own profound desire to dwell within the sight (grapheme) and sound (phoneme) of language, to be himself within the echoing call to be someone else, to be present through the (absent) dead and the distant, those who are available only through the words which they become.

To return to an earlier point, Kyōka's unflagging belief in language and literature makes problematic attempts to place stories such as "The Order Book" in a discourse of fantasy, if by the fantastic we mean to indicate that which is "beyond nature." Although it is entirely possible (and necessary) to call the ghosts in the author's work figures of speech or beings that occupy a territory beyond the borders of positivism, the assumption that the real itself is not figurative or knowable without recourse to imaginative construction is one that Kyōka would easily reject. We sense with every reading and rereading of the author's work a heightened regard for figurality in general. In an essay entitled "Flying Blossoms, Falling Leaves" ("Hika rakuyō") written in 1898, Kyōka earlier declared his belief in ghosts by suggesting their affinity to geisha and, therefore, his attraction to both.

It is at dusk when *mono* are most horrible (*sugoki*). This is when the evil spirits and specters come out to do their work. Note how this also happens to be the time when geisha gather together in the brothels. By the wee hours of the morning, the world belongs to monsters. They occupy the universe and, without giving a thought to the world of human beings, frolic about, devoting themselves to whatever suits their fancy. (28: 301)

At a time when both the phonocentric thrust of Western science was reformulating the limits of sight and insight and the culture of Yoshiwara was in decline, this simple belief in evil spirits was retrograde. Despite an unflagging attack from his detractors, Kyōka would persist. Eventually he would feel a need to explain more fully the influence of ghosts upon his writing. But while writing "The Order Book," he was not yet able to articulate what he knew intuitively as a writer. Similarly, Hakuchō and other critics were better at pointing out the skillfulness of Kyōka's eccentricity than at finding a plausible explanation for it.

The plot is, as usual, improbable, but because of the author's skill in matters of design and structure, from beginning to end it is consistently a story of fantasy. . . . Whatever we may say about the strange unnaturalness of much of Kyōka's work, his skillful use of this sort of material guarantees his place as a member of the *bundan*. If he were to take his poetic inspiration from daily life, he would not be able to display this ability.[5]

Here we must understand "daily life" to mean a rational, quotidian reality that held meaning because of its place within the larger late-modern project of realism. Yet, to state the obvious, Kyōka's daily life did not necessarily coincide with Hakuchō's, and we cannot say with perfect surety that he was not in fact drawing from experience.

If Hakuchō granted Kyōka his niche in the world of Meiji letters, others were less willing to see beyond the anachronism.

This may be a ghost story, but as a fictional narrative it is unnatural to an extreme. First of all, for the courtesan to be immediately filled with the desire to murder her lover upon hearing that he wants to end their relationship is unnatural. Also, a man's looking into a mirror and feeling repentant enough to treasure it afterward is one thing, but for his widow to polish and then send it as a gift to her nephew, who is in the middle of his going-away party, is, once again, unnatural. Finally, for Owaka to fall in love with him at first glance, then to be immediately filled with the desire to kill him, is perhaps the most unnatural thing of all. What begins unnaturally ends unnaturally. I will grant that even things that are unnatural can be interesting when presented in a skillful way, and we have to give Kyōka credit for his ability to do this. Yet his characters are always the same. They have no wisdom, no discernment, no common sense. Their ability to fall in love in one glance and then to murder at a moment's notice are, like the circumstances in which we find them, never anything but strange. Kyōka has departed from the correct path of the novel, where all characters should come alive through the changing circumstances in which they are found. He entered the wrong path and now has gone yet a step further by entering the ghost path. In dragging in ghosts from the previous century, the author is a bit ill.[6]

Kyōka, writer of ghost stories, is both wrong-headed and spiritually sick.

As we will see, Hakuchō's attitude would become more sympathetic as he came to understand how the strangeness of Kyōka's writing flowed naturally (and even plausibly) from the author's emotional circumstances. At this point, however, he was unwilling to allow Kyōka his own way of creating meaning.

"When listening to a ghost story told by a skillful raconteur, one finds a certain amount of weirdness interesting. . . . But this view of life is shallow and does not get at the truth of the human situation that lies hidden."[7] Hakuchō wanted depth. He required the exposure of the sort of truth that is concealed and, therefore, needs the author's skills of representation. Of course, Kyōka, too, sought something true. But he felt no compulsion to make it anything that could not be present as a surface. His characters have "no wisdom, no discernment, no common sense."

Suzu

Sometime during the first few months of 1902, Kyōka suffered a bout of dysentery and, after a stay in the Tamura Hospital in Tsukiji, left Tokyo for the resort town of Zushi on the Shōnan Coast to the south of the city. He had spent a summer there before, in 1890, and now returned to the sea to escape the oppressive heat of the city and to convalesce.

The trip took approximately three hours by train. Once in Zushi, he rented a small two-room house that had been built specifically for renting out. One room was eight tatami mats in size, and the other was six. There were no bathing facilities, but the house was situated in the mountains and provided an excellent view of the seashore and of the ocean beyond. He stayed here from July to September and described his summer home for his readers in this way.

At night, the fireflies sadly announce the approach of fall. Their lights flicker faintly here and there among the paddies of rice that sway in the wind. Behind the lattice fence draped with morning glories, the moonlight shines through the trees on the hill and glows elegantly upon the sleeves of my summer kimono. A flight of stone steps ascends a series of hills. Beneath the trees, on the dark, moss-covered hilltop, stands a Buddhist pavilion that houses the Benevolent Kannon. The temple is called Kanzōin. At the base of the cliff, dark and terrible, the creeping plants grow so thick you can see the stars shining even at midday. The people living here call it Dragon's Valley.

The rental house in which I am living is located in a place called Sakuragaoka, an easy climb from the Funekoshi Road. . . . From my kitchen I can see Mt. Fuji. The dew-laden leaves of the rose of Sharon are faintly crimson. In the darkness of night, lantern lights from the thatched farmhouses glow like fox fire. From the foothills toward Ikego comes the pounding of fulling blocks and the song of a peasant walking the distant paddy levees on his way to meet his lover. Now that we are on the autumn side of the Festival of Lanterns, the pathos grows deeper. (28: 337–8)

Despite his promise to Kōyō, Kyōka kept seeing Suzu. She came to his home in Zushi two days a week. Their meetings were kept secret in deference to the Master, but their ongoing relationship was widely known among Kyōka's friends. Again, we do not know the particulars of why Kōyō disapproved. Some speculate that if Kōyō had had a daughter of the appropriate age, she surely would have become Kyōka's wife.[8] There is no way to know if this would have actually happened, but a marriage of professional convenience would not have been unusual for the time.

On the subject of Itō Suzu, the other Four Devas—Fūyō, Shun'yō, and Shūsei—all sided with Kōyō. Perhaps this is why the secret was so difficult to keep. Rumors persisted, and Kōyō decided to visit Zushi. He arrived unannounced. Kyōka and Suzu realized he was on the way only when they spotted him walking the path that wound up the hill from the station to their house. Rushing to get rid of all signs of her presence, they hurriedly straightened up. Just before Kōyō reached them, Suzu ran off to hide at a neighbor's house.

Without entering, Kōyō sat down on the veranda to catch his breath. As he talked with Kyōka, he noticed a woman's underskirt hanging on the clothesline and inquired about it. Struggling for an answer, Kyōka told him that it belonged to Hattori Teruko, Teraki Teihō's good friend, who had come visiting and had stayed behind to clean the kitchen. Kōyō, who was no stranger to the brothels, could see that the garment had no strings and was the kind only geisha wear. He scolded Kyōka roundly but did not mention Suzu again during his visit. Already, he was growing weak from the lingering illness that would eventually take his life.[9]

There were other visitors to Zushi. Shun'yō came to stay for two or three days at a time. Of the Four Devas, he was the hardest drinker. Kyōka and Fūyō also indulged regularly. Shūsei enjoyed alcohol the least of all. In anticipation of their visits, Kyōka had stocked up on Kikumasa, which he procured from the Aokidō in Kanrakuzaka. Dipping into Kyōka's provisions, Shun'yō would get drunk and torment Kyōka by singing out, "'The grass on the bank withers underfoot, but revives with the loving dew.' That's what Kyōka's island woman sings all year long, right Izumi?"[10] The island referred to here is Suzaki, a brothel in Fukagawa that Kyōka and the others frequented. It is the setting for "A Tale of the Southwest Quarter" ("Tatsumi kōdan," 1898).

Returning to Tokyo in the fall of 1902, Kyōka spent the winter months at his home in Enoki-chō. By March of the following year, he was ready to move into a larger house. It would be a place where Suzu could stay permanently. A photograph shows Kyōka, his grandmother, and his brother at this home (see Fig. 13). In the second autochronology, Kyōka writes of the move. "March 1903. We move to Ushigome Kagura-chō. In May, Suzu moves in. This was made possible by the kindness of my childhood friend Yoshida Kenryū" (1: vii). Perhaps out of deference to Suzu, Kyōka omits the details of Yoshida's involvement. She had already been spending two days a week in Zushi and was unavailable to fulfill her responsibilities in Tokyo. That must have caused serious complications. We can only assume that others were willing to look the other way, since Suzu was far from financially independent and was not really in a position to do as she pleased. Seeing his friend in such a desperate situation, Yoshida, later the president of Hiroshima Normal School, put up some money so Kyōka and Suzu could see each other more easily.[11]

Their problems were far from over, however. As before, the romance had to be discreet. Whatever Kyōka did to keep their love a secret, we know from Kōyō's diary that he soon discovered that his favorite disciple had still not gotten rid of his "prostitute." According to Kōyō's account, Suzu moved in as early as April, not in May as Kyōka remembered it.

April 14, 1903. Cloudy. Exhausted. I had a masseur come in the afternoon. . . . For lunch I ate five bantam eggs and a bowl of yogurt. My fatigue is severe. I had Fūyō come in the evening to discuss some editing questions. Afterward, we paid Kyōka a visit. (I learned he was keeping a prostitute, and went to express my disapproval.) He tried to hide the truth from me. I lost my temper and came home. Fūyō came back at ten. I sent him to check out the situation again. I called Kyōka and his brother to my bedside and chastised them. It was midnight by the time I sent them home.

April 16, 1903. Warm. Drizzling rain. . . . My stomach is improving. The stars came out at night. Kyōka came in the evening. I went with him to his house and met the woman Momotarō, who told me she would move out the next day. I gave her ten yen.[12]

In effect, Kōyō paid her off. She left, as agreed, but, as we shall see, she did not stop loving Kyōka simply because Kōyō wanted her to disappear. A photograph shows Kyōka as he looked during this period of disagreement (see Fig. 14).

In *A Woman's Pedigree*, a story that Kyōka wrote four years after Kōyō's death, the details of his separation from Suzu are presented quite differently. Instead of the ten yen noted in Kōyō's diary, Sakai Shunzō, who is mentor to the story's hero, Hayase Chikara, makes the alimony considerably more generous: "three crisp ten-yen notes." The difference has been interpreted variously. Some hold that by increasing the sum, Kyōka attempted to show how difficult it was for Kōyō to send her away. Katsumoto Seiichirō took the opposite position: that Kyōka's story was written in revenge and represents an effort to point out Kōyō's miserliness.[13]

Katsumoto was one of Kyōka's strongest detractors, and he openly worked to discredit Kyōka's loyalty to Kōyō. Still, we should not dismiss the possibility of Kyōka's anger and resentment. The story takes another significant departure from what we know about Kōyō's handling of Kyōka's relationship with Suzu. In *A Woman's Pedigree*, the geisha Koyoshi works with unflagging energy to bring the lovers Chikara and Otsuta together. But we know that the character on which Koyoshi is based is Kōyō's lover Oen. And we also know that she was highly critical of Suzu and probably had much to do with Kōyō's rejection of her as a possible wife for his protégé. Finally, as already mentioned, Oen was also a Kagurazaka geisha. Although she and Suzu worked out of different houses, it is quite likely that Oen had heard rumors of Kyōka's plan to make Suzu his partner. Despite the obvious sincerity of Kōyō's feelings for Oen, this was something he never intended for her. Thus, it is speculated that the envious Oen worked to poison Kōyō's opinion of Kyōka's lover.[14]

Whatever Kōyō actually knew about Suzu, his interference could only have been regarded as an attempt to deny Kyōka's passionate attachment to this woman who so perfectly fulfilled the role of his dead mother's proxy on earth. As sympathetic as some readers would have Hayase's mentor be, that Kyōka and Suzu were embittered by Kōyō's refusal to acknowledge their love seems undeniable.[15] Like the act of lying to his mentor, the writing of this story (which we will examine later more carefully), as well as Kyōka's subsequent handling of his relationship with Suzu, was filled with ambivalence. Suzu moved in with Kyōka immediately after Kōyō's death, but her name was not entered into the Izumi family's registry for quite some time. (In fact, she retained her status as a registered geisha until 1905 and continued working even after she began living with Kyōka in Tokyo.)[16] Kyōka, who later offered ritual tea every day to a hanging scroll of calligraphy that Kōyō had given him, visited his teacher's grave frequently but never let Suzu approach it.[17] In the end, she was not required, or expected, to pay her respects to this man who died before accepting Kyōka's love for her.

Kōyō's Illness, "Of Flowers and Herbs"

Kōyō entered the University Hospital in February 1903 and was diagnosed as having stomach cancer. He was released in late March and stayed at the home of his wife's brother, until the beginning of April.[18] Upon returning to his home in Yokodera, he spent the remaining months of his life in and out of bed. His stomach pains grew more frequent from about July, when he began taking medicine to relieve the pain. The analgesic was not long-lasting, however, and his struggle to complete *The Gold Demon*, which was still being serialized in the *Yomiuri News*, was painful and exhausting. While he was working on the manuscript, which he would leave uncompleted, no one else saw it but Kyōka. Kōyō had him read it out loud so he could hear what he had written. Kyōka later remembered one of their final meetings with each other:

> "Is Izumi here?"
> He served me the season's first tea in his study.
> "Help yourself to these sweets. I just finished this. Read it to me, will you?"
> When he was relaxed, he would take off his socks and sit cross-legged in a stylish pose, even when he was at someone else's house. But when he was at his desk, he usually sat up straight with his legs beneath him. . . . His eyes, bloodshot from having stayed up all night, were shining and penetrating. On his lips were the gentle traces of a smile.
> As I say this, I feel as though I should straighten my collar and sit up. Even now I feel he is near me. (28: 580–81)

On May 11, the *Hōchi News* and other Tokyo newspapers made public the severity of Kōyō's condition.

> Ozaki Kōyō and Kōda Rohan have long been known to the world as the two morning stars of the literary firmament. In particular, we pray that Kōyō's splendid prose will continue to adorn the *bundan* with a never-ending brocade. The Master, however, is now stricken with stomach cancer and has had to discontinue writing in order to devote all his energy to the healing process. As his illness daily grows more severe, the concern that his students show for him is extraordinary. Searching for ways to comfort their Master, Kyōka, Fūyō, and Shun'yō have decided that each of them will write a story to dedicate to Kōyō as he lies ill. For over three weeks, they have been working day and night, shaping their words and developing their thoughts, each producing a masterpiece worthy of their mentor. They have presented the collection to Kōyō. In due time, the anthology will be published. Proceeds from its sale will be used to help defray their teacher's medical expenses.[19]

Kyōka's contribution to this effort, a lyrical story entitled "Of Flowers and Herbs" ("Yakusō tori") was published in the *Niroku Herald* from May 16 to May 30, 1903. With Kōyō's illness in mind, Kyōka drew from the archetype yet again, deepening familiar images with Buddhist ones in order to create a narrative powerful enough to subsume the particular agony of his mentor's decline within the greater meta-story of watery trespass and a man's need for a woman's saving powers.

The hero, Kōsaka Mitsuyuki, is a medical student. He has wandered into the mountains to pick herbs for a relative who is in critical condition and dying. With this figure of the desperate Mitsuyuki, Kyōka suggests the limits of medical science and the necessity of a journey away from the masculine, ordered world of civilization and into the more chaotic, feminine depths of "nature." As we have seen, the mountains are a place of both miracle and murder. The young woman who becomes his guide to the verdant heights of Maiden Moor is from Futamata (or trail fork) village, a name that also suggests the modern/anti-modern split made incarnate in the figure of Kōsaka himself.

At first encounter, she mistakes Kōsaka for a pilgrim since he is chanting passages from the *Lotus Sutra*'s "Book of Healing Plants" (Chapter 5) as he walks. Kyōka uses the sutra to establish the principal images of the work: moisture-filled clouds, grasses, trees large and small, myriad grains, and healing herbs. From what we know, we can see why Kyōka chose this particular sutra, with its emphasis on sacrifice and its inclusion of the unusual admission that even women can be reborn in the Pure Land. As important as the scripture is to the overall shape of this short narrative, however, the *Lotus Sutra* is not precisely "the foundation from which this work grows."[20] The base remains the archetype, and the particular portion of the sutra quoted in this story provides a separate grid of imagery superimposed on already established iconographic poles so that the theme of miraculous healing can be situated within the larger narrative of trespass and return. In the adjustment that takes place between these two constellations of visual signs, the images are fructified and expanded as the words that carry them are made to fuse beneath the poetic burden.

Kyōka's sensitivity to what he would later call the *myō*, or wonder, of language is steadily growing. Here, water, the principal image of horror, is affirmed in a way more positive than we have seen before. As introduced by the sutra, rain is nothing less than a metaphor for Buddha's benevolence. Water is love. It falls evenly upon the land. It soaks the earth and makes the abundance of grain and healing herbs possible. In a dramatic reversal of the author's personal reality, even the flashing lightning and rumbling thunder that Kyōka dreaded with inhuman passion become signs of salvation and kindness: as set down in sutra, upon seeing and hearing them, "all living beings are filled with joy."

In terms of the narrative, the storm that moves toward us comes not to destroy but to sustain. Of course, this more benevolent water exists only within the sutra. The larger story that contains the scripture retains Kyōka's usage: water is enabling, perhaps, but always terrifying. Against the hope provided by the Buddhist verse, water retains all its horrors, a point that the dying Kōyō, who read and even corrected the story as it appeared in the newspaper, could not have failed to miss. As Kōsaka and this young woman make their way deeper into the mountains, he relates an experience of twenty years earlier in which water signifies the border to a world in which miracles happen, although only at the price of bondage and death. As usual, a beautiful young woman dies, in order to pay the price of the miracles. In the end, the savior presented here for Kōyō's benefit is, in style, unmistakably Kyōka's private comfort.

We have already noticed a similar narrative structure in *The Holy Man of Mt. Kōya* and "The Order Book." By using the device of a story within a story, Kyōka is able to fuse present time with remembered time. The ultimate effect of this maneuver is a denial of temporal order in favor of a spatial sense of visual ritual. When Kōsaka was nine (Kyōka's age when his own mother died), his mother fell hopelessly ill. Desperate in his desire to help her, he ventured deep into the same mountains to find the single flower that "blossomed pure red." This was the only plant that could save her, and the passage to the spot where it grew took him across two rivers. "Through the clear, black water, the deep blue of the river's depths showed no bottom. Our boat was sucked toward huge boulders that loomed ahead. The cliff was frightening, the water deep" (7: 611) There was also a rainstorm. "From the moment we crossed the river, the mountains began to vomit clouds. In the water of the paddies here and there, the black clouds came and went" (7: 612).

Kōsaka found the miracle-working flower. As a result, his mother lived for another five years. But the price of her cure was the life of another young woman—beautiful, kind, giving—who met Kōsaka in a mountain village along the way and guided him to the sacred space. Reflecting the ambiguity of water imagery—the import of the sutra working against the larger tragic force of the story—their moment of triumph was ruined by a band of mountain brigands who kidnapped them and let Kōsaka return to his home only because the young woman agreed to marry the leader of the gang and to spend the rest of her life in bondage. Kōsaka returns "like the dead returned to life" and presents to his mother the flower that he received from the hand of the young woman. Knowing the price that has been paid for his mother's recovery, he is filled with grief, an emotion remembered all too vividly as he, now twenty years later, makes the journey a second time.

The resolution of the story is a metamorphosis. The enormity of the author's emotional need to remember his dead mother and to save Kōyō from meeting the same dreaded end forces the miracle of one thing changing into another. As the time frame of the flashback and that of the overall narrative collide, the young woman who has led him into the mountains this second time becomes the one who led him there before.

The sunlight cut through the undergrowth, where the shadows of the grass glowed blue like the moonlight upon the sutra scroll. As he walked ahead, reading the verses, the holy writings became marked with colors, coming and going as butterflies in play—here crimson, here yellow, there purple, white passing by—like cherry blossoms flowering and scattering throughout the four seasons.

Suddenly the heavens opened, and his body was enveloped in clouds. A wondrous fragrance distilled upon his sleeves as he looked at the drifts of snow-white flowers to see sparkling points of crimson and green. Quickly, the colors separated, each becoming a petal of a blossom or a leaf. The steadily blooming flowers of Maiden Moor surrounded him with their scent and blossomed within his heart.

The flower girl set her basket down, then paused a moment to rest. She removed her hat, so he could see the pale skin of her neck and hairline. Dark and shiny, her hair was pinned up with one small flower. Pausing amid the whiteness of the chrysanthemums that were scattered about the hem of her kimono, outlining the edges of her sleeves, she waited for Kōsaka. Her smiling face was beautiful, stately. Pierced by her gaze, he no longer felt like the man who had been telling her his story. He forgot himself. No longer able to remember his own name, he became a nine-year-old boy.

"I got so involved in your story, it took longer than I thought. The moon will be out soon. Until then, could you please help me fill my basket with flowers?"

She spoke as if she needed his help. Kōsaka, on the other hand, felt as if she were a god and he was in her service. He picked a chrysanthemum on his left, a peony on his right. His hand plucked the Chinese bellflower in front of him, a morning glory behind him. Again, he repeated the details of the story—how they crossed the river, the robber's house, saying farewell to the young woman who sacrificed herself for him. By the time he had finished, the basket had disappeared beneath a wealth of blossoms.

The moon appeared, and he fell down on his knees to pray. His words were heartfelt as he peered again and again into the darkness. His eyes searched the moor. But all he could see was the faint illusion of fragrance and clouds and snow and purple, all taking shape and blending into the color of night.

Ready to abandon hope, he fell to the ground. Now with despair in his heart, he saw her standing next to him with her hands together in prayer. The single flower in her black hair was crimson in the moonlight.

Kōsaka bowed and worshiped at her feet.

She reached down and held his hand. He put his arms around her knees and looked up, pressing his cheek against her sash. She gazed back. Her kind, graceful face was bathed in moonlight. She turned her face to the side, and her hair came cascading down. In her hand was the same crimson hairpin that she once put into his trembling collar when he was still a young medical student. He was spellbound.

"So we meet again. Use this, and the one you're thinking of will be cured completely."

He released his hold on her and held the stem of the pin. As he did, the woman's sleeves rose in the air, and her body moved like a shadow into the distance of the blossom-filled moor.

He stood to follow after her. But she continued on toward the peak of the peony-covered cliff, shaped like the head of a huge, white elephant. As she quickly rose into the sky, as if to enter the clouds, he caught one glimpse of her beautiful eyebrows, then suddenly found himself alone on the windless, moonlit moor.

Kōsaka fell to his knees.

Using the crimson flower to mark the page, he spread the sutra out on a huge peony. He pressed his hands together in prayer and began reading from the "Book of Healing," and continued through the night. (7: 626–28)

Here the familiar colors of red and white are made to carry a complicated symbolic weight. Both appear with obsessive frequency, almost as words of a mantra. They reflect not only their importance to the erotic and violent nature of Kyōka's imagination but a Buddhist import as well. Grace, enlightenment, beauty, purity—all are suggested by the moon, an important religious symbol, which here is both compromised and heightened by the constant need for white to denote a woman's skin. Red is also taken in two directions. As the color of blood and erotic passion, it here signifies, especially as expressed in the central image of the moon-brightened flower hairpin, an erotic beauty that has the power to heal. "The single flower in her black hair was crimson in the moonlight." It is as if the confluence of Buddhism with Kyōka's personal narrative of erotic salvation anticipates an aesthetics of blood sacrifice like that so deeply embedded in, for instance, the Judeo-Christian tradition. In this even larger archetype, a savior endures suffering and sheds blood in order to save others (who purify themselves by drinking that blood and eating the sacrificial flesh).

A largely secularized, postwar readership has been reluctant to recognize Kyōka as a religious writer. And yet the hesitance of the Japanese critics to explore this obvious intersection between belief and language, icon and image, remains an impediment to their understanding of works like "Of Flowers and Herbs," which so clearly advanced Kyōka's literary style by virtue of their impassioned if ultimately frustrated response to despair. In this case, the context of the story could not be clearer, although the narrative itself leaves room for various interpretations. Given the general lack of pronouns, we will never know the gender let alone the particular identity of the one who Kōsaka is thinking of, the one, that is, he has come into the mountains to save. Considering the provenance of the story as an offering to the dying Kōyō, however, it is reasonable to assume that Kyōka had someone like his mentor in mind. If so, the crimson hairpin finds an analogue in this story itself, this object of healing that, as it turned out, did not have the power to turn death away. We know that Kyōka actually did search for herbs in the neighborhoods of Tokyo.[21] But that, too, proved futile.

The inability of literature to heal the sick does not change its status as a means to an important end. Kyōka required the healing powers of language. Not only did he continue to write throughout his lifetime, but he also returned to the same narrative archetype again and again. For Kyōka, the flow of language from the brush to page brought him to a state of emotional intensity sufficiently strong to counter the constant pull of fear. This state of equilibrium was short-lived. As an affirmation of ephemerality itself, Kyōka's writing is saved from the tedium of falling blossoms and dew-drenched sleeves by the undeniable sense of desperation that suffuses practically every word he wrote. If literature was a process that made the continuation of his own life possible, it was made all the more intense (and modern) by its nature as a self-conscious form of bliss.

Kōyō's Death

By October, Kōyō's condition was critical. On the twenty-ninth of the month, his physician indicated that he might not last through the night. Telegrams were immediately sent out, and his family and friends quickly gathered. By midnight, Kōyō's condition had not improved. Everyone but his closest associates—Kyōka, Fūyō, Sazanami, and Ishibashi Shian (1867–1927; one of the original founders of the Ken'yūsha)—returned to their homes. At three in the morning, Kōyō spoke his parting words to his wife, his wife's mother, and his wife's younger brother. Afterwards, he had asked that his disciples, who were waiting in the three-mat room by the *genkan*, come up and say their farewells. They would drink one last cup of wine together. Kōyō passed away late the next evening.

Kyōka would later write of Kōyō's death in a short essay entitled "Master Kōyō's Final Fifteen Minutes" ("Kōyō-sensei seikyozen jūgofunkan," 1903).

October 30, 1903, 11:00 P.M. The situation takes a turn for the worse. I go upstairs and remain in the adjoining room. Ishibashi, Maruoka, and Kuga are there.

From one ear to the next pass the sounds of whispering, like dull, weak flashes of lightning.

Kōyō's room is silent. We hear not a sound, save for an occasional sob and the rasping tick of the clock.

Between the rooms are four sliding doors. At one end, a narrow crack appears, as Kōyō's wife comes and goes every four or five minutes. A young nurse, dressed in white, wears a look of hopelessness on her face. Quietly, unsteadily, she passes like water through the lantern light. She stands in the hall with the doctor, and they exchange words privately.

The rain beats down.

At exactly 11:10, the doctor comes in. There is anguish in his expression as he explains that the injection he has administered to the Master no longer has any effect.

The wind blows stronger.

The rain falls in waves.

From this point on, we hear only the faint sound of someone coughing. At that moment we are all filled with horror. We hold our breaths but can hear nothing, not even a sigh.

A short while later, a nurse appears through a crack in the sliding doors. She exchanges glances with the doctor, and they both disappear into the other room.

Ishibashi takes a chair, no longer able to stand. He looks up at the ceiling then down at the floor, to the right, then to the left. He seems more dead than alive.

The whispering gradually increases. It becomes more tender and deep, like fleeting sounds of the tide rushing in and out beneath the moon. It is 11:15. I am unable to say more. (28: 347–48)

The account ends in silence. Out of respect for his mentor, Kyōka lets Kōyō's death hang on the moaning of the storm and the flood of moonlight. Quite in contrast, Tokuda Shūsei included a number of details that give us a much clearer sense of the dying man's final moments.

At the doctor's pronouncement late that night, messengers and telegraphs were sent off to relatives and close friends.

People began trickling in, taking their places around the sick man's bed.

"My god, what's happened?" exclaimed an artist with a bad heart as he came running in, pale and wheezing heavily.

The patient was awakened from his coma by his morning injection, and when his eyes suddenly opened wide, the faces of those crowded around were mirrored in them. A quietness, funereal yet uncertain, filled the room. The footsteps of guests ascending and descending the stairs as quietly as possible added to the tension, giving the patient an awful intimation of what was to come.

As the fit of delirium gradually subsided, Sasamura's [the protagonist of Shūsei's story] teacher was able to converse for short periods with members of his family. His voice was fairly calm. But his mind was pitifully disordered, out of delirium or perhaps because of rage. Was it because he was unable to bear the excruciating pain brought on by impending death? Or was it a childish fury against a fate he could no longer hope to escape? He screamed. A stream of nonsense came from his mouth in a high whining voice.

When his suffering eased, he returned to his normal self. He even dozed off from time to time. In his lucid moments, he made last requests—that his wife be escorted to a hot spring resort to recover from the exhausting months of nursing him, or that his body be donated to medical science for autopsy.

"Death will at least mean an end to the pain," he observed with a sad smile.

"Bring your ugly faces here," he yelled and looked around with clouded eyes to pick out his students who drew near.

"Eat awful-tasting food. I want you all to live as long as you can."

Muffled sobbing came from his wife and another woman who were clinging to his hips.

The room upstairs, crowded with guests, suddenly grew silent, as if all had stopped breathing at once. Most of those behind the inner circle were standing.

Sasamura's teacher drew his last breath late that night. (3: 116–18)[22]

Kōyō's parting admonition to his students that they "eat awful-tasting food" means only that they should avoid the gourmet food that Kōyō thought had contributed to his disease. The great mentor, if we can trust Shūsei's account, maintained his sense of humor until the very end.

Shūsei's version of Kōyō's death is more informative and, in this sense, more powerful than Kyōka's. But this was precisely why Kyōka objected to it. To him, Shūsei's slavish commitment to realism was crass and distasteful. In fact, this passage from Shūsei's autobiographical novel *Mold* (*Kabi*) infuriated both Kyōka and Fūyō so much that they broke with Shūsei. How could he so indiscreetly write about Kōyō's whining delirium? Their friendship, if it ever existed, was officially over. They cut Shūsei off.

This is not to say, of course, that Kyōka's own account lacked detail. In "Master Kōyō's Final Fifteen Minutes," the press of time and the sorrow of parting are noted with a strange accuracy, as if the flow of minutes and seconds is the enemy, robbing the writer of his master's presence. In "Of Flowers and Herbs" the harsh reality of time's passage is moderated by space and image—the storm, the moon, and so forth. Here, what makes the focus on time seem even more obsessive is our knowledge that these last few minutes with Kōyō may not have been a part of the author's experience at all. According to Teraki Teihō, Kyōka was not present when Kōyō died. During the final days of Kōyō's decline, his students took turns being at his side. Kyōka, it seems, was at home eating breakfast when the news came. Teraki states that he happened to be at Kyōka's residence. "I had reason to visit Kyōka's home and was there when a messenger came rushing in to announce that Kōyō had passed away. Kyōka, still holding his rice bowl and chopsticks in his hands, began wailing like a child. I was surprised."[23]

If this account is true, it tells us much about Kyōka's posture as a writer. The truth of absence (whether the one missing was Kyōka's mother, or father, or Ozaki Kōyō) required the invention of presence. Absence was horror, and presence, however short-lived, was its antidote. But what sort of presence must this be? Surely, it was a difference in fictional stance as much as it was Shūsei's actual description of Kōyō's final decline that angered Kyōka. Shūsei's use of realistic detail effectively establishes the presence of the narrator (and his observed object), even though that narrator's presence is to some degree effective precisely because of its distanced attitude. The presence of Kyōka's narrator, whom we are to assume is the author himself, is one that skirts around the ineffable horror of death by speaking, literally and figuratively, of atmosphere. While strongly felt, it is, in the end, Shūsei's point of view that seems more penetrating and convincing. Perhaps the comparison reminded Kyōka that he had not been present (as he would have liked), and, beyond this, that his literary presence at the side of the dying Kōyō had never been and would never really be anything more than yet another flowery fiction, however emotionally necessary.

Whatever the answer to this question, it was never unclear which of his students Kōyō himself preferred. At Kōyō's funeral, on November 2, Kyōka represented all the disciples by reading the following memorial. For Kōyō, an author who began his career with a declaration of the playfulness of language, the memorial seems an appropriately polysemic unraveling of "autumn leaves" (*kōyō*).

Here eighteen of your students have gathered to bid you farewell—our sleeves touch each other, drenched with tears. Could it be true that you are leaving us? Were it possible that you might linger, we would clutch at your robes. We would hold fast to the skirts of your kimono. We look together upon your face, and if it were in our power we would bravely give our lives in place of yours. Yesterday, the rain of a godless month fell cold. Today, we see your name in the autumn colors and are filled with sadness. You have gone and will not return. Knowing we cannot begin to repay you for your many acts of kindness, we send your body to the grave. No words can express our grief. You dwelt in the world of the living for only thirty-seven years, yet your name will live for a thousand years to come as we pray for your peaceful rest. These are our words, expressed in sadness to the noble spirit of our beloved mentor, Ozaki Kōyō. He will continue to give his brilliant color to literature's forest, for seven seasons, a hundred seasons, a thousand seasons to come. (28: 599)

CHAPTER 10

Flight to Zushi

∾

1904–1906

Naturalism, a New Era, and
The Elegant Railway

Kyōo's death marked the end of an era, not only for Kyōka, now without a mentor, but also for the *bundan*, which had already begun moving in new directions. The transition was commemorated with a funeral sufficiently grand for a writer who had sought, and with *The Gold Demon* had achieved, a voice that could speak to an entire nation. According to Tayama Katai, the narrow streets around the Ozaki residence in Yokodera were so crowded with rickshaws, horse-drawn carriages, people, and flowers that "it was almost impossible to walk."[1] The funeral procession began there and traveled down Kagurazaka-dōri, along the moat to Ichigaya and Yotsuya-misuke, to the huge graveyard in Aoyama. Approximately a thousand people attended the ceremony.

It had been Kyōo's good fortune that his career had coincided with the development of a national readership. Like Tokutomi Rōka, Kyōo had written the right sort of thing at the right time. Both were successful in taking advantage of a developing bourgeoisie and the growing literary market. By the end of 1903, the buying and reading of fiction had come to identify a certain subculture. The Meiji reader felt compelled to become familiar with the topical issues of the day—tuberculosis, romance, capitalism, colonial expansion—and increasingly saw itself as a part of a definable (if divided) national whole. An awareness of the possible contribution of literature to Japan's continuing development as a modern nation partially explains why Kōyō's real successor, despite the continued existence of the Ken'yūsha writers and regardless of Kōyō's traditional regard for the transmission of art from mentor to disciple, was perhaps not Izumi Kyōka but Tayama Katai.

Katai, who had accused Kōyō of taking on students to bolster his position, was quick to see the benefits of posing as a follower himself. In February 1904, he published an essay in *The Sun* entitled "Candid Description" ("Rokotsu naru byōsha"). In this treatise, considered the official clarion call of the naturalist movement in Japan, only Kōyō is singled out with the honorific term *sensei*, and this despite Katai's publicly expressed opinion of the Ken'yūsha group as writers of "gold-plated literature." Perhaps this deference demonstrates nothing more than the anxiety of influence, but that there could be influence at all is a point worth considering. As implausible a successor as Katai might seem at first, his declaration that "everything must be candid; everything must be true to the facts; everything must be natural" is not far from Kōyō's position on what makes writing good.[2] Kōyō favored simplicity. "Writing gorgeous, striking, wonderful prose is something that appeals only to a beginner's eye. On the other hand, fluent, simple prose, where no passages stand out from the others, is extremely difficult to write. It is not an easy goal to achieve."[3]

Kōyō's ideal resonates with what Katai would come to call "technique without technique" (*mugikō no gikō*) and "objective description" (*heimen byōsha*). Certainly, Kōyō was inspired more by the realism of Saikaku than by that of Zola. Yet, Kōyō's work helped prepare an opening for Katai and the naturalist movement, whose influence steadily increased from this point onward, reaching a peak in 1908 during the aftermath of Japan's war with Russia. Also suggested in this call for "simple prose" are Kōyō's mixed feelings about Kyōka's style, which attempts to be "gorgeous, striking, [and] wonderful" at every turn. We only have to recall Kōyō's comment to Shūsei that "Izumi's writing is wrongheaded"[4] to wonder what Kōyō really thought of Kyōka's elaborate prose.

Still, Kyōka had the satisfaction of knowing that Kōyō's last critique of his work was full of praise. On his deathbed, Kōyō had read the manuscript for *The Elegant Railway* (*Fūryūsen*) and enthusiastically approved of Kyōka's (not-so-compelling) attempt at a best-seller. The first half of the novel, the longest that Kyōka would write, was serialized in *The Citizen's News* (*Kokumin shinbun*) from November 24, 1903, to March 12, 1904; and its continuation (*Zoku fūryūsen*) was published in the same paper, from May 29 to November 5. Reminiscent of earlier pieces such as *Crowned Yazaemon* and "The Poverty Club," this rambling expose of Meiji-period corruption and hypocrisy, a story of the struggle between the bad who are actually good and the good who are actually bad, is filled with violence—stranglings, stabbings, drownings, rapes, arson, and on and on.[5] We are left to wonder what it was, precisely, that Kōyō found so praiseworthy about a work that does not convey the author's intentions to the reader. As a popular novel, it is not engaging. As a work of art, it is not as polished as works that followed, such as "One Day in Spring" ("Shunchū," 1906) and *A Song by Lantern Light* (*Uta andon*, 1910).

Perhaps it was simply Kyōka's attempt to write for a wider audience that pleased the ailing Kōyō, who was undoubtedly concerned about, and perhaps even envious of, his student's ability to carry on without him. To judge from Kyōka's comments on the novel, what impressed Kōyō the most about the work was the amount that *The Citizen's News* was willing to pay for it.

October 1903. As Master Kōyō's situation grows worse, I and his other students take turns at his bedside during the night. Around the fifteenth of the month, the cries of insects in the frosty darkness continue as the night grows late. At the first light of dawn, when the cold dew covers the ground, I am at the Master's bedside.

"I hear you're publishing a piece in *The Citizen's News*. Do your best. How much are they giving you, by the way? A yen?"

"No. A little more."

"One and five *sen*?"

"A little more."

"Two yen?"

"Master, a little more."

"Two and two *bu*. Three yen? You should be grateful." His back is covered with bedsores. He leans back and looks at me for the longest time. "Do your best." (28: 590–91)

The vagueness of this passage allows us to read the emotional tone of Kōyō's comments variously: that he was surprised that one of his students could command such a high price for a manuscript, that he was proud of Kyōka's accomplishment, that he envied his success, that he doubted Kyōka could pull it off successfully, that Kōyō realized that his own powers were failing. Given Kyōka's care with all matters relating to his mentor, however, this cryptic passage may be a thinly veiled criticism of his mentor's (still) patronizing attitude.

Whether Kōyō felt Kyōka equal to the challenge or not, the opportunity to reach as wide a readership as his mentor had now presented itself. During the months of January and February, Kyōka stayed up practically every night working to finish the manuscript. It was his habit to write at night and to rise late the next day. Prior to beginning a project, he experienced "labor pains," an anguish that began the creative process. Once he started writing, this torture subsided, and he worked quickly and steadily. The *Citizen's News* had been publishing a novel by Kawakami Bizan, but its serialization had been irregular at best. The eventual cancellation of Bizan's work forced Kyōka to write faster than he had planned, and the paper's apology to its readers only intensified the pressure to perform. "Needless to say, this long work by Kyōka will make up for the shortcomings of the previous piece. It is sure to satisfy our readers."[6]

It is difficult to know how appealing the novel was to the general reader, especially since the work had to compete with news of Japan's war with Russia. Taoka Reiun, who had long been sympathetic with Kyōka's work, was among those who were satisfied. In a review that includes an unmistakable barb directed at the naturalists, Reiun noted Kyōka's already well known ability "to make the uncanny seem real," and added that *The Elegant Railway* established him as one who now had the facility "to make poetic and mysterious the vulgar truths of real life."[7]

The vulgar truths of which Reiun speaks are, beyond the forms of brutality already mentioned, the construction of a railway line to the hinterland of Ishikawa prefecture (of which Kanazawa is the capital). The railroad was an important part of economic development and figures prominently as a symbol in the literature of this period. Kyōka, who would later find travel by rail one of life's great pleasures, presented the image in a way that reveals the suffering and human misery that were too often the cost of modernization. This is Kyōka's articulation of the last gasp of an agricultural society being overwhelmed by an industrial one.[8] The impenetrable mystery of woods and steeply rising mountains, the places Yanagita Kunio was discovering to be a repository of traditional narrative and custom, are, as a matter of "real life," penetrated by a railroad line and, more specifically, a bridge over the Tedori River, which the engineer Minakami Kikuo has come to build. Minakami aligns himself with a gang of hardworking, hard-living construction workers. They call themselves the Elegants (*Fūryū gumi*), a connection that explains the first half of the novel's enigmatic title. Together they are led to numerous acts of violence by Oryū, the daughter of a former domainal lord, and her lover, a philosopher named Muraoka Fujita, who, having feigned suicide, has retreated to a hideout deep in the mountains. The Elegants' principal target of attack is Ōyama Godaifu, a wealthy entrepreneur who pretends to be building houses for the poor but is actually pocketing the funds. As such, he is the villain of this story. He can be numbered among the many crass capitalists of the sort Kyōka has previously condemned.

Godaifu's wife, Mikiko, is the slender thread that binds the many scenes of this seemingly endless work together. She was once Minakami Kikuo's lover, and it is largely Kikuo's resentment of her that makes him sympathetic with Godaifu's enemies, Fujita and Oryū. Mikiko eventually realizes her husband's hypocritical attitude: the poor are no better than animals. At the same time, she also happens to be the romantic interest of her adopted son, Wakasugi Kono-suke, who is also wronged by Godaifu, who rapes and drowns Wakasugi's older sister Otsuma. At Otsuma's funeral, Mikiko concludes that she cannot continue to endure her life with Godaifu and asks Fujita to kill her. He obliges and strangles her with a purple cord from Konosuke's drum. Thus, when the first train finally arrives in Kanazawa, signaling a new stage of development and economic hope for the region, Mikiko's corpse is its first cargo. She is joined in death by practically everyone who figures importantly in *The Elegant Railway*. Oryū, who is captured and held at Godaifu's compound, pretends to submit to his sexual advances but tips over a lamp and burns Godaifu's mansion to the ground. Thus, this 670-page novel ends as Otsuma's husband, Kariya Shugaku, driven mad by the horror of what he has witnessed, tells the tale of Godaifu's death by fire.

It is easy to see why the huge and sprawling *Elegant Railway* is so often referred to as Kyōka's *Water Margin* (*Shui-hu chuan*). This famous Chinese novel, translated into colloquial Japanese in the Edo period, continued to be popular well into the late-modern era. More specifically, *The Elegant Railway* shares a number of loose connections with Takebe Ayatari's (1719–74) version of the long and often violent Chinese novel.[9] The appeal of *The Water Margin* to Kyōka at this particular point in his career becomes obvious when we compare his position with Ayatari's and consider these two works in the wider context of what was being written at the time of *The Water Margin*'s introduction to Japan in the eighteenth century.

More than any other text imported from China, this work stimulated the development of both *yomihon* (a relatively more readerly and word-centered text) and the illustrated kusazōshi, two subgenres of Edo-period fiction that have length as their common attribute. What attracted the early-modern writers such as Ryūtei Tanehiko, Santō Kyōden, Takizawa Bakin, and others to *The Water Margin* is precisely what attracted Kyōka as well: this rambling narrative showed practitioners working in a tradition of briefer and more visual works how to write longer narratives. Length mattered because the market mattered. That longer narrative forms did not develop easily from a growing need to say more or to speak in a more linear and discursive fashion is demonstrated not only by the dominance of illustration in so many genres of early-modern writing but also by the fragmented and, if anything, relatively more disconnected and episodic nature of the Japanese versions of this Chinese work. Indeed, many of the numerous eighteenth- and nineteenth-century works with the word *suikōden* in their titles have little to do with the original, save a tendency to ramble adventurously.[10] Given the lyrical tendencies of the Japanese narrative tradition, the requirement for length, whether modeled after this Chinese model or the many Western novels being translated into Japanese during the Meiji period, was not easily satisfied.

Kyōka's closeness to Edo-period writers, creators of narratives that were still densely pictorial and largely unresponsive to the ways in which words would be required to establish psychologically rounded characters, illustrates why, in the age of the *kindai shōsetsu*, *The Elegant Railway* fails to hold our attention. Despite the author's attempt to write a long and coherent work, there is no narrative glue that creates a whole from the sum of its parts. Had Kyōka been writing during the Edo period, he would have shared more with Kyōden, whose yomihon do not have the brilliance of his more heavily illustrated texts, than with Bakin, whose kusazōshi were less compelling than his famous "reading books."

Even helped by the broad outlines of *The Water Margin*, Kyōka's attempt to replace Kōyō as a national writer fell pitifully short. The delaying of Mikiko's enlightenment and her suicide-murder are not satisfying justifications for the work's length. Her resemblance to Kōyō's Hazama Kan'ichi, who in *The Gold Demon* similarly makes the wrong decision and chooses money over love, is more than a coincidence, for here again Kyōka was exploiting yet another proven formula of popular fiction. Needless to say, preferring money over love is a formulation that is only tangential to Kyōka's narrative paradigm, which he seems to have temporarily set aside. I am not arguing, of course, that the only legitimate way for Kyōka to write was for him to reproduce his archetype and that anything else was necessarily a species of falseness. But it is clear that Kyōka's vision was by this point tightly, even obsessively, focused, and that this work seems like a diversion. What did carry over into this work from the archetype of trespass is its iconography—the already established meanings of mountains, rivers, and so forth—but because the form of the narrative significantly departs from the pattern, these images do not seem to have an amplifying power.

Motivated by the desire to become a more topical writer, Kyōka decided to model Muraoka Fujita, the philosopher-robber, after Fujimura Misao, a student of philosophy whose sensational suicide at the Nikkō Kegon Falls became a topic of national interest.[11] Fujimura died on May 21, 1903, after carving a farewell message on the incomprehensibility of the universe on a tree. The statement was reprinted in the papers to tragic effect. Copied out and memorized by young men throughout Japan, it spurred a rash of suicides. By August 1907, as many as 185 people had either attempted or succeeded in throwing themselves into the same waterfall.[12] Kyōka's journalistic use of such a sensational contemporary event has deep roots in the early-modern penchant for topicality. In this case, however, it fails to serve Kyōka well because its affirmation was also a denial of the meta-story and of his most compelling reasons for writing. In this sense, Kyōka's creativity differed from that of Chikamatsu, who was able to exploit current events by weaving them into the formula of his own obsessions. In comparison, Kyōka was more purely modern because his own fictional world was already becoming too personal and too perfectly self-motivated to accommodate with sufficient ease the type of stories that Kōyō's readers found most interesting.

In short, Kyōka could not write like Kōyō, nor would he ever be able to address the same audience. His master was gone and could not be recaptured through imitation. Perhaps because Kyōka realized the difference that separated them, he never again wrote another novel like *The Elegant Railway*. Neither did he ever again show as much interest in philosophical figures such as Fujimura and in extended contemplations of "the vulgar truths of real life." These were topics he relinquished to Katai and the naturalists, who seemed more than willing to explore them and to fill the vacuum created by Kōyō's departure. As for the completion of the unfinished *Gold Demon*, Kyōka left the project to Fūyō. Out of respect for his colleague and for their mentor, Kyōka never read the novel once it was finished.

Kite's Death, "A Female Visitor," and Retreat to Zushi

Kōyō had held his students together by the strength of his personality, and his death seemed to allow the differences between them to grow more acute. Shūsei reconsidered his position and declared himself a "born naturalist."[13] Fūyō similarly converted to tenets of naturalism, and as early as December 1907, he could declare, "Our frame of mind when we were writing novels as Kōyō's students and the way we feel about literature today are as different as clouds and mud."[14] At the time, conversion probably seemed the only way to survive as a novelist, a fact to which Kyōka could attest, since the leading literary magazines were beginning to close their pages to him. "At the time, the magazines and journals that offered Kyōka space were the *Yamato News* (*Yamato shinbun*), the *Tokyo Morning News* (*Tōkyō Asahi shinbun*), *Mita Literature* (*Mita bungaku*), *Literature Club*, *The Central Review* (*Chūō kōron*), the *Illustrated Women's Journal* (*Fujin gahō*), *Women's World* (*Fujokai*), *Human Being* (*Ningen*), and so forth, which, with the exception of perhaps two or three of these, were all at that time non-literary magazines of the second order."[15] Beleaguered by the powerfully articulated theories of the naturalists that were featured in the newspapers and attracting the notice of society at large, Kyōka was dealt another blow when his grandmother Kite passed away.

Kyōka recorded the event and his own general state of ill-health in the second autochronology.

> Meiji 39 (1906) [*sic*], 2nd month.
> I lose my grandmother.
> Meiji 39, 7th month.
> My health continues to deteriorate. We rent a house in Tagoe, Zushi, and go there to recuperate. What began as a summer's stay eventually stretches to four years. I eat practically nothing but gruel and potatoes.

Kyōka recorded the dates incorrectly. We know from other sources that his stay in Zushi lasted from July 1905 until February 1909, and that his grandmother died on February 20, 1905, one year earlier than he indicated.[16]

Meboso Kite's death was the decisive factor in the physical and mental deterioration that led to Kyōka's stay in Zushi, which lasted much longer than he originally intended. Of all the members of his family, Kite had been the one with whom Kyōka had lived the longest. He had known his mother for only nine years, and his father for twenty-one. In comparison, he had shared thirty-two years of his life with his grandmother, who had been a steady and sorely needed source of emotional support. Upon his father's death, she had been the one who encouraged him to leave the family in Kanazawa and return to Tokyo in order to concentrate on his career as a writer. As soon as he established himself as a writer, he welcomed her to Tokyo. Since the age of nine, she had been his only real mother; and losing her proved to be a severe blow.

The novelist and playwright Kubota Mantarō (1889–1963), who would become one of Kyōka's closest friends, affirmed Kyōka's status as Kite's "favorite grandson."[17] In Kyōka's grief over her death, he began "A Female Visitor" ("Onna kyaku"), which he finished only after his move to Zushi. *The Central Review* published the first two chapters in June 1905, but the subsequent installments did not appear as planned. The interruption, rare for Kyōka, suggests the seriousness of his physical decline. An editorial comment accompanying the publication of all five chapters of the work in the November issue of *The Central Review* noted this and apologized. "Despite the fact that Mr. Izumi went off to Zushi for reasons of health, the editor was unreasonable enough to press him for new work."[18]

The major portion of this story is a dialogue between a lacquer artisan named Kin and Otami, a relative of Kin's wife who is visiting Tokyo along with her five-year-old son, Yuzuru. While Kin's wife and the maid are out of the house, he confesses his love for Otami, remembering a time when they were both living in Kanazawa and she provided him with the emotional support he so desperately needed.

"I'd stay at your house until late. We'd say goodnight, and I'd leave. Sometimes you were already dressed for bed. But even when it was cold, you wouldn't mind seeing me off. . . . On my way home, I'd pass along the edge of the moat. Although I knew you were already asleep, I'd be tempted to throw myself into the moat. I knew that as soon as I started slipping over the edge, you'd grab me from behind and say, 'Kin-chan, what are you doing?'

"I wanted to die. But I also desired to be saved. When I passed by that dreadful place, I was able to stay alive only because I knew, even though you were asleep, that you would never fail to come to my rescue. Thanks to you I'm still alive. To me, you're not just someone who's helped me. You're the one who saved my life." (9: 483–84)

A letter from Toyoharu to Teru, dated April 25, 1901, shows that Meboso Teru visited Tokyo with her son and stayed for several days while Kyōka was still living in Ushigome Minami Enoki-chō. "A Female Visitor" is obviously based on this visit. If this remembrance of Teru in "A Female Visitor" sounds familiar, it is because the work is a reformulation of Kyōka's attempted suicide, as described in the 1885 story "The Night Bell Tolls." Kyōka's return to this dark period of his youth suggests the extent to which his grandmother's death shook him. Confronted by loss, he remembered and wrote about both the pain of losing a family member and the desire to be saved. Elsewhere he described this state of mind in the darkest terms. "I couldn't tell day from night. I never slept well, nor did I ever feel that I was wide awake. I had only the vaguest notion of who I was."[19] He did not elaborate on the exact nature of his illness, neither here nor in the second autochronology, except to say that for the next four years he was capable of eating only "gruel and potatoes."

Teraki Teihō remembered Kyōka's sickness: "Ostensibly his illness was gastrointestinal. But looking back, I see that he suffered from a neurosis of the most advanced sort. Kyōka came to fear food. His belief that everything he ate would damage his digestive system became an obsession with which he had to deal. From this point until his death, he refused to eat anything that hadn't been cooked, either boiled or broiled, for at least twelve minutes. As a result, his diet came to be extremely restricted."[20] Eventually he would eat only food prepared by Suzu, who knew exactly what he would and would not accept, and how he required things to be cooked. Everything had to be overcooked, sanitized to the core by heat. Raw fish was out of the question. So were lobsters, because they fed on the decomposing flesh of the drowned. Other animals, including shrimp, were simply too grotesque to be palatable. As a novelist, he could write of grotesqueries—the eating of snakes and the drinking of another's blood—but as a consumer he would allow himself to consider few things more daring than soggy noodles.

Aside from his days in Kanazawa following his father's death, the Zushi years were the darkest of Kyōka's life. It was in this beleaguered state, however, that he sharpened his sense of language so that, with the sound of the waves of the Shōnan Coast in his ears and the sight of wooded mountains in his eyes, his understanding of the metaphoric nature of words deepened sufficiently to lead his imagination to where no other late-modern Japanese writer cared to venture. Tokyo was three hours away by train, and the aggressive clamor of the naturalists could continue without his contributions to the debate about the transparency of language and its ability to present reality without distortion. Plainly, it was fear rather than the will to achieve descriptive accuracy that continued to drive his literary vision, dissuading him further of the advantages of perspectivalism and the desirability of objectivity in art. In the age of the emergence of the individual and of what has been called the "discovery of landscape," Kyōka was not a discoverer in the same sense as the realists. He, too, was finding a self. He, too, was torn by the process of becoming aware of becoming aware. Yet this split did not necessarily prepare him to embrace those supposedly universal systems of truth that would give absolute authority to his authorship. In his case, the modern fracturing of the self produced doppelgänger but not the splitting of subject from object, interior from exterior. In providing a more obviously visual, presentational alternative to these more rigorously discursive structures of representational discourse, he anticipated the world of the modern*ists* and, beyond that, the post-structural critique.

"One Day in Spring" and a Language Beyond Language

Although the Shōnan Coast was beginning to attract more attention as a summer escape for Tokyoites, Tagoe Village, where Kyōka and Suzu lived, was still not much more than a farming community. By the time of Kyōka's arrival, the region (generally known as Zushi) had already been made famous in a literary way by Tokutomi Roka, who moved there in 1897 and wrote his famous novel, *The Cuckoo* (*Hototogisu*, 1898–99), a story about a naval officer's wife who is divorced because she contracts tuberculosis. Kōyō's *The Gold Demon* and Roka's novel were the two most widely read works of fiction during the late Meiji period. In 1907, having written "Nature and Humanity" ("Shizen to jinsei," 1900) and *A Chronicle of Recollections* (*Omoide no ki*, 1900–1901), Roka moved to a farm in Chitose on the northern island of Hokkaidō. Despite his relocation, Roka's associations with the Shōnan Coast remain strong even today.

Kyōka and Suzu's home was the right half of a small duplex. The other unit was occupied by a hairdresser named Chōno, who received customers at her residence.[21] The building itself belonged to a man named Kurokawa, who resided in Kamakura farther down the coast. The land belonged to a young man in his twenties named Ubukata Rin, whose residence was behind the Izumis' on the banks of the Tagoe River. Ubukata married in 1907 and had a son, Seiji, the following year. Kyōka, who disliked children, secluded himself in the small room on the second floor, where he wrote. Suzu, who never became a mother, spent a lot of time playing with the child.

After Ubukata Seiji's death in 1946, his widow Haru retold her husband's account of Kyōka and Suzu's life at this time. "There was no plumbing in the house, and so they would send a maid or a young student to replenish their supply of water. Suzu, who always had her hair done up in a maidenhair coiffure, was very beautiful. It seemed, though, that she didn't know the first thing about housework. When the two of them, Kyōka and Suzu, went out together, they both wore gold, wire-rimmed glasses. He would always wear a kimono."[22]

That Kyōka and Suzu stood out from the local crowd is obvious from this and other accounts. Suzuki Ryū, who was in his teens during the Izumi's stay in Tagoe, had a more favorable impression of Suzu than of Kyōka, although he remained cautious of both. "While I was waiting to get my hair done, Suzu would appear holding a smoking pipe and a tobacco bowl. She would be dressed in a tightly woven, shiny cotton kimono with a collar. She was about ten years older than I and spoke with an affected downtown accent. She was very sociable. I also saw her husband from time to time. He wasn't that tall and looked like a clerk for some merchant family." According to Ryū, the people in the village used to tell their children that they must not become like that man Kyōka—doing nothing every day and wearing fancy clothes.[23]

Although weakened by his illness, Kyōka continued his job in Tokyo, but on a reduced scale. He returned to the city eight days a month to attend to his duties as an editor at Shun'yōdō. Otherwise, he lived in quiet seclusion with Suzu, whom he had never stopped seeing, not even after Kōyō's intervention. Now that Kōyō was dead, there was nothing to stop them from living together once again. In Zushi, the two of them were joined by a maid and a live-in student named Maeda.[24] Teraki describes their life together:

Kyōka liked to fish. That is to say, he put in his share of time along the Tagoe River, waiting to catch a big one. When he smoked, he would never let his fingers touch the part of the cigarette that went into his mouth. He'd tip the pack upside down and shake the cigarettes until he could pull one out with his lips. Then he would light up. . . . But when it came to fishing (baiting the hook was Maeda's job, of course), he had a different attitude about getting dirty. I was surprised to see that he didn't mind if his hands or his fingers or even his whole body started smelling fishy. But that just shows you how somber, lonely, and gloomy his life in Zushi was.[25]

There were few visitors and few distractions. Although his ailments slowed the pace of his output, he wrote well when he was finally able to work again. His best work from this period leads us with well-turned phrases and striking images across the border of transgression to an aesthetic denouement that is more often a state of suspense than an increased clarity. Never quite sure of our bearings, we are nevertheless made aware of both the private, idiosyncratic world we have entered and also the vast emotional territories stretching out from it in every direction. Reduced to a diet of gruel and potatoes, the recuperating Kyōka followed his instincts faithfully enough to fashion an impressively visionary idiom. It is hard to say whether the well-tuned ambiguity of his Zushi stories should be considered the cause or the result of emotional instability, but the truth of their genuineness and power is incontestable. Perhaps this is because Kyōka no longer had to strain to create such a language; as he later admitted, he was living and writing a dream. From the reality of his fear emerged the plausibility of the implausible.

Kyōka himself noted the beauty of his madness.

Meiji 39, (1906) 10th month.
I publish "One Day in Spring" in *New Fiction*.

> In a nap at midday
>   I met my beloved,
> Then did I begin to believe
>   In the things we call dreams.

Rain leaks into our room, owls call from the trees. The wind snaps the branches of the zelkova. It pierces the roof and stabs at us through our ragged bedding.

The reeds scatter about our frost-cold pillows. The crab spiders gather and scamper over the tatami.

I complete the sequel to "One Day in Spring." A butterfly? A dream? I am practically in a trance. I read and enjoyed the poetry of Li Ch'ang-chi. (1: viii)

Their address was Zushi 954 or 957, which today would be Zushi City, Zushi 5 chōme 9–328. At the time, the area was swampy, thus Kyōka's mention of reeds and crab spiders.[26] The butterfly allusion refers to Chuang-tzu's famous dream in which he sees himself as a butterfly. Awakened from the dream, he cannot be sure if he is Chuang-tzu, who dreamed he was a butterfly, or if he is a butterfly, who is dreaming he is Chuang-tzu. The butterfly image, the leitmotiv of "One Day in Spring," links the story to this well-known formulation of how we know what we know and how we distinguish between what is real and what is not. These questions are the same issues voiced by the ninth-century poet Ono no Komachi, whose poem about believing in dreams figures prominently in both the chronology and in this story. If we are happy with our dreams, why should we not believe in them? This question was also being raised

by the naturalists, although in a very different way. Tayama Katai and others
chose to deal with the problem of indulgence and mania from a more "scientific"
perspective.

The structure of "One Day in Spring" is reminiscent of those Noh plays
with multiple versions of the same protagonist. In his original metamorphosis,
the hero is a nameless visitor from the city who has come to Zushi for an extended stay and lives in a flat near the station. On a warm spring day, he sets off
for a temple, the Gandenji, located high in the hills that overlook the village of
Zushi and the Shōnan Coast. He goes to worship the figure of Kannon housed
there. As other critics have allegorically read this temple visit, his movement is
away from civilization and toward a more primitive past that is being quickly
erased by the progress of modernity. The conflict between the modern present
and a less "enlightened" past is a concern familiar to us from *The Elegant Railway*.
But here flight from the modern is much more clearly the sort of trespass required by Kyōka's archetype, which looms in the background.

Zushi is both old and new, and thus a perfect setting for this confused
search for Japanese identity. At the turn of the twentieth century, the area
around Zushi was beginning to gain a reputation as a summer home for, especially, Westerners, who built villas along the Shōnan Coast, plied the water in
sailboats, and showed the Japanese how to enjoy the beach as a place of recrea-
tion. At the same time, the mountains rising from the quickly developing
shoreline were riddled with tombs and grave markers that had been there since
the Kamakura period. This forsaken space was, in Kyōka's day, a popular gathering place for the homeless and disenfranchised. As a conjunction of the traditional and the modern, the dead and the living, and the failing and the prosper-
ous, this site could not be more appropriate.

On his way to visit the temple, the wanderer is initiated both to the mystery
of this sacred yet haunting space and to the power of the season. Trees are
blossoming, and birds are singing loudly. His approach reminds us of the Kōya
mendicant's entry into a forbidden realm. He sees a snake in a rape field, another crawling into a two-story house along the road, a farmer tilling his field,
two weavers outlined by the bright yellow of rape blossoms, and a line of pack
horses bringing new stones to repair the flight of steps that leads up the hill to
the main temple. The wanderer is "enclosed in a triangle" formed from the lines
connecting the snakes and the horses. The geometric framing of this territory
suggests Kyōka's visual emphasis and points ahead to the way in which he will
emphasize the graphic elements of language in order to establish this landscape

as a formation of irreality. It is a hauntingly static spring, an atmospheric countryside that exists in order to call existence into question.

Later, the landscape will be interpreted for the wanderer by Tamawaki Mio,
the story's heroine.

"It's almost impossible to tell you how this sunny spring day makes me feel. It's like
talking about a dream. This quiet sadness. Can't you feel it? It's like seeing the most
vivid part of a dream, don't you think? It reminds me of when I was two or three, riding
on my nurse's back, looking at a festival swirling around me.

"I feel more vulnerable in the spring than in the fall. That's why I feel so damp. This
isn't sweat. It's something the sun has wrung from my heart. Not pain, not distress.
More like blood being squeezed from the tips of a tree's tender leaves, as though my
bones are being extracted and my skin is being melted. Yes, that's the perfect expression
for times like this. I feel like I've turned into water, as though what's been melted of me
will soon disappear, and that there will be tears—though neither of sadness nor of joy.

"Sometimes you cry when someone scolds you. Other times you cry when someone
comforts you. But on a spring day like today, your tears are of this latter kind. I suppose
they're sad. Yet there are different types of sadness. If fall is the sorrow of nature, then
spring is the anguish of human life."[27] (10: 308–9)

Enveloped in such a dreamscape, the wanderer makes his way up the steep
flight of stairs to the main hall of the temple complex. There he finds the poem
by Komachi mentioned above pasted on one of the pillars, along with the many
other name tags left by countless pilgrims who, having seen a higher reality,
have left these as signs of their faith. They are a language of worship and imagination, "proof that their spirits had passed this way." As a note to his naturalist
critics who wanted to remove artifice from art, Kyōka used this opportunity to
draw a comparison. "If the donations published in the newspapers and the lists
of donors posted at the temples are realism, these name tags are romanticism"
(10: 228). Kyōka set what he perceived to be the crassness of the former against
the loftier, spiritual concerns of the latter. That is to say, his immediate objections to the naturalists focused not so much on questions of mimesis as on their
related inability to "put the lid on things that are ugly" (28: 687).

The dilapidated state of the once-splendid building speaks of Buddhism in
decline, and no one is more aware of the deterioration than the lonely priest
who mistakenly assumes the wanderer is yet another tourist come to look at the
temple's icons as works of art rather than objects of worship. Hungry for company, the priest offers tobacco, a place to sit and rest, and, most important, the
story that forms the body of Part I. The wanderer, a man of leisure, accepts the

hospitality. As the two of them relax together, gazing out over the village and ocean below, they enter into a conversation about "idol worship," a topic made relevant by a growing rationalism, which, as suggested by the priest, has led to the near-extinction of his temple and the once-sprawling complex of buildings that covered the mountainside. The solidly built yet dilapidated main hall, as well as the Buddhist statues it houses, are traces of the past, one of many forms of language that Kyōka put forward in order to connect the living with the dead. Both blurring and heightening the distinction between life and death, language becomes its own subject. It divides itself in its service to romanticism and realism, in the desire to signify widely, on the one hand, and narrowly, on the other. Words and images generate meaning by both erasing and establishing difference. Again and again, Kyōka returned to this issue.

This compulsion explains the first exchange between the priest and the wanderer over the status of Buddhist images. This is, at its deepest level, a disagreement over the ascendance of phonemic rhetoric over graphemic expression, as fostered by the positivistic impulse of modern realism. The priest's simple phonocentrism is set against the wanderer's understanding of a semiotics of belief. Despite a recent resurgence of interest in religious matters, the priest cannot believe that the debate has anything to say about the wooden images that he has unsuccessfully been trying to maintain.[28] Thus Kyōka must make the wanderer, not the priest, defend the necessity of icons.

In the visitor's view, the time for Buddhism to flourish again has come, and to deny the value of idols is to misunderstand the important role that images play.

"But how could we possibly do without idols?" the wanderer responded. "Without images, what would we have to believe in? Your mistake, Sir, is in calling them idols. They have names, every one of them. Shaka, Monju, Fugen, Seishi, Kannon. They all have names."

"It's the same with people," the wanderer continued. "If they're strangers, they mean nothing to us. But let's give them names. With a name a person becomes father, mother, brother, sister. And in that case, would you still treat them like strangers? Idols are no different. If they're just idols, they mean nothing to us. But the one here in your main hall is Kannon. And so we believe in it, don't we?"

He pointed to the main hall. "You could say a carved figure is nothing but wood or metal or earth, decorated with gold, silver, and gems to add color. But what about people? Skin, blood, muscle, the five organs, the six organs, join them together, add some clothes, and there you have it. Never forget, Sir, that even the most beautiful woman is nothing more than this."

He faced the priest. "But then you'll say that people have spirits and idols don't. But, Sir, it's precisely our understanding of the spirit that causes us either to lose our way or to find it, to feel threatened or to gain peace. To worship, to believe. How can you practice archery without a target? Even acrobats and jugglers have to study. So to those who say they don't need idols, I have to ask, 'Is it enough to yearn for your beloved, to love and to pine for someone without ever thinking you'll be together someday? Is it all right to never see her? And if you do see her, then is it acceptable never to speak to her? And if you speak to her, wouldn't you want to touch her hand? And if you touch her hand, would it matter if you never slept together?' Ask them that.

"The truth is that you'd want to embrace the one you love even if it can only happen in your dreams. Come now. Even if it were a fantasy, you'd still want to see the gods, wouldn't you? Shaka, Monju, Fugen, Seishi, Kannon. Tell me that you aren't thankful for their images."

The priest's face became animated and his eyes shone so that the wanderer could almost count the points of stubble around his smile. "Well said. Most interesting."

The priest put a hand on his knee and touched the other to his forehead. "*In a nap at midday / I met my beloved, / Then did I begin to believe / In the things we call dreams.*" He quietly mumbled the lines of the verse pasted on the pillar. (10: 237–38)

The wanderer is led to the substance of Komachi's poem by way of this debate, because Kyōka chose to deepen the issue of dreaming and identity by broaching the question of what a language of belief might be. In few other stories is Kyōka's interest in the ability of words to name the dead (and thus give life to the living) more obvious or more artistically productive. If there is a language of reality—a discourse that secures meaning through reduction and debate—is there not also one of irreality, which seems as knowable (and as desirable to know) as its more "rational" other? Is the inviting presence of the Buddhist statue anything more than a convenience? Is the body anything more than a temptation? And beauty anything more than a distraction?

Rejected by the naturalists and devastated by the death of his grandmother, Kyōka validated the truths of dreaming by continuing to write. Perhaps his illness made it clear to him that nothing is accomplished without the illusive permanence of images, that nothing is made better without the fix of language. No love is satisfied. No one can be saved. Without images—whether statues, poems, or words—there is no beginning, even though, once begun, there may be no end to the chain of signification, no sense to be made of the relativity that is eventually produced. Even if the perfect names for all things could be found, there still would be no way to guarantee the stability of the relationships among them. There would be no becoming one with that which we love, regardless of the fact that the possibility of blissful union is so very imaginable.

Perhaps for this reason, Kyōka's story suggests that true fulfillment is obtainable only in death. Yet even this possibility, however necessary, is shrouded in doubt. This skepticism generates the overwhelming sadness of spring that we feel in Kyōka's landscape—a rise of activity that is static, an atmosphere that is "strangeness made spatial."[29] In his dreamlike, trancelike state, Kyōka, who was making daily trips to worship the Kannon at Gandenji, came to insist on both unencumbered love and peaceful death, although the former is impossible in its lived details and the latter is (and will always be) unknown. Thus Kyōka's search for comfort is reduced to the realm of propositional knowledge and a question that pretends it is a surety: "If it is in our dreams that we meet the people we love, who wouldn't dream as much as he or she could?" (10: 290).

Komachi's poem is about believing in such dreams, and Kyōka's story, which takes this belief a step further, is concerned about finding words capable of naming such a conviction. The wanderer's argument that everything has a name is ironic, since the poem itself can be seen as an idol, like the image of Kannon, a material convenience that has no signifying force if not read properly. The statement is also ironic because the wanderer himself has no proper name. In fact, of the main characters in "One Day in Spring," only the heroine, Tamawaki Mio, is named by the author. This general sense of namelessness allows the melding and confusing of identities—which is the real work of this narrative—to take place. Through his own reading of the poem, in other words, the wanderer discovers someone else's story that turns out to be about himself.

To keep his guest at the temple, the lonely priest tells the story of how a certain gentleman came to live at the temple cottage, met a woman named Tamawaki Mio, fell passionately in love with her, became obsessed with her captivity as another man's wife, went off into the mountains one night to meet her, and embraced her. The uncanny resemblance between wanderer and gentleman suggests that they are somehow versions of each other, a possibility the priest intimates when he tells the wanderer, "He was a man like you." When the wanderer learns that Tamawaki Mio lives in the very house he noticed earlier being invaded by a snake, we more strongly come to feel as if the outcome of the gentleman's story will be his own destiny. Listening with great interest, the wanderer reaches a point of confusion when he sees himself seeing himself.

This happens when the gentleman and Tamawaki Mio meet in a *yagura*, a rectangular tomb cut into the mountainside, that has been converted into a stage.

"She wore a robe and a sash that was wrapped several times around her waist. Her bare feet were as white as frost, and she, still facing away, bent her knees, as if collapsing to the stage.

"Again the wooden clappers sounded. *Kan.*

"The gentleman stood transfixed. Then someone quickly stepped forward, brushing his back as he passed. It was a black shadow.

"'Is someone else here?' he thought. But how could it be? And yet the shadow staggered onto the stage and sat down, back to back, with the woman. When it looked his way, the wanderer saw his own face. It was he."

"It was who?"

"The gentleman himself. Later he told me, 'If that were really I on that stage, I should have died there.' I remember how he sighed and turned pale." (10: 283–84)

This splitting of one's identity—a double doppelgänger, as it were—seems to question the coherence of self-identity.[30] For Kyōka, it is a defamiliarization that mirrors the metamorphic wonder of language and, as such, cannot be extracted from the artifice of art. It is here, at this moment of intense imagination, that Kyōka introduces a new language that is intentionally opaque, a severe test of poetry.

"He couldn't stop looking. His flesh was leaping, and his blood was on fire. He saw himself twist around and look rapturously at Tamawaki Mio's back. He saw himself use the tip of his finger to trace a peak and then a line, making a triangle on her pale robe.

"The gentleman's heart was filled with ice, his body was soaked with cold sweat. The woman, Tamawaki, kept her head bowed.

"Next, he drew a square. I mean, he watched himself draw a square. His finger touched her knee and began to tremble.

"Then he drew a circle, a round line on her back; and just as he was completing the figure, the wind gusted, sweeping the earth and gouging the sky. The torchlight down in the valley vanished completely, leaving a bright, delicate pink. Was that the beach? Or the color of the ocean? As he stood looking, he heard the rustle of leaves and scattered coins swirling in the wind. He realized that four or five people were huddled together, sitting close behind him, and that they, too, had been watching.

"The color of the woman's face shone through her bangs, making her look all the more attractive. A smile formed on her lips as she leaned back, resting against his leg, using his knee for a pillow. Her black hair flowed down as she looked up, and the white of her bosom appeared. Under her weight, the man fell back, and the stage slipped down and down into the earth." (10: 284–85)

In the original text, these figures *are* figures—△ □ ○—standing out from the already visually rich scripts of *kanji* and *kana*. They are totally figurative: graphemes without phonemic partners. They are words without sounds, characters without readings. Having *only* names—triangle, square, circle—they approach pure figurality, quite in rebellion to their need to signify and name reality. Their specific referents, if any exist, are not easy to know, since the set of possibilities is so vast. In short, they are not words in an everyday sense, for the very point is that their use is original and, therefore, appropriately faithful to the human need, absurd though necessary, to want to know what we cannot know. Like stones in a Zen rock garden, the figures may signify widely. Or, to the contrary, they may be tied specifically to the beloved of one's dreams. As pronominals, they are both common and proper in their naming function.

No wonder, then, that attempts to interpret their meaning have run from the archetypes of the Jungian collective consciousness to geographic particularity.[31] Like figures in a mandala, they are cosmological.[31] Reminiscent of the *go-rindo* or stone death markers found in the tombs and around the temple, they are marks of seduction, a non-transparent language expressive of emotional change, unfettered signs that do not yet have the ability to establish meaning through difference.[32] They are expressive of a "death pact" between the gentleman and Tamawaki Mio.[33] They are a pledge made in another dimension, a posthumous name possibly inspired by Sengai's famous painting of the cosmos, which Kyōka had seen.[34]

There is a limit to the usefulness of trying to connect these figures with an established hermeneutics or iconography. Again, they are not words in any established sense, because they lack readings and knowable referents. Certainly, the significance of their figurality is that their use must be original and, therefore, faithful to the unknown quality of what we most want to know but cannot. Although we might not realize what they signify in particular, their narrative importance is more than obvious by the time the story has ended. If the first half of the story leads us by way of the Komachi poem to a presentation of these figures, the second half is an encoding of them that leads us in *renga*-like fashion to other poems and to a visual sort of open-ended resolution.

Having learned that the gentleman committed suicide a few days after seeing himself drawing these figures on the woman's body, the wanderer decides to take his leave rather than accept the priest's invitation to guide him to the spot where the unfortunate lover threw himself into a watery cave. On the way down the hill, he ponders what he has just heard, realizing that, like Chuang-tzu and the butterflies, he can no longer easily distinguish between what is true and what is false, what is real and what is illusion.

He had just seen a dream, but then—

What about dreams? he thought. He felt as though he were seeing one now. If you wake up and realize you were asleep, then you know you were dreaming. But if you never wake up, how could it be a dream? Didn't someone say that the only difference between the mad and the sane is the length of one's periods of insanity? Like waves that grow wild in a blowing wind, everyone has times of madness. But the wind soon calms, and the waves end in a soothing dance. If not, then we begin to lose our minds, we who ply the seas of this floating world. And on the day that we pray for repose yet find no reprieve from the winds, we become seasick. Becoming seasick, we quickly go mad.

How perilous! (10: 289)

Although the wanderer is just beginning to lose his bearings, Tamawaki Mio is already quite mad. Bedridden with grief, she is tortured by the promise of love that tempts her toward the world of the dead, the only place where she will be able to meet her lover. The wanderer, having been warned of her dangerous beauty, tries to avoid her. But he cannot. She saw him pass by her home earlier that day—this man who looks so much like her dead lover—and has been waiting at the bottom of the hill to thank him for sending a farmer to remove the snake from her house.

They meet. Like the priest, she has much to say. Illuminated in the spring sunlight, she speaks of the cruelty of spring and about how she cannot be with the one she loves. Her lover's promise to her, the figures that he wrote on her body, reappear when the gentleman discovers them in her notebook.

He laughed innocently as the notebook fluttered open in his lap. The pages were like butterfly wings in his fingers. And there, written in pencil, was—

His face suddenly went pale.

They were written large and small, dark and light, all in confusion. Some were half-drawn, others misshapen, others trembling, some abandoned. He saw nothing but triangles, squares, and circles.

"What do you think? The people around here think I'm quite an artist. I come out to this embankment and this is what I do. Better than just sitting here, pretending I'm guarding the valley. My sketches are well regarded, you know. I was even thinking of bringing some brushes and art supplies out and setting up shop right here in the grass. Don't you think they're good?

"This triangle is a mountain, this square a rice paddy, and this circle is the ocean. You can think of them that way. Or maybe the triangle is a doll of a young woman or a samurai dressed in a kimono, the square a body, and the circle a face.

"Or maybe it's something beneath the surface of the waves. If you ask the artist what she thinks these figures are, she'll say she doesn't know. And then you can make an arrogant face. Or else you can worship them as the posthumous name of the deceased."

The wanderer finally spoke up. "Posthumous name? What is it? Tell me the name!"

"Master Triangle, Round Round, Lord of the Square." (10: 319–21)

The △ □ ○ are the language of an undifferentiated reality, symbols of dreams and madness and death, unreserved in their proliferation of possible meanings and identities. Despite this lack of coherence, however, their emotional force is all too clear to the wanderer, who desires one thing and one thing only. "What is it? Tell me the name."

When he hears "Master Triangle, Round Round, Lord of the Square," he knows he is spared, since he does not recognize the name as his own. This knowledge establishes the beginning of difference and thus makes meaning possible. He knows that his fate is not Tamawaki Mio's, which he understands only too well. By writing the figures on Mio's body, the gentleman of the priest's story distinguished himself from the wanderer by naming his passion for her. He signed a death pact, which he has honored though she has not. Triangle, circle, and square are his will, a final statement of his earthly passion, a promise he leaves with her. His writing of the name is a step he dares to take because of Komachi's poem and the promise it suggests. Dreams are real. Lovers will meet again.

For Mio, the triangles, squares, and circles are similarly expressions of love, but her incessant scribbling of them expresses her lack of faith in the promise of the Komachi poem. Tormented by voices and by the dark, pounding, yet strangely dry showers of this mysterious spring day, she is far more skeptical than her lover. It is doubt, not passion, that has driven her mad. Thus, she uses the figures differently, not to commit herself to love (and death) but to divine the truth of the afterlife, employing them as a poem of pure imagery— which provide a purely associational link between Komachi's poem and a third one.

To progress beyond Komachi's poem, she must borrow the strength of yet another poem.

> Should I have the chance
>   to see you again,
> I would comb the four seas—
>   diving deep as the sea tangle.

This poem by Izumi Shikibu is her answer to the many triangles, squares, and circles she has scribbled in her notebook. She gives it to a young boy, one of two lion dancers who happen to pass by on their way to the ocean. And he, by unwittingly sacrificing himself in her service, delivers the message to the land of the dead.

From atop a sand dune, strewn with seashells, the wanderer, having left Tamawaki Mio behind, witnesses the death of the young dancer, who innocently swims out to sea with the poem still tucked into his lion's mask. He disappears into the water and does not resurface.

They didn't find the body. It wasn't until the next day, with the low tide at dawn, that they discovered two people on the rocks at Cape Nakitsuru, the exact spot where the man who had stayed at the temple last summer was found. The boy's head was like a jewel, pressed against the woman's breast, the red lion's cape still wet and tangled around her white arm. Beautiful and alluring, Tamawaki Mio had finally discovered the destination of the dead.

The wanderer would never forget how they had parted at the embankment, how he looked back and she, holding her purple parasol to the side, her black hair weighing down upon her as she watched him walk away. As the sand on the beach spread and drew back soundlessly, hollowing out and filling back in, he thought of how the waves must have ravished her. From the sand there appeared only beautiful bones and the color of shells—red of the sun, white of the beach, green of the waves. (10: 333–34)

Like the triangle, circle, and square, these shells, too, are language. They form the fourth and last poem in the sequence. Belief (Ono no Komachi's poem) leads to promise ($\triangle$ $\square$ $\bigcirc$). Promise leads to conviction (Izumi Shikibu's poem). And conviction leads to death (the final verse of shells in the sand, the beautiful bones that speak silently from the dead, a lonely and condemning skeleton, a trace of life and passion that can, and must, be read in whatever way possible).

We know from a letter that Kyōka wrote to his brother, Toyoharu, on October 30, 1906, that the death of the young lion dancer was central to his conception of this story, and that he wrote it in two parts—"Shunchū" and "Shunchū gokoku" (One day in spring, part two)—only because of poor health.[35] The meaning of that death is obvious. We have only to consider the archetype to understand that the watery demise of the boy and the gentleman and Tamawaki Mio expresses the author's will to conflate maternal and erotic love. By now, we know that the expression of this desire is hardly a new accomplishment. What is new, however, is that by writing "One Day in Spring," Kyōka found a way to propel himself beyond the natural limits of the Japanese language to express the beautifully haunting truth of love. Echoing "The Order Book," this expression is the truth of *mono*, things speaking for themselves: red sun, white beach, green waves. These are the intermingling of *iro*, as color and eros, with the steady mystery of nature as it leads all life inexorably toward death and to whatever might lie beyond.

CHAPTER II

The End of Desire

~

1907–1908

A Woman's Pedigree

Zushi proved to be a balm for Kyōka's ailments. He continued commuting by rail into Tokyo each week as his job required, but he postponed his permanent return to the city again and again. His nerves needed the solitude of mountains and surf. His soul required the near daily walks to the Gandenji, where he prayed before the statue of the benevolent Kannon. The verdant and still largely undeveloped Zushi was a place set apart from Tokyo and the activities of the bundan. It provided a needed form of separation, just as Kōyō's death had provided another. Without Kōyō's support, he was like a branch cut from a tree, vulnerable to the latest developments that had given the naturalists a position of prominence. On the other hand, he was living happily with Suzu, no longer concerned about his teacher's disapproval of his love for the woman who bore his mother's name. So strengthened was he by her companionship that he finally dealt with the bitterness of the so-called Momotarō incident by writing a story based on Kōyō's mistreatment of the geisha who was now his wife. Although some readers have been reluctant to read revenge into *A Woman's Pedigree*, perhaps for fear of defiling Kyōka's image as the most faithful and adoring of Kōyō's students, it is difficult not to notice the toxins hidden here.

The provenance of the story is a confusion. Tobari Chikufū, who was in charge of the literary column for the *Yamato News*, asked Kyōka to write a story for the paper. Chikufū knew of Kyōka's work because they had collaborated on a translation of Gerhart Hauptmann's *The Sunken Bell—A German Fairy Drama* (*Die versunkene Glocke—Ein deutsches Marchendrama*). Some time in 1906, after finishing the play, he made the trip to Zushi from Tokyo. According to one source, Kyōka had already begun to write about his forced separation from Itō Suzu and their eventual reunion as lovers. If we can rely on this account, Kyōka felt that what he had to say about the difficulties of his own romance would be inappropriate for a newspaper novel, and asked Chikufū for any ideas.[1] Chikufū happened to have heard a story about a pickpocket that might lend itself well to the present need. Kyōka heard him out with much interest.

The story Chikufū told was about a certain Iwamasa Kenzō, a high school friend who had a successful bureaucratic career as a superintendent of customs in Hakodate and later in Taiwan, then one of Japan's newly won colonies. Although successful as an adult, Iwamasa had been a pickpocket as a youth. He had been rescued from this life of crime and set upon a more wholesome path by a scholar of German letters, who pitied him enough to provide for his future. Inspired by this narrative and perhaps made sympathetic to Iwamasa's story by his own year of wandering in Tokyo, Kyōka reorganized his material and within two weeks began to write *A Woman's Pedigree*. In the main, it is a story about Hayase Chikara, a pickpocket who wages war against the hypocrisy and affectation of a certain Kōno family. Into this larger framework, Kyōka incorporated a biographical account of how Kōyō forced him to choose between the love of Itō Suzu and a relationship with his mentor. This side story of disappointed love was meant to be a subplot within the former, yet there are obvious reasons why it is this secondary narrative that most people think of when they hear the title *A Woman's Pedigree*.

Apart from the dramatic potential of the subject matter, the work's popularity owes much to the accessibility of the writing. In filling Chikufū's request, Kyōka obviously knew that he needed to please a wider audience, and he chose topical themes: love and marriage, adultery and deception, revelation and fall from social grace, the importance of the family. Also contributing to the story's readability are its relatively simple narrative devices and generous portions of dialogue, which in their wit and attractiveness reflect Suzu's intimate knowledge of the Tokyo vernacular. The story's domestic realism makes it seem a hiatus in the author's persistent deepening of the archetype. Yet its overriding

ly ask that she

et rid of me.

happy. Hayase,

nfailing sense
ove. Romance
Hayase: "Take
empt for Ha-
erly suggested
ne right thing.
ving seen and
The Yushima
completely in
y a subsidiary
amily. Even if
to deny that
ange suggests
sfaction with
According to
gures in only
low to admit
oted the new
Sugako, but
the principal
ever felt that
rmed on the
s that Kyōka
ite about his
eir disagree-
y the forced
with Kyōka's
adequacy of

ale protago-

ins familiar. Indeed, A Woman's Pedi-
re open version of the same aesthetic
ture work. Being less structurally and
y in Spring," it only seems less securely
he Elegant Railway in its quotidian na-
work in that it is more personally felt.
ations, when the story began its run on
page, or the "human interest" section,
attention, however, that it was moved
eighty-fourth installment; and there it
published on April 28. What readers
d to determine precisely, but part of the
nanner in which the work was almost
as early as September of the following
being performed in Tokyo. Written by
hers, this rendition focused on the dis-
ver Suzu, a topic to which Shun'yō had
circle. As in the original story, the focus
with Otsuta but, rather, on his dealings
s interpreters were intent on highlighting
ntually included a scene not found in the
Yushima Tenjin, this supplement focuses
are forced to say farewell.

after Kyōka) announces to his lover, a
hi (modeled after Suzu), that their love
them by Hayase's mentor, Sakai Shunzō

you.
ff? Is that it? That's what you say to a geisha,
die. You might as well tell your Ivy [Tsuta] to

aptation for the stage, Kyōka was asked to
f the manner in which he presents Otsuta's
zu's pain, then we are still left to deal with
tent) Kyōka meant this to be a criticism of
word kireru in the passage above implies).

Otsuta's understanding and nobility pain Hayase, who can o~~
forgive him for his slavish obedience to Sakai.

Otsuta: I understand. And when he said that, you told him you'd
Hayase: Forgive me. I'm sorry. I did promise him.
Otsuta: Then you said the right thing. As your wife, you've made m~~
you did what a man has to do. (26: 229)

Otsuta can be so accepting of her fate only because she has an
of who she is. Whatever happens, she is committed to true
makes her transcendent. She is Kyōka's ideal. She is able to tell
care of yourself. And don't worry about me" (26: 232). If her cor
yase's mentor is not clearly articulated, it remains, of course, bit
by the way Otsuta as his wife (*nyōbo*) tells him that he has done ~~

Kyōka wrote this additional scene in September 1914, after h
written about Shun'yō's version of the original story. Entitled '
Temple Grounds" ("Yushima no keidai"), this contribution is
keeping with Shun'yō's intent to emphasize what was supposed
development to Hayase's vengeful involvements with the Kōno
we might wish to clear Kyōka of the charge of revenge, it is har
the shift of focus away from the Kōno family is extreme. The cl
the extent to which Kyōka himself was convinced that his dissa~~
Kōyō's treatment of Suzu was the most crucial part of the whole
the playbill published for the first performance, the Kōno family
the sixth of the seven acts.[2] Despite this obvious shift, Kyōka was
the truth. He commented on the play on November 1908 and r
emphasis. He claimed the original story is *primarily* about Kōn~~
this is a disingenuous statement. "In my original story, Sugako is
heroine and Otsuta has a supporting role. Answering for both, I ~~
Otsuta was the main attraction, but, strangely enough, when perf
stage it seems like a play about her" (28: 436). One interpretation
made such a prevarication because, from the start, he wanted to w
conflict with Kōyō but did not want to draw public attention to t
ment.[3] Certainly, the structural weakness of the story, especia~~
connections between the first and second halves, has more to do
lack of courage in addressing the topic at hand than with the i~~
Chikufū's pickpocket idea.

The major contours of the original story are as follows. The ~~

nist, Hayase Chikara, hears from a fishmonger named Me no Sōsuke (modeled after the Izumis' fishmonger in Zushi) that Kōno Tomiko, wife of Kōno Hide-omi, former surgeon major general, once had an affair with a stableman while her husband was away on duty. Hayase himself, we soon learn, also has some-thing to hide. A former pickpocket saved from a life of crime and poverty by a scholar of German named Sakai Shunzō, Hayase works as a translator for the General Staff Office. When his friend Kōno Eikichi, son of Kōno Hideomi and Tomiko, comes to investigate his mentor's background, Hayase is angered by his probing. Eikichi is interested in marrying his mentor's daughter Taeko, but wants a thorough investigation of physical, emotional, and financial matters first. This is the source of the story's title, *Onna keizu*. Kyōka was trying to criticize the notion that a woman's worth depends entirely on the quality of her pedigree (*keizu*).

Hayase has a number of reasons for disliking the Kōnos. First of all, he is protective of the Sakais, because he owes his livelihood to them. In addition, he is privy to the Kōnos' dark secret and is, therefore, contemptuous of the hypoc-risy of their investigations. Especially vexing is the arrogance of Sakata Reino-shin, a "teacher of morals," whom the Kōnos have asked to mediate in the on-going negotiations between the two families. Hayase will later become entangled with Sakata, and as a result he will lose his job and be banished from Tokyo. But certainly, and this is the fourth and most profound source of Ha-yase's abhorrence of the Kōnos, his belief in the principles of love, as Kyōka articulated earlier in the essay "Love and Matrimony" (1895) and in the story "Maidenhair" (1896), makes him ill-disposed to arranged marriages.

Kyōka was as passionately in favor of romance as he was against the institu-tion of marriage. In his view, matrimony robbed women of all rights to work out their personal happiness and subjugated them to the demands of their partners. Kōyō, who probably rejected Suzu because she was inappropriate, can hardly escape criticism, even though in the story Sakai Shunzō is also a victim of Reinoshin's probing questions about Taeko's worthiness. For all his postur-ing as a man about town, Kōyō thirsted for respectability. As mentioned, he himself was openly involved with the geisha Oen (Murakami Machi), though never to the detriment of his marriage. (During his final decline, his wife and Oen nursed him together at his bedside.) His conviction about marrying well was borne out by the betrothal of his daughter to a naval officer, for instance.

Because of his very different attitude toward matrimony, Kyōka employed Chikufū's pickpocket motif in a surprising way. While Hayase is traveling with

Sakata, a thief named Manta steals Sakata's wallet and, to escape detection, drops it into Hayase's sleeve. This is the first suggestion of Hayase's questionable past, and the unraveling of this incident leads to Hayase's eventual undoing. First, however, Hayase is made to suffer because of another discovery. Sakai finds out about his ongoing affair with Otsuta, and delivers the ultimatum made famous by the story's adaptation for the stage. In the novel, Sakai's objections are intense and obdurate: "It's not a question of right or wrong. Even if I'm asking too much, that shouldn't matter. Maybe I'm being heartless. Who cares? Let the girl bear a grudge, let her cry. These are your teacher's orders. Break off with her! It's either me or the girl. That's all there is to it" (10: 488–89). In accordance with his mentor's wishes, Hayase parts with Otsuta, whose life falls apart and ends tragically.

Meanwhile, at the school she attends, Taeko learns that Hayase has lost his job because of his part in the theft of Sakata's wallet. Taeko, who was brought up like a sister to Hayase, clips the article about a "German scholar pickpocket" from the newspaper, not believing what it says. That her concern for Hayase is something more than sisterly becomes obvious to her father, who breaks off the discussions with Sakata when it becomes clear that Hayase and Taeko have fallen in love. Hayase, it seems, loves everyone, and everyone loves him. With varying degrees of sincerity, he becomes emotionally involved with Otsuta, Taeko, and, as we see in the second half of the story, with all the daughters of the Kōno family as well. As Sakai Shunzō sees it, the solution to Hayase's attachment to Taeko is to send him back to his hometown of Shizuoka.

In Shizuoka, Chikara meets and, while plotting the downfall of the Kōno family, becomes familiar with Sugako, an extravagant woman who is Kōno Eikichi's younger sister and the wife of a certain Shimayama, a respected professor of science. Back in Tokyo, Taeko visits Otsuta, who, still suffering from her separation from Hayase, has become ill and bedridden. Taeko also happens to meet Koyoshi, a geisha and one of Otsuta's supporters. And it is here that Kyōka's sympathy for the Sakais, and therefore for Kōyō, becomes most ambivalent. The reader learns that Taeko is, in fact, not Sakai Shunzō's daughter by his wife but the illegitimate child of Koyoshi, Sakai's lover. Koyoshi is modeled after Oen, who clearly disliked Itō Suzu. In the story, Koyoshi tries to get Otsuta and Hayase together, but we know that in actuality Oen helped to turn Kōyō against Kyōka's lover. Her appearance here as Otsuta's confidante and supporter could, then, clearly be interpreted to be a damning irony.

At this point, the fishmonger Me no Sōsuke re-enters the story, reminding us of a secret that Hayase is now prepared to divulge. Hayase advances his plan to destroy the Kōno family by telling Michiko, the Kōnos' oldest daughter, the truth of her birth. She is the illegitimate child of her mother Tomiko and the stableman Teizō. At Michiko's request, Hayase takes her to see her real father, who is now aged and dying in a hospital. Being the least aristocratic by birth, Michiko is the most sympathetically drawn of the Kōno daughters. The snobbish Sugako, in comparison, is repulsive. Fatally attracted to Hayase, even though he is working to bring about the downfall of her family, she is finally demeaned by her adulterous relationship with him.

While in the hospital, Hayase learns that Otsuta, his true love, is on her deathbed. He does not go to her, but his mentor, Sakai Shunzō, does. Having had a change of heart, Sakai visits Otsuta to express his apologies, but it is much too late. Awakened to the importance of love and wracked with contrition for having destroyed her relationship with Hayase, Sakai tearfully tells the dying Otsuta to think of Hayase in the next life. She dies in Sakai's arms. Taeko, Sakai's illegitimate daughter, takes a lock of Otsuta's hair to Hayase.

In the story's climactic scene, Hayase rehearses all the ugly secrets of the Kōno family to Kōno Hideomi, who is devastated by the revelations. By destroying this family, Kyōka wanted us to understand that the underlying source of everyone's unhappiness is the family system itself and its destructive pressures to shore up respectability, prestige, and wealth through matrimony. Having traded emotional honesty for security, the Kōno family finally loses its soul and destroys itself. Kōno resigns from his post. His two daughters, the illegitimate Michiko and the deceived Sugako, commit suicide by drowning. And in melodramatic fashion, Kyōka's hero, too, ends his life. "Clutching Otsuta's black hair, Hayase heroically took his life by drinking poison" (10: 747).

Had he been alive to read it, Kitamura Tōkoku would have approved of such an ending. By his own suicide, Tōkoku meant to communicate that there is no place in this world for those who truly understand the rapture and sorrow of love and beauty. On the face of it, Kyōka seems to have agreed. Yet as it turns out, he had misgivings about letting the story speak for itself. When the chapters of the story were published in two hardback volumes by Shun'yōdō in June 1908, Kyōka added twenty-one lines to the ending that have the effect of undermining the entire work. The addition is represented as Hayase Chikara's final testament, sent to Kōno Eikichi. In this testament, Hayase admits to his lowly status as a pickpocket and denies that Eikichi's mother had an affair with

Teizō, the stableman. Furthermore, not only does he confess that he felt justified to do all within his means to bring down the Kōno household, but he goes so far as to affirm the family ideology that Kyōka loathed. "I express my deepest respect for the strict ideology of the family system" (10: 749). This reversal of Hayase's character is an enigmatic ending to an already puzzling story. When the work was republished as a part of the collected works in 1915, Kyōka deleted the testament, giving no more explanation than "I added it carelessly because of my circumstances."[4] Although Kyōka never made the details of these circumstances explicit, many have been tempted to speculate about them, especially because the models for the story's characters were particularly obvious.

As already mentioned, the biographical ties are many. Hayase Chikara is a shadow of Kyōka himself. Otsuta is based on Itō Suzu. Sakai Shinzō is modeled after Ozaki Kōyō. Koyoshi is Oen. And Me no Sōsuke is based on the Izumis' fishmonger in Zushi. The models for the members of the Kōno household are also easy to trace. Kōno Hideomi is patterned after Uchida Masa, a wealthy physician who lived in Hamamatsu. Kōno Eikichi was inspired by Masa's oldest son, Akira, whom Kyōka disliked intensely because he constantly talked about his mother, and Sugako by Masa's daughter Kin.

Kin also happened to be the model for Omiya in the New Year's party scene in Kōyō's *The Gold Demon.* Among Kōyō's circle, she was known as "Lady Gold Demon." An ardent fan of Kōyō's, she invited him to attend a card party at the home of a friend, some time around 1894, and it is this occasion that Kōyō later remembered in his novel. Uchida Kin, then a student, went on to marry Wadatsu Yotarō in 1897. She then moved to Nagoya, where Wadatsu was the head of the Nagoya telephone exchange. Kyōka first met her there on February 4, 1902. As an editor of *New Fiction,* he had been asked by Gotō Chūgai to travel to Ise with Shun'yō to hunt up a story. They stopped in Nagoya, taking with them letters of introduction from Kōyō. Welcomed as Kōyō's associates, Kyōka stayed at the Wadatsu home while Shun'yō stayed with another friend.

Kin's son, Wadatsu Kiyoo, remembered Kyōka's visit.

Ishibashi Shian had taken Kyōka to one of the brothels in Nagoya, from which a messenger came bearing a note. "Lost my glasses. Out of money. Morning is approaching. Please come and get me." When my father went to bail him out, Kyōka was sitting alone in the storage room, looking very forlorn. Afterwards, we had a laugh at his expense. Kyōka was very nearsighted and couldn't function without his glasses. I can still picture him clearly. We were invited to someone's magnificent summer home shortly thereafter, and Kyōka walked right over some persimmons that had been set out to dry. It was a most embarrassing moment."[5]

Kyōka apparently maintained close relations with the Wadatsu family even after the publication of the story and they moved to Tokyo. Kiyoo remembered him as "an interesting, amusing man, who was always saying silly things. He liked *sake*, but unless it was boiling hot he wouldn't touch it. Neither would he eat anything that hadn't been boiled or otherwise cooked through to the very center. . . . The older maid in our house would often laugh and exclaim, 'What a bumpkin!' We lived in Yotsuya, and Kyōka's residence was in Kojimachi. Since it wasn't far, he came over frequently."[6]

This picture by Wadatsu Kiyoo contradicts the opinions of many, including Uchida Masa's nephew Uchida Tōru, who suggested that *A Woman's Pedigree* permanently damaged the relationship. Tōru presented a very different interpretation: "The plot was patently false, but the characterizations and the places described matched in the smallest of details, and so it is easy to imagine how the main line of my family was greatly shocked and displeased. Hearing about their reaction, Kyōka probably added the twenty-one-line epilogue when the story was published as a book in order to obscure the connections."[7]

This, then, is one explanation for the testament. In order to salvage an already damaged relationship, Kyōka added an ending that denied, or at least cast doubt upon, what had been presented as the hidden secrets of the Kōno family. But if this is so, why did Kyōka decide to delete the testament when the work was reprinted for the collected works?

A second explanation for Hayase's testament is structural. The addendum has the effect of tying the various subplots of the story together, even though in a forced manner. The critic Katsumoto Seiichirō's assessment of both the story and this final attempt for coherence was harsh: "Most of the second half is nothing but an assorted collection of loosely-screwed-together junk. With or without Chikara's testament at the very end, the general structure of the story is flawed beyond repair."[8] Itō Sei suggested that this vacillation is inherent to the work in general. It reveals what might be construed an inability on the author's part. "The motive behind *A Woman's Pedigree* is, as with *Worship at Yushima*, Kyōka's dealings with Itō Suzu. But the plot becomes fragmented, and the work ends in confusion. What Kyōka most wanted to write was the pain he felt in being caught between Suzu and Kōyō. But he couldn't express this feeling honestly, and so the work is a failure."[9]

It is precisely this lack of honesty that places *A Woman's Pedigree* in the broader context of Kyōka's development as an artist. Kyōka's inability to speak more openly about his pain emerges as an issue only because the more realistic style of this work forced him to write about marriage and the trauma of his separation from Itō Suzu more discursively than he cared to do. The quotidian aspects of *A Woman's Pedigree* make us expect clarity and the sort of detail that Kyōka was unprepared to give in full. He could not repress the desire to write about just those things that troubled him most, including his relationship with Kōyō, but this more straightforward style forced him from the house of poetry into the daylight of prosaic scrutiny. Ultimately, his lack of honesty is essentially a failure of courage, a timidity better expressed by obscuring forces, such as the formulaic pull of the meta-story and the ambiguities of poetic diction. As the confessional, more courageous I-novelists were showing, it was also a result of a general lack of experience with the artistic articulation of the individual will.

As suggested above, even this domestic novel about topical matters flows from the same artistic source and is governed by the same principles of morality as Kyōka's more haunting works, such as "One Day in Spring." In comparison, *A Woman's Pedigree* suffers to the degree that it is rhetorically inappropriate to that source. If, as in Akutagawa's formulation, Kyōka's morality is aesthetic, grounded deeply in the same fear that allowed him access to the metamorphic powers of language, the lack of honesty in *A Woman's Pedigree* pointed out by Itō Sei is expressed in the way the substories compete with each other rather than work synergistically. It is also evident in the way the story's meaning is undercut by Hayase's final testament. These obvious structural problems follow from the author's heightened sense of fear, in its widest sense. In this case, it *was* translated as both hatred and respect for a mentor, both dread of and delight in the monogamous fulfilment of romantic love, both distaste and fascination for the life of the privileged.

In other words, Kyōka is working against himself in ways that are only more obvious than before. Living in fear, he was not brave enough to close himself off to the comforts of poetry. Although he criticized the naturalists for lacking the human decency (*ninjō*) to conceal the sordid aspects of life, he was like them pulled toward the compulsion to reveal a hidden truth. Through the failure of *A Woman's Pedigree*, he took another step toward perfecting his art by confronting that point at which vacillation and the will to confront all things must transform itself into ambiguity. Here he learned the critical point at which the wonder (*myō*) of figurative language replaces the denotational strength of realism with a discourse that promises fulfillment by engulfing both the honesty *and* the dishonesty of human relationships. In other words, by stopping short of embracing the expressive ambiguity of mythic realities, Kyōka allowed the less noble side of his personality to appear without its usual facade of grotesquerie. Given his inability to launch a clear and sustained criticism of Kōyō or the Uchida family (and the privileged life that Kyōka both deplored and enjoyed), ambiguity was unavoidable.

The various versions of *A Woman's Pedigree* allow us to place Kyōka within a larger context of realistic writing. The vacillation found in Kyōka's original story was replaced by the more forceful and honestly critical version supplied by Shun'yō. And it was Shun'yō's version, not the original story, that was influential within the cultural landscape of Meiji Japan. Indeed, the play *A Woman's Pedigree* became a signature piece for the *shinpa* theater, which was itself a modern compromise between mimesis and the *kata*, or established forms of traditional stage performance. The realism of the new theater had the effect of clarifying the critical aspect of Kyōka's work, thus distorting the original story and making Kyōka seem more forthcoming about his relationship with Kōyō than he had intended.

As we might expect, both story and play received harsh criticism from those close to Kōyō's family. At her husband's funeral, Kōyō's wife had been apologetic to Kyōka for the way her husband had dealt with Suzu.[10] Yet it seems that Kyōka was slow to forgive. When Kōyō's wife later fell into financial difficulty and took her husband's diaries to Kyōka, he refused to buy them on the grounds that he did not deserve to have such august belongings in his possession. According to Katsumoto Seiichirō, who eventually ended up with the diaries, Kyōka's rejection of her plea for help left Kōyō's wife in tears, not because of Kyōka's "famous lack of feeling" or because of his "famous stinginess" but because "she was sensitive to the cynical criticism implicit in Kyōka's treatment of her husband as a god."[11] In Katsumoto's view, Kyōka was Kōyō's most severe and relentless critic. His reputation as a devoted protégé was false, merely a facade.

We may not be as ready as Katsumoto to see Kyōka's apotheosis of Kōyō as cynical. But we must at least wonder if, indeed, Kyōka himself saw his worship of Kōyō as a form of criticism. Perhaps the vacillation apparent in his treatment of Kōyō's widow was in some sense as natural as fear. Kyōka's failure to enter Suzu's name on his family registry for many years, for instance, can be interpreted as either an expression of respect or an insult. (Or perhaps he simply did not care enough about the institution of marriage to bother filling out the forms?)[12] More clearly ascerbic is the way Kyōka inflated Kōyō's payoff to Suzu from ten yen (as recorded in Kōyō's diary) to "three freshly printed ten-yen bills" in the story. Was Kyōka trying to make Kōyō seem generous? Or was he suggesting, quite to the contrary, that Kōyō was cheap? Ten yen was worth a great deal more then than now, certainly. Yet even at the time ten yen was a laughably small amount to offer to Suzu, who could not, in the end, be bought off at any price. Even Kyōka, who had come to the city from Kanazawa, knew the usual cost of such a transaction.

Taking such matters into consideration, Katsumoto softened the criticism leveled against Shūsei, the usual target. In Katsumoto's account, he becomes the brighter background against which Kyōka's dark regard for Kōyō becomes apparent.

Kyōka broke off relations with Shūsei . . . because Shūsei criticized Kōyō. But Kyōka himself was always critical of Kōyō. Not only this, he was forever fighting with his mentor and was even vengeful toward him. Kyōka's manner of criticism was different from Shūsei's, that's all. . . . In my opinion, Kyōka . . . faulted his mentor with his entire being, with his works, his everyday life, with an entire lifetime of behavior. For Kōyō, this was certainly the most disagreeable kind of criticism he could possibly receive. . . .

Kyōka's criticism of Kōyō was bitter, an extended war. He was cold as a snake, unrelentingly perverse. Shūsei's was human; Kyōka's was satanic. In the end, both authors prevailed over Kōyō. Shūsei had no ill-feelings toward Kōyō but naturally surpassed him at some point. Kyōka, on the other hand, never let go of his problems and was warped in his victory, having a deep-seated ambivalence in his heart.[13]

"The Grass Labyrinth"

If the ambivalence of *A Woman's Pedigree* was born of fear, the profundity of that emotion drove Kyōka to continue searching for that point at which awe and horror find perfect expression in language. In all fairness to Katsumoto's critique, had Kyōka not been so obstinate, there would have been no victory. Surely, the issue of his unrelenting perversity cannot be so easily dismissed. It is perhaps more accurate to say that his obsessions led to the creation of a beautiful anxiety, a literary miniature of delicate proportions, a pattern established by a few images that lie at the center of a vast universe. At their best, Kyōka's writings capture that moment of mystery when we find ourselves before a familiar strangeness, when we gain access to places we did not know how to reach, when the impossible becomes possible, and when memory becomes identical with awareness.

If *A Woman's Pedigree* did not create such a space of mystery, Kyōka's next major work did. "The Grass Labyrinth" ("Kusa meikyū," 1908) is one of the author's most successful stories. Stated simply, its intensity derives from what Mishima Yukio praised as Kyōka's sincere "pursuit of nothing save the drama hidden in the deepest recesses of the author's soul."[14] As Mishima noted in another context, Kyōka's endless search for one thing, the message formally expressed by the archetype, is an expression of sincerity that rewards the reader with "a pleasant and pure continuity."[15] This sincerity expresses itself in the repetition of this meta-narrative, which in turn establishes an ontology that makes Kyōka's fiction distinctive among late-modern visions of the world. It allows for the apparent seamlessness of this sphere and the one beyond. To be sure, other writers would write about the supernatural, such as Edogawa Rampō (1894–1965). None, however, handled the blending of the mundane and the sacred with such mastery and profundity. Rarely clumsy or forced, the drama "always present" in Kyōka's heart oriented "every word" he wrote.[16]

This attitude of belief and desire is not only always present, it is the basis of all that becomes present. It is, in other words, the insistent and originating notion that those images most important to us in an emotional way can and must be available for contemplation and even adoration. Belief is by nature originating. It is always concerned with the possibly sure. Consequently, faith is as resilient as madness, whether or not we agree with the need to perceive necessity in every human action. In Kyōka's case, we must measure his insistence in a way that appropriately illuminates not only the structure of his art but also the tradition to which it belongs. Mita Hideaki makes the point that the two-dimensionality of European romanticism, the visible world of the physical and the invisible world of the spirit, is an inappropriate basis for understanding Kyōka's aesthetics. Surrealism is a closer analogue, since in Japan the "real" world and the world of spirits are held to be coextensive and cotemporal. Accordingly, there can be no clear bifurcation of the normal and the heightened, of the here and the there, since this begs a falsely Western ontology. In other words, if the frequent presence of the supernatural is a quality of Kyōka's work, it is also defining of the cultural context in which he wrote.[17]

Whatever the validity of this general claim, in the end we are better off adjusting the boldness of this comparison with the West by individualizing

Kyōka's madness as Mishima and the scholar-critic Noguchi Takehiko do. Along with these two readers, we benefit by placing Kyōka's work at that juncture where a culture of (visual) presence is strongly critiqued by the influences of representation. The author's desire for the dead to be made available was contested by the antifigural thrust of the real as conceptualized at this particular point in time. However persuasive the claims of positivism, however believable the absence of the supernatural, however systematic and universal the vision of perspectivalism, the force of the ghostly tradition was neither easily nor fully suppressed. If the naturalists were successful in doing away with the apparitions of old Edo, the centrality of the supernatural was again taken up by postwar writers such as Mishima, who in his "What Is a Novel?" discussed Yanagita Kunio's *The Tales of Tōno* (*Tōno monogatari*) and argued that, in essence, the other world exists and that a novel of any worth ought to make that other world available through the inclusion of supernatural events.[18]

Mishima's formulation of the novel as an expression of the supernatural is as sympathetic to a work such as "The Grass Labyrinth" as it is condemning of the naturalists and of what Mishima called the "desert of modern Japanese literature" that supposedly surrounded Kyōka. Whereas European naturalism had developed within a culture of science, early-modern Japan had not accepted to the same degree the metaphysical underpinnings that would make such a reductive and universalizing worldview immediately tenable in the late-modern era. As many have pointed out, Japan's version of the realistically encountered truth was yet another variety of concept without roots, reaching the height of influence just as Kyōka wrote "The Grass Labyrinth" and a number of critical essays that expressed his differences with those whom he called "those naturalists who won't let me earn my keep."[19]

The compelling force of this second of the Zushi masterpieces focuses on the "irrational" issue of belief. As a statement of the author's faith, it problematizes the reading of Kyōka's imaginative flights as *merely* fantasy since, as Noguchi points out, Kyōka believed in the existence of the other world that he so earnestly worked to establish by writing.[20] The seriousness of his imagination was yet another consequence of the contest between fright and reverence. Ultimately it was the strength of Kyōka's need to believe in something that made him understand the powers of language well enough to make "The Grass Labyrinth" "beautiful to the point of wretchedness, filled with a metaphysical sadness."[21]

No previous work so thoroughly expresses Kyōka's stated desire to connect himself with the greater reality. In an essay entitled "My Attitude" ("Yo no taido"), published in July 1908, only six months after the publication of "The Grass Labyrinth," Kyōka stated this now clearly understood purpose for writing. "I don't want to write about reality (*genjitsu*) as reality, but to go through reality to reach a greater power" (28: 696). A slightly earlier essay, published as "A Few Remarks Regarding My Fondness for Monsters and Memories of My First Published Work" ("Bakezuki no iware shōshō to shojosaku") in May 1907, explains what this greater power might be.

I believe that there are two supernatural powers in this world. If I had to give them names, I would call one the power of Kannon, and the other the power of evil spirits. In the face of either of these forces, human beings are powerless. . . . On the one hand, I have a profound fear of evil spirits. On the other, I believe in the tremendous protective powers of Kannon. (28: 677–78)

Taken out of context, this passage can be misleading. If "human beings are powerless," Kyōka nevertheless felt that it was possible to negotiate one's fate in the face of these two overwhelming forces. He did this by way of language, whether through the power of its sound or through its visual potential. He wrote of the blessed noise of sutras being chanted and of the mysterious presence of the word as it existed in the form of his mentor's manuscripts. To illustrate this second point, he described his habit of circumambulating the mail drop three times and then looking back once whenever he mailed a manuscript for Kōyō. He followed this ritual in order to free himself from the fear of misplacing something so important as the written word.

But then Kōyō-sensei saw my disgraceful behavior and berated me: "Why are you doing such an unsightly thing!" And that was the end of that superstition. I had complete trust in my mentor, and a scolding from him was for me a manifestation of Kannon's power. Through this incident, I learned that the power of religion was not so much a matter of doctrine and that it had a great deal to do with human character. (28: 679)

To state what has long been obvious, the emotional realities expressed by the archetype were fundamental to Kyōka's literary quest, especially to his need to harness the power of language in order to secure a state of equilibrium vis-à-vis the destructive powers of hideousness, sickness, and death. Consequently, the naturalists' insistence on draining literature of artifice made little sense to Kyōka, who saw that "words are, to begin with, a type of artifice," laden with history and meaning, possessing a connotative force that is, in the final analysis, one's only means to survival (28: 694). To affirm this poetic power is to use language to one's advantage, to practice the manipulation of words with a believer's devotion to establishing a sense of that which is whole and beautiful and worthy of adulation.

The wholeness that Kyōka sought was not an affirmation of his situation's limits but an emotional intensity that exploited the associational powers of language in order to transform absence into a state of presence and to free himself from fear by making the dead live again. Kyōka came to use words to this end by stating the (normally) impossible and thereby calling attention to language and its limitations as a purely denotative system.[22] In order to establish the mythic reality of the archetype, the denotative function of language was suppressed so that its connotative potential could establish ties with a felt reality that escaped empirical proof. In short, where the realists wanted transparency, Kyōka embraced opacity. The realists sought to narrow the possibilities of reference through observation and analysis; he sought to increase them through an imaginative synthesis. Disregarding the agenda of the mainstream, Kyōka made the distinction between what is and what could be less clear by insisting that, in keeping with his attraction to the enabling powers of one thing's connecting with another, the tenor and vehicle of metaphor be interchangeable and that the ontological status of both be similar.[23]

In setting out the various relationships of the archetype, "The Grass Labyrinth" takes us beyond metaphor or, perhaps better stated, into the very process of metaphor itself. It is a story about metamorphosis, dedicated to making the apparitional available through a transforming (or bakemono-esque) play of language. Here the binary structure that forms the stable and well-balanced ground of phenomenology begins to fail. Just as the vehicle/tenor binarism begins to break down, so do pairings of the profound and superficial, substantive and trivial, natural and artificial. All give way in order to establish an idiosyncratic order that is decorative yet saturated with meaning, extravagant yet expressive of sincere purpose. Like the language of a Noh libretto, the words of this story gradually and inexorably build toward their enactment of the drama first played out in the author's soul.

In this instance, Kyōka formulates the performance as a quest by the protagonist to hear a song that his mother once sang to him. Since she died when he was a boy, Hagoshi Akira, the protagonist, remembers it only vaguely. He is, nevertheless, dedicated to encountering the *form* of it, which he knows he will be able to recognize. Having traveled for five years, engaged in a search for which he has sacrificed all, he never doubts that he will be able to translate his vision into language, and that his words will then magically become the song (and the dramatic moment) of his most profound desire.[24]

Akira describes the object of his quest in a way that draws attention to its description.

A dream? A reality? A phantasm? It is like a melody that takes shape before the eyes but has no form upon the tongue. Gentle, nostalgic, and sad, it is filled with love and emotion, full to the touch, clean and cool, making one shudder with its terror. It is like an ecstasy, like the rending of your heart. If I may use a metaphor, it is like sucking a pure and fragrant nipple while still in the womb. It is the feeling you get upon seeing the beauty of your mother's breasts. (11: 269)

The longing is familiar, for it is obviously shaped by the incidents of Kyōka's childhood and formed by the archetype, which insists that the boundary between the lived and the written be confused. We know that this vaguely remembered object of Akira's search, for instance, was actually one of Nakata Suzu's favorite songs.[25] It properly belongs in this story because her death produced the emotion of loss that manifests itself as this linguistic transformation, which Kyōka had originally titled "A Children's Song" ("Temari uta").

Kyōka claimed to have no clearly articulated rationale for why works such as "The Grass Labyrinth" are filled with monsters.

It's simply a matter of emotion. All along I've received many words of advice from Fūyō and others. But I can't simply stop having this emotion. I've had people say to me, "If you're going to put monsters in your stories, wouldn't it be better to have them appear in some awe-inspiring setting, in some mysterious valley deep in the mountains, rather than in the middle of Tokyo?" . . . But I prefer to have monsters appear right in the city, within the sound of streetcar bells.

In short, monsters (*obake*) are the concretization of my emotions. Among the children's street songs that I used to hear so often as a young boy, there were some very cruel ones: the snake this, the viper that, the one about the rich man's daughter who did this and that.

When I take the time to think about it, the transcendent beauty of those songs pierces my heart, and a subtle, indescribable emotion wells up within me. Sometimes the feeling turns into "The Grass Labyrinth," at other times it becomes a bakemono. There's really not much to explain.

In sum, I don't follow any particular ideology. The call of the artist isn't to write theory but to create works of art. While I deride those who have been seduced by theory, I must avoid being taken in myself.

And so I repeat. Naturalism is fine. Neither do I object to romanticism. Expressionism is equally acceptable. The only needful thing is that a writer produce works that hold together. I want to experience art that is perfect. (28: 697–98)

In short, "The Grass Labyrinth" began as a cruel yet beautiful song that produced an intense desire for that language which would make such feelings present themselves plausibly. This fundamental emotion of loss is familiar to us by now. Concerned with Akira's search for this once heard but not forgotten song, the story is a convoluted and labyrinthine psalm of Kyōka's longing for his dead mother. Its structure is complex: the outer passages form several secondary stories that lead to the center in roundabout ways, requiring numerous tellers and a listener through which the reader gains access to these various subplots. Kyōka's protagonist only gradually occupies the inner sanctum of this labyrinth, and the slowness of the journey functions to ensure the story's emotional fullness.

As in *The Holy Man of Mt. Kōya*, a wandering priest leads us through the narrative. To establish an obvious comparison with Noh, Shōjirō is the *waki*, the witness, the hearer. At a teahouse along the Shōnan Coast, he learns from an older woman who serves tea and dumplings to passersby that this area is haunted. In the waters offshore several swimmers have mysteriously drowned. And at the water's edge are found the so-called *koumi ishi* (literally, child-bearing rocks), which reproduce spontaneously but refuse to share their fecundity with the old woman, who is barren and bitter.

Kyōka floods the reader with such images of round and spherical objects, the *tama* that are, if we can rely on the etymologies put forward by Orikuchi Shinobu,[26] both spirit and sphere. They function narratively in two ways: first, their visual associations allow the story to expand as other images come into play; second, these images are tied to past experiences that become narrated as parts of the larger story. The image of the woman's dumplings, for instance, provides our connection to a certain Kakichi, a deranged man who provokes her to tell Shōjirō about the circumstances of his madness: how he became drunk, was helped by the woman's husband, Zaihachi, and then encountered a beautiful young woman. Because he misreads the young woman's kindness toward him, mistaking her compassion for sexual interest, he suffers the consequences. She is a typical heroine—kind yet alluring, available yet forbidding. When he makes advances toward her, actually doing what the Kōya priest was only tempted to do, she strikes him with her fan. Looking into her face, he calls out "Bakemono," and from this moment he is never again sane.

Singing a children's song—"To where, I ask, does this road lead? This narrow road, this dangerous road. To Tenjin-sama's land it leads, this narrow,
narrow road"—this wraithlike woman, Kyōka's "monstrous" female, walks off
in the direction of the Akiya Mansion, the second home of a local leader and
man of means named Tsurutani. By way of another strand of narrative, we
learn that Tsurutani recently handed over the care of the house to his son,
Kitarō, who, upon returning to the area from Tokyo, brought two women with
him: one his wife and the other his mistress. Both were pregnant. Both died in
childbirth, along with their babies. Unable to cope with his grief, Kitarō killed
himself, leaving the mansion deserted and haunted.

It is this mansion that becomes the inner sanctum of the narrative maze.
After hearing of these deaths and despite what the old woman has told him
about the haunted house, Shōjirō feels compelled to go there in order to perform a Buddhist memorial for the spirits of the dead. There he meets Hagoshi
Akira, Kyōka's typically idealistic protagonist, who has been led to the same
mansion by a ball (*temari*) that he found floating in a river as he was passing by.
He is, once again, on a quest to find the song that his dead mother used to sing;
and since that song is a *temari uta* (one sung by the players as they bat a ball
back and forth) he is not without reasons for wanting to investigate this coincidence. Traveling upstream, he comes to the mansion, which is hidden in a sea
of grass and surrounded by woods and strands of spider's web. This is a sacred
place, a cocoon in which the other world will become present.

A veil of smoke. A mist. The entire area was dyed by the setting sun. The tips of the
pine trees above and the roots of the willow trees below were surrounded by the murky
waters of the Yu River. Between the path and the mansion, a wide bank of fog rose into
the air, making the upper edge of the foundation stones to appear as if floating on the
mist. Because the fog in the dark reaches of the forest floor was visibly much thicker
than anywhere else, the Black Gate Mansion seemed to be floating in midair. (11: 229)

Driven by his obsession, Akira occupies the mansion, undaunted by the
strange events that unfold around him. Although the ball disappears, he remains to hear the song that will accompany it. As he waits, he witnesses a flurry
of supernatural events—tatami mats moving, lamps floating and spinning in
the air—but they do not persuade him to leave, since he is no ordinary traveler
and because this world of metamorphosis is, after all, the end of his desire.
When Shōjirō appears at the mansion, Akira relates what has happened. He
tells of his five-year quest and also recounts a story about his childhood friend,
a girl named Ayame, who was kidnapped by the gods (*kami kakushi*) one even-

ing, never to be seen again. She is one of a few people who knew the exact words to the song that his mother used to sing. She happens to be, of course, the same mysterious woman who drove Kakichi mad, one of many Kyōkaean heroines reminiscent of the "young women of the neighborhood who told me stories" noted in the second autochronology.

Given these associations between Ayame, Akira's mother, and the sought-for song, we should not be surprised that Kyōka has the young woman come through the veil to sing the song. A visitor from another world, she embodies the threatening yet captivating lyrics. She is a complicated though hardly unusual composite of condemning temptress (the woman who caused Kakichi's madness), alluring sexuality (Akira's childhood friend now a young woman), and loving protectress (Akira's mother). The melding of these identities in one figure is both the story's *raison d'être* and, once again, a fundamental requirement of the larger narrative pattern.

Ayame belongs to the world of the dead and thus joins with other monsters in their desire to see Akira leave the mansion. Unlike them, however, she is moved by his longing for his dead mother and thus fulfils the emotional requirements of the archetype. When she approaches Akira as he sleeps inside his mosquito net with the intent to harm him, his mother, who is also a citizen of the other world, fears for her son. Sensing her concern, Ayame gives up her original plan.

In honor of the love between mother and son, and in deference to the incest taboo still strongly at work, she and her kindred spirits play a game with the ball. The temari has reappeared. As they bat it back and forth, their play transforms the room itself into a brocade of language, as if the multicolored strings that make up the ball unwind and reweave themselves in different patterns. Shōjirō, Akira's alter ego, witnesses this amazing transformation. While Akira dreams, Shōjirō watches, although unwilling to remain trapped within the labyrinth that is clearly the womb suggested in Akira's description of the song.

"The time has come for me to leave. Although such matters are certainly childish to you, dear Priest, please allow us to show our affection by playing one game for Akira. So then—" Ayame called, and, like a butterfly suddenly escaping from a paper-covered lampstand, one of the young girls, with short hair and a petite nose, brought the ball upon her sleeve. Taking it from her, the beautiful young woman held it in her palm and gently stroked the large, crimson bud. Such is the world of the spirits! Holding her sleeve between her teeth, she tied the trailing portion up with a cord.

A graceful smile formed on her lips as she said as if lost in rapture, "Surely you don't expect me to play alone? Everyone come, and let's play together!"

Encircling the mosquito tent that covered the sleeping Akira were the beautiful bellflower and lemongrass, the tender bush clover and yellow lady, the bell-ring and the cricket. Together their voices sang—

> In the swamp a rising snake
> Is thinking of the plans she'll make,
> Young Princess of King Hachiman,
> The daughter of cruel Hachiman.
> In her hands two jewels she holds,
> And on her feet are shoes of gold,
> Cruel daughter of King Hachiman.

The walls and sliding doors become maple leaves; the sitting room becomes a brocade spun from the ball. The thickly falling foliage surrounds the lantern and turns its glowing light into crimson. Cross-stitched into the color is the falling snow of countless hands, white here and white there. As their fingertips heartlessly brush against the priest, his hands dance of their own accord.

> Bring him to the temple
> To learn his holy call.
> Our Priest is a Pleasure Priest,
> From the veranda he did fall.
> The ball flies up. It falls. They bat it upward again. (11: 329–30)

Singing the song "To where does this road lead?" Ayame takes her leave, abandoning her desire to have Akira come with her to the land of the dead. Structurally speaking, this is the way it must be. Kyōka has advanced considerably from the unfinished manuscript for "The White Witch's Tale," which ended abruptly at the point the seduction began. A fully successful encounter would result in satisfying desire, which would mean that there could be no return to the reality of loss, and therefore neither eros nor the continued guarantee of meaning through continued use of the archetype. However much Kyōka played with death, he was not ready to die. Relying heavily on the suspense of the erotic, one thing he could not risk was completion. If it is true that Kyōka sought the eternal by doing away with strictures of time, it is equally clear that he could not do away with death by simply conjuring up the deceased.

In a more obvious way than demonstrated in either *The Holy Man of Mt. Kōya* or "One Day in Spring," "The Grass Labyrinth" advances the formulation that heightened eroticism calls for increased weirdness.[27] The required metamorphosis of language—the linguistic concretization of emotion made necessary by the mythic structure of the archetype—is in this case aided by the story's complicated structure. Of course, these many layers of narration emphasize the lack rather than the presence of late-modern perspectivalism, which attempts to describe and explain the created reality of a work with reference to a single, totalizing system of knowledge. The multiplication of narratives suits Kyōka's denial of such a system, since they contribute to the establishment of as many as three different time frames: first, the narrated past (Kakichi's madness and the deaths of Tsurutani Kitarō, his wife, and his mistress); second, Akira's account of his childhood and spiritual quest (as told by Shōjirō); and third, the present time of events in the Akiya Mansion.

To return to the comparison with Noh, the narrative pace, at first slow and meandering, builds inexorably in pace and intensity toward the final epiphany, in which every word and image becomes laden with reverberations of every other word and image. Especially in the final pages, we encounter a forced obscuring of the usual semantic borders that separate and thereby establish meaning by creating clear-cut boundaries of difference. The rhetorical progression is appropriately from one of hearsay to one of experience, from what Shōjirō gleans about past events to what he directly experiences at the Akiya Mansion. This story is, in essence, about the presence of things desired. At issue in every subplot and image are the traces of Kyōka's profound sense of loss and his compulsion to provide answers to the enduring question of what can and cannot be gained through belief and ritual. That is to say, the rhetoric of transformation (which attempts to make bakemono real) becomes essential, since the question of emotional survival depends on an oscillation between disappearance and appearance.

The description in this story is not realistic. There is no carefully measured exterior, nor is there a psychologically profound interior that exists as a counterpoint (and interpretive source) of that which can be seen. Kyōka gave us a surface so obviously distorted by the opacity of language that we are forced to consider the way in which a literary text is nothing but words at play. Again, Kyōka's point of view is elegant and clear. Literature is artificial, and consequently its correspondence to the everyday world is a fabrication, made in accordance with the will's need to establish the appearance of connection. Whereas a more representational discourse attempts to conceal the capriciousness of this constructive will, proclaiming as natural (or at least predictably stable) systems of correspondence between signs and referents, Kyōka revealed human intentionality through a formalistic and even decorative mode of expression. It is a superficial style designed to highlight the eccentricity of desire.

Physically ill and emotionally overwrought, Kyōka perceived that the object of both archetype and language must be to make present that which he *felt* to be missing. To this end, the powerful figurality of language was not something to be denied but embraced. For him, even the emotional encoding of words was clearly relational and, therefore, in need of the larger structures of myth. To the extent that language requires form and that meaning is born of this collusion, the naturalists' casting of the superficial or decorative as less meaningful (because it is less deeply systematic) was, for him, a misguided notion. If discovering a reality beyond the vagaries of language is taken to be the project of fiction, how could anyone possibly see what is there (or see what one wants to see) if the visual habits of realism constantly compel the writer to look at the world with an eye for systems of ordering that are themselves not necessarily present? As the wanderer in "One Day in Spring" argues, even if the metaphysical (including the system of thought which holds that there is no such thing as metaphysics) matters to us, how can we possibly know or express it without recourse to formulaic and metaphorical devices?

Where is the epiphany in this sort of formalism? If by enlightenment we mean the comprehension of a more general formation of knowledge, Kyōka's protagonist gains no new vision. At the same time, it is easy to see how the decorative prose of "The Grass Labyrinth" represents a deepening of Kyōka's faith in art. Akira and Shōjirō survive the attack of bakemono because of their belief in art, but the attack itself results from the same unintimidated belief.[28] No doubt this conviction seemed laughable to the naturalists, whose fascination with the sordid had the effect of marginalizing Kyōka's work. Yet Kyōka's sincerity had led him to his own style, and to a poetic power that was impossible to deny. As one critic saw it, only Kyōka could write this sort of story.

The bundan is a great ocean. The waves of realism are upon it, and winds of naturalism are blowing. Those passengers who do not wait for the boat named "The Correct View" are swept out by the wind and surf. Calling "Progress!" and "New Wave!," they are carried away. What a flurry of activity!

"The Grass Labyrinth" is from the brush of Izumi Kyōka, a writer who has learned nothing from the activities of the boatmen. As for the plot, the story begins when an itinerant priest, Shōjirō, stops at a teahouse on his journey around the country. . . . He learns from an old woman, who is tending the shop, about the haunted Akiya Mansion, and is asked to bring the power of the Buddha into the matter. The language is abstruse, the events mysterious. Yet both reinforce each other and move the reader with a sense of ghastliness. For me to continue even with a plot summary would be like smearing feces on the head of Buddha. I set my feeble brush down here.[29]

To other critics, already tired of the rawness of the new realism, Kyōka represented a safe haven.

Having fallen into silence for some time, Izumi Kyōka, the hope of the romantic school, now gives us a new novel, the result of a half-year's recuperation. . . . It is a ghost story of the kind only Kyōka can write. Each word and phrase is filled with an eerie ghastliness and has the power to make the reader's flesh shiver with horror. His style abounds in poetic spirit, far beyond the abilities of his novelist peers. These days, with this false flourishing of the carnal novel, coming across a good story of such subtle and profound quality is like hearing the sound of footsteps in a lonely valley.[30]

Another admirer of this story was the young Akutagawa Ryūnosuke, who encountered the work as a middle-school student. He found "The Grass Labyrinth" so compelling that he stayed up through the night reading it, completely disregarding his preparations for the exam he was to take the following day. As we will see, Kyōka would have a great influence on Akutagawa and other writers of the next generation, who for various reasons were also ill-disposed to the work of the naturalists. Kyōka's gift to them was to provide an alternative to realism. Their gift to him would be their steady support, whether emotional or financial, or both.

CHAPTER 12

Perfecting Art

∿

1909–1910

Signs from the Other Side

Bolstered by the successes of "One Day in Spring" and "The Grass Labyrinth," Kyōka was now confident enough to write openly about his methods and about his fundamental disagreement with the naturalists. In December 1908, he published the essay "Letting Go" ("Mukō makase"), in which, for the first time, he described his thoughts about the creative process.

The urge to write comes upon me when a new feeling or some accidental incident makes just the right connection with an idea I've been keeping in my head. In other words, I get the urge to write when some old idea comes together in a felicitous way with a new one, thus taking on an interesting form that I wouldn't have conceived on my own. Then I feel as though I can't help but write. Of course, this feeling, the desire to write, the need to create, is something that everyone has. I should think that without feeling this way, one wouldn't be able to write. (28: 698)

Kyōka was convinced that certain powers were unavoidable, and so it is not surprising that he should characterize himself as one inspired. His creative method required receptivity to the world beyond his control: the "other side" or what he here calls *mukō*. Although Kyōka conceived of the writing process as requiring the lack of a previous plan, the works themselves indicate that what he thought of as an extemporaneous process of creation was deeply grounded in the archetype. This larger structure of meaning looms in the background to give shape and pattern to Kyōka's imaginative freedom. Certainly, for all his insistence upon unpredictability, the writing process is a controlled form of chaos. Even if the role of the meta-story seems to be in tension with this process of appealing to the "beyond," there is no better way to explain how Kyōka's spontaneity could be so repetitive and, in the larger context of his life's work, so predictable.

The smallest noises, such as the ringing of a bell, sound as if they are coming to me from another world. Even the sound of a tofu peddler's call seems as if it's coming from a place far separated from the world of reality. I'm writing along, and the echo of striking objects comes to my ears from far away. There are times when it immediately becomes a part of the story. This explains why things happen that I could never have predicted—the unexpected flashes of mystery, the unpredictable turns that a story takes. . . .

When I'm writing, I don't have everything planned out. I'm inclined to leave everything to the other side (*mukō*) once I take up the brush and finally start writing. By this, I mean that I try as much as possible to avoid forcing myself upon the work. (28: 699)

As borne out by "The Grass Labyrinth," one obvious result of letting go in this manner is a fragmented and impressionistic style. Clearly, Kyōka's responsiveness to the other side did not lend itself easily to a linear, carefully constructed plot or to lucid exposition, since the writer's stance vis-à-vis the source and matter of inspiration is supposedly passive and secondary. And yet this claim to be led by other powers must be reconciled with Tanizaki's admiration of Kyōka as one of a few Japanese writers who could structure a novel skillfully. As already mentioned, the powers to which he refers are neither random nor out of balance with each other.

Kyōka's suppression of the persona of the writer as manifested in a creative work must be understood in the context of the confessional I-novels that came to dominate Japanese literature at this time. The prominence of the I as narrator, an assertion of the function (if not the actual identity) of an author, is one of many aspects of the new literary culture that flourished with the rise of naturalism. The emergence of the confessional first-person narrative is, like the development of omniscient third-person narrative, the result of a new awareness of the imagination, heightened by the visual extravagance of image-laden, Edo-period gesaku texts that, in turn, engendered the phonocentric reaction of the genbun itchi movement. The "discovery of landscape" in the second, accelerated stage of Japan's modern development is but one aspect of this new awareness of the mind's ability to see and to control this power to imagine in ways that conform to ideological systems. The binary subject/object split that provided the basic structure for the dominant late-modern episteme was made necessary by conceptual systems that endow the viewer with astounding cognitive powers at precisely that atomizing and contradictory moment when the viewer gains authority by surrendering to larger systems of truth and verification (such as perspectivalism, nationalism, social Darwinism, and so forth). That so many Japanese writers gravitated to this position of first-person narration reflects, certainly, their sensitivity to this paradox, their reluctance to identify one's personal and localized vision with universal (third-person) systems. Kyōka's method of *mukō makase* is a similar denial of universality, but its nature is hybrid and complex, because it is simultaneously an affirmation of a higher order that rewards the will to power by fueling the needs of self-consciousness with the potencies of an ancient iconography. Despite the highly personal nature of his writing and despite his constant desire to formulate a narrative scheme that would allow him to pursue his eccentric vision, Kyōka did not write in the first person. This reluctance sets his work apart as being more openly artificial and fictional than those written by his peers.

Kyōka felt that the naturalists' focus on the unadorned truth was essentially unresponsive to the very source and purpose of art. The presumption that one could observe and copy reality without distortion resulted in a type of writing that is stilted and limited. And yet this vaguely articulated criticism of realism is not particularly well considered when we think of the ways in which the spontaneity of Kyōka's work is similarly contained by other measures of truth. As unpredictable as "letting go" might seem, it is still very much a river meandering within a well-defined floodplain. The syntax of images, though not used on every occasion, is far from arbitrary. In fact, what Kyōka called a lack of planning was possible precisely because, on a much deeper level, the foundations of personal myth and the traditional patterns of iconography that manifest themselves in his words were already firmly in place. As Noguchi Takehiko has argued, these forms established a grammar appropriate to the paratactic accumulation of these associative units.[1] This grammar allowed Kyōka to indulge in a remarkably consistent image of himself as mediated by the archetype. Like the writer, the protagonist is guided rather than guiding. Rather than suffer the trials of others, he is more often the cause of suffering. In sum, Kyōka's heroes are loved more than they love. If there is a lingering weakness, it is here.

Kyōka returned to Tokyo in February 1909. The short story "A Messenger from the Sea" ("Umi no shisha"), first published in July 1909, just after Kyōka's return to Tokyo, presents the clearest demonstration of the consequences of this passivity toward the other side. A story redolent of the watery coast of Zushi, "A Messenger from the Sea" was published not in *New Fiction* or one of the usual outlets, but in *Writing World* (*Bunshō sekai*), then being edited by Katai, who penned the journal's manifesto and continued as editor until 1913. Given *Writing World*'s steady support for the naturalists and Kyōka's reputation as a romantic, this particular matching of writer to publisher may seem surprising, but Kyōka published several pieces in Katai's magazine. To judge from their common concern for setting down one's ideas about writing, it is possible that "A Messenger from the Sea" was meant to be a demonstration of Kyōka's writing methods, however anti-naturalist in spirit.

There can be little agreement on this point, however, as long as the exact nature of this piece remains a matter of debate. One Japanese scholar feels that the story is essentially a *shasei bun* or literary sketch and, as such, was acceptable to Katai as an example of realistic writing.[2] At first reading, this assessment seems plausible. The piece does share many qualities with prose-sketches by such writers as Masaoka Shiki (1867–1902) and Sakamoto Shihōda (1873–1917): a relatively unimportant plot; a narrator who functions as an observer; and, most crucial, an objective, spare mode of descriptive writing. Compared with other of Kyōka's more fanciful and convoluted stories, "Messenger" does stand out as a possible, rare example of object-observing prose.

But Kyōka was adept at changing his style to suit his audience, and although he seems here to have accommodated the realists, a closer look at the story reveals the point at which he was unable to compromise. The manuscript especially gives clear evidence of his feel for language: what he believed words to be, and what he felt he as an artist could and could not do with them. Seemingly realistic in spirit but not actually so, "A Messenger from the Sea" is particularly important because it reveals the nature of Kyōka's style of realism and an understanding of language that separated him from most other writers of his time.

The plot of the story is simple. It is dusk and quickly growing dark. A man walks along the head of the Tagoe River. There are woods, patches of reeds, clouds in the sky, a cliff, and a Buddhist temple. There is water everywhere.

The narrator comes to a wooden bridge whose rotting timbers creak and cry like birds beneath his feet. Beyond the bridge, among the reeds, is a second bridge, nothing more than a plank thrown across a tidal pool. He begins to cross the water and notices a shape in the small pond. It moves, rises, sinks. It swims impudently across the reflection of his face on the water's surface. It is a jellyfish. To the narrator, however, it is an *umi bōzu*, a monstrous "ocean monk," which, according to legend, appears during storms at sea to assault the unaware. Angered by its audacity, the narrator plucks a reed and tries to impale it. The water suddenly begins to rise, forcing him to flee for the safety of the creaking bridge. The water eventually surrounds him. Riding the surge, the jellyfish waits by the bridge in anticipation. In the growing darkness, the moonlight shines brightly on the temple cliff. The story ends with this contrast of dark and light.

Believing in the sanctity of words, Kyōka carefully preserved his manuscripts. It is possible, therefore, to study his choices as a writer, and to know on a word-to-word basis how his stories were written. In this case, we can see how he worked to polish an earlier draft. A study of the original reveals that almost all the changes at the final stage of the manuscript's preparation were deletions rather than additions or lengthy rewritings. Punctuation, which was added liberally by others at later stages of the story's printed life, is the only exception. Practically all other changes indicate a process of paring.[3]

The significance of these processes is suggested by the deletion of the copula in three places: at 12:216.12, 12:217.9, and 12:218.6 (the numbers refer to volume, page, and line in the Iwanami *Kyōka zenshū*). These alterations truncate the sentences in which they occur, making them end with nouns. This common rhetorical device, *taigendome*, contributes to concision and enhances the resonating value of the nominal. *Hibiku oto de aru* (It was an echoing sound) becomes simply *hibiku oto* (echoing sound), to give one example.

This propensity to emphasize the sentence's nominal force is also enhanced by a second type of alteration: deletions of demonstrative adjectives, at 12:212.9, 12:213.11, 12:218.4, and their variations, at 12:216.3 (*sono mune ni*) and at 12:218.12 (*sono kage*). As words with little connotative strength of their own, *kono* and *sono* are extraneous, whether their function is to delimit (with *kono*) or to redelimit (with *sono*). These words function to indicate distance from the speaker. As crutches for ordering the writer's imagination, they are cast aside as the story assumes its shape and the author tries to rid the narrative of unnecessary limitations caused by the felt presence of a denoting narrator.

The point being contested in the manuscript is just this balance of limits. Through a third type of deletion—the trimming of superfluous explanation—Kyōka's choices of what and what not to limit become increasingly clear. At 12:216.13, for instance, the narrator is standing on the bridge, trying to determine the source of the birdlike song he hears. His statement "Ah, something is making the bridge boards squeak" (*Aa, hashi-ita ga dōkashita kikai de, kishimu n'da'* あゝ，橋板[はしいた]がどうかした機会[きかい]で、きしむんだ [the kana enclosed in brackets are *furigana* in the original]) is trimmed to "Ah, the bridge boards squeak" (*Aa, hashi-ita ga, kishimu n'da* あゝ、橋板[はしいた]が，きしむんだ). This small but important adjustment shows how Kyōka subverted discursive narration. Again, at 12:217.1, the narrator's description of the tidal pool, home of the jellyfish, was similarly trimmed to convey a sense of concreteness and presence by deleting the phrase "when the river runs" (*kawamizu no toki*) from "Only when the tide rose did it fill with water; when the river runs, the pond ebbs." (*Shio ga agete kita toki bakari, mizu o tataete, kawamizu no toki ni wa hite shimau* 汐[しほ]が上[あ]げて来[き]た時[とき]ばかり、水[みづ]湛[たた]へて、川水[かわみづ]の時[とき]には干[ひ]て了[しま]ふ). This trimming represents no loss of meaning since the phrase is replaced with the concise (and visually pleasing *kanji* for) *mamizu* (眞水[まみづ] "fresh water"). "When the tide rises, it fills with water, and at fresh water, the pond ebbs." Although the revised sentence is less descriptively clear, it is more vivid. Given a choice between clarity and emotional forcefulness, Kyōka consistently chose the latter.

Similar adjustments are found at 12:217.7, in a description of the plank bridge thrown over the pool. "It was nothing more than a plank, carried over, thrown down, and placed there for future use" (*Kore wa mata, wazuka ni ita o motte kite, nagesuete oki ni suginu* これは又[また]、纔[わづ]かに板[いた]を持[も]つて来[き]て、投[な]げ据[す]へておきに過[す]ぎぬ) becomes "It was nothing more than a plank, carried over and thrown down" (*Kore wa mata, wazuka ni ita o motte kite, nageta ni suginu* これは又[また]、纔[わづ]かに板[いた]を持[も]つて来[き]て、投[な]げたに過[す]ぎぬ). And at two different points, descriptions of the jellyfish are similarly altered: at 12:218.5, "Its overall color was a faded reddish yellow" (*zentai no iro ga usukaba de* 全體[ぜんたい]の色[いろ]が薄樺[うすかば]で) becomes "It was a faded reddish yellow" (*zentai ga usukaba de* 全體[ぜんたい]が薄樺[うすかば]で); at 12:218.9. "Without a bottom or middle or top, it fluttered in a straight line, having just put on flowing, sheer silk" (*usuginu o kaketa tokoro o katsuide* 薄衣[うすぎぬ]を掛[か]けた

ところを被[か]ついで) becomes "Without a bottom or middle or top, it fluttered in a straight line, wearing flowing, sheer silk" (*usuginu o katsuide* 薄衣[うすぎぬ]を被[か]ついで). Similarly, at 12:218.12 "It was small, but this pond" (*chiisaku wa atta ga, kono ike* ちいさくはあつたが、此[こ]の 池[いけ]) is reduced to "This pond" (*kono ike* 此[こ]の池[いけ]). The effects of these changes are to remove judgments that could only be made by the narrator ('placed for future use,' 'small') and to eliminate any dilution of the description ('its overall color,' 'having just put on').

By making such changes, Kyōka was trying to make the reader experience a scene as directly as possible. The task, of course, is difficult since a narrator is required and the reader's access to what this narrator sees cannot be direct. There are, however, ways to limit the sense of mediation rather than strengthen it, as required (though often disguised) by the perspectival conceits of representational discourse. If, as shown in the examples given above, discursive comment about things external to the narrator is restricted, so too are comments about the narrator's perception. This fourth category of deletion does away with the distracting workings of his mind; and consequently *de wa nai ka to omou* (I was inclined to think; 12:212.4), *yappari* (just as I thought; 12:214.3), *nani* (what?; 12:214.10), and *nani gokoro naku* (with no specific purpose; 12:217.14) all disappear beneath the author's revising brush. What the narrator feels (or, more precisely, what the writer feels about what the narrator feels) is irrelevant in a narrative that above all seeks direct, unanalyzed access to the power of words.

The relative unimportance of the narrator's analyzed emotion is emphasized by a fifth type of deletion in the manuscript. Again, the narrator must be present: he is the eye through which we see, and, no less important, he is the principal actor in the story's dramatic situation. Yet Kyōka consistently strikes out words that call attention to the narrator's functions. With the view of the reeds and woods before him, with the rotting planks of the bridge beneath his feet, the narrator decides to commit himself to more adventures: "and when I finally stepped forward one step, again came the cry *kiriri*" (*yagate hitoashi fumidasu, to mata kiririri to naita* やがてひと足[あし]踏出[ふみだ]す、 と又[また] きりりりりと鳴[な]いた). Kyōka later reduced this to "and when I finally stepped forward, again came the cry *kiriri*" (*yagate fumidasu, to mata kiririri to naita* やがて踏出[ふみだ]す、 と又[また]きりりりりと鳴[な]いた; 12: 213.1–2). "One step" is one detail too many. At 12:213.8, the verb "to step" (*fumu*) is deleted for the same reason. And at the story's climax, as the narrator flees

toward the bridge (12:221.13), the adverb "hastily" (*awatadashiku*) is crossed out
to ensure that the emotional content of the description is not weakened by a
facile comment about the one who is also playing the part of describer.[4]

These changes are more than simply matters of concision, and Kyōka is
doing more than what any stylist might do. The question of how he went about
editing the text opens us up to other elements of the text that suggest much
more is happening. In other words, to understand this process of editing as
simply a matter of concision would be to ignore a distinctive and important
aspect of Kyōka's epistemology. Through the various deletions mentioned
above, Kyōka was trying to delimit the narrator rather severely because the
existence of a seer within the text limits access to what is being seen: not an
external landscape but words themselves. In this case, the words are objects in
themselves, words as pictures. Their referential aspect is weakened in favor of
what has been called an "impressionistic" method of establishing narrative
space, a tendency found even in overtly realistic writing that modulates the
fictional strength of late-modern Japanese prose.[5]

Finally, Kyōka's response to the word as an image is also supported by the
manner in which the story holds together thematically. By looking at the manuscript, we discover that the water and moon imagery, warp and woof of "A
Messenger from the Sea," both come from a single word, *kurage* (jellyfish),
which is a compound of two Chinese characters for ocean and moon (海月).
The story's various water images—the sea along the Shōnan Coast, the Tagoe
River, saltwater, freshwater, tidal pool, the quickly rising tide that threatens the
narrator at the end of the story, and the jellyfish itself—are brought to life
through the metamorphosis of the original word/image. As a study of this
manuscript illustrates, Kyōka achieved access to the story's deepest levels by
transforming one word into another.

Kyōka's alterations at 12:221.10, for instance, are especially crucial because
they mark the beginning of the story's catastrophe—the point at which the
identity of the jellyfish (or the narrator's emotional perception of that identity)
is transformed. In the Iwanami text the sentence reads: "The voice of the water
was heard, as if shooting through the surf, galloping along" (*to yagoe o kakete, shio
o ite kakeru ga gotoku, mizu no koe ga kikinasaruru*   と矢聲[やごゑ]を
懸[か]けて、潮[しほ]を射[い]て駈[か]けるが如[ごと]く、水[みづ]の聲
[こゑ]が聞[きき]なさるる). But originally Kyōka had something else in mind:
it was the jellyfish's voice, not the water's, that the narrator heard. The manuscript once read: "The jellyfish shouted out, the jellyfish shot through the surf"

(*to [kurage ga] yagoe o kakete, [kurage ga] shio o ite kakeru ga gotoku, mizu no koe ga kikinasaruru*   と海月[くらげ]が矢聲[やごえ]を懸[か]けて、海月[くらげ]が潮[しほ]を射[い]て駈[か]けるが如[ごと]く、水[みづ]の聲[こゑ]が聞[きき]なさるる). *Kurage*, indicated by my brackets, is written and then crossed out twice, so that, in the end, the voice becomes the ocean's not the jellyfish's.

In understanding this change, we must consider the visual component of the words, how 海月 has become 海, how one word has formed from another. Calling this a metamorphosis of language, a bakemono-esque transformation, might seem an exaggeration of common poetic practice. Certainly, we must wonder about the extent to which one word can form from another rather than simply connote another. That is to say, the propagation of imagery might be understood more simply as a coming together of related elements rather than as a creation of new ones from old. This prudent sense of poetics follows from our experience with alphabetic writing systems that predispose us to think that the ties between words are abstract, that they are bound to each other primarily by semantics, phonetics, and grammar rather than by their physical and visual characteristics. Since we think of words in alphabetical writing systems as essentially transcriptive of what some have called the logos, these systems tend to camouflage the materiality of words. Through their simplifications, they deny the corporeality of language and reduce the physical presence of the grapheme to a by-product of signification. Although this phonocentric regard for scripts tends to dismiss the word's physical mutability and, therefore, any linguistic patterns that might follow from it, a visual poetics of language, where words belong together because they *look* alike, not only exists but strongly supports what we know about Kyōka's fetishistic regard for the word as image. Given the author's words about the "concretization of emotion," the power of visual connotation also helps to explain his emotionalist attitude toward the process of description.

Even if the phonocentric supplanting of illustration and pre-modern iconography forced Kyōka to do without pictures and to work within a cultural context that favored the realists, Kyōka had only to look at the words on the page to see that the outlawed monsters of the gesaku tradition were still at hand. Kyōka discovered that the visual wealth of the pictocentric tradition had taken refuge in the body of language. In the sentence that follows the previous quotation, the jellyfish, whose voice just became the ocean's, begins releasing light from its body "like a pine torch lit in the dragon's palace" (*To miru to, ryūgū no taimatsu o tomoshita yō ni, kare no karada ga donyori to hikari o hanatta*

と見[み]ると、龍宮[りうぐう]の松火[たいまつ]を灯[とも] したやうに、
彼[かれ]の身體[からだ]がどんより光[ひかり]を放[はな]つた; 12:221.10).
What is happening here? Having become the ocean, the jellyfish now turns into
the moon; thus, its luminous powers. Still later the jellyfish will change into an
umi bōzu 海坊主, whose shaven head is, in like fashion, an image of brilliance
and roundness.

The point to understand here is that all these words evolve from each other
because of their visual qualities, whether of the image *as* the word, or of the
image *of* the word. That is to say, 海月 becomes 月, which suggests the moon-
headed 海坊主. A close look at Kyōka's writing reveals the extent of artifice in
this narrative that has been able to pass as a realistic sketch. It is realistic in the
sense that the story expresses Kyōka's word-bound sense of the real. Having
access to the manuscript, we come to grasp how profoundly "A Messenger from
the Sea" is a game of language. For example, the first mention of the moon, the
second part of the word *kurage*, occurs early in the story, as the narrator describes the cliff below the Genmu Temple. In the darkening evening, the cliff
glows "as if the moon were dwelling within." This association of cliff, temple,
and moon is echoed in the final line of the story: "On the whetstone surface of
the Genmu Temple cliff, the moonlight suddenly flashed" (*Genmuji no itadaki
naru to no gotoki iwao no omo e, tsukikage ga satto sashi* 玄武寺[げんむじ]の
頂[いただき]なる砥[と]の如[ごと]き巖[いはほ]の面[おも]へ、月影[つき
かげ]が颯[さっ]とさした). Within this frame of moon imagery, the metamorphosis of the jellyfish into an umi bōzu and a number of other more subtly
handled references to the lunar images are contained.

The first of these occurs at 12:220.10 with a phrase "floating and sinking"
(浮[う]いつ沈[しづ]みつ ; *uitsu shizumitsu*), which brings to mind a famous
scene from the *Tale of the Heike* (*Heike monogatari*) in which the Genji bowman
Nasu no Yoichi dashes out into the waters at Yashima on horseback to shoot
down a fan held aloft by a Taira lady. The red fan is decorated with a gold sun,
which Kyōka perhaps associated with the moon image. As the waves move the
Taira boat, the fan bobs up and down (*uitsu shizumitsu*), like the jellyfish in the
tidal pool. Yoichi pierces it with his arrow and wins everyone's praise, quite
unlike Kyōka's anti-hero whose reed misses its mark. In "A Messenger," the
narrator leaves himself open to reprisal. The waters rush. He runs for safety.

The second and more obvious indirect reference to the moon is an incomplete quotation of one of Mukai Kyorai's (1651–1704) verses. At 12:217.14, a line
mentioned earlier, the narrator crouches on the plank and peers down into the

tidal pool. "Here, too, am I at the cliff's edge, as if sitting on a bench, leisurely gazing down at the incoming tide" (*Iwabana ya, koko ni mo hitori, to, suzumidai ni kaketa yō ni, soko ni ite, sashite kuru shio o nagamete shibaraku tatta* 岩端[いはばな] や、ここにも一人[ひとり]、と、納涼臺[すずみだい]に掛[か]けたや うに、其處[そこ]に居[い]て、さして来[く]る汐[しほ]を視[なが]めて 少時[しばらく]經[た]つた). Kyorai's poem reads: "The edge of the cliff / here too is one / viewer of the moon" (*Iwabana ya, koko ni mo hitori, tsuki no kyaku* 月の客). The phrase *tsuki no kyaku* (moon viewer) is omitted from Kyōka's sentence, but the author's reason for including a fragment of the poem is obvious: to the eyes of Kyōka's narrator, jellyfish and moon are interchangeable manifestations of the same linguistic matter.

In sum, "A Messenger from the Sea" is essentially an interweaving of the two parts of the jellyfish's body: ocean and moon. It is Kyōka's visual response to the word *kurage*, a bakemono, a concretization of his emotions. If *The Holy Man of Mt. Kōya* established the structural archetype and intimated, especially in its waterfall scene, the type of language that would be required for the fullest expression of the archetype, this obscure but important story, written in response to the theoretical musings of the naturalists, marks Kyōka's rigorous refinement of that language. Having affirmed the visual playfulness of words in this radical way, his methods as an artist were now developed enough to allow him the confidence to return to the theme of love and to write brilliantly of its confluence with art. The result would be *A Song by Lantern Light* (*Uta andon*, 1910), his most accomplished work to date and a story thought by many to be his finest.

Kuwana, Art, Love

Kyōka's new home in Tokyo was located at Kojimachi Dote 3 Banchō. The small, single-story house had four rooms and was situated at the base of a cliff dressed with a wall of fitted stone. Atop the cliff was a mansion. Kyōka's house, hidden in the shadows below, was built in a slight depression and rarely caught the direct rays of the sun. The surrounding garden was small, approximately twelve square yards.

In the Banchō house, Kyōka saw less of the sky and none of the picturesque Shōnan Coast. Still, he was content to be back in Tokyo. This was the time of new beginnings, not only for him but for many others who had also become weary of the tenets of naturalism and were ready to try different methods and to propose new purposes for the narrative arts. The vitality of this movement is evident in the way coterie journals flourished over the next three years. In

January 1909, Mori Ōgai began *Pleiades* (*Subaru*). In October of the same year, Kitahara Hakushū (1885–1942) established *The Roof Garden* (*Okujō no teien*). In April 1910, Mushanokōji Saneatsu (1885–1976) organized *The White Birch* (*Shirakaba*). The following month saw the beginning of Nagai Kafū's *Mita Literature* (*Mita bungaku*). In September 1910, *The New Current* (*Shin shichō*), which had been idle for a time, resumed publication with Osanai Kaoru's selection of Tanizaki Jun'ichirō's "The Tattoo" ("Shisei"). The following year, 1911, Hiratsuka Raichō (1886–1971) was instrumental in bringing about *Blue Stockings* (*Seitō*), which became an important outlet for writing by women.

Kyōka's most formal affiliation with this countermovement was the Literature and Art Reformation Society (*Bungei kakushin kai*), which was established in March 1909, after his return from Zushi. Gotō Chūgai, editor of *New Fiction*, was its founder and the author of its charter. Kyōka dubbed the monthly gathering the "Kinpira kai," after Gotō's given name, and the term quickly gained currency among the other members. Tobari Chikufū, the playwright, and Hirezaki Eihō were among the members. So was Sasakawa Rinpū, whom Kyōka personally invited to join. Most of the members, however, were critics rather than artists and writers, and as the years passed and the group's influence waned, Kyōka found himself mixing more frequently with members of the *Mita bungaku* crowd—especially Minakami Takitarō (1887–1940), Kubota Mantarō, and Satomi Ton (1888–1983)—who were a generation or so younger.

The Literature and Art Reformation Society, like *New Fiction*, reflected Gotō's objection to the (naturalistic) notion of writing about reality without the guidance of ideals. Hoping to come up with an antidote for the poisons of naturalism, the members of this group made a number of lecture tours into the provinces. Although the efficacy of such forays proved to be limited, it was while traveling in the company of like-minded persons—Chūgai and Rinpū, especially—that Kyōka found himself freed of the emotional weight that had forced him to take refuge in Zushi. Writing about a trip to Kuwana, Chūgai described a relaxed and even entertaining Izumi Kyōka.

Kyōka got drunk and demonstrated what he had just learned about eating clams from one of the waitresses. He would tickle the underside of the clam shell with his fingertips and strangely enough the meat would come out of its shell without a fight. Fascinated by this newly learned skill, he would tickle clam after clam. Everyone roared with laughter.[6]

While on a trip to Ise, from November 18 to November 25, Kyōka came upon a sight that was, to use the phrasing of "Letting Go," the new combined with the old. According to Chūgai's account, the group reached Kuwana late one moonlit November evening. They got off the train at Kuwana Station, then traveled by rickshaw to an inn at the head of the Ibi River.[7] It is with a description of this scene that Kyōka begins his famous *A Song by Lantern Light.*

On a cold night in mid-January, there came the sound of a single muffled voice reading from Book 5, Part I, of Ikku's famous *Shank's Mare.*

> Many were the sights and tastes that delighted our two travelers as they viewed the massive, *daikon*-shaped pillars of the sacred Atsuta Shrine and partook of the local cuisine: boiled radishes cooked with miso. Continuing on, they ferried themselves over seven miles of choppy waters until they arrived with thankful hearts in the safe harbor of Kuwana on the Bay of Ise . . .

> The sky was clear, the stars bright enough for a night of cold-water ablutions. As two travelers crossed the bridge over the railroad tracks, their shadows stretched out over the moonlit landscape. They exited the Kuwana Station, looking at the flickering lanterns of the town and at the forms of the winter-stripped trees that appeared here and there before them. (12: 596)

This night scene of Kuwana, lying cold and still in the moonlight, reveals much about Kyōka's rendering of the natural world. Blended with passages from Ikku's *Shank's Mare*, the well-known Edo-period travelogue about two comic figures making their way from Edo to Kyoto, this description establishes a textual site for the lyrical fusing of emotion and nature. Kyōka wrote of the need for just such an imaginative understanding of the natural world in "Truth's Foundation, Imagination's Embellishment" ("Jijitsu no kontei, sōzō no junshoku," 1909).

> When looking at nature, a scene of extraordinary beauty is sometimes created when the writer's mind is allowed to figure into it. This is the imagination at work. Needless to say, I do not agree with those who feel that the imagination can be excluded from a work of art. It is impossible to create art by simply setting down what is there, exactly as it is. (28: 733)

This opening description of moonlight introduces the first of forty-six occurrences of the word "moon" throughout the eighty or so pages of this story. As a part of nature, the image blends with three other "texts" and cannot be separated from the question that Kyōka is pursuing: love and the role that art plays in making love possible. From the Zushi period, the harmonious blending of art and nature is a hallmark of Kyōka's fiction.

Again, the sight of Kuwana at night can be considered one of those new stimuli about which Kyōka wrote when describing his writing method as a process of mukō makase. The original germ for the story, the old material slowly incubating in his mind, was the ostracism of a famous young Noh actor, who was cut off by his family because of his extreme arrogance.[8] Kyōka no doubt had this incident in mind when he was later inspired by the sight of the town at night. Upon seeing the moonlit scene, he returned to Tokyo and began writing immediately, finishing the manuscript in a month's time. The story appeared in the New Year's edition of *New Fiction*. A preview in the December issue of *New Fiction* gives the title as *The Diver's Dance (Ama no mai)*, suggesting that he might have had the story's final scene, a rendition of the Noh play *The Diver (Ama)*, in mind even before he embarked with Chūgai, Chikufū, and Rinpū on the lecture tour. The title that Kyōka first wrote on the manuscript was *Song of Hakata (Hakata uta)*, which was crossed out and replaced with *Uta andon*.[9] The new title, which literally means "Song Lantern," indicates an emphasis on setting and reflects the impression that the sight of Kuwana's streets at night, dimly lit by the glowing paper lanterns and by the moon shining above, had on Kyōka. The progression from *Ama no mai* to *Hakata uta* to *Uta andon* helps us read the enigmatic "Song Lantern." The Hakata song, which is sung by the protagonist Kidahachi, is like the moonlight that falls upon the dimly glowing lanterns that hang eerily in the night-stilled streets of Kuwana.[10] It is this melding of song and moonlight, and their envelopment of the lantern (a death image), that provides the grounding for the work's notable lyricism.

Kuwana became the stage upon which Kyōka made his characters act out a number of text-bound performances. The one we encounter at the very beginning is patterned after that section of *Shank's Mare* in which Ikku's protagonists Kitahachi and Yajirōbei arrive in this small town near Ise. Kyōka never tired of *Shank's Mare*. In fact, he carried this book about travel and the sorts of adventures one might encounter as a "charm against evil spirits" (*mayoke*) whenever he traveled (27: 530). Here he used Ikku to establish a lighthearted mood, which gradually darkens as the allusions shift to another text. Even as Ikku's work provided comic relief, however, Kyōka is using lightness to foreshadow anguish. He is preparing us for a later allusion to the passage in which Kitahachi and Yajirōbei become separated in Ise Yamada. From the beginning, he is setting the reader up on a deep and almost hidden level for Onchi Kidahachi's solitary travail and his estrangement from his uncle, Onchi Genzaburō.

The other text that Kyōka incorporated at length is the Noh play *The Diver*, whose images of water, blood, and jewels (*tama*) reintroduce the familiar Kyō-kaean motif of a mother's sacrifice for her son. This play, in which a woman dives to the bottom of the ocean (the land of the dead) and cuts open her belly in order to secure the success of her son, is a classical inspiration for the arche-type. That one of Kyōka's most powerful works should end with a dance from this play follows naturally from his obsession with the process of trespass into watery territory. Beyond this, the inclusion of the play also expresses the esteem that Kyōka had for his mother's family, who were professional Noh musicians of the Kadono school. The Noh drama also provides structure. As Yoshida Seiichi pointed out long ago, much of Kyōka's work follows the *jo-ha-kyū* (in-troduction, development, and frenzied denouement) pace suggested by Zeami, starting slowly and building in tempo and intensity toward a climax, as we have already seen in, for instance, "The Grass Labyrinth."

These connections aside, perhaps the most important debt that Kyōka owed to the Noh theater is its ontology. Highly allusive and intertextual, the Noh text establishes a world in which both the fusion and confusion of linguistic and ontological elements is not only possible but absolutely essential to its artistic and philosophical intent. Consider, for instance, how a banana plant might serve as the protagonist of a play, the realm of sentient beings being extended to include the world of plants and other material objects. In Kyōka's own words, "In the Noh plays, it is often the case that nature is the protagonist (*shite*) and human beings the deuteragonist (*waki*)" (28: 734). Ultimately, it is this sense of equality that grounds the polysemic and allusive texture of this work, with the result that, like a well-written Noh play, everything about *A Song by Lantern Light* seems to fit, even if in unexpected combinations. Simply put, this story is a remarkably rich synthesis of things that Kyōka handled well as a writer: the lyricism of *Teriha Kyōgen*, the mystery and metamorphosis of *The Holy Man of Mt. Kōya* and "One Day in Spring," and the world of the geisha as in *Worship at Yushima, A Woman's Pedigree*, and "The White Heron" ("Shira-sagi," 1909).

To return to an earlier point, Kuwana allowed this to happen. The town at night supplied Kyōka with a setting that was more than simply a setting. As stated in "The True Value of Description" ("Byōsha no shinka," 1909) and suggested by the spate of essays about writing that he set down in 1908 and 1909, a setting should be something more than merely a "prop" (*dōgu*). The space of a story is as important as the characters residing within it and should be kept in balance with them. Indeed, because the choice of setting usually precedes and, therefore, determines the creation of a story's characters, setting is in a way more crucial. For Kyōka, it establishes a fictive space that allows access to something other than observable reality. Thus Kyōka's credo: "I don't want to limit myself to describing reality as reality. I want to go through reality to gain access to a much greater power" (28: 696).

A Song by Lantern Light is a demonstration of just such an attempt to go beyond the observable to tap greater powers. In this case, those forces are love and art, as manifested in both their destructive and their restorative potential. Because of art, Kidahachi contributes to the suicide of a blind artist named Shōzan whose inflated reputation as a local Noh performer angers him. Kida-hachi is a haughty young man who has studied at the knees of Japan's masters from his childhood. While visiting Kuwana, he secretly seeks Shōzan out and listens to him perform. He makes a fool of the blind man before his own daughter, and as a result Shōzan hangs himself, leaving a suicide note in which he curses Kidahachi's posterity to the seventh generation. When his uncle and mentor, the famous Noh performer Onchi Genzaburō, learns of this incident, he disowns Kidahachi, who is left to make a living as an impecunious street musician.

Art has the power to kill. It can lead to estrangement and poverty. On the other hand, it is only through art that Kidahachi demonstrates his remorse and achieves atonement. He gives his knowledge and skill, and therefore his love, to the hapless Osode, Shōzan's daughter. After her father's death, she is sold by her mother-in-law to become Omie. As a geisha, she lives a life of constant suffering. She is not especially talented and has no art to offer her customers. She also suffers in her role as a geisha because she takes seriously Kidahachi's earlier warning to her: "Even if it means your life, never let yourself become a man's plaything" (12: 670). He wrongly thought she was Shōzan's mistress. Upon encountering her after her father's death, he learns of her misfortune and agrees to teach her his art. In the very grove where her father hung himself from a pine tree, he secretly instructs her. He becomes a "demon." Possessed by his work, he shoves and positions her body with his own hands. They eventually part. She has received his gift, however, and it is through her perfect perform-ance of the jewel-taking dance of *The Diver* that he is later reunited with her and with his uncle.

This moment of reconciliation unfolds at the Minatoya, an inn near the river's mouth. Following a performance in Ise, Onchi Genzaburō and Henmi Hidenoshin, otherwise known as Sessō, a famous Noh drummer, are staying the night in Kuwana on their way back to Tokyo. Calling himself Yajirōbei after Jippensha Ikku's famous character, Genzaburō talks his partner into calling in a geisha to relieve the loneliness of the evening. It turns out that all but one, Omie, are already engaged at a farewell party being held for a group of young soldiers about to go off to war. Omie makes her appearance but has little to offer in the way of expected amusements. She cannot sing. She cannot play an instrument well. She can do only one thing: a dance from the Noh play *The Diver*.

This is an unexpected accomplishment for someone of her profession. Before these men, who doubt her truthfulness, she begins the diver's dance. Stunned by the strength of her performance, Genzaburō realizes that there is only one person in the world who could have taught her this dance so well. They question her and learn how she met and was instructed by a certain street musician who pitied her. When she resumes the dance, Genzaburō and Sessō accompany her in honor of the noble act of repentance that Kidahachi has done. Sitting in a noodle shop not far away, the drunken Kidahachi hears their music. He hurries to the Minatoya. Standing outside the inn, he begins to sing, reunited through this performance not only with Omie but with his uncle as well. Knowing that he has been forgiven, he is able by way of his song to vanquish the ghost of Shōzan that has been a constant and haunting presence.

If *A Song by Lantern Light* is steadily and simply focused on these modulations of love, the manner of presentation is anything but straightforward. Bringing together such a wealth of material—the ostracism of a young Noh actor, Kuwana at night, the Hakata folk song, Ikku's *Shank's Mare*, and the Noh play—Kyōka organizes these sources within a complicated structure of two interweaving plots that, because of their extreme effectiveness in combination, won him a reputation as one of the few Japanese novelists who knew how to structure a novel.[11] The two stories flow concurrently from two different sites: one is the noodle shop, where Kidahachi relates the story of his past to the shopkeeper's wife; the other is the nearby Minatoya, where Onchi Genzaburō and his traveling partner are staying the night. The narrative focus shifts back and forth in linked-verse fashion, one unit playing off an association or image presented in the previous one. In addition, the two narratives are made more complex by the various flashbacks related at both places. At the noodle shop, where Kidahachi is sitting with a blind masseur, he tells of how he visited the blind man's home to hear him perform and explains why he considers himself the enemy of all blind masseurs. At the inn, not far down the darkened street, Omie responds to Genzaburō's request and relates the details of her trials as an artless geisha and how she was pitied by Kidahachi, who led her into the woods and secretly taught her to dance the jewel-taking scene from *The Diver*.

Kyōka develops these two strands a chapter or two at a time, shifting from one to the other. But in the final chapter, as the tempo of the narrative quickens, both come together. The reader progresses from the witty repartee of the comical world of Ikku to the solemn mystery of the Noh theater, from a railroad station and the world of mass transportation to the Dragon's Palace at the bottom of the sea. Heightened by this transition and gradual development, the final scene is accelerated in pace and charged with the joy of reunion and reconciliation.

"Listen!" exclaimed a single voice. As he looked in the direction of the Minatoya, Onchi Kidahachi, rising star of the Noh theater, obscured by exile, rose from the stool where he had been sitting and placed one foot down on the dirt-floored entryway of the noodle shop. "That's Sessō playing his drum!" He leaned forward and held his chest. Grabbing a towel, he quickly covered his mouth and coughed up a spot of blood. He threw the towel down and grabbed the blind masseur by the right arm. "Curse me if you want, Blind Man. But you're coming with me to the Minatoya! This is what you've been waiting for. Now you'll have your performance." He jerked the masseur to his feet, and together they quickly stepped into the moonlight.

Coming to them from down the street was the sound of Genzaburō's voice, singing the accompaniment to Omie's dance.

> Down into the waters deep
> Down to where the dead ones sleep,
> I looked about and there I saw
> The gleaming tower of jade.
> In it lay the precious jewel
> 'Mid flowers bright and beautiful,
> With guardian gods there keeping watch,
> Eight dragons at the gate.
> Wicked fish and crocodiles
> Swarming 'round with vicious smiles,
> How was I to stay alive,
> To taste the breath of day?

> 'Twas no surprise when came to me
> Thoughts of home and family,
> Memories of my foolish son,
> Amid the crashing waves.

At that moment, the intense feelings of her heart overflowed. And the knot of her coiffure came undone, and her lustrous black hair spilled over her shoulders. Tortured by the waters, illuminated by the flickering lantern light, she made each movement with utter perfection as she danced upon the *tatami* floor, an ocean clearly shining against the train of her kimono.

> I know my son remains alive,
> So does his father yet survive.
> Still, parting thus
> Brings sadness great to bear.

Remembering the one he had vowed never to remember again, Genzaburō became choked with emotion. His voice began to fail. But just then, from outside the Minatoya, came the voice of another, resonating in the room, taking up the melody just where it had begun to fade. Like a rainbow, the voice suddenly flooded Omie with a white brilliance as she struggled to continue the dance.

Now it was Kidahachi, her beloved, singing to her every movement.

> Tears now rushing to her eyes,
> With resolve she starts to rise . . .

"This is it. Don't falter now." Genzaburō suddenly rose from his seat and steadied Omie's back with his hand. Gaining confidence, she placed the wave-patterned sleeve of her kimono on the old man's arm and quickly brought her fan up and touched it to her dark, glistening hair. The clouds painted on the silver fan met with the shadow of her lover, reflecting a brilliant light that made the lanterns dimly flicker as she continued.

Dance the dance! Sing the song! Joining the secret notes of Sessō's accompaniment, the waters of Kuwana Bay sounded like a thunderous drum, and the river nearby added the higher pitch of lapping waves. Towering in the moon light, as if seated around a stage, the snow-covered peaks of Mt. Tado, Gozaisho, Mt. Kama, and Kamuri witnessed the performance.

The night was still. The town of Kuwana cold and frozen. Listening to the final notes of the flute that traveled through the wintry sky, Onchi Kidahachi found himself alone. Singing beneath the shadows of the Minatoya's eaves, his silhouette was blue and his shadow dark. The moon that brightened the roof tiles splashed his face with the silvery light of a fan. One fan touching another, two sides of the same, Kidahachi and Omie joined together.

She brought her hands together in prayer, as he continued the song.

> "Extend to me your saving light,
> Through the course of this black night,
> Let your powers join with mine,
> Oh, Kannon, Merciful One."
> To her head, she touched the blade,
> Now left, now right, all guardians fade,
> With steps ahead, death's price now paid,
> Into the Dragon's Palace!

Here the singing and dancing stopped.

"Carry me home, Shōzan." The exhausted Onchi Kidahachi, having performed before the dead man's ghost, seemed to climb upon the back of the large, shapeless shadow that had been crouching next to his legs. Finally, he had vanquished his enemy.

Such was the song of lanterns, such was this tale of moonlight. The moon-brightened road leading away from the inn was a white line, set off by lanterns flickering dimly here and there. In the darkness was a crowd of people, among them blind men walking with sticks. (12: 675–77)

The reunion of Kidahachi, Omie, and Genzaburō is mediated by art. They do not actually meet each other, except through their common performance, and the story's conclusion suggests that they will never come together again, face to face. Sick yet vindicated, Kidahachi will continue his wanderings until he dies. But there has been a spiritual meeting of hearts, and the effect of their joint performance of the diver's sacrifice is clear. Realizing that Kidahachi is penitent, Genzaburō expresses his forgiveness when he sings the words "my son" (*waga ko*). He also accepts Omie, referring to her as Kidahachi's wife. Omie, in turn, realizes more fully that Kidahachi's art has become a part of her and that the dance is an expression of his love. Finally, Kidahachi, having performed before the ghost of Shōzan, is able to overcome the curse that has plagued him since his disinheritance. He defeats the monstrous blind man, a manifestation of his own feelings of guilt and regret, by singing about this mother who is willing to do anything for the sake of her beloved son. This is done, of course, in accordance with a familiar requirement: the salvation of a young man that requires the presence of a beautiful woman and the endless love of an equally beautiful mother.

The concluding lines of this story have long been a puzzle for readers, since it is not clear who we are seeing or from what perspective we are seeing them. Given the structure of the narrative and the emphasis upon the setting as a means to express the transcendence of love and art, the anonymity of the "crowds," probably those who have come to bid farewell to young soldiers, and of the blind masseurs working the streets, is most likely a final salute to the moonlit landscape of Kuwana. It is as if the camera moves back and opens with a wide lens for one last look at the larger picture, a world in which the sighted go off to kill and the blind remain behind to give pleasure to the body.[12] In Tōgō Katsumi's words, it is as if Kyōka meant to frame the story in order to draw attention to its perfection. It is as if he wanted to say to the naturalists, "Look at this. This is the power of art."[13]

CHAPTER 13

A Space for the Dispossessed

1910–1923

The Banchō House

Kyōka and Suzu moved once again in May 1910, this time to Kojimachi Shimo 6 Banchō 11. The house would be Kyōka's home for the next twenty-nine
years, until his death in 1939. It was a two-story, wooden structure, situated
directly across a narrow street from the Arishima Mansion, Satomi Ton's large
complex of high walls and spacious gardens and a stark contrast to Kyōka's
modest yet "chic private dwelling, appropriate for a trueborn gesakusha."[1] One
entered by opening a latticed door and stepping up from the street into a small
portico, which is shown in Fig. 15. A cabinet for shoes was on the right, and
to the left was the entrance into a small, three-mat room in which the telephone
and a small bookcase were kept. Dangling from the ceiling was a square
paper lantern, on which were written in green the character for Izumi and Kyōka's *genji-kō* or incense mark. This emblem denotes the "Autumn Excursion"
chapter of *The Tale of Genji* and was an obvious allusion to Ozaki Kōyō's pen
name, "Autumn Leaves." The poet Yoshii Isamu (1886–1960), a frequent visitor
to the Banchō house, phrased the sympathy between door and lantern in this
way:

The lattice door of Kyōka's house opens.
Hearing the sound,
Again afresh, the autumn night.[2]

Straight ahead was a four-mat tea room furnished with a long hibachi, a low table, and a cupboard. Directly above, cracks in the ceiling boards were covered with strips of white paper that Kyōka and Suzu had pasted there to prevent dust and rat droppings from sifting through. Dangling near the lightbulb in the middle of the room was a dried ear of corn, there to protect the house from thunder and lightning. In the left corner was the Buddhist altar, and to the right a flight of steep wooden steps. Through the sliding door to the right was an eight-mat sitting room, furnished with a standing mirror and a chest of drawers. In one corner was the god-shelf to which Kyōka paid obeisance each morning. Directly ahead, behind another set of doors, was the cooking area, brightened by a skylight and equipped with a refrigerator, a sink, and a gas burner. Here, shelves for the storage of food were designed to be taken down every night so that rodents and insects could not crawl over them. Access to the bathing and toilet areas was through a sliding door in the back of the kitchen. The urinal was covered over with a sheet of paper so it could not be used. (Kyōka could not abide the thought of stray drops splashing on the walls or floor. In fact, he especially hated the flush urinals of the sort found in Tokyo's buildings and would catch a cab home to urinate in the cleanliness and privacy of his own home.)[3] Behind the house, visible from the eight-mat room and enclosed by a tall bamboo fence, was a small backyard, which contained a bird-house for sparrows and a pole for drying clothes.

The steps to the second floor were steep and narrow. They were washed down with three separate rags: one for the top third, one for the middle third, and another for the bottom third. (The rationale here was that the heavily used stairs were too dusty to be thoroughly cleaned by one rag alone.) The second floor was divided into one 4-mat room at the top of the stairs and one 8-mat room accessible through a wall of sliding doors. The four-mat room usually contained nothing in the way of furnishings except a folding screen covered with gold foil and decorated with the colorful covers of Ryūtei Tanehiko's *The Fake Murasaki, the Rustic Genji*. The larger room, Kyōka's study, was arranged so that he could look up from his writing table into the Arishima garden. He sat on a thick cushion and faced a wall of four shoji and glass doors that could be opened to let in the light and air. To his left was a stand, a lamp, a hibachi, and a wooden box that contained his smoking pipe and a supply of the small, colorful paper tubes that Suzu made to cover the mouthpiece of the pipe. These tubes, like the paper covers that also lined the urinal downstairs and other points in the house that others were likely to touch, were for sanitary purposes. All such paper covers were replaced at regular intervals so the house would stay germfree. To his right was a long table covered with a dark cloth. On the cloth were two cases that held his ink and writing brushes, a small, blue glass vial that contained the water he used to sanctify his manuscript pages, and two crystal rabbits. Many other rabbit figurines, large and small, sat in front of the staggered shelves (*chigaidana*) that filled the space next to the alcove. Kyōka was born in the year of the cock, whose opposite sign is the rabbit. Convinced that he would be protected from danger if he collected specimens of his opposite sign, he eventually acquired an impressive number of rabbits.

It was to this home, beginning from around 1916, that a number of the most prominent writers of the next generation began to visit regularly. Their numbers included Satomi Ton, Minakami Takitarō, Tanizaki Jun'ichirō, Kubota Mantarō, Yoshii Isamu, Satō Haruo (1892–1964), and admirers who "gaily opened the door to the reclusive life of a somber Izumi Kyōka."[4] Although famous for both his fastidiousness and parsimoniousness—when Kyōka went out drinking with his friends, either someone paid for him or everybody paid for his own—he showed a real interest in these men and welcomed them into his home (so long as they did not make a mess). He was an important figure for these writers, who found the extreme realism of the naturalists wanting; he was someone of similar artistic sentiment around whom they could rally. Even so, his position within the bundan was never as central as Kōyō's had been. These younger writers did not need his support in order to find opportunities to publish, nor were they formally his students. If anything, he was too intensely focused on his own work to become a real mentor to anyone.

A Turn to the Theater

Without the vociferous dominance of the naturalists, Kyōka would not have been as appealing to this younger generation of writers. Neither would he have survived Kōyō's passing away by finding a niche for himself in the theater that other writers, including members of this younger group, pushed him toward. His involvement with the stage began as early as 1895. *Noble Blood, Heroic Blood,* published jointly with Kōyō in November 1894, was quickly adapted for performance by the shinpa theater by Kawakami Otojirō (1864–1911) and performed under the title *Taki no Shiraito* at the Asakusa Komagata Theater.[5] The play immediately became a great success, although it did little to help establish Kyōka's name as a writer because Kawakami credited neither Kyōka nor Kōyō for writing the original text. In fact, Kawakami had the audacity to advertise the play as having been derived from "a Russian novel,"[6] a point that Kōyō loudly protested. As a response to Kōyō's strident demands that the authors of the original work be acknowledged, the opening of the play was delayed but not canceled.

When *Taki no Shiraito* played before full houses, it won both popular and critical approval. Kawakami's adaptation was heavy-handed, but he did an excellent job of conveying Kyōka's melodramatic story of Taki no Shiraito's self-sacrifice for Murakoshi Kin'ya. The reviewer for the *Morning News* (*Asahi shinbun*) was unqualified in his praise of the production.

Kin'ya's encounter with Taki on Tenjin Bridge is the showpiece of the play. Both actors quoted verbatim from the novel, so the dialogue from *Noble Blood* leapt from the page and into life. . . . [The courtroom] scene was so intensely emotional that this reviewer could not restrain his tears. Before the whole audience, Kin'ya magically assumed the form of the coachman he had once been, as he turned a pistol to his breast and killed himself. A *tour de force!*[7]

Kawakami, who played Murakoshi Kin'ya, added an extra dose of drama to what Kyōka had in mind for the original story. By changing the final scene to include the very act of suicide, Kawakami provided a heightened sense of closure and more turbulence than even a lyrical writer such as Kyōka had been willing to supply.

Perhaps the inherent theatricality of Kyōka's stories explains why, especially after this first success, his work continued to be indispensable grist for the shinpa mill. *Taki no Shiraito*, in particular, continued to be performed frequently and became one of the mainstays of this new form of stage performance.[8] A number of other adaptations for the stage followed. Prior to the Taishō period and the beginning of Kyōka's own career as a playwright, *A Tale of the Southwest Quarter* was staged at Tokyo's Kawakami Theater in June 1900. *The Holy Man of Mt. Kōya* appeared at Tokyo's Hongō Theater in September 1904. A stage version of *The Vigil* (*Tsuya monogatari*, 1899) made its debut in Osaka's Asahi Theater in August 1906, followed the next month by *Worship at Yushima*. The

Elegant Railway showed in July 1907 at the Hongō Theater. *A Woman's Pedigree*, which also became a shinpa standard, was first performed at Tokyo's Shintomi Theater in September 1908. *The White Heron* showed at the Hongō Theater in April 1910. In March 1911, *Shamisen Moat* (from "Shamisen-bori," 1910) made its appearance at Tokyo's Miyato Theater. And in May 1912, *Love Suicides in the Southern Quarter* (from "Nanchi shinjū," 1912) was performed at the Shintomi Theater just five months after the original story appeared in print.

Kawai Takeo (1877–1942), who played the heroine in *Love Suicides*, noted the importance of Kyōka's work to this new form of theatrical performance, which attempted to be more mimetic and less formalistic than kabuki. "Shinpa would never have been born, had it not been for the influence of the Kyōka plays [*Kyōka mono*]. . . . If one counted not just the plays he wrote but the plots we borrowed from his other stories, the sum would add up to an incredible number. As you know, the Master's prose and dialogues are difficult. The ears of the masses were not attuned to his writing, and so the novels were performed in thoroughly plagiarized form, one after another."[9]

The tension between Kawai's statement and the review quoted above suggests the real inconsistencies in Kyōka's relationship with the theater. Whereas the reviewer appreciates the manner in which the original text comes to life on the shinpa stage, Kawai's regard for the difficulty of the original material becomes a rationale for a "thoroughly plagiarized" version. In truth, the originals required much simplification before they could be performed. Kyōka, who was eventually prompted to begin writing plays for himself, seems to have both accepted and rejected this need for the mediation of others. The stage presented him with the opportunity to express himself more accessibly and more memorably.

On the one hand, he was openly displeased with Kawakami's 1900 production of *A Tale of the Southwest Quarter*. After Nakano Nobuchika, who played the role of the boatman in the play, had traveled to Zushi to request that Kyōka allow the adaptation to be staged, Kyōka wrote a follow-up letter to him in which he stated, "As for your planned performance of my work at the Hongō, although it is my policy to reject all requests for the performance of my work, when I saw you in person it was impossible for me to say no. I hope, however, that you will now get the gist of the matter" (29: 309). In other words, the real answer was no. In his critique of a 1902 performance of *Taki no Shiraito*, Kyōka criticized Nakano and others for being driven not by the emotional requirements of the story but by how things would look to the audience. Nothing came out right. The moon over the Asano River, like the crucial meeting of Taki and Kin'ya on the Tenjin Bridge, was too bright. The Chinese knife-thrower's clothes were too blue. The denouement was too graphic. "What an ending! Kin'ya sopping up his blood with a tissue, doing all he could to make a show of himself" (28: 662). Speaking of the theater more generally, he criticized shinpa actors for being too rushed. "The problem is that they are in a hurry to advance the plot and do not take the time necessary to savor the lyricism of a scene." This tendency to move carelessly ahead was also apparent, Kyōka claimed, in film, which was growing ever more popular (28: 736).

Whatever his criticisms of actors, Kyōka's growing involvement with the stage was closely tied to his personal involvement with these men who made a living by acting out the scenes he imagined. He eventually befriended Kawai, but never liked Kawakami. The latter got his start as a propagandist for the Liberty and Human Rights movement, but later abandoned his attempts at political theater in order to capitalize on the growing interest in seeing topical events presented on stage. He and his wife, Sada Yakko (1892–1946), the "first woman" of late-modern theater, became internationally famous when the two toured America and Europe, performing exotic snippets of kabuki for appreciative turn-of-the-century Western audiences. Upon returning to Japan, they remained in the limelight by introducing the Japanese to the plays of Shakespeare, Ibsen, Maeterlinck, and Sardou. Their influence waned, however, with the rise of the Seibidan, a more conservative shinpa troupe that challenged and eventually prevailed over Kawakami's and Sada's more thoroughgoing commitment to realism. As originators of the larger movement, Kawakami's group had departed significantly from convention by having Sada Yakko and other women perform women's roles. In reaction, the Seibidan revived the traditional role of the *onnagata*, the male impersonator of female roles. Kyōka preferred this. He complained that the voices of untrained actresses grated on his ears "like nails scratching against a pane of glass" (28: 839).

Had it not been for this revival of the onnagata, Kyōka might not have been drawn to the people who eventually opened up the world of theater to him. At first, his involvement was limited to making suggestions to those who adapted his stories, but soon he began going to the theater to comment on the details of production. He met and conversed with actors, and eventually came to see the possibilities of the stage for his own artistic purposes. Here was a natural outlet for his work at a time when the dominance of the naturalists made it increasingly difficult to publish his sort of fiction. Although his development as a playwright was initially slow, during the Taishō period, his production of stories and novels tapered off noticeably as he focused his energies on writing for the stage.

Among those male actors who specialized in playing female roles, one man in particular appealed to Kyōka's own poetic sensibilities. "Among shinpa actors, I like Kitamura Rokurō (1871–1961). He is intelligent, and his artistry is solid. Among today's players, when it comes to knowing the proper spacing that should exist between actors on the stage and how to deliver lines effectively, he is perhaps the best. His voice isn't what I could call outstanding—a bit too mannered. But his enunciation is clear" (28: 735–36). For Kyōka, actors like Kitamura and Takada Minoru (1871–1916) stood out from the crowd. Their more refined sense of aesthetics and strong stage presence allowed them to take the time necessary to let the audience savor the lyricism of the script. That is to say, the magic of language continued to be Kyōka's point of focus even after his attention turned to writing plays.

Kitamura was a dandy. Born in Nihonbashi, he was an Edokko, a "Jewel of Fire," as his sobriquet had it. His career took him to the Kansai area, where he worked for over ten years to establish his reputation as a member of the Seibidan (along with Takada, who had left Kawakami's group) before returning to Tokyo to perform. As a young man, he enthusiastically read both Kōyō's and Kyōka's work and even sent a fan letter to Kyōka while still living in the Kansai area.[10] The two did not meet until 1906. Kitamura made his farewell performance at Osaka's Asahi Theater in May, and then moved back to Tokyo at the end of the month. He made his debut at the Hongō Theater on June 5 with a performance of Shun'yō's *Mistletoe* (*Yadorigi*). While the play was still running, Shun'yō accompanied him to Kyōka's house for an evening visit.

At that time, Kyōka was spending most of his time in Zushi, not Tokyo, but he did maintain a residence in Kagurazaka and was, as already mentioned, commuting to the city because of his job with *New Fiction*.[11] His meeting with Kitamura went so well that the young actor became a regular visitor to Kyōka's home in Zushi, where he sometimes stayed the night.[12] Their close relationship came to have great significance for the development of shinpa in general since most of the numerous *kakinuki*, or selected scenes, that Kyōka wrote for the shinpa stage were done because of some connection with Kitamura.[13] Perhaps the most famous example is the "Yushima Temple Grounds" ("Yushima keidai") scene, which we have already considered. Kitamura had played the role of Otsuta when Shun'yō's adaptation of Kyōka's novella opened at the Shintomi

Theater on September 29, 1908. Dissatisfied with Shun'yō's version, Kitamura personally asked Kyōka to rewrite this crucial moment when lovers part. Kyōka agreed. When *A Woman's Pedigree* was performed the second time in 1914 at the Asahi Theater, Kitamura was involved in another production, which made him unavailable for this part that Kyōka had written especially for him. Only after several requests did Kitamura give his permission for another actor to use the new script. He later performed the scene when the play was produced for a third time, in November 1916 at Kyoto's Minami Theater. Today, "The Yushima Temple Grounds" has become one of the most popular and frequently performed scenes of the shinpa repertoire, often standing alone as the abbreviated essence of the entire play.

Shinja the Great

Through such adaptations of his work, Kyōka came to know several of the most famous *onnagata* of the first half of the twentieth century—not only Kitamura and Kawai, but also Kitamura's protege Hanayanagi Shōtarō (1894–1965). Kawai's associate, the actor Fujizawa Asajirō (1866–1917), was the one who gave Kyōka his first commission to write an entire play. The offer came as early as 1904. The completed script was to be performed as part of a double bill on September 1904 at the Hongō Theater. Kyōka responded to the request by writing *Shinja the Great* (*Shinja Daiō*, 1904), a reworking of the earlier story "Water Rail Village" ("Kuina no sato," 1901). As it turned out, Fujiwara and Kawai found Kyōka's drama impossibly difficult to perform.

Kyōka set the play in a secluded village near Takefu, the general setting of the equally supernatural "The White Witch's Tale." Act 1 is not so weird. Oyamada Tōru, a newspaper reporter, visits the village. From an old woman, the hero's mother, he hears about the water rail, a bird for which the area is famous. He also learns of a local shrine dedicated to Shinja, the great ruler (*daiō*), who is a female dragon spirit, an *aragami*, or "terrible god," who "steals men's good fortune and curses them in return" (25: 12). As he is about to leave, he meets the heroine Oshun. She was previously the fiancée of the young hero, Matsusaburō, but now she is the mistress of Kuramochi Densuke, a wealthy landowner and the villain of this play. Like Taki no Shiraito, she has become a courtesan in order to provide a needy young man, the ailing Matsusaburō, with money for his studies. It is a warm day, and because she is wearing a double-layered kimono, Oshun takes off one and leaves it there. When Densuke and his live-in thug, Ōgaki Shōta, find the kimono, they pull Matsusaburō from his bed, accuse him of sleeping with Oshun, and beat him mercilessly. Taking the kimono with him, Densuke swears that he will find and punish Oshun. Matsusaburō follows after them with a knife. He attacks Densuke but is overwhelmed by Shōta and left for dead. The act ends as Oshun, discovering Matsusaburō, holds him in her arms.

Act 2 transports us to a very different world. Densuke and Shōta are pillaging Shinja's shrine for any objects they might be able to sell as antiques. In their search for a commercial form of the past, they find nothing but junk, assorted remnants of a long-forgotten age when people once had faith in the gods. Densuke breaks the head off a dilapidated statue of the Buddha and out pours black smoke. When the fumes clear, Shinja the Great and her cohorts—the headless Buddha, a monkey, a white fox, a weasel, an old man (*okina*), a paper doll, and a drum—gather to confer about Densuke's punishment. Meanwhile, Oyamada finds Matsusaburō, who is looking for a place to die, and tells Matsusaburō to leave everything to him.

The third and final act takes place at Densuke's residence. Shōta and Densuke have found Oshun, who has nearly drowned. They carry her in and tie her to a stone lantern in the garden of Densuke's estate. In a gradual escalation of violence, Shōta beats her. When Matsusaburō appears, he is tied to a pine tree and is pummeled by Densuke's men. Oyamada, witnessing this brutality, calls out to Shinja the Great to intercede and show her power. A flood occurs, and Shinja's supernatural cohorts run wild in the garden. Densuke drowns. Matsusaburō and Oshun survive to acknowledge Oyamada's hand in saving them. To their "As you please, we wait for your instructions," Oyamada replies, "Don't ask me. Ask Shinja the Great."

When Kyōka submitted the piece, Fujizawa met with Kawai, Takada Minoru, and the actor Satō Toshizō (1869–1945?) to discuss what they should do with it. The play's annoying didacticism aside, Kyōka had created too many characters for the piece to be easily performed. In the original casting, Takada was to be both Kuramochi Densuke and the haggard Buddha. Kawai was to play both Oshun and the paper doll. And Satō was to be Oyamada and the white fox. In the end, Fujizawa and the others decided not to produce the play, citing the difficulty of casting, especially in connection with the play that was to precede it on the program. Instead of *Shinja the Great*, they decided to substitute an adaptation of *The Holy Man of Mt. Kōya*, which had already been completed and was waiting to be performed. They did not want to alienate Kyōka and invited him to help with the props. While helping in this advisory role, he published *Shinja the Great* in *Literature Club* (*Bungei kurabu*). The play was not performed until March 1914, when Fujizawa played Matsusaburō, and Kitamura performed the part of Oshun.

The rejection of Kyōka's first play was undoubtedly due to more than casting difficulties. Compared with the more realistic stories that the shinpa theater had already appropriated as their own—such as *Noble Blood, Heroic Blood* and "A Tale of the Southwest Quarter"—*Shinja the Great* marked a significant departure from what Fujizawa and the others had expected. The original "Water Rail Village" takes place in a misty, hidden world of mystery and fascination. It succeeds as a story by creating a space for the uncanny, a goal that seems to have been Kyōka's principal concern, both for the story and for the play. As a vehicle for the supernatural, *Shinja the Great* suggests what would be borne out by the plays yet to come. What Kyōka instinctively sensed as the essence of the theater was its spatial and symbolic function as an otherworldly site for reunion, violence, and cataclysm. The stage was, to recall the map of Kyōka's childhood world in Kanazawa, yet another bridge to the other side of the river. It was a structure that fulfilled its role by providing access to the other world, and was another means of trespass.

Shinja the Great is not a finely crafted play, but its importance to Kyōka's artistic development is obvious. It establishes a lasting pattern. It shares a structure with two later plays, *Demon Pond* and *The Sunken Bell* (*Chinshō*, 1907): two worlds, one sacred and the other profane, are established in order for a battle to be waged between them. In this twofold space, "passion confronts reason, faith meets skepticism, and the primitive ethos of the wilderness is oppressed by the materialistic values of modern Japan. Romantic love, in short, is pitted against society, but its advocates are as supernatural as they are antisocial."[14] As a place of mystery, the stage provided Kyōka with a position from which he could launch an attack on the day-to-day world in which we live. From here on, the attack would be more passionate than ever.

Once again, as a consultant for the production of *The Holy Man of Mt. Kōya*, Kyōka gained direct exposure to the details of theater performance.[15] Yet it is clear that he was not seeing the shinpa stage as it was: a late-modern sphere of psychological realism that had pulled away from and then was cautiously moving back toward the world of kabuki. Rather, he saw it for what it could be: a space that would indulge his imaginative commitment to the meta-story and to the need to wander ever more boldly in the realm of the dead. The major problem with production was simply that Fujizawa and others could not physically go where Kyōka's imagination wanted to be. For this reason, a number of his plays, though ostensibly written for the shinpa stage, were performed only much later or never performed at all. Clearly, the supernatural elements were problematic. They were, as well, lingering elements of a pictocentric, proto-psychological episteme and its predilection for monstrous display that served Kyōka's more formulaic and mythic vision so effectively. That the sacred should be so graphically demarcated from the profane illustrates the futility inherent in Kyōka's vision of a late-modern world. Yet this separation is neither surprising nor always obvious. The intermingling of natural and supernatural beings and the metamorphic possibilities that this coexistence presupposes was hardly Kyōka's invention. To repeat an earlier point, it was an ontology familiar to those who knew the Noh stage, to say nothing of the various genres of ge-saku that form the more immediate sources of Kyōka's iconography.

Kyōka had reason to know the world of the Noh theater well. His mother's older brother was Matsumoto Kintarō, a well-known performer of the Hōshō school. Born in Edo during the final years of the Tokugawa shogunate, Matsumoto was originally Nakata Kintarō but married into the Matsumoto family, which had long served the shogunate. When Tokugawa Yoshinobu retired to Shizuoka during the tumultuous years prior to the fall of the regime, Kintarō went with him. With the revival of the Noh theater in 1884, he moved back to Tokyo. He had a stage built in his home and began to teach his art to others.

When Kyōka first came to the capital to apprentice with Kōyō, he had no idea that he and his uncle were living in the same city. He had assumed that Matsumoto was still in Shizuoka and discovered otherwise only upon reading about him in the *Yomiuri News*. In a letter to his father dated July 9, 1892, he wrote of a visit to see his mother's younger sister Tanaka Kin, who was staying at the Matsumoto residence in Kanda Sarugaku-chō 2 chōme 11 banchi.

Overjoyed, I rushed over by rikisha to the Matsumotos'. Both Uncle Kintarō and Auntie Kin were happy to see me. She told me, "It's like meeting Suzu and Toyoki [Kyōka's maternal grandfather] again." Kin took my hand and tears came to her eyes. Kintarō, his wife, and his cousin were also there. He's now a Noh actor of the Hōshō school, which is second to none. They treated me like royalty. They told me that I should consider their home as my own, that I should feel free to come over any time. When they asked why I hadn't visited as soon as I arrived in Tokyo, I didn't know quite what to say. (29: 286–87)

Kintarō died in 1914, but Kyōka, who was only nineteen when he first visited the Matsumotos, had many occasions to see him perform. From this exposure, he gained a deeper sense of the sort of metamorphic and sacred space that he would try to create on the shinpa stage.

If his first attempt was faltering, Kyōka was nevertheless driven to write another play. Judging from the advertisement he wrote for his second play, *Love's Fire* (*Aika*, 1906), he had already at this early date come to sense the exciting possibilities of the stage. As he himself asserted, *this* play would set the world right by providing a proper space for the passion and resentment of the dispossessed.

In order to break from the evil habits that have come to plague today's theater—tastelessness, dryness, puerility, crudity, and inconsistency—I shall demonstrate how majestic, mysterious, profound, and ghastly a script for the stage can possibly be. My poetic and powerful words will be in harmony with the rhythms of nature, showing a complete grasp of structure and technique that is free and unhindered, each word arising like a plucked string of the *koto*, each phrase like the rolling surf. It shall be nothing like those powerless scripts that care only for plot, lazy writing that denies the power of the brush. With a story that has been lying dormant in my mind for many years, one that has now risen up to its moment of full maturity, I shall awaken the world of letters from its dogmatic slumber and brush the cobwebs from minds of all readers. In short, *Love's Fire* will be an uncompromisingly unadulterated Japanese play. I do not know whether the theater is capable of performing such a wonder. But is this not what drama should be? (28: 647)

As it turned out, Kyōka was right to wonder whether anybody could perform the play. It was an unconditional failure. Far from awakening everyone from their plot-mongering malaise, the seemingly endless and punishingly lyrical *Love's Fire* gained absolutely no admirers. A long and tangled appreciation of love's power, it has never been performed to this date. Indeed, Kyōka's closest friends singled it out as quite possibly the worst thing he ever wrote.

The badness of the writing is not difficult to understand if we consider the larger purposes of Kyōka's artistic career. He perceived drama as an essentially lyrical art, one that could further his desire to create an archetypal world to bring to fruition the promise of presence. Whether encountered as an actual stage in works such as "One Day in Spring" or *A Song by Lantern Light*, or as the suggested space of drama as in *The Holy Man of Mt. Kōya*, the stage (in this expanded sense) is always made manifest by language of a heightened though still descriptive nature. The problem is that when the stage is present as a physical, visually perceived space, the need for such description becomes questionable. Drawn by the potential of just such a place, Kyōka had, by the time of *Love's Fire*, yet to find an appropriate language to complement this more obviously theatrical mode of visuality. This worst of all his plays, then, fails because it tries unnecessarily to replace the spatial and visual lyricism of the stage with the narrative lyricism of the stories. By trusting his instincts, he had actually come closer to the mark with the earlier *Shinja the Great*. He would eventually return to the supernatural world of *Shinja*'s Act 2 in order to find the proper coordination of language and theatrical space, but only after his one and only experience as a translator. Only then did he gain a suitable approach to the visual directness and material presence of the sought-for stage.

Gerhart Hauptmann

Japanese scholars often point to Gerhart Hauptmann's (1862–1946) *The Sunken Bell—A German Fairy Drama* (*Die versunkene Glocke—Ein deutsches Marchendrama*, 1896) as a decisive inspiration and model for the plays that follow.[16] Kyōka became involved with the translation of Hauptmann's work at the bidding of Tobari Chikufū, who had earlier arranged for the publishing of *A Woman's Pedigree* in the *Yamato News*. Chikufū, an ardent Nietzschean and promoter of German romanticism, had come up with a rough translation of the play, which he asked Kyōka to render into an appropriate style of Japanese. To judge from the earlier and later manuscripts of the play, Kyōka's part in nativizing the text was considerable. In a letter to Chikufū, Kyōka said as much. "Your translation is so interesting that I've thrown myself into the project, working day and night, despite the heat. Still, it's not going as well as planned. I've been over it with the greatest of care. But there are places that seem a little stiff. I've taken the liberty to do some experimenting here and there" (29: 365). In very general terms, Kyōka converted Chikufū's more classical, formal wording into a colloquial idiom.

Kyōka's interest in the project is not surprising. Hauptmann's play concerns itself with familiar problems: the need to love and the compulsion to follow one's dreams by way of artistic endeavors. Hauptmann was a leading proponent of naturalism in Germany, but the realism of his *Sunken Bell* allowed much room for the supernatural; as in *Shinja the Great*, it was the mixing of worlds that Kyōka seemed most driven to accomplish. As the play begins, pagan mountain spirits sabotage the installation of a Christian bell, which gets thrown off its wagon and plunges into a deep lake. Heinrich, the bell's creator, is injured in the accident and nursed back to health by the beautiful Rautendelein, a nymph of the forest. Even though they belong to two different worlds, they fall in love, and it is the impossibility of this union that unites and antagonizes the denizens of both the natural and the supernatural worlds. Heinrich eventually allies himself with the mysterious sphere of the mountains, despite appeals from his parish priest and village elders that he come to his senses and return to his religion and family. Although he is willing to abandon these, he will not give up his craft. He sets up a new forge and plans the casting of another bell, to be dedicated to "the palace of the fir trees, beloved of Freya." Despairing of her husband's paganism, Magda drowns herself in the lake and, as an angry spirit, rings the sunken bell that haunts Heinrich with its sound. Heinrich is dealt a further blow as wood and water sprites steal Rautendelein away from his side and destroy his mountain forge. In order for Heinrich to be with her again, he must drink a potion that will cost him his life. Hearing her voice calling his name from the well where she is imprisoned, Heinrich cries out, "Ah, the sun. The sunrise. The sunrise! Ah, the night is long." He dies as the new day begins.

Heinrich's purgatory reminds us of the fate of numerous Kyōkaean protagonists. They, too, are drawn from the real world by the lure of desire and beauty, although the territory into which they trespass is not totally welcoming. By manipulating metaphors of the real and of the world beyond, Hauptmann challenged Christian orthodoxy. Following suit, Kyōka attacked the brutish systems of late-modern capitalism. Whatever the targets of their criticism, the universe as presented by both Hauptmann and Kyōka is bifurcated, vertical, and hierarchical. The valley and village are a world of order and family life, but to Heinrich they come to represent a repressive hell. The height of mountains is naturally sacred, filled with fairies, goblins, and pagan deities, a world of irrationality, chaos, and, finally, death. As a critique of conventional morality, Hauptmann's play could be (and was) attractive to both the romantic and the naturalist.

Although many Japanese scholars have suggested that Kyōka's involvement in the translation of this text was an important influence on his further development, equally evident is the way in which the direction of Kyōka's career as a playwright was already apparent in his very first play, *Shinja the Great*.[17] This point is overlooked, possibly because the tendency to cite European sources for Japan's modernity follows from a Eurocentric bias that has long provided definition (and, therefore, justification) for studies of the late-modern. To this point of view, it makes sense that Kyōka's inspiration should come from the West, even though, should we wish to continue in this critical mode, we ought to say that Hauptmann's influence is certainly more direct in the case of Tayama Katai, for instance, whose *Quilt* (*Futon*, 1907) was clearly modeled after Mori Ōgai's translation of *Lonely People* (*Einsame Menschen*, 1889–90). Five years earlier, Tayama Katai read an English translation of *The Sunken Bell* and was attracted to the play's critique of orthodox morality and to its "cynical view of life" (*enseiteki jinseikan*).[18] Kyōka's debt to Hauptmann is less explicit.

On the other hand, it is undeniable that the work of translation influenced Kyōka's awareness of style and his search for an appropriate language for the stage. Kyōka's hybridized idiom was not universally appreciated. Hasegawa Tenkei (1876–1940), another important figure in the naturalist movement, took exception to the translation done by Chikufū and Kyōka. Tenkei found the first two acts, which appeared in the May and June issues of the *Yamato News*, "so inept that I am rendered speechless." According to Tenkei, the beauty and lyricism of the original German had been lost. Hauptmann's verse had been replaced with a "plodding and vulgar vernacular" that had reduced the noble Rautendelein to "a sex-crazed nurse, just out of girl's school."[19] Possibly in response to Tenkei's scathing review, publication of the remainder of the play was canceled.

In an unusual move for him, Kyōka responded publicly to Tenkei. He defended Chikufū, who had borne the brunt of Tenkei's criticism, by taking full responsibility for any faults in the translation. The admission, however, was not necessarily a confirmation of Tenkei's critique. Providing his own close reading of precisely those passages quoted in the review, Kyōka wrote at great length to show that his stylistic choices had been faithful to the spirit of the original. The most important thing about a script, he argued, is that it allows each character to have his or her individuality. As for Tenkei's impression of Rautendelein as foulmouthed and lascivious, Kyōka reminded his critic that she is a child of nature, wild and mannish. Having her speak a more classical and literary idiom, as Tenkei had suggested, would have been inappropriate and even comical. To support his contention, he supplied numerous examples of varying levels of formality and even a sample of rhyming verse to show why none of them would work (28: 399–416).

Chikufū also responded to Tenkei, though much more sharply. It was true that the original was written in verse, but this did not mean that it was not also colloquial and personal. Had Tenkei read the original German, which he obviously could not, he would have realized that this was true.[20] In fairness to all concerned, the language of the theater, like that of the novel, was evolving quickly in Japan and had yet to stabilize. This fact alone explains a large part of the disagreement over *The Sunken Bell*. Hauptmann's work, coming as it did from another literary tradition, straddled the border between realism and fantasy, between formal and informal language. Thus, its translation into Japanese required nothing less than a reformulation of existing literary categories. The result was a new, unfamiliar diction, which Tenkei resisted.

Osanai Kaoru's reaction was less acerbic but not that different in thrust from Tenkei's. Since the work of translation is difficult, Osanai wondered why Kyōka had bothered to translate a "verse drama" (*inbun geki*) rather than a "prose" (*sanbun*) or "realistic drama" (*shajitsu geki*) in the first place. This pairing of prose with realism and verse with fantasy was, in essence, the root of the problem. In Osanai's opinion, Kyōka had not only committed an error of style but one of judgment as well. The world of the sunken bell was removed from the quotidian and, therefore, more given to poetic expression. Although it was Kyōka's tendency to gravitate toward figurative language, he had, after the obvious failure of the lyrical *Love's Fire*, taken Hauptmann's play in the opposite direction. As for the matter of bad judgment, by choosing to work on such a play at all Kyōka continued to resist the realistic spirit of the day.

Yanagita Kunio and *Demon Pond*

Kyōka did not appreciate Osanai's second-guessing his reasons for translating Hauptmann. Even if his motivation was not obvious to others, it was clear to him. By confronting the issue of new categories, he had let *The Sunken Bell* bring him a step closer to finding a way to make the stage a viable space for the drama in his heart. He could not deny the growing rationalism of the day. Yet for him, the swell of positivist thinking seemed to make the need for the world beyond reason that much stronger. This is nowhere more obvious than in his growing interest in the work of Yanagita Kunio, who in his study of legend and folklore made Kyōka even more aware of and attracted to the supposedly outmoded rhetoric of metamorphosis.

As noted above, Kyōka first met Yanagita around 1896, while visiting the First School dormitory of his hometown friend, Yoshida Kenryū. He modeled a minor character in *Worship at Yushima* after Yanagita, whom Kyōka described there as a member of the privileged intellectual class, the sort of young man that he himself was not. Yanagita went on to become a bureaucrat, taking advantage of the social structure that rewarded him for having graduated from the First School. He had always had strong literary interests, particularly a fondness for poetry. When his parents died in 1896, the year he entered the First School, he

grieved deeply for his mother, losing interest in everything but reading literature and taking extended trips to remote regions of Japan. Despite its reputation as a seminal text for anthropological studies in Japan, Yanagita's *Tales of
Tōno* is also a consciously artistic work, distinguished for its elegant language
and imagistic style. With this collection of legends, he sought to express the
world beyond external appearances, thus aligning himself closely with Kyōka's
view of things. He did not actually travel to Tōno to gather the stories, but
heard them from a friend, Sasaki Kizen, who had grown up there and learned
the oral tradition through his parents and grandparents. With the Grimms'
fairy tales in mind, Yanagita wrote down what he had heard from Sasaki and
used his own funds to publish 350 copies, which he distributed to friends.

Katai dismissed *The Tales of Tōno* as an extravagance of affected rusticity.
Obviously, Yanagita's work was too impressionistic and sentimental for a more
straightforward presentation of the sort of "local color" that Katai and other
naturalists sought.[21] Kyōka, however, appreciated not only the ambiguity and
suggestiveness of the work's imagery but the underlying notion of a coextensive
world of gods and men that was expressed by the tales: *kami* (gods) are in the
world, here and now. "What I feel from reading this tale is not only the
strangeness of events and the phantasmic nature of things. Also expressed in
the interstices of silence are the scenery of the land, the customs, and the colors
of the trees and grass" (28: 465).

In writing his next play, *Demon Pond* (*Yashagaike*, 1913), Kyōka affirmed the
worldview expressed in *The Tales of Tōno*. Not only does he present as coextensive the worlds of human and divine beings, but he uses the figure of the anthropologist to explore the interconnected issues of man's relationship to legend
and the problem of belief. Modeled after Yanagita, a young ethnologist, Hagi-
wara Akira, has disappeared on one of his legend-gathering trips into the
countryside. His colleague, Yamazawa Gakuen, manages to find him living in
a remote mountain village in Echizen. Gakuen learns that Akira has settled
there with a young woman named Yuri and that he cannot return to the city
because he feels obligated to continue the ritual bell-ringing that Yuri's father
performed until his death. The rationale for the ritual is contained in a local
legend, the subject of Akira's study. A Buddhist saint, in order to prevent the
flooding of local villages, once confined a dragon goddess in a mountain pond.
A bell was erected at that time and was to be rung three times each day to remind the goddess of her promise to suffer the containment. Although the local

people themselves no longer believe in the legend, Akira, who has come to them from the city, loses his distance from the object of his study. He not only finds the story believable, but he gives himself to the tradition, taking it upon himself to strike the bell each day in order to keep the villagers alive.

Akira explains his relationship to the story.

As you know, I set off for the North Country hoping to gather tales from the countryside. But the fact is that I myself have become a part of one of those stories. They say a witch can take a mountain and put it in the sea, or turn a man into a tree, a rock, or the rock into a leaf. . . . Just by coming here, no doubt *you've* become a character in a story. As for me, well, I've gone a step further. I've become a story, nothing more and nothing less. (25: 597)

In this way, legend, place, and identity are bound together through a vaguely intimated process of metamorphosis. The world of the mountains is decisively powerful. It transforms all trespassers into characters of the legends that remain here, untouched by the withering sun of rationalism. It forces all, even the sophisticated urban intellectual, to belong to its legend-space, which gives identity to those who live in it.

This is precisely the space that Kyōka was seeking by writing for the theater. Just as figures from the other world appear easily in legend, so too do they easily take a place on stage. Certainly, the physical reality of this territory of performance encouraged Kyōka to make stories true by acting them out. As in the early *Shinja the Great*, in *Demon Pond* the members of the supernatural realm make an appearance. Shirayuki, the dragon princess, "is dressed in an undergarment of snow-white gossamer, and a pale blue court robe with a long train dyed into scarlet flame patterns. Her obi is black satin decorated with a silver fish-scale appliqué design. . . . Her skirts are sweeping, her black hair is longer than she is tall. She wears silver slippers on her feet. A metal scepter protrudes from her obi and glitters like a jewel. A letter scroll dangles unfurled in her hands, trailing on the ground" (25: 619–20). As a monster, Shirayuki is resplendent.

She is also frustrated. She pines for her love, a serpent contained in another pond. Neither can go to the other without flooding the world of human beings, and as an indication of her mounting resentment, she has caused a serious drought. Desperate for water, the villagers force Yuri to become the mock sacrifice in a ritual that will supposedly end the curse. They try to abduct her and make her ride naked upon an ox, but Akira and Gakuen intercede. As the fighting escalates, the ideological differences between those who believe in the legend of the bell and those who do not become clear and insurmountable. Both Yuri and Akira are mortally wounded in this battle against brutish men. In his last moment, Akira, who knows no one will ring the bell once he has died, calls directly upon the dragon goddess to avenge them. Immediately, the dragon princess sends a deluge that destroys everyone except Gakuen, who survives to tell the tale.

Although the human and supernatural figures occupy the same stage, they do not do so simultaneously. Each group is controlled by two separate though intertwining stories that do not merge until the end of the play. For this reason, many critics have faulted the work. Muramatsu Sadataka, for instance, draws a comparison with *The Sunken Bell*, where Heinrich and Rautendelein freely interact with each other. He concludes that Hauptmann's treatment is better, and that a later play by Kyōka, *The Castle Tower*, is the author's best because it seamlessly incorporates one world into the other.[22] That Kyōka was quickly moving toward a conception of the stage as a perfectly coextensive sphere for both the natural and supernatural is undeniable, but, as we will consider shortly, the seamlessness of these worlds is problematic as a measure of their aesthetic quality, which depends upon the tension inherent in the *possibility* of such a merger.

Presentational Theater

In 1913, Kyōka wrote a total of four full-length plays. One of these, *The Sea God's Palace* (*Kaijin bessō*, 1913), unabashedly belongs to the other world and is set from beginning to end in the sea. Its stage is from the outset the realm of the dead, the end rather than simply the means to a world of absolute value. It is as if Kyōka chose to begin *The Sea God's Palace* where *Demon Pond* left off. Immediately establishing an aqueous realm for lovers, the play provides absolute distance and perspective on the world of the living. If in *Demon Pond* men were described as "tailless apes," (25: 621), here the critique is even more acerbic and condemning. Because the point of view originates in supernatural coordinates, the suggestiveness of earlier plays is replaced by an unambiguous tirade that is less effective artistically, albeit more forceful.

A beautiful young woman is sacrificed by her father to the God of the Sea. The father is an impecunious fisherman, who gains a fabulous harvest of fish and a bounty of other treasures in exchange for his daughter. As the curtains open, she has just survived a harrowing journey from her home to the Sea God's exotic underwater palace. Disheveled and disoriented, she eventually realizes that the preparations are being made for her marriage to the deity. Consonant with her status as a typical sacrificial heroine, she must agree to the marriage that has been forced upon her. Her ties to the living are still not perfectly severed, however, and she requests permission to return to the land of the living to show her father that she is not dead but, like him, better off than before. The Sea God reluctantly allows her to go, but warns her that she is no longer the same. Her fellow villagers, and even her father, who has demonstrated his pitifully greedy nature by trading her away for material wealth, will not see her as a woman but as a dragon, a creature of the sea. She is, in short, dead to him, a member of the other world. Not wanting to believe this truth, she makes the return voyage only to discover that the Sea God's prediction is true. Resigned to the fact that she cannot live anywhere else but in the sea, she goes through with the marriage.

The alteration in the young woman's perspective, her realization that even her father cares more for money than for her, is the simple point of this play. Commenting on what he has done, the Sea God's minister notes, "Beauty's father is as mortal as the rest. Since he alone won the luck of the sea and piled up a mountain of gold for himself, he has cared nothing for the misery of others" (26: 39). When the Sea God asks, "Is human desire satisfied with so little?" the minister answers, "He's actually one of the more grasping ones. By trading an only daughter for the treasures of the sea, he proved himself a bit more greedy than most. I'm of the understanding that human beings do some amount of selling and trading among themselves—soft, plump, white flesh, wrapped in flaming silks, and steamed" (26: 40). Kyōka seems to suggest that giving a daughter in marriage is not so different from paying a prostitute for her erotic values of red and white. In either case, money buys the service.

On the other hand, the Sea God is also a party to this trade in flesh. Consequently, his kingdom is not a paradise but a realm that is uncanny and incredible precisely because of the honesty of its logic. A perfect understanding of romantic love may be available only to "poets and painters," but even its consuming power follows from a sadistic, cannibalizing force. When the Sea God considers earthly precedents for the way in which his bride is being trailed down to the ocean floor, he considers the suffering of Osan, one of the adulterous heroines of Ihara Saikaku's *Five Women Who Loved Love* (*Kōshoku gonin onna*), to be not only fitting but beautiful as well. And when the Sea God realizes that the fisherman's daughter is unappreciative of his gifts to her, he thinks nothing of killing her. "Killing a beautiful woman's not much more than plucking a flower. Scattered petals here, a stem there. Just toss the pieces in a jewel-box. Now, kill her, I say!" (26: 75). Perhaps, as Kasahara Nobuo suggests, Kyōka's sense of the beautiful ultimately flowed not from goodwill but from malice.[23] This may be another facet of the aesthetic grounding of Kyōka's ethics, noted later by Akutagawa.

The Sea God and the fisherman's daughter are united in love, but they participate in a romantic ideal that, in destroying conventional and humanistic definitions of love, is not possible in this world. Thus, the palace beneath the sea might be a place where total freedom reigns. Still, it is far from utopian. It is more precisely an alternative, disorienting universe that exists apart from the normative one of domestic attachments and betrayals. It allows us to see reality for what it is because it is honest about the conditional (and, therefore, compromised) nature of erotic love and about the provisional nature of the signs by which we come to understand it.

Kyōka's stage and the lyrical language that prevails there underscore the important point that our access to the real world is always first an affirmation of signs. When, for instance, the Sea God desires to know more about the world of human beings, he must consult his in-house professor, who is a comically learned man. Upon reference to the savant's extraordinary collection of books, all things become language.

The Sea God: (*Sitting down on the table*) That's quite a book you have there.
The Professor: This encyclopedia was commissioned by the French emperor Napoleon, a world-class bibliophile, just as he set off to invade Spain in 1808. In order to keep up with the times, he ordered Barville, then the Head of Libaries, to compile these thousand volumes, each bound and boxed. Forty for religion. Forty for epic poetry. Forty for drama and sixty for other kinds of verse. Sixty for history. One hundred for novels. Each volume printed in the so-called duodecimo. Your good sister Otohime heard of the production and acquired her own copy. As many as a thousand pages finely spun from a single lotus thread. Ten thousand pages, each folded over once, one hundred twenty folios stitched together to make one volume. And when one opens these books to the subtle light of our ocean country, all creation—starting with the human race and including every element of the universe: flora, fauna, mineral—turns into finely printed characters on the page. Not only that, but words emit the primary colors so that nouns, pronouns, verbs, auxiliary verbs, both subjects and predicates, punctuation marks, each in their several ways all glow in various tints upon the pure whiteness of the opened page. (26: 48)

Otherwise, the real world is seen through a looking glass that allows this underworld to see what is going on above. From within the sea palace, the Sea God can view that domestic space from which the fisherman's daughter came and to which she attempts a return. Because of Kyōka's growing confidence in writing the other world into existence, this domestic sphere is not present in any form other than this passing reference to it.

In short, the conceits of reality have vanished from the stage; in their place Kyōka proposed a dramatic mode of being quite unlike that to which the theatergoers of the day were becoming accustomed. Although he continued to write shorter scenes of a more domestic order throughout this period, Kyōka's major work as a playwright was to exaggerate the uncanny aspects that he put forward in *Shinja the Great*. Given his personal closeness to Kitamura Rokurō and his knowledge of what his talented friend could and could not do as an actor, Kyōka's departure from the "geisha pieces," the bread and butter of shinpa performance, can only be understood as a subtle though unmistakable critique of popular drama as it was developing at the time. Earlier, Kyōka had turned away from a workable formula for fiction in order to further his artistic explorations regardless of cost when he stopped writing "conceptual novels" in order to pursue the formation of the archetype despite the critical success of "Night Patrol" and "The Surgery Room." But, then again, in the larger context of dramatic performance in Japan at the time, Kyōka was only one of many who was not sanguine about the future of shinpa.

The decline of shinpa came as rapidly as its development. By September 1915, its future survival had become doubtful enough to warrant an entire issue of *The Drama Pictorial* (*Engei Gahō*) to be dedicated to the question "Will shinpa survive?" The world of the theater was changing rapidly in the wake of Stanislawski's theories of dramatic performance. In Japan, Shimamura Hōgetsu and Matsui Sumako's production of Maeterlinck's *Interior* (*Naibu*) and *Mona Vana* in September 1913 had a great impact upon the world of drama. Even Kawai Takeo broke with shinpa drama to establish the Public Troupe (Kōshū Gekidan), which performed translated plays from Europe, including Berlin's *Practicing MacBeth* and Hugo von Hofmannsthal's *Elektra*.[24] The performance of Kikuchi Kan's (1888–1948) *Father's Return* (*Chichi kaeru*) in 1917 indicates the extent to which European realism—after the style of Ibsen, Wilde, and others—continued to challenge shinpa. Kyōka, of course, was moving in exactly the opposite direction. If anything, the successes of Hōgetsu and Kikuchi made his plays seem all the more irrelevant and strangely out of touch with the times.

The Castle Tower

In 1917, Kyōka wrote what many consider to be his best play. *The Castle Tower* (*Tenshu monogatari*) follows naturally from *Shinja the Great*, *The Sunken Bell*, *Demon Pond*, and *The Sea God's Palace* both in the importance placed upon beauty and the unshakable trust with which the other world is presented. Like these plays, it too was deemed unacceptable for the audiences of the day. It was not performed until 1951, and even then its reception was uneventful. On the other hand, its performance in the 1970s was decisive in initiating the so-called Kyōka boom, which led to the critical re-evaluation that raised the author to the status of a leading literary figure. It was with this revival of *The Castle Tower* that Kyōka's resurrection began.

As in *The Sea God's Palace*, the stage is simply a part of the world beyond. In decided contrast to the horizontally oriented, wide but shallow kabuki stage, the imaginative space of *The Castle Tower* is vertically arranged in order to express the ontological theme it problematizes. It is a privileged place from which we look down upon the world with ridicule and contempt. Kyōka described the stage setting as follows:

> The fifth story of a castle tower. Pillars to the right and left. The stage is extended toward the audience in the front and on both sides, creating a raised platform covered with elegant mats of rice straw. Along the outer edge, a length of scarlet cord is tied from pillar to pillar with butterfly knots to represent a balustrade. Scarlet cords also serve as balustrades for a steep flight of stairs that rise to the ceiling at stage left, rear. On the other side, stage right, there is a door for another stairwell going down. . . . Just beyond the balustrade in front, a tiled roof and the tops of trees are visible. Similarly, the tips of a thick stand of trees skirt the front of the stage. (26: 451)

The action of the play takes place far above the barbarous world of human life, which is completely invisible to the audience. Dwelling in the towering heights of Himeji Castle, Princess Tomi and her retinue live in a beautiful yet misanthropic world. Their space is marked off by drum cords, much like the cave of Amaterasu was set off by *shimenawa* or ropes of rice straw. Like the underwater realm of *The Sea God's Palace*, this stage is only tenuously connected to the world of humankind. Rather than a magic looking glass, we see a stairway, an emblem of passage and symbol of that marginal space which provides the potential for conflict, change, and growth. Reflecting the continuing concerns of the archetype, the trespass of a mortal into this sacred, upper space by means of these stairs provides the dramatic thrust of the play. In this case, the other world is more in accord with the archetype than the ocean bottom of *The Sea God's Palace*: here a woman presides and a man transgresses.

The time of the play is "unclear, sometime during the feudal ages, late autumn, between the hours just before sunset and midnight." The entrance of Himekawa Zushonosuke, a young falconer who dares to climb the castle tower in search of his lord's prized falcon, establishes the necessary comparison between the higher and the lower, the supernal and the vulgar. Can he survive in this strange environment in which the young girls in Princess Tomi's retinue fish for flowers? Once he enters this upper space, he cannot go back unchanged. This is a foregone conclusion of the meta-story. In this sense, his is a one-way journey. The truth of his situation is emphasized by the song that the young girls sing as they dangle their lines over the edge of the tower. It is a tune familiar to us from "The Grass Labyrinth," which was similarly about the quest for total presence, for the impossible safety of the womb, and for the transcendental love of a young and beautiful and dead mother.

> To where, I ask, does this road lead?
> This narrow road, this dangerous road?
> To Tenjin-sama's land it leads, this narrow, narrow road. (26: 451)

This popular children's song, which dates to the Edo period, is a dialogue between a traveler and a border guard who attempts to block her way. Passage through the barrier at Hakone, an important divide between the two cultural spheres of Kantō and Kansai, was allowed only when sufficient cause was given for the trip, such as the death or illness of a relative. And even then, return was strictly prohibited. Consequently, there is a foreboding finality about the song and the atmosphere that it lends to Kyōka's stage.

In *jo-ha-kyū* fashion, the play builds slowly toward its denouement. It is driven more by the logic of imagery and streams of poetic language than by the requirements of plot. Indeed, the first third of the play is nothing more than a playing out of the various images associated with young women's fishing. Dew is the bait, and flowers are the catch—all articulated in a flood of verbiage designed to mesmerize and transport the audience to a world that is clearly beyond daily experience. Images of dew yield to those of rain as Princess Tomi enters, wearing a straw raincoat and surrounded by a lingering cloud of brilliantly colored butterflies. She appears at the staircase and gives an account of her outing in the world below, recalling how she called upon her friend "Miss Yuki of Demon Pond" to send a storm to rout Lord Harima's obstreperous hunting party, thus clearing the way for the visit of her sister, Princess Kame.

With Kame's arrival, the images of fishing take on a more sinister tone. As a gift for her sister, Kame brings the severed head of Takeda Emonosuke, lord of the castle where she resides. Takeda is none other than the brother of Lord Harima, ruler of Himeji Castle in which Tomi lives in an abandoned tower that no human being has dared enter for the past hundred years. The castle and the territory it controls may be expressive of the power of men, but the tower itself is a woman's world, in which the only masculine presence is a huge lion's head that decorates the center of the stage in totemic fashion. Kame's gift of a man's head is an easily readable sign of disdain for the men they have left behind. In the decapitated man's throat is a fish hook, said to be the cause of his death. By it we are to understand that he is Kame's catch for her sister and that his blood is his *tsuyu*, a homonym for both dew and juice, suggestive of both bait and blood. When the container for the head is opened, it is discovered that Takeda's "juices have spilled" (*tsuyu ga demashita*) (26: 465). By way of wordplay such as this, the drama progresses, no doubt flying past many in the audience in the same way that the dense complexity of a Noh libretto escapes all but the most well prepared.

Not wanting to present a soiled gift, Cinnabar, a male member of Kame's retinue, orders that it be cleaned up even though Tomi insists that things be left alone. The gory job falls to Long Tongue, an elderly attendant woman with a monstrously long tongue. Her willingness to serve is all too enthusiastic.

Cinnabar: I'm afraid our present's been defiled. Lest I be accused of following the ways of the unscrupulous fishmonger who douses his rotting bass with buckets of fresh water, old hag, give it a wipe. Won't you make it presentable for the Princess?
Tomi: (*With pipe in hand she studies the head.*) No need to worry. The bloody ones are even tastier.
Long Tongue: Spilled broth and garbage juice. No need for seasoning. Filthy! Oh, my eyes, you filthy thing! I'll have you cleaned up in no time. (*Dressed in a red pleated skirt, she crawls forward on her knees. Gripping the bucket with her wrinkled hands, she throws back her gray hair, opens her mouth wide, revealing rows of blackened teeth, and with her three-foot tongue begins licking blood from the face of the freshly severed head.*) Filthy! (*Slurping.*) Filthy! (*Slurping.*) You filthy thing, you. Oh, you filthy, delicious thing. You filthy thing. Oh, filthy. Oh, and so tasty.
Cinnabar: (*He lunges between the old woman and the head.*) Hey there, old hag. Keep your teeth off! There won't be anything left for the Princess's dinner. (26: 465–66)

Although rare in the novels and stories, this sort of gruesome humor can be found in the plays, where the world of monstrosity is allowed to speak for itself, as it were, and to be itself. Such comedy is encouraged by the visual force of the stage, which allows such grotesquerie to take on its most shockingly quotidian form. If humor finds a place in Kyōka's prose, it is mainly in the later works, such as *The Plum Blossom*. The earlier stories reflect a gravity common to most works of late-modern Japanese fiction. If the rise of the authoritarian author requires that serious matters be treated in somber ways, the increased visuality of the theater allows for more immediacy, which then has the almost counter-intuitive effect of allowing a more "human" range of expression. In this instance, Kyōka's famously pathological fear of any form of uncleanliness becomes the genesis of a joke. Taboo is broken with hilarity as the long-tongued hag licks the severed head clean with an extravagance to match the strength of the author's natural aversion to (and therefore his perverse interest in) anything so violent and repulsive.[25]

Why Princess Tomi and her sister are interested in the consumption of men's heads becomes clear later. Like Oscar Wilde's Salome, the women in the tower are driven by jealousy and the need for revenge. Their world is above and separate from the world of men for the same reason that Kyōka's heroines are superior to the men they must save. Once again, it is female suffering that allows the world to exist at all, and Kyōka wants to commemorate this debt. His recognition of the inequality women must suffer allows this dramatic reversal of punishing subject and punished object.[26] It is not from Wilde, certainly, but from the ancient trope of the *onryō*, or vengeful ghost, that Kyōka derives a rationale. Tomi, we learn, died a tragic and wrongful death. To escape the constant warfare of "feudal" times, she fled to a local sanctuary wherein a lion's head was enshrined. Rather than be taken alive and raped by warriors, she bit off her tongue and died. Moved by her fate, the lion held her in his lap and licked her face clean of blood while shedding tears of sympathy.

This, then, explains the presence of the lion's head at center stage. The figure symbolizes a male-yet-sympathetic principle that is granted a central place in an otherwise female realm. As in the other plays, Kyōka has established a tension between the mundane and the sacred, the male and the female. The world of the castle tower must be no less hierarchical than the male world below. Yet its order is essentially subversive of historical reality, an idealized alternative to business (and warfare) as usual. The lion's head exists, once again, as a visual sign of the way in which these two worlds can be bridged. It is through the character of Himekawa Zushonosuke, however, that we best understand the difference and distance that separates war from love. His dramatic trajectory is toward the lion's head and to the place where he and Princess Tomi will come together in order to express their mutual love and receive both the opprobrium of the world and the sanctification of art.

Before this can happen, however, he must discover his better nature and allow Princess Tomi enough time to become convinced of that nature for herself. He climbs into the tower for a mundane reason: to find his master's falcon, which was driven astray by the very storm that Princess Tomi brought upon his master's hunting party. As his lord's falconer, he is responsible for the bird's loss and will be executed if he fails to bring it back. And so, propelled by duty, he dares to enter this forbidding space. By her reactions to his visit, we know Tomi is truly a typical Kyōka heroine. She must sympathize with his oppression. Twice he attempts to return to the world below, and twice he discovers he cannot. Knowing he can no longer live among his fellow warriors, she takes it upon herself to protect him, even to love him. When Lord Harima's constables ascend the tower to take him, Zushonosuke and Princess Tomi declare their passion for each other and take shelter in the lion's head. Sensing their hiding place, the constables attack the lion. They aim at its eyes with their spears and finally blind it.

At the same moment, Zushonosuke and Princess Tomi also lose their sight. But they are spared when Tomi sends the constables away with the head of Lord Takeda, which the men fear to be the head of their own lord. Tomi knows the offering will vanish as soon as it leaves the castle and that the men will immediately return to kill them. Realizing their fate, they prepare to commit double suicide. But then enters Tōroku, a carpenter, who appears at their moment of greatest despair.

Tōroku: Beautiful children, don't cry! (*He walks directly to the lion's head and strokes it.*) First, allow me to open your eyes.
(He takes a chisel from his pouch and touches it to both of the lion's eyes.)
Tomi and Zusho: Ah!
Tōroku: How about it? Now you can see. Ha, ha. Now your eyes are open. There's joy in your open eyes. Laugh. Be merry! (*He laughs.*) (26: 497–98)

Their sight restored, Tomi and Zushonosuke learn that this artisan is the very one who originally carved the magical lion's head. He grants them peace and bids them to be merry. The play ends with this strange intervention.

The Castle Tower presents a clear view of Kyōka's hierarchy of being. Princess Tomi and Zushonosuke may be beautiful and far superior to the inhabitants of the male-oriented world below, but it is this artisan whom Kyōka enshrines as all-powerful. Others pale in comparison to this man who with a stroke of his chisel can restore sight and make a life of everlasting love possible. Far below are brutish men and an ugly, bellicose world of leaders and followers. Towering above is the realm of love and beauty. Tomi dwells here as yet another heroine victimized by the mundane. Zushonosuke likewise survives in the castle tower because of his beauty. And Tōroku prevails because he, like the peasants who are also described sympathetically, is still connected with the world of nature.[27] His name, Tōroku, or "Peach Six," suggests this affinity. Similarly, Himekawa Zushonosuke's appellation is a conglomeration of those elements necessary for the sustenance of Kyōka's imagination: women, water, and books.

This strange figure, Zushonosuke, is a shadow of the author's father. Kyōka had already paid him homage in "The Divine Chisel" ("Shinsaku," 1908), a short story about a man's attempt to regain his love by making a perfectly carved figure.[28] His reappearance here is perhaps one reason why Kyōka felt so strongly about having *The Castle Tower* performed. After its completion, he is said to have announced, "If someone would perform *The Castle Tower*, I would charge nothing. I would even send a gift."[29] But, as already mentioned, no one felt compelled to grant his wish, and the play was not performed until the 1950s. The delay notwithstanding, today it is one of the author's better known works, and its popularity has helped dispel the commonly held image of Kyōka as a writer of more domestic pieces such as *Taki no Shiraito* and *A Woman's Pedigree*. Compared with these more realistic pieces, Kyōka's plays of metamorphosis are both more challenging and more memorable. It is also true, however, that despite the ingenuity with which Kyōka expressed his unequivocal ideal of romantic love, these works suffer from a certain flatness and stridency.

Wild Roses and Creeping Despair

Perhaps stridency is the price that Kyōka had to pay for so wholeheartedly accepting the stage as the home for his wildest imaginings. There is little suspense in such a world, and none of the tension that gives the uncanny its usefulness as a narrative force. Indeed, Kyōka purposely reversed the assumptions upon which an aesthetic of the uncanny usually operates. If we suspected as much in the stories, here in the plays the function of art as a means to undermine reality becomes all too obvious. The richness of Kyōka's language creates an alienating effect: the more poetic the diction, the more outlandish the scene described. Since the commonplace and normative are under question, they are rendered more poetically than the supernatural or surreal, which are tagged in the plays by plainer forms of diction. In other words, a certain plainness of language prevails precisely because this is already the otherworld: nothing extraordinary needs to be established by the "distortion" of poetic diction. In this narrow sense, the powers of art are missing from a stage that has become increasingly ritualistic in function. Only this ritualism explains why *The Castle Tower* ends so mechanically—*deus ex machina*. Only this tells us why deliverance is supplied by an artisan rather than an artist.

For the late-modern spectator, Kyōka's ritualistic regard for supernatural forces poses the issue of acceptance and rejection without providing a sufficiently cushioning rhetoric of persuasion. Confronted by Kyōka's lucidly intentional reading of metamorphic wonders, we are coerced into viewing a field of visual signs that are supposedly believable by virtue of their lack of ambiguity. Without giving ourselves to the more participatory mode of reading that such heightened visual display makes necessary, our encounter with, especially, Kyōka's plays of metamorphosis leads us to the criticism voiced by the novelist and playwright Ikuta Chōkō (1882–1936), who remarked that Kyōka's taste for monsters threatens to "deteriorate into an idealism which is mere child's play."[30] This is to say that Kyōka's "fantasy" suffers from the clarity of his mature vision of the world and from the powerful finality of his contribution to the late-modern critique, which moved the site of drama from the marginal riverbank to the carefully equipped and lighted stage.[31]

Although seldom discussed, another of Kyōka's most powerful plays was written five years later, toward the end of the Taishō period and a few years before the last of Kyōka's attempts as a playwright. *Wild Roses* (*Yamabuki*, 1923) is an attempt to reinstate both the marginal space of Japanese drama and the role of the artist. It makes a return to a more representational mode, letting us maintain an "objective" distance between ourselves and what is happening on stage. At the same time, it clearly reflects Kyōka's experience with the visual presence of the metamorphic plays. *The Castle Tower* is the product of Kyōka's idealism, whereas *Wild Roses* flows from his resignation. Its visual spectacle does not invite us into the space of ritual. Rather, it presents an intense and probing examination of ritual as a vehicle for transgression and atonement.

The world of *Wild Roses* is exaggerated in its simplicity. Two short scenes introduce four characters: a shop owner, a puppeteer, a woman, and a painter. The time is late spring, the season of blossoms. As the curtain opens, the puppeteer, Heguri Tōji, is drinking alone. He is inebriated and obviously unhappy, punishing himself for a past that the audience has yet to discover. He speaks irreverently about the Buddhist ceremonies that are taking place nearby. With a festival going on at the neighborhood temple, who will pay any attention to his puppet show? He orders drink after drink yet is not so drunk that he cannot admire the three cherry trees in full bloom outside the shop. The blossoms provide a point of transition, leading to the woman and the painter who stop to admire them.

She is twenty-five years old and beautiful. Traveling alone, she is escaping from her husband, Count Koitogawa. The Count is a penniless member of the aristocracy, interested more in her money than in her. Their marriage is miserable. Persecuted daily by her mother-in-law, she finally flees in order to follow the painter, Shimazu Masa, a lover from before her marriage. To the painter she confesses her love and tells him that without his love she will become like the dead carp she has just discovered in a nearby stream. When he refuses to become involved, she gives herself to the puppeteer, whose self-loathing, we now learn, results from his murder of a young woman many years ago. Murderer or not, she chooses him as her new partner. In their misery, she promises that "for the next ten years, the next one hundred years," she will do whatever he wants, "morning and night" (26: 525).

What he wants most is to be punished for his transgression. He asks to be beaten; and she obliges by pounding him with her umbrella. If she cannot have the painter, she will marry the old puppeteer.

I had no where to go, and nothing but death to look forward to. But now I've found myself. (*She turns, showing her resolve.*) I'll go with this old man. He admits to killing a woman and now wants to be whipped day and night. On behalf of the women of the world, I'll clear away their pains of revenge. He worships his Shizuka Gozen, a woman of great beauty. I was born a woman. So by way of this old man, I'll let the dust of sorrow and retribution cover me. Just as he picked up the carp, rotting in the ditch, now I'll have him handle my flesh, weak and fallen. (26: 530)

To commemorate their marriage, she and the puppeteer eat the remains of the dead carp. The painter is their witness. As the two go off, he reflects upon what he has witnessed, questioning its reality.

Yes, this is the world of demons. Or could it be a dream? No, this is reality. (*He stares at the woman's sandals.*) Maybe I should throw everything away. My body, my name. (*He picks up one of the sandals. Anguish shows on his face.*) No, I have my work. (*He throws the sandal away.*)

The sounds of the storm end.

Temple bells ring in the night. (26: 535–36)

The bizarre encounter leaves the painter a wiser man: he has learned something about matters of the heart. But in being led to question reality, Shimazu's decision to linger behind in a familiar world is filled with both regret and resignation. The same was true of the wanderer in "One Day in Spring." But now the usual answers no longer feel like answers. It is as if this special house Kyōka has made for the dispossessed has been mortgaged. For one thing, the lessons of Buddhism are starting to erode all others away, including the sustaining assertions of the archetype. It is no longer possible to tell which is more monstrous and hideous, the reality we imagine or the one we live. This is precisely why Akutagawa Hiroshi, son of the famous writer and one of the most sensitive producers of Kyōka's plays, would later reframe these questions in a way with which Kyōka would certainly have agreed. "Some comment about the fantastic nature of Kyōka's plays. But in fact they are only reflective of reality. What could be more hideous than Japan during the 1930s and the 1940s?"[32]

Besides keeping him in the public eye at a time when his popularity as a novelist continued to wane, access to the space of the stage also allowed Kyōka to express the monstrosity he saw more openly and more honestly than ever before. The exposure to this seductively powerful place of transformation made him bold. Yet he also seems to have been startled by the evanescence of his own conclusions. In this final scene in *Wild Roses*, we get a foreshadowing of the years ahead. Although Kitamura Rokurō, now a solid friend and supporter, described a man enjoying his maturity—"These days, Izumi smokes cigars and drinks wine. He's become sophisticated, but in sentiment he's the same as ever, a most pleasant person."[33]—in fact, the years ahead would be hard ones for Kyōka. He continued to get financial backing from Minakami Takitarō, his patron and friend. There was no suffering in this sense. There was, however, a spiritual trial. Although the painter in *Wild Roses* could pronounce with satisfying finality "I have my work," Kyōka himself would come to suspect that even literature might not have the power to save him.

CHAPTER 14

Among Friends

1915–1927

The Mature Eccentric

Kyōka's interest in writing for the stage waned after 1917 and *The Castle Tower*.[1] He had written stories throughout the Taishō period while working on the plays, but it was not until around 1918 that he again concentrated on writing prose. His intense involvement with the theater had lasting effects, however. Due to his experimentation with the stage as a place for the dispossessed, his later fiction acquires an even more ghastly, intensely visual tenor. The 1915 story "Will-o'-the-wisp" ("Kakegō"), for instance, illustrates the direction of this shift. A grotesque account of a man's encounter with a diseased and betrayed woman, "Will-o'-the-wisp" is guided by the familiar contours of the archetype as it quickly moves toward visual excess.

The ocean was even drearier. As the deathly calm of evening passed into night, the water became heavier, more oppressed, a molten copper that coated the beach.

Striking and spreading, the sea broke into pieces. It approached then slid away, waves boiling, seething. Muted and hushed, the black water undulated, occasionally throwing a wave upon the sand—a gush of indigo lightning falling upon purple, blanketing the beach with a blue light and suddenly flaring as if doused with oil. Before Mamiya, the ocean was a twisted, tormented volcano. . . .

The dark blue water grew huge in the sky, throwing up its legs, blasting, gnashing its purple fangs against all that obstructed—the cliffs, the grass, the sand. Its waves were the writhings of a poisonous dragon, its spray the heated flame of vengeful spirits fished and tyrannized by the billion.

Although its ghastliness was quite beyond comparison, let us compare the sight of this ocean to something gentle in the extreme—a glowing firefly, fluttering delicately around hydrangea blossoms at night. (16: 478–479)

If Kyōka's involvement with the stage heightened the metaphoric intensity of stories such as "Will-o'-the-wisp," it also seems to have stirred in him a desire to write longer works that allowed him to reflect and meditate upon past events. The impressive length of the longest of the Taishō period novels might simply be a result of greater maturity, a development of past strengths quite apart from anything imparted by the new training of the theater. Yet there is something suddenly both more fluent and more orchestrated about the novels of this later period, as if Kyōka's understanding of the world beyond and its connections with events of the present had in fact been stimulated by the new spatial configurations afforded by the stage. In both *The Peony's Song* (*Shakuyaku no uta*, 1918), his third-longest work, and *Women of Acquaintance* (*Yukari no onna*, 1919), second in length only to *The Elegant Railway*, the role of memory and the models for the characters are particularly obvious, suggesting an increasingly strong autobiographical interest. Narratively speaking, their length follows from the prolixity of the flashback, an encoding of the present with the past, a rhetorical mode particularly well suited to the Buddhist notion of karma (*innen*) that was coming to preoccupy Kyōka even more intensely.

In the case of *The Peony's Song*, many of the remembered events were relatively recent. Particularly important was a November 1916 meeting with a young man who was to become one of his closest associates, Minakami Takitarō (Abe Shōzō). Kubota Mantarō, who was a disciple of Osanai Kaoru and already one of the leading figures in the anti-naturalist Mita school, brought Minakami to the Banchō house. Kubota had been introduced to Kyōka through Ikuta Chōkō at a Noh performance sponsored by the journal *The Cuckoo* (*Hototogisu*). He had visited Kyōka for the first time either in December 1914 or during the first two months of 1915, and his purpose in calling was to appeal for help. Kubota had been asked by his friend Minakami, who was studying abroad at the time, to send him everything that Kyōka had written, and he had come to track down a number of hard-to-find, earlier publications. Impressed that someone was such an ardent reader of his work, Kyōka invited Kubota to stay for dinner. Kubota let his own likes and dislikes be known: "I told him frankly that I didn't care for his monsters. When he asked me what I did like, I told him promptly that I admired 'A Female Visitor.'"

At the time of their meeting in 1916 Minakami had just returned from studying abroad for five years in the United States and England. His interest in Kyōka had begun sixteen years earlier, when he read *The Maki Cycle* at the age of thirteen. His own first published work, "A Child from the Heights" ("Yama no te no ko," 1911), shows the influence of this series of stories and also of Kyōka's *Teriha Kyōgen*. It focuses on a young and privileged boy who escapes from his wet nurse and makes friends with the less wealthy children in his neighborhood. It lyrically describes his sadness upon being taken from their company and follows the story of one of the young girls he met, who is sold to a geisha house. Nagai Kafū liked the story and published it in *Mita Literature*. Kafū also published his next work, for which Minakami used a pen name for the first time. Reflecting his devotion to Kyōka's writings, he created a nom de plume by combining the first and last names of two Kyōka characters: the valiant Minakami Kikuo in *The Elegant Railway* and poor-boy-turned-aristocrat Chihaya Takitarō of "Black Lily."

Minakami, the eldest son of the founder of the highly successful Meiji Insurance Company, followed his father as its head. Because of his wealth and willingness to use his considerable means to further literary causes, such as bankrolling the publication of *Mita Literature*, he became as much Kyōka's patron as his protégé. In the 1928 autochronology, Kyōka mentioned Minakami.

June 1918.
I publish *The Mandarin Account* (*En'ō chō*), a new monograph. Last spring I had received an advance from the publisher, but couldn't come up with a manuscript. Minakami, who saw me crying in my cups, told me that his pocket change was more than my advance. "Just give the money back!" With his friendly encouragement, I finish a draft. (1: x)

Perhaps in appreciation for Minakami's friendship, a portrait of him appears in *The Peony's Song* as "a sexually attractive man with money and power." Having read and acquired every piece Kyōka ever wrote, Minakami must have known that without his abiding appreciation of the arts, these same qualities would have led to his immediate rejection. He was, after all, a businessman of Taishō Japan, perfectly suited for a role as antagonist.

Women of Acquaintance

Women of Acquaintance is one of Kyōka's finest and most comprehensive works. In this long novel, Kyōka includes all the major themes as well as all the principal players: himself, his father, his mother, his grandmother Kite, his wife Suzu, his cousin Meboso Teru, and his childhood sweetheart Yuasa Shige. The women have appeared in earlier pieces, though usually in combination with each other, overlapped and combined to form an ideal image of womanhood. Although the same sort of melding occurs again in *Women of Acquaintance*, it is noticeably modulated by a historical, autobiographical impulse that emerges at this point and deepens the somber tone of Kyōka's mature work. Since the original energy for the archetype was the trauma of lived events, we might say there is a biographical element even to Kyōka's wildest imaginings. Yet with the further development of his fiction toward more intensely imaginative variations of the meta-story, a stronger tendency toward documentation also appears. In the past, Kyōka had resisted the desire to draw too frankly from his own experience: too strong an autobiographical interest had unmistakably contributed to the misguided methodology of the I-novel and its obtrusive first-person. Yet even Kyōka's commitment to artifice eventually dwindled, despite his lack of regard for the tenets of Japan's realists.

Kyōka never used a first-person narrator. Yet the hero of *Women of Acquaintance*, Asagawa Reikichi, is clearly a thinly disguised proxy for Kyōka himself. The novel begins when Asagawa returns to his hometown of Kanazawa after learning that construction of a new park has made it necessary for him to move his parents' graves. He leaves his wife, Okitsu, in Tokyo and, while arranging for the removal of his parents' remains to the capital, re-establishes himself with various women of his acquaintance. One is his resourceful cousin and childhood friend Okō (modeled after Meboso Teru). Another is Tsuyuno, whom he met while staying with relatives at a hot springs in Ryōnai. And a third is his childhood sweetheart Oyō (modeled after Yuasa Shige). She is married to a wealthy Kanazawa merchant and is suffering from facial disfigurement, having accidentally ingested the poison of an insect.

What should be a fairly simple matter of arranging with the family temple for the removal of the remains becomes complicated and even dangerous when Tsuyuno visits Okō's residence, where Reikichi is staying. She is working as a domestic servant for a local political figure and newspaper owner, Daigōji, a typically evil villain: politically powerful, wealthy, yet crude and of limited intelligence. Because Tsuyuno fears punishment if she returns to Daigōji's home, Okō and Reikichi encourage her to take shelter, first with them and later in the home of her former wet nurse, who happens to be a member of the *burakumin* class. Daigōji and his men discover Reikichi's involvement and make it impossible for him to return to Tokyo as scheduled. In an attempt to escape possible violence, he and Tsuyuno finally seek refuge at Shiragiku, an isolated valley in the mountains that surround the city.

Reikichi has been to Shiragiku before. As a child, he was once saved from a runaway horse by a peasant girl, Shimo, who threw herself over him and was trampled to death. With regret and as an expression of their gratitude for the young girl's sacrifice, Reikichi and his mother made the trip to her village on horseback. Years later, as he journeys toward the "haunted valley" a second time, he notices another woman on the far side of the river. Oyō is on her way to bathe in the pure waters of the same valley, hoping they will cure her affliction. She is the woman he has longed for all his life, and, true to the pattern, his image of her becomes confused with that of his mother. With her in sight, the true meaning of his return to his hometown becomes clear. His is a journey into the past, a reunion with his dead mother that is aided by other women who protect and are protected by him along the way. He sacrifices everything for this all-encompassing passion. Reikichi crosses the river, leaving Tsuyuno behind. He eventually reaches Shiragiku and meets Oyō. There he is attacked by Shimo's father, Jinjirō, a madman beaten to insanity by his own father as punishment for trying to see his mother's nakedness. Reikichi dies of his wounds, but not until Okitsu arrives from Tokyo. Tsuyuno commits suicide. Okō grieves.

First published in *Women's Pictorial* (*Fujin gahō*), the novel stands as Kyōka's fullest and most protracted affirmation of the archetype. Its fullness results from Reikichi's ability to remember and to be loved by so many women. He is, of Kyōka's many protagonists, the most fulfilled. As Kasahara Nobuo has argued, the hero's obvious egotism and the childish intensity of his desire to require the continual sacrifice of others brings many sacrificial women to his side.[2] The amplitude of Reikichi's desire certainly matches the author's. Yet this instance of the modern search for self had to be an obliteration of that same self. Especially here and in the later works, desire becomes problematic if we consider how Buddhist notions of cause and effect preclude the possibility of existential freedom. Ultimately, the will to be loved in such a context can only become a yearning for cause and effect itself, that absolute fact of interrelatedness that allows in its denial of existential presence the possibility of a rhetorical one. Human will reinforces the freedom of those connotative associations that join all things by means of an utter lack of freedom. In turn, this interconnectedness is an essentially allusive reality. In this sense, Kyōka resolves the paradox of presence—a wish for the unchangeable in a world of change—because he is able to establish a narrative strategy in which memory can be readily commingled with action. In the imaginative text, everything is ultimately present, but always as yet another (necessary) delusion. Here the meaning of fiction, as it is created at this breaking point between artifice and remembrance, and between imagination and documentation, is that which becomes both more "fantastic" and more "real" at the same time.

Reikichi is acquainted with so many women because the world of *Yukari no onna*, as suggested in this title, is a fictive sphere in which karmic connection (*yukari*) serves as an unimpeachable structuring device in an otherwise amorphous reality. Karma defines psychological space by establishing interconnection and relationship. As a structuring principle, it is as general and expansive as the counternotions of illusion and flux. Whereas a more positivistic framing of the world might require the analytical strengths of plot and plausibility, the premise of delusion upon which a Buddhist perception of reality is based is well expressed by the polysemic tensions common to the Noh libretto or to Kyōka's visual style. The similarities between Kyōka's work and Noh drama continue to be obvious. Not only is the text constantly injecting the past into the present, but it also progresses by first posing a series of riddles by which the story develops. The method is similar to the "cutback" in cinematography. It is this non-linear and sometimes antitemporal quality that, relying upon a plastic sense of space, is best expressed through corresponding metamorphoses of visually understood images.

It was precisely this desire to pull bits of the past into the present that made Kyōka return again to Kanazawa. Twenty-eight years after leaving for the capital, the pull of his hometown was still strong. The very name of his protagonist, Asagawa Saikichi, is drawn from the names of the two rivers that flow through the city, the *Asa*no and the *Sai*. Moreover, the names "Kanazawa" and "Kaga" appeared in the original manuscript, only to be deleted or replaced at later stages.[3] Despite the obfuscation, there can be little doubt of the story's setting. When Shun'yōdō published the story as a book in 1921, the painter Komura Settai (1887–1942) supplied a fictional map that showed the relative positions of the places mentioned—Mukai Yama (Mt. Utatsu), the Asano River (Asa in this case written with a different character), the train station, and so on—without specifically identifying Kyōka's hometown itself. Few readers were actually fooled. One reviewer, Mizuno Akira, who had never been to the city, wrote, "I could vividly see the mountains and graveyards of Kanazawa as if they were right before my eyes."[4]

Although his hometown continued to be an important anchor for his soul, Kyōka did not necessarily depict Kanazawa in a favorable light. He expressed positive feelings for the women remembered in association with the city, but he remained generally critical of the city and its social organization. Not only does Reikichi speak disparagingly of his hometown in the opening passages of *Women of Acquaintance*, but other characters and subsequent events underline precisely those aspects of life in Kanazawa that Kyōka found most distasteful. A summation of exactly what he most disliked is voiced by Maezuka Gonkurō, a member of the burakumin caste, who protects Tsuyuno from Daigōji and his thugs and accepts Reikichi as a friend. "No place discriminates on the basis of wealth, family background, and personal status like this town" (19: 424). Kyōka did not dislike aristocrats as such. His aversion was toward what they represented: the arrogance of local authorities and the obsequious "castle town mentality" of the lower classes.[5]

To an anthropologist like Yoshitani Hiroya trying to understand the social structure of Kanazawa in the years following the Russo-Japanese War, *Women of Acquaintance* is a text that shows the "attack" of the empowered (governmental) class upon the "darkness" (*yami*) of those on the periphery: the merchants, the denizens of the temples and brothels, the peasants, and the outcastes.[6] Indeed, this mapping of Daigōji's incursions into Reikichi's sphere of acquaintance makes a pattern of invasion clear. The aggression originates at the center—from Hirosaka, the topos of governmental power—and moves west toward the neighborhoods on either side of the Asano River. Such is the political geography of Kanazawa, as well as the aesthetic geography described in Chapter 1. They are similar because Kyōka, who grew up in this castle-town environment that was still ordered by rigid class distinctions and by discrimination based on "wealth, family background, and personal status," defined himself and his literary work in terms of this bifurcated space. As an artist, he made use of the tensions that existed between them. And this, as much as nostalgia, explains his continued interest in Kanazawa as a setting.

Kyōka's art is born of inequality, a point made clear by this congruence of political and aesthetic geographies. If the movement of governmental intrusion is from the center to the margin, so is Kyōka's spiritual journey. His neighborhood, as established by birth and by his upbringing as an artisan's son, already lies on the margin. Even this margin has its periphery, however. It is the far side of the Asano River, where the disenfranchised dwell. The structure of the archetype finds its original pattern here: the Asano River forming a watery barrier to the other side, a commingled world of the sacred (as represented by mountains—especially Mt. Utatsu with its numerous temples and graveyards), the artistic (as made present by the seasonable availability of space for temporary stages on the riverbank) and by the more permanent presence of the entertainment quarters, and the "polluted" settlements of the supposedly nonhuman. Reikichi's progression is to this other side, a world of danger, of magic, of possibility, of death. The far bank is his dead mother's abode, a spiritual home away from home. It is also the retrogressive, not-yet-rational, mountainous, sacred preserve of myth that is, because it retains the possibilities of belief and salvation negated by modernity and reason, an enabling site of trespass, reunion, beauty, and bliss. No one understood this better than Yanagita Kunio, who became one of Kyōka's most avid readers.

Kyōka's open sympathy for the outcastes who live on the other side is colored by both idealization and resignation. In his heart, Kyōka must have harbored feelings of sympathy and discrimination toward the "unclean." His fascination with pollution was displayed with shocking clarity in the fish-eating scene of *Wild Roses* and in the blood-drinking scene of the short story "The Blood-Tempered Sword" ("Yōken kibun," 1920). For Kyōka, defilement was always an exploitation, made beautiful by its very structure of clashing opposites. The same must be said of his treatment of women, the stated topic of this novel. For they, too, properly belong to the opposite bank, to the world of spirits. Like Tsuyuno, they are tortured and unappreciated by those whose more aggressive instincts have procured for themselves material wealth and social status. For weaker men, as we well know by now, they are a spiritual necessity.

Outcastes and Kawabata Yasunari

Hinin and burakumin appear in a few other stories. In every instance they are aestheticized and placed on the side of good. The heroine of "The Blood-Tempered Sword," an arresting but infrequently discussed story, is a hinin. In the story's climactic scene, Omachi commits suicide while performing ablutions in a river. She attempts to cleanse herself of her impurity because of her desire to be loved by Seizaburō, a handsome young man whom she mistakes for a "normal" person and therefore someone far beyond her. Because she is "non-human," her cleansing is futile. And so, in resignation, she stabs herself and lets her defiled and defiling blood flow away in the current of the river in which she stands.

> "Are you in pain?"
> "No." Her voice faded away.
> "What happened?"
> "It hurts a little . . . here."
> She raised a trembling arm, the elbow bent and deathly white against the water, and pointed to her chest through her padded kimono. Her fingernails were crimson, and her fingers like small white fish swimming in a trail of blood.
> "I stabbed myself just now, when I entered the river. There's nothing I can do now, so let there be no regrets. . . . I'm able to talk to you only because of the power of Fudō. When I think upon your words and how your concern has unraveled the knot of my heart, I feel as if I'm melting and flowing away. Watch out! Don't get near my blood, or you'll be polluted. Don't let it touch you. You'll be polluted. It's the blood of a hinin! Of an eta!"
> She opened her silk kimono, and from the wound beneath her breast gushed a scarlet stream. . . .
> "Who cares about pollution? Let me have your blood!"
> Seizaburō writhed with passion. He grabbed her hand in his and pulled her into his tight embrace. Before the color faded from her lips, he put his mouth to her bosom and greedily drank her blood.
> He fell to his knees in the river. Holding erect the frozen blade that reflected the snowy whiteness of her face, he sucked the clots of blood from its tip.
> It was at this moment, with the smell of her life on his tongue and lips, that he grasped the hidden secrets of sword-making. . . . He was the young man who later became the famous sword smith, Kiyomitsu, a man who publicly disclosed to all the world that he himself was an outcaste. (29: 127–28)

Kyōka sympathetically portrays the uncleanliness of Omachi, a wandering minstrel whose occupational attire is red and white. A typical heroine, she must sacrifice herself. Her blood, spilt for the sake of others, contributes to Seizaburō's understanding of himself and, therefore, to his development as one who knows and can create beauty.

Kyōka's aesthetics of the margin affirms a long-established pattern of art being born at the riverbank, society's no-man's land. At the same time, the author's traditional sense of geography implicates ancient prejudices that persist to the present day. For instance, discrimination against hinin and burakumin, also the topic of Shimazaki Tōson's *Broken Commandment* (*Hakai*), continues even though the pollutions associated with occupations such as butchering animals and tanning leather were reconsidered during Japan's encounter with the West and its different standards of food and clothing. Kyōka's sympathetic rendering of these marginalized groups comes not so much from his stance as a social reformer but from a poetics that requires the sort of beauty that is born of suffering. As such, the shedding of Omachi's blood has limited relevance as a social critique, although its role in the archetype could not be more obvious.

When we lay the political and aesthetic maps of Kyōka's hometown over each other, we see that if the people of the far bank are fated, so too are Kyōka's protagonists. Having left the present to enter the past, having departed from civilization to journey into the hinterland of Shiragiku, having seen his mother's image, met his eternal love, crossed the Asano River, and endured a violent storm, Asakawa Reikichi, the hero of *Women of Acquaintance*, must die. As always, the salutary effect of this fictional trespass is not long-lasting. Still, for the author, it was real in its effect and, in this case, more broadly conceived and elaborated than usual. Perhaps the novel is unnecessarily sustained. Extensive trimming occurred between its serial publication in *Women's Pictorial* and its subsequent emergence as a book, but there is still much that could be pared without weakening its impact. Occasionally, we may wonder if the many reminiscences brought together here could possibly mean as much to Kyōka's readers as they did to him.

Even so, many have found the novel to be highly accomplished and, if anything, underappreciated. According to Kawabata Yasunari, Kyōka's obscurity was near-total by this point in his career. "I remember that when *Women of Acquaintance* first appeared, it drew no attention from the bundan." Yet for Kawabata, "it was only Kyōka's work that I read hungrily, my heart pounding inside my chest."[7] Six years later, upon publication of the collected works by Shun'yōdō in May 1925, he wrote again about this work, describing the author as "a visionary who creates with the most possibly beautiful language the most possibly beautiful world." This is a "land of beautiful monsters" that "two out of ten cannot abide." It is "too beautiful," which meant for Kawabata, who was just beginning his own career and consciously trying to read new relevance into Kyōka's work, that it was simply "too Japanese." For the young Kawabata, Kyōka was a model to emulate. "There are very few like him; throughout his long career as a writer, he has never lost the freshness of motivation. Whenever Kyōka writes, he feels the desire anew, never losing the purity of his motives. . . . He is a natural-born artist . . . who does not tire of his dreams." As a dreamer, Kyōka had for Kawabata no significance as a social critic. "It is quite impossible for this lyrical romanticist to analyze reality. He does not give us a critique of it. One sometimes gets the impression that he does not even taste reality. He never doubts. He only believes and enjoys. Thus, he has no philosophy. If he had, it would be called a philosophy of lyricism."[8]

Kawabata's motivation for writing so enthusiastically about Kyōka becomes increasingly clear as the values of Japan, beauty, and self gradually coalesce, and as he locates in Kyōka's work a "new glorious possibility for the Japanese language." As we will see, Mishima Yukio and Tanizaki Jun'ichirō would similarly anoint Kyōka as the bearer of the Japanese tradition, and for many of the same reasons. In Kawabata's reckoning, the beleaguered tradition is represented by Kyōka's ability to "decorate life" and to hold in reverence those who have passed on to the realm of the dead. Focusing on the novel, Kawabata praises the powerful and convincing portraits of three women of acquaintance: "Okō is chivalrous and charming. Tsuyuno is lovely and grand. And Oyō is lofty and noble. Each of them is more beautiful than anything on earth." He commends, also as traditional and worthy, Kyōka's regard for his ancestors as expressed in Reikichi's attitudes toward his grandmother, his father, and especially his mother. "Kyōka's predilection is to view only the most traditional and beautiful aspects of the ethical principles and emotions that developed between people and also the relations that bind them, not just the reverence with which we consider our ancestors but the relationships between parent and child, husband and wife, lover and lover, neighbor and neighbor, master and disciple."[9]

In short, *Women of Acquaintance* could not have been a more engaging work to Kawabata Yasunari, who found it necessary to distance himself from just that sensibility which had condemned Kyōka to obscurity. If we can trust Kawabata's reading of current literary trends, Kyōka was largely dismissed by the writers of his own generation but had come to be "read once again by the central figures of the bundan, his value newly discovered." Speaking for this younger generation, Kawabata declared, "We younger writers will read Kyōka in a new light and refresh ourselves from the everlasting spring (*izumi*) that he is."[10] As we shall see, the spring began to fluctuate after *Women of Acquaintance*, but not, however, until Kyōka had written some of his best short fiction.

Tanizaki Jun'ichirō and "Osen and Sōkichi"

One of the "younger writers" whom Kawabata had in mind was Tanizaki Jun'ichirō, soon to become one of the leading literary figures in Japan. Kyōka was Tanizaki's senior by thirteen years. They first met in 1911, at a New Year's party sponsored by the *Yomiuri News*. Among the writers, painters, and critics present, Tanizaki was a newcomer, both pleased and nervous about having been invited for the first time. As he remembered it, "I fell on my butt" when Kyōka, already an established writer, came walking by. Tokuda Shūsei made the introductions: "Izumi, you like Tanizaki, right?" Kyōka, who was already drunk, managed only to say, "Oh, Tanizaki."[11]

In fact, Kyōka had read Tanizaki's stories and liked what he had sampled. Among their shared interests were a fascination with the color white, an unfathomable yearning for mothers, and an extreme devotion to feminine beauty. (Of all of Tanizaki's works, Kyōka most praised *The Arrowroot of Yoshino* [*Yoshino kuzu*], probably because it, too, is a remembrance of a mother, in which the whiteness of paper is the whiteness of Tanizaki's mother's thighs.) Like Nagai Kafū, who promoted Tanizaki by publishing his work in *Mita Literature*, he was considered an aesthete, a member of the so-called Aesthetic school or *tanbiha*. Kafū's "The Work of Tanizaki Jun'ichirō" ("Tanizaki Jun'ichirō no sakuhin"), published in the November 1911 edition of the journal, praises him for "the mysteriousness that derives from physical horror," "the utter urbanity of his sensibility," and the "perfection of his prose." Quite clearly, Tanizaki showed an affinity with Kafū, whom he discovered as an "artist of similar sentiment" upon reading *American Story* (*Amerika monogatari*). Nonetheless, Tanizaki's first widely acclaimed story, "The Tattoo," was probably inspired by Kyōka's "The Grave Writer" ("Higedaimoku," 1897) rather than by anything that Kafū had written.[12] As described by one Japanese critic, the influence was twofold, "Kafū was Tanizaki's father, and Kyōka his mother."[13] Obvious differences separate the three, but we can identify a shared appreciation for Edo culture and also a passionate regard for artistic style.

It was not until some years after the New Year's party that Tanizaki became professionally involved with Kyōka. Having begun his career as a playwright, he was hired in 1920 by the Taishō Motion Picture Company to produce screenplays, including one based on Kyoka's "Sands of Katsushika" ("Katsushika sunago," 1900). Set in Tokyo's Fukagawa district, an area interlaced with numerous rivers and canals, the story is about a young geisha, Kikue, who is so devastated by the death of a famous kabuki actor, Onoe Kitsunosuke (after Onoe Kikunosuke), that she tries to kill herself. Dressed in a robe given to her friend Onui by the deceased actor, she plunges into a river, only to be fished out by an elderly boatman, Shichibei. In the story's final scene, she stands upon the Hōrai Bridge. Chanting "Hail to Amida, Buddha of Light," she offers the robe to the river and watches it disappear in the distance, slowly sinking in the stream.

We have no account of what Kyōka thought of the production, although he did mention the occasion of their meeting in one of the autochronologies. "I meet Tanizaki Jun'ichirō about a movie" (1: x). A few years later, when Tanizaki moved from Tokyo to the Kansai area after the Great Earthquake of 1923, their contacts fell off; before that, however, they had already become friends. Anecdotal evidence suggests that Kyōka and Tanizaki frequented a shop called the Hatsune, a *tori ryōriya* that specialized in cooking fowl. Because of Kyōka's various eating phobias, sharing a boiling pot with the ravenous Tanizaki posed considerable problems. Before Kyōka dared eat any of the morsels slowly cooking in the hot broth, Tanizaki would devour them. Kyōka would then add new ingredients to the pot, only to watch Tanizaki snatch them away as well. Kyōka is said to have used his chopsticks to concentrate a certain number of chicken pieces on his side of the pot and then to have made his strategy perfectly clear to Tanizaki. "From here this way is mine. You eat on that side."[14]

Kyōka must have admired Tanizaki's vitality. Although he himself could never be so comfortably indulgent, Kyōka was not above learning from someone who was so obviously at home within the world of the senses. Some see the masochistic tone of the later plays, as noticeable in *Wild Roses* and *Warring States, Rice with Tea*, as Tanizaki's influence.[15] Perhaps this is so. It makes sense that Kyōka's response to Tanizaki's sensualism should tend toward cruelty since, as guided by the archetype, any movement toward the opposite sex necessarily results in violence and death. In their conscious violation of taboo, Kyōka's acts of trespass are much more limited than Tanizaki's fictional acts of sexual indulgence. The distinction between them is the difference between flesh and wood, between the smell of skin and that of blossoms. The mother-longing (*hahagoi*) and youth of Kyōka's heroes do not usually lead to sexual encounters such as that experienced by Tanizaki's Tadasu in "As I Crossed the Bridge of

Dreams." For all their similarities and their mutual admiration, Kyōka and Tanizaki had very different things to say about human sexuality. Flowing blood is more color than warmth for Kyōka, since his work, reflecting a more picto-centric framing of reality, is not so obviously dependent upon the teleological structures of plot that Tanizaki learned from Conan Doyle and other Western masters of manipulation. In Kyōka's work, the body has no weight. It is not yet a territory of the late-modern mind's linear process of discovery.[16]

In other words, Kyōka's men are not mature since they are driven by an archetype that requires an enduring state of sexual inexperience. This will change, however. As Kyōka moved closer to Tanizaki's position of experience, the resulting denial of the meta-story meant nothing short of a crisis for Kyōka as a person and as an artist. For now, however, he was still playing with the inherent danger of ingesting something that, though necessary, might be pol-luting and life-threatening. The appearance of food in titles from this period, for instance, can be understood as both a playful code sent to young friends such as Tanizaki—"Here's something tasty for you!"—and a subtle invitation to the beauty of violence. In each case, with "Osen and Sōkichi" ("Baishoku kamonanban," 1920), "The Osprey's Sushi" ("Misago no sushi," 1923), and *War-ring States, Rice with Tea* (*Sengoku chazuke*, 1926), the shedding of blood is central to the narrative satisfaction of each.

This point is easily demonstrated. The enigmatic title of the famous short story "Baishoku kamonanban" includes a name of a dish (*kamonanban*) that consists of strips of duck meat served with scallions atop noodles and broth, served southern barbarian (i.e., Portuguese) style. The juxtaposition of the words "prostitute" (*baishoku*) and "duck noodles" (*kamonanban*) probably refers in an oblique way to Osen, the story's heroine. Having saved the young pro-tagonist Sōkichi from slitting his throat with a razor, Osen works as a prosti-tute, selling her flesh, in order to provide food and nourishment for him. He becomes her adopted son (and possibly her lover). She sacrifices even her sanity for his education and success. In his debt of gratitude for what she has done, Sōkichi seeks to end her suffering by bringing a razor to her hospital bed.

If *Women of Acquaintance* represents the height of Kyōka's longer novelistic style, stories such as "Osen and Sōkichi" and "How Beautiful Without Eye-brows" ("Mayu kakushi no rei," 1924) represent the peak of Kyōka's polished short-fiction style. "Osen and Sōkichi" flows easily and is well cadenced, but it is structurally little more than an assortment of established pieces, joined to-gether with transitions that are often confusing to a reader who does not realize that Kyōka is drawing from an established archetype. Kyōka began the story with a glance and a rapid deployment of the images that carry the necessary code and little else. Knowing exactly what he wanted to write, Kyōka wasted no time in getting to the point.

I'm embarrassed to say that the first thing that caught his eye was the scarlet of her crepe undergarment, bright as flame and dappled with cinnabar. Her skirts weren't folded back but hiked up high and held between her knees, allowing the crepe slip to flow softly down, hugging her white ankles, which were apparently being spared the kimono's unpleasant wetness. On her bare feet, so white they brightened the crimson around them, the woman wore thick, lacquered clogs, fastened with wisteria-colored thongs and splashed with mud. With one thigh twisted in and feet slightly pigeon-toed, she sat in a corner of the waiting room as the rain continued to fall. (20: 238)

Again, we encounter the familiar combination of red and white, reminding us of the ways in which eroticism and violence are always entangled and ever present. If these colors indict Kyōka for exulting in the female image for his own narrowly conceived purposes, it is hardly surprising that during his day most of his readers were women. Those who were fans regarded him as an empathetic figure, one of a few male writers who could describe (and therefore express his understanding of) female suffering.

Osen is introduced in a way that piques both erotic interest and pity. We eventually come to a deeper appreciation of her derangement, but initially Kyōka shows us only the wildness of clothes, exposed legs, and brilliant color—all expressions (judging by Sōkichi's desire to distance himself from them) of a disturbing though inherently mesmerizing sexuality. Waiting at the crowded train station, Hata Sōkichi begins reconnecting himself to Osen through visual signs that pull the past into the present. "Noticing the color, he became the protagonist of this story."

Hata is a famous physician on his way across town. He is trapped in the waiting room because of an untimely rain that has turned Tokyo into a sea of mud and, more specifically, by the failure of his train to come on time. His first impulse is to get away from the crimson lady, but there is something familiar and attractive about her. It is her eyebrows, "incomparably lovely, gentle, and well-shaped." A familiar metonym for both feminine and masculine beauty, eyebrows have a heightened importance. Not only does Osen have lovely eyebrows, but, at a later point in the story, she intercedes so that Sōkichi's do not get shaved off. The importance of the image is clear, for from the moment it appears Sōkichi begins to associate Osen with his mother, "the woman who gave him life." Later, the image will suggest the moon, similarly beautiful and curved. "Sōkichi felt as if he had suddenly swallowed the crescent moon, and that it was sparkling in his heart with a precious, joyous light." As the moon, it also forms an additional link, through the name *nono-sama*, which can refer to either the crescent moon or to the Buddha.

> "Look, the moon," she said. "The Buddha."
> He never forgot that moment. The half moon seemed to be descending from a black cloud, its light shining upon the treetops of the ginkgo towering above, like the gentle contour of his dead mother's breast. (20: 262)

To Kyōka's imagination, eyebrow, beautiful woman, mother, moon, Buddha, and breast belong to the same family of images. They counterbalance the color red by adding an element of motherliness to the erotic, thereby making Osen far too inclusive and complicated to be easily identifiable as either madonna or whore.

Image engenders image. The rain continues to fall. When there is enough water, the story's outer narrative frame fractures and sloughs away. Then, like a sprout swelling from a seed, the story within the story emerges. And as it does, the Mansei Bridge Station suddenly and without warning becomes a water-going vessel. "His heart pounded like the sea, and the train station turned like the deck of a great ship until its bow pointed straight toward the Myōjin wood, which now seemed close enough to touch" (20: 245). This and other passages would be difficult to understand if we did not remember the function of water in Kyōka's work. They come directly from the narrative archetype—a woman, a young man, water, and so forth—and are locked into place by Kyōka's need to save himself through narrative repetition. As such, they are not often explained in the text, but, rather, are used to move the story ahead in a connotative fashion. They are employed for their considerable burden of established associations. As a consequence, the story develops in preconstructed pieces, held together by the associative forces that link image with image.

The power of this highly visual process of creation is demonstrated most clearly in those instances in which the story's fragments overwhelm Kyōka's ability to place them in some sort of narrative order. Once the image of the ship appears, for instance, the visual associations, and therefore the narrative that makes use of them, begin to progress too quickly for even the writer to manage them:

"Sloping down in that direction. That's Myōjin Hill."

In the house to the right and all the way to the end of the alley—

On the morning of that fateful day, Sōkichi had had one of his friends shave the boyish beard from his face. And that evening in the Myōjin temple grounds, he put the same razor to his throat!

But wait. I'm losing control of the story. (20: 245)

In a few sentences, the outline of the entire story pours forth: we progress from water to hill, to the house at the end of the alley, to beard, to temple ground, to razor. Overwhelmed by the too-rapid progression of visual associations, Kyōka chose to make his passive position with respect to these images perfectly clear. "*But wait. I'm losing control. . . .*" Of course, his admission is also a challenge. Once again, for those unfamiliar with the archetype that ties such images together, the text dissolves into a seemingly random collection of vivid yet incomprehensible pieces.

The autobiographical impulse of *Women of Acquaintance* is carried over to "Osen and Sōkichi." The body of this story, anticipated by this watery prelude, is a remembrance of Kyōka's life between November 1890 and October 1891, from the time he left Kanazawa to study with Kōyō until he met him and was taken in as his protégé. He was penniless during this period and changed residences numerous times, drifting between Tokyo and Kamakura. The hardships of those days are recorded here in relation to this woman that Sōkichi has accidentally met at the train station. Suddenly, he is only seventeen years old, living with a group of vagabonds, "people who, through indolence and dissipation, had been forgotten by the world." On his way back to their shared residence in a tenement house, as he carries a bag of rice crackers recently purchased from a neighborhood shop, he gives in to his hunger and makes a mistake that will nearly cost him his life.

He paused at a landing where the path up the hill was so steep he could reach out and touch the steps before him. Shielded only by a thin covering of ginkgo leaves and the branches of the firs and Chinese nettles towering far above, Sōkichi faced the drainage ditch that ran along the cliff and partook of forbidden fruit for the first time in his life. He chomped down on the hard crackers like a horse clamping down on a bit. How wonderfully delicious! (20: 255)

Sōkichi thinks he is out of sight, but his deception fails. He soon discovers that he was in full view of at least one of the people in his group, Small Plate

Heishirō, whose laughter fills pages in the original text, as if the story were a transcription of a raconteur's performance. Eating the crackers might seem like a small offense, but to Sōkichi it is not: he has shown that he cannot be trusted, that he is not really part of the group. Humiliated before Osen, to whom he is secretly attracted, Sōkichi tries to kill himself that evening. The place is the Myōjin Temple. Osen, mistress of the leader of the group, is the one who saves his life.

> "What are you doing? What do you think you're doing?"
> She seemed like a wondrous bird with a beautiful woman's face, sweeping down from the trees to grab his sleeve. He was leaning back against the trunk of a ginkgo tree that was being used as a corner post for one of the empty stalls behind the main temple. Just as he was about to slash his throat, Osen came. She wrested the razor from his hand. Everything seemed like a dream. (20: 261)

Kyōka probably found inspiration for this bird/woman image from Mantei Ōga's *Eight Lives of Siddhartha, a Japanese Library*, one of the illustrated texts in his mother's library, and a work he himself later sought out and purchased. As noted above, the image first appeared in the early story "A Bird of Many Colors"; it finds further amplification here. As Ōga did in this kusazōshi, Kyōka also took advantage of the transformational, plastic nature of visual signs. Consequently, the story's characters lack delineation and interiority; the semantic border between one image and another is vague and ill-defined—bird blending with woman, one connotation linking and melding with another. If the more transparent language of realism sought to clarify by excluding semantic possibilities (and thus provide a context for the observable object), Kyōka's visual tropes work through a grossly opaque and generic process of inclusion. They invite ambiguity, allowing Osen to be mother and lover at the same time. She is savior and temptress, a complicated figure who is nevertheless too formulaic to be considered a psychologically differentiated character.

The story jumps ahead. No obvious transitions are provided. Sōkichi and Osen are living together in a cheap tenement building. Returning home from school, he brushes shoulders with a man, a client, who is hurrying to get away. The door opens. Osen's bedding is laid out on the floor, telling us that she has just slept with the man for payment. In the figure of Osen, the distinction between the erotic and the nurturing, prostitute and mother, is blurred, since Kyōka insists that she must provide in *every* way while remaining above reproach. This is socially impossible, however, and as a result, Osen suffers. She must bear not only the public stigma of prostitution, but also the private burden of being a nurturing woman. Her fate is to be available to the needs of the less-than-resourceful men in her life. In the fullness of her sexuality, Osen is both oppressed and exalted. Her insanity and the double suicide suggested by the conclusion indicate, surely, what Kyōka held to be both the difficulty and beauty of this role.

In a scene reminiscent of the erotic tenderness of Tamenaga Shunsui's *Plum Calendar* (*Shunshoku umegoyomi*, 1832), Osen grills rice cakes for Sōkichi while telling him the story of the lovely but ill-fated Urazato. The allusion foreshadows her own fate, as the numerous connections between "Osen and Sōkichi" and Urazato's story, Tsuruga Wakasanojō's "Crow at Dawn, a Dream of Light Snow" ("Akegarasu yume no awa yuki," ca. 1772), are played out. Like Countess Kifune, Tamawaki Mio, and Osen, Urazato is also a kept woman. As punishment for attempting to escape from the brothel, she is bound and tied to a pine tree that stands in her compound's snowy garden. While her life slowly drains away, she dreams of her lover, Tokijirō, sneaking over the rooftops, coming to rescue her.

In both the written and the staged versions of *Akegarasu*, Tokijirō's head is covered with a bandanna. Without offering much in the way of explanation for the reader, Kyōka retained the image but employed it differently. He did not send a lover to rescue Osen but an officer of the law, a representative of the Meiji patriarchal order that provided a sinister backdrop for so many of his stories. He jumps over the back fence and arrests her for moral indiscretion. He tethers Osen, then leads her off to jail. Heartbroken and vulnerable, the sobbing Sōkichi follows after.

Osen hung her head without looking back. But then she turned, and Sōkichi, looking into her face, saw her eyebrows.

The young man was speechless.

"Sō-chan. I'll give you my spirit."

She folded it as the policeman pulled her along. Soon it was there nestled in the palm of her hand, a crane of white tissue paper.

"Follow this to wherever it takes you." She blew her warm breath into the bird and it came to life. With the marks of her lips showing faintly red against the crane's bluish white body, the bird flew among the floating blossoms, dancing in the air as it led Sōkichi to the gate where he was taken in. (20: 267–68)

Again, we encounter the bird image, magically providential. Again, we find the colors red and white. And once again we notice Kyōka's radically concrete sense of cause and effect: having blown her spirit into the crane, Osen literally loses her mind. She and Sōkichi become separated by her arrest. But, inspired with her breath, the paper bird takes to the air and leads Sōkichi to the people who take him in and help him become Doctor Hata, the famous surgeon of the story's opening paragraphs. He is, to make the obvious connection, a type of gentleman familiar to us in the figure of Doctor Takamine (literally, Towering Peak) from "The Surgery Room."

Once again, the story leaps forward, returning us to the original time frame of the narrative. Sōkichi, convinced that the woman in the waiting room is Osen, persuades her attendants to let him take her to his hospital. Another leap, and the story ends with his visit to her private room. The story concludes as he kneels beside her bed and places a razor in her hands. It is a vague attempt at closure. Kyōka did not tell us what happens. But if we recall the meta-story, the conclusion is clear. In a final demonstration of red and white, and in the spirit of Miyoshino and her lover Inosuke, who killed themselves with a razor, Osen and Sōkichi will end their lives together. Doing so, they join, among many others whose lives end violently, Countess Kifune and Takamine of "The Surgery Room," Tamawaki Mio and her lover in "One Day in Spring," and Tsuyuno and Reikichi of *Women of Acquaintance*.

Earthquake and
"How Beautiful Without Eyebrows"

The Banchō house was noticeably damaged by the earthquake that struck the Kantō area on September 1, 1923. Although it was left intact by the tremors, Kyōka and Suzu could not stay there. A fire soon broke out in the neighborhood. The two of them and the woman who was helping with the housework quickly escaped to a nearby park, fleeing over earth that was still rolling from aftershocks. The wind, strong and from the south, quickly spread the flames through the crowded neighborhoods of wooden buildings, sending clouds of smoke and waves of embers into the sky.

Altogether, they spent two days and two nights in the park, waiting and watching to see if the winds would bring the fire their way. Occasionally, they would leave this temporary refuge and return to their home. The maid was the first to go back. She returned to the park carrying two bottles of grape wine, one of Kyōka's Western indulgences. It had been her original intention to bring back *sake*, but in her hurry to get out of the house she had tipped the bottle over and spilled its contents. The wine was to be used to wash and disinfect any wounds they might have. Uninjured, Kyōka and Suzu each drank a glass, then shared the rest with their neighbors.

Later, as people started to go back to their homes to retrieve valuables, Kyōka himself returned to the house and brought back a small molded figure of Kannon and a brass children's identification tag that his father had carved for him as a child. Terrorized by the fire and destruction, he waited with these amulets in hand until it was safe to return. His home had been spared the fires that had swept over the city, but Tokyo would never be the same. Tanizaki's reaction was to flee to the west, where he began a new life in the Kansai area. But Kyōka had no intention of going back to Kanazawa or of moving elsewhere. He had tried his best to become an Edokko, and even though many of the last vestiges of old Edo were destroyed by the earth's convulsions and the flames, he would not leave his mother's city even though she herself was buried in Kanazawa.

Undaunted by the earthquake, Kyōka published a story in May 1924 that would mark the apex of his career as a short-story writer. "How Beautiful Without Eyebrows" ("Mayu kakushi no rei") is a work of impressive complexity that successfully brings together several strands of image-centered narrative to produce an astonishing resonance in which the plausible and implausible, past and present, real and imagined, no longer have meaning as categories except in their ability to shed such parameters of meaning. Compared to "Osen and Sōkichi," the open displays of the author's choices are here so well integrated by the style of narration—stories within stories within stories—that the unexpected juxtapositions and the sudden ending seem to flow naturally from the accumulation of images, which moves confidently and powerfully toward the denouement. Like practically all the works mentioned here, the story has yet to be translated into English.

The story begins as Sakai Sankichi, named as a friend of the narrator, is traveling by train along the Kiso Road, which winds through the mountains of Nagano prefecture. Kyōka himself took a similar trip in December 1914 and stayed in an inn called the Tokuriya located in the village of Narai, the setting for this story. His habit was to read Jippensha Ikku's *Shank's Mare* while traveling, and like the protagonists in *A Song by Lantern Light*, Sakai also patterns himself after Ikku's Yajirōbei and Kitahachi. He is on his way to Agematsu, but a disappointing night in Matsumoto has made him feel particularly close to the hapless Kita and Yaji, and he makes a last-minute decision to get off the train in Narai.

We know that this is going to be a place of strange happenings because it is raining when Sakai alights from the train. He walks away from the station and passes by two modern-looking inns before entering one with a look of age about it. He is warmly welcomed and led to a room on the third floor, Crane Number Three. Unlike the night before, the food is good, including a plate of thrush that are baked whole. He inquires about the tiny fowl, a delicacy of the area, and asks Oyone, the maid, if it would be possible to have the cook prepare another round, this time not baked but served in a boiling pot of broth. Oyone leaves, and Isaku, a dark and lonely man, comes to confirm Sakai's order. He is the cook, and their conversation leads to his relating a strange incident. A geisha from Tokyo came to the area to catch thrushes. She and a few men set up a net and at sunrise were successful in snaring a number of the birds. They built a fire and immediately began to cook them, but when the geisha bit into one, her mouth began dripping with blood. Upon wiping her mouth with a handkerchief, it became bloody, and her head suddenly floated into the sky.

The next morning, Sakai hears a noise outside and sees Isaku standing motionless by the edge of the garden pond. Sakai's guess is that Isaku is trying to keep the egrets from eating the fish, but he is only partly right. As Sakai reflects upon his good fortune in coming to this inn, it begins to snow, another subtle yet important sign of the increasingly strange events yet to come. Unprepared to accept the possibility that he has wandered into a world far stranger than his ability to comprehend, he blames his stomachache not on the thrushes he so heartily consumed but on the noodles he ate in Matsumoto two nights ago.

He decides to stay longer in Narai and changes his third-floor room for a less imposing one on the first floor. As he prepares for a nap, he again sees Isaku staring at the pond. He hears the sound of running water, still another omen of things to come, and on one of his trips to the toilet discovers that three water taps have been left on. He closes all three and returns to his room. Soon after, he hears the noise again and discovers that the three taps have been opened again. He turns them off, only to find later that someone has turned them on again. The matter of the taps is bothersome but simple to explain. The running water is meant to raise the level in the pond since the low water has made the fish more vulnerable to the birds. Structurally speaking, this incident of the taps is important to the progression of the story because it ties together images of water, birds, and prey and establishes an atmosphere of suspense that continues to build as the story progresses.

Sakai decides to take a bath. He enters the bathhouse by way of a rounded bridge that, as we have seen in other stories, serves as a passage to the other world. The bathhouse is dark, lighted by only one dimly glowing lantern

As Sakai began to untie his sash, he thought he heard the splash of someone in the bath. The rush of water running in the sink suddenly stopped.

He hesitated.

Any time was fine. He had told Oyone to let him know when the bathing room was free. There probably wasn't anyone in there. Just in case, he retied his sash and stepped forward. He put his cheek to the door, just above the glowing lantern. As he peered in, the light near his sleeve that had turned dark suddenly became bright again. The light became a birthmark, and the comma-shaped swirl on the lantern infused itself gloomily upon his cheek. Just at that moment he heard the sound of someone moving in the water. Then from somewhere came the scent of plum blossoms, the fragrance of makeup, warm and moist.

"A woman." (22:468)

Sakai retreats to his room, where he chats with Isaku about the birds who come to eat fish from the pond. The unconscious identification of these two men as fish, and of the woman as a bird of prey, makes itself felt in a subtle though persistent way. When Sakai suggests they watch the pond together, the two are joined in a common bond of fear. Thoughts of birds outside and of the woman inside (the bathhouse) mix and merge, until a strange woman suddenly appears in Sakai's room. She sits before a mirror and fixes her makeup. She covers her eyebrows and asks, "Does this become me?"—a question that brings to our attention the woman's desire to be someone's partner in matrimony. (The shaving off of one's eyebrows is associated with marriage.) The proposition can only have the effect of making Sakai feel more vulnerable. Just as he hears the sound of birds' wings flapping outside his window, Isaku enters.

At this point, Kyōka complicates an already complicated story by inserting a story within the story. A tale of a beautiful though unhappy woman named Otsuya, it explains Isaku's obsession with the pond and his heightened sense of vulnerability. As we suspected all along, his constant attention to the water is something more than simply a concern for the fish. He is trying to save himself from desire and madness. In a chilling moment that is reminiscent of the doppelgänger in "One Day in Spring," Isaku sees himself approaching the spot where he and Sakai are sitting.

"Sir, sir. The lantern. Look there! On the bridge to the bathhouse. That's me, coming from the other side. And there beside me. Otsuya."

Sakai clenched his teeth.

"Calm down! There's nothing to be afraid of. Nothing. She's not after you."

Above their heads, the electric lightbulb turned into a swirling comma, black and floating in the air. Over the smoldering coals of the brazier hung a glowing lantern.

"Does this become me?"

Suddenly the room was a lake, with flakes of snow, like white bellflowers blossoming on the water's edge, falling in confusion upon the matted floor. (22: 496)

The appearance of Otsuya's ghost and the immediacy of her utterance "Does this become me?" narrow the time frame of this narrative to the simple present, a moment of reunion when the living meet the dead and those who think they are still alive see themselves as being already dead. Having narrated the past into the present, Isaku is simultaneously on both sides of the bridge that very literally connects this world with the one beyond. Ultimately, all things become present as everything is reduced to the emotional reality of the writer, who brings the story to this sudden climax.

As we have seen in earlier stories, the intensity of this lyrical moment is expressed not only by the doppelgänger and the appearance of the dead but also by metamorphosis, in this case a lightbulb that becomes a lantern and a room that becomes a lake. The powerful ending of this story follows from a number of factors that Kyōka brought together with amazing skill: the sustained repetition of key words and images such as the number three, birds of prey, various manifestations of water, and lanterns; the manner in which the past is brought into the present by a structure of flashbacks and stories within stories; the way the various narrative strands that form this story are condensed and abbreviated; and the associative and visual manner in which these units are linked. Perhaps most fundamental to this extraordinary ending is the manner in which Kyōka pushes the tense-less quality of the Japanese language to its extreme, denying a past that is anything more than memory and a future that is any more than desire and speculation.[17] A more discursive style—an insistence on third-person narration and a more authoritative use of the distancing and stabilizing past tense—would have required many more pages to achieve a comparable effect. Certainly, many more transitions would have been needed. As it stands, the fragmented, dense, and shifting nature of this narrative requires, contrary to what the length and complexity of the synopsis just provided might lead one to expect, only about fifty pages.

As is true of Kyōka's best work, this story clearly expresses his stated desire to pass through reality to reach a more profound state of being. The gradual and steady accumulation of imagery finally leads to an ontological rupture and the overwhelming of the denotational by the connotational. And yet the desta-bilizing effect of this narrative, powered as it is by the masochistic fear of be-coming prey to the woman/bird, signals both the fullness of the archetype and the beginning of its deterioration. As Takakuwa Noriko's reading suggests, the desire to punish adultery brings these otherwise unrelated characters together. That is to say, this story is essentially about man's ambivalence toward fantastic punishment. It is about a fear of the supernatural that is also a desire for tor-ture. As before, the death of women makes the ascension toward sacred death possible. Each appearance of the supernatural, each violent act, each loss of life, brings men closer to that which they irresistibly want yet profoundly fear. This spiraling progression toward the other world of death and (possible) bliss es-tablishes the structure of eroticism as Isaku and Sakai move inexorably toward a sublime sexuality. Otsuya's taking off her clothes, her bathing, her putting on makeup, constitutes a transition to another world. Her question "Does this become me?" (*Niaimasu ka*) is asked from her location on the "other side." It is directed to those men who are still lingering in reality, and its effect is to feel what is real by sensing something beyond.[18] To the extent that this seduction is horrible, Kyōka's men have, like Kyōka himself, matured considerably. Hav-ing become mature in their sexual desires, they now face a terrible crisis. For if they are no longer boys, how can the structure of the archetype continue to preserve them?

The Complete Works and Akutagawa Ryūnosuke

It is a curious fact that Kyōka's departure from the safety of the meta-story began just as the decision to publish his collected works was made. In March 1924, two months before publication of "How Beautiful Without Eyebrows," Kyōka met over dinner with Minakami to announce the project and to sound him out about helping. Minakami's initial reaction was negative, not because he was unhappy that Kyōka was being honored by having all his works reprinted but because he had misgivings about Shun'yōdō. He respected the house for having publishing some of the most famous works of Meiji literature: Kōyō's *Passions and Griefs*, Ōgai's translation of Hans Christian Andersen's *Improvisato-ren*, Rohan's *The Five-Story Pagoda* (*Gojū no tō*), and Kyōka's *Worship at Yushima* and *Teriha Kyōgen*. Moreover, he was more than willing to recognize their steady support for Kyōka over many long years. As a businessman, however, he felt that the management of the company was sloppy. He was of the opinion, which he left unstated, that if it were simply a matter of sales and distribution, Kyōka would be better off with another publisher.

Kyōka was not totally forthcoming either. He only slowly got to the reason why he had asked Minakami to meet with him. Would it be possible for him to join a committee of advisors who would help guide the Shun'yōdō project? The other members would include Osanai Kaoru, Tanizaki Jun'ichirō, Kubota Mantarō, Akutagawa Ryūnosuke, and Satomi Ton. Minakami's name would be added to this distinguished list not as an editor but as a "patron." Without knowing what exactly to say in reply, Minakami toasted Kyōka's accomplishment. Together they talked until late into the night.

When Minakami later approached Kubota and Satomi about the undertaking, they knew no more than he about its progress. Summer passed and autumn arrived. Finally in December, Kyōka asked them all to attend a planning meeting. Tanizaki and Akutagawa were absent. But the others drafted a proposal, which included the following points:

It is decided that:
—Osanai Kaoru, Tanizaki Jun'ichirō, Kubota Mantarō, Akutagawa Ryūnosuke, and Minakami Takitarō will hold meetings and serve as advisors regarding all administrative matters;
—this committee will also be allowed to serve as advisors on financial decisions;
—the leader of this committee will be Minakami Mantarō, who will convene the meetings according to the schedules of the other members;
—the members of the committee shall receive no salary, and all expenses will be their own;
—besides producing memos, they should make suggestions relating to the progress of administrative matters;
—the names of the members of the committee will not be published in the collection, although they will be allowed to be published in other publications;
—a quorum shall consist of three or more members;
As for the Complete Works
—the collection shall be called the *Kyōka zenshū* (The Complete Works of Izumi Kyōka);
—all the author's works will be included;
—novels, plays, and essays (including *haiku*) will be grouped into three divisions and presented according to their year of publication;
—the number of volumes will be determined by first collating one volume of the gathered material, then proceeding in the same way for other volumes; hence, the number of pages as well as the number of characters per line will be decided afterward;

—the works to be included in a particular volume will be determined by the time of advertisement;

—the typeface will be chrysanthemum;

—the cover will be designed by Okada Saburōsuke;

—the calligraphy for the title will be written by the author;

—a chronology of works will be included;

—if at all possible, a photo portrait of the author will be included in each volume;

—author's prefaces and advertisements will be included with the work;

—publication will begin March 1925 and the deadline will be May 5;

—we recommend that the liaison with the editorial office be Hamano Eiji and that Komura Settai be involved in all matters.

Kyōka presented the proposal to Wada Tokutarō, who immediately agreed to almost all points.[19]

It was Kyōka's suggestion to have Okada (1869–1939) do the artwork. Okada had designed the cover for *The Grass Labyrinth* when it initially appeared as a single volume from Shun'yōdō in 1908. Kyōka had been impressed with his work, although we must wonder why Komura Settai, who had illustrated many more of Kyōka's books than had Okada and was said to be closer to the author than anyone except Suzu, was not chosen for the job.[20] Apparently the committee wondered, too. They suggested that Settai be consulted in all matters. The editor Hamano Eiji was the committee members' choice for liaison because they wanted someone with good managerial skills, an ability that, once again, Minakami felt was all too rare at Shun'yōdō.

The work of gathering materials began immediately. In the end, it was impossible to find everything Kyōka had published over the years. Some of the magazines had been lost and were unavailable even in Minakami's extensive private collection, which became the main source for first printings. In order to take full advantage of this archive, an office was set up in Minakami's home. As Komura Settai described it, "Minakami's efforts were extraordinary. His home in Banchō, the so-called Genroku Mansion, became an editorial office. All the materials that he had taken such pains to collect—the monographs, clippings from newspapers and magazines, even the advertisements that Kyōka had written for his upcoming publications—were generously offered for the project. If Minakami had not been so dedicated (*seijitsu*), we would have run up against many more difficulties."[21] Hamano went to Minakami's home daily. Kyōka and the members of the committee also had access to the office and came and went freely. As the work progressed, Minakami became increasingly involved in the process.

The first volumes appeared in July 1925, four months behind schedule. A party to celebrate what should have been the beginning of publication was held the evening of March 1 at the Shiba Kōyōkan, an upscale establishment (named for the fall foliage rather than Kyōka's mentor), decorated with maple leaf patterns throughout. More than eighty people met in a large Japanese-style room. Each sat behind small lacquered tables placed in a large U-shape. Sasakawa Rinpū began the evening with a welcome speech, and Kyōka responded with a few words. The novelist and writer of children's literature Suzuki Miekichi (1882–1936) led the group in a champagne toast to Kyōka and Suzu; this was followed by a speech by Satomi Ton. As described by those present, the evening was a tremendous success. "With Satomi Ton's speech fanning the fire, the evening became lively. There were songs from [the geisha] Torayuki and Toramaki, and then a *nagauta* from Nihonbashi's Susue and Tomikiko. There was joy in the faces of the eighty or so who were present, illumined in the resplendent light of spring lanterns. Perhaps there was something in the air, but everyone's heart burned with passion, making it an evening of beauty that the bundan has not seen in recent years."[22]

Kyōka himself sang a *kouta* to shamisen accompaniment, and Suzuki Miekichi did a "catching-loaches-in-a-basket" mime. Hanayanagi Shōtarō came an hour late, and joined with the actor Kawaguchi Matsutarō to do a performance in the style of the Peking Opera. (Kitamura Rokurō was in Osaka beginning rehearsals for a new performance and could not attend.) Later, when Hanayanagi was drinking with Kubota Mantarō and Akutagawa, the novelist and playwright Okada Yachio (1883–1962) commented on what a splendid time the threesome seemed to be having: "You look like a drinking sandwich." Upon hearing this, Yoshii Isamu added, "Yes, a sandwich. But somehow that thing between the bread doesn't look too tasty." To this, Kubota is said to have retorted, "You got it. We're a vegetable sandwich!"[23] A photograph from this period taken at the Kōyōkan shows Akutagawa, Kubota, and others gathered around Kyōka (see Fig. 16).

The party ended with Sasakawa Rinpū recounting his memories of Kyōka and giving thanks to "the young people," the best of the coming generation, who had joined in the work of making the collection possible. Sasakawa later described the occasion as "an unprecedented gathering of practically all the most famous writers of the day, coming together to acknowledge the publication of Kyōka's complete works. No doubt they were brought there by the power of Kyōka's mysterious and beautiful words. They shared the same calling as writers, even though they were very different from Kyōka. To his credit, this was so. Unassuming, unpretentious, humble, kind, and affable, he has drawn others to him."[24] Among the writers present were Tokuda Shūsei, Orikuchi Shinobu, Yoshiya Nobuko, Kikuchi Kan, Yanagita Kunio, Yamamoto Yūzō (1887–1974), and Minakami Takitarō. And, as always, a number of painters were among those who gathered around Kyōka, including Kaburagi Kiyokata (1878–1972), Komura Settai, and Hirezaki Eihō.

In commemoration of the publication, Hamano Eiji edited a special edition of *New Fiction*. Entitled "Izumi Kyōka, Genius," it appeared in May, a few months after the celebration. Akutagawa contributed the preface for the collection, celebrating the achievement as "not only one of the great events of our age, but a grand achievement of art, now and for a hundred generations to come."

Among writers both living and dead, Kyōka-sensei, master of letters, walks alone. Possessing a genius that is brilliant and invigorating, he is capable of describing a beautiful woman and capturing her essence with language—a peony wafting its fragrance before the Taishin Pavilion. With thoughts pure and supernal, he writes of gods and demons and journeys within the realm of the marvelous. . . . The appearance of Kyōka's world (*sekai*) is not only one of the great events of our age, but a grand achievement of art, now and for a hundred generations to come.

Sensei has woven a tapestry of more than five hundred stories, plays, and essays. Its warp is the elegance of three hundred years of Edo culture—a kaleidoscopic imagination that flows from a modest heart. Its woof is the totality of Japanese emotion—a moment's reflection that gives birth to immortal poetic sentiment. Truly his is a brocade made in heaven, beyond the ability of human hands. Before a backdrop of the ancient—warm and full of grace, gathered like aquamarines in Sensei's heart—the modern flows from his brush like pearls, whiter and more brilliant than ever before. . . . He has articulated numerous aspects of the most recent thought from the Occident. . . . Can we not compare his work with that of the great French romantics? In quality, his writings are a seven-jeweled pillar that supports the heavens, surpassing the skill of Mérimée. In quantity, they are like the mythical linden tree, comparable in volume to the works of Balzac. How great is Sensei's work!

His eminence follows from an abundance of natural talent. And yet, at least half of the matter is the courage with which, for more than thirty years, he has steadily pursued his consuming devotion to literature. . . . With the rise of naturalism, the masses blindly followed the crowd. Delighting in the dust of this world, they saddened the cranes that preferred to soar among the heights. Enamored with mud and sand, the naturalists frequently troubled the ancient dragon. But Sensei alone resisted and fought against the decline of romanticism. Faithfully, he took upon him the mantle of his mentor, Ozaki Kōyō. His feelings of ostracism and his desire to walk alone are easy to imagine. We who make a living by crafting words cannot know the full value of a swift horse by simply hearing it neigh in the marketplace, yet countless are the times when we have been encouraged by the sight of the white crane circling above the moors as we watched from afar. Now the divine wind has dispelled the fog, and what was once pushed off to the margins has now become the center. Ah. Without suffering many trials, would Sensei's work have been possible? We shade our eyes with our hands and gaze up at the clouds of good fortune that cling to the tower of Izumi Kyōka. We cannot contain our cheerful thoughts and broad smiles, yet neither can we staunch the deep welling of tears.[25]

This famous characterization of Kyōka and his career did much to form critical reception of his work in the years to come. By introducing the term "Kyōka's world" (*Kyōka sekai*), Akutagawa understood Kyōka's accomplishment as an eccentric and totalizing imagination, a world unto itself. He could not help but pitch Kyōka against the competing sphere of the naturalists, who had occupied the mainstream of modern Japanese letters. Such an appreciation reflects, most certainly, Akutagawa's own dislike of the naturalist "masses." The encomium is also expressive of the comfort he took in Kyōka's stubborn dedication to his artistic vision. Struggling with his own failing trust in the powers of language, Akutagawa wanted to believe that the difficulties Kyōka faced had worked to his benefit, that he had prevailed, and that the tables had now turned. The writer who was once ostracized and relegated to the margin had now taken his place at the center.

What Akutagawa could not express in this finely crafted preface found voice in a less polished though no less influential article that appeared on May 5 and 6 in the *Tokyo Daily News*.

Upon the publication of Kyōka's collected works, I would like to step away from my position as one of its editors in order to speak as a critic about the author's work. The first thing that ought to be said is that Kyōka-sensei's writings frequently put forward a certain argument. This might sound heretical to the author's devoted readers, but it is true especially of the longer works, such as *The Elegant Railway*, *The Vigil*, and *A Woman's Pedigree*. The argument he presents flows from an ethics based on poetic justice. Those who do not see it will probably discover in its place a traditional sense of chivalry. But I do believe that this sense of ethics stands outside the realism of the Ken'yūsha. Not only this but it also falls outside the purview of what the naturalists did, which in turn did not fit within the boundaries of the Ken'yūsha writers.

Compare, for instance, Ozaki Kōyō's *Passions and Griefs* or his *Gold Demon* with Sensei's writings. In Kōyō's work, morality is a matter of rhetoric, whereas Kyōka's is generated by a certain archetypal plot. Kyōka's concerns were unknown to Kōyō. And the reason the naturalists have had so little to do with Sensei is not solely a matter of rhetoric. Today's bundan, dominated as it is by the naturalists, sees naturalist tendencies even in the work of Oguri Fūyō. Indeed, they even try to put a naturalist face on Nagai Kafū. Ultimately, the reason they don't also try to make Sensei's works fall into this same stinking category is because they cannot deal with his halo of poetic justice.

This sense of justice first colored Sensei's work long ago, as early as "The Poverty Club" (an early work being anthologized for the first time in the complete works). According to Otan, the female protagonist, charity is not necessarily a virtue. As long as giving serves the self-justification of the wealthy, it must, in fact, be considered evil. Even at the risk of starvation, the poor discover happiness in their united rejection of charity. My interest in such a sense of ethics does not follow simply from this fact. Isn't this ethical position, which pervaded Sensei's works throughout the 1880s and 1890s, the same as that which propels the proletarian literature of today?

This same moral force also has much to do with Sensei's love of the supernatural—of spirits and monsters. Certainly, Sensei's early works were unable to dispense with evil spirits. The bat in the story "The Bather" ("Yuna no tamashii," 1900) is an excellent example of an evil spirit. But after this point, elements of the supernatural are heightened in an ethical way. Within the dim light of mystery, the bald Buddha in *Shinja, the Great* and Akuzaemon of "The Grass Labyrinth" stand in judgment of our sense of good and evil. Their manner of measuring sin owes little to the study of ethics. Rather, theirs is a judgment based solely upon a poetic justice that appeals to our emotions. Nevertheless, or perhaps I should say precisely because this is so, Kyōka's writings display a beautiful majesty that can be found nowhere else. *The Castle Tower* is one of the most perfect examples of this type of work. From the age of *Tales Present and Past* (*Konjaku monogatari*), our literary tradition has not suffered from a lack of supernatural elements—even in the early-modern period we have Akinari's *Tales of Moonlight and Rain*—yet who besides the protagonist of a Noh play can give such majesty to the world of spirits?

The second point I would like to make is that Sensei's writings are enriched with a unique rhetoric. This is not to belabor the obvious, but I do believe that Sensei's prose is more distinctive than what the world usually calls distinctive. No other Meiji-Taishō writer uses in the same work so many types of language: colloquial, classical, Chinese poetic diction, and even nouns. If we had to search for someone comparable, we would have to look to the genius of the Muromachi period [Zeami] who gave us the Noh plays. Of course, this quality has placed Sensei outside the ranks of any grouping within the bundan.

I was going to write about a third item, but I see that I am running out of room.

For the two reasons I have mentioned, it was easy enough for the bundan to put Sensei away (*satsu*). In its rejection of difference and its love of similarity, the literary world is no different from the world at large. When bravely going against the trends of the times, a writer must realize that his place within the bundan, even if he feels no direct threat to his life, is a very fragile thing. And yet, it was a mistake for the bundan to kill Sensei. The fifteen volumes of *The Complete Works of Izumi Kyōka* that have just appeared prove his victory over his critics. I say this not only on behalf of Sensei's most avid supporters, but also for those cold-blooded fellows like myself who cannot believe in poetic justice. That is to say, by putting down these poorly conceived words, I publicly declare my personal opinion on the matter. Should my remarks on Sensei's work invite his derision because they have led even to a discussion of proletarian ethics, then all I can do is wait for his forgiveness.[26]

Here Akutagawa once again denounced the naturalists as the ones who did wrong to "put [Kyōka] away." If the comparison was to the French romanticists in the preface, in this newspaper article it is to other texts and writers of the Japanese tradition—*Tales of the Present and Past*, Zeami, Ueda Akinari—a genealogy of the supernatural that places Kyōka beyond the "stinking category" of naturalism. It is upon this picture of a beleaguered, abandoned, yet ultimately victorious Kyōka that later scholarship on the author's work will build. By establishing the essence of this world as an ethics largely based on aesthetic concerns, Akutagawa laid the foundations of Kyōka criticism for years to come. This is not to say that others had not already addressed the same qualities in Kyōka's work. But no one had done so as memorably.

Minakami, among others, immediately realized the importance of Akutagawa's comments. As one of the editors of the collected works and as Kyōka's most devoted fan, he attempted to pen his own summation of Kyōka's achievements. Although his essay did not reach the light of day, it reads as follows.

Izumi Kyōka's is an art of longing and resistance. In its longing, it incessantly pursues all beauty and truth, even unto the far reaches of mystery. In its resistance, it endlessly reviles all that is ugly and evil about the world. Childhood, Edo, women, pride, chivalry—these are the objects of his flamelike yearning. Authority, vulgarity, inelegance, greed, the unshaven face—these are fated to receive his ridicule and scorn. He nurtures justice and charity in his heart. Beneath his feet, he tramples injustice and indifference. A yearning for the beloved rules all he does. The ideal of an all-conquering love shines eternally throughout his life's work. A master of the romantic tradition, he has written hundreds of works, all imbued with this basic spirit of yearning and resistance. Truly, his writings are wonderfully colorful, like paintings done with words, like music. Yesterday and today, east and west, has anyone had an equal command of language? Fortunate enough to be living in the same period as the author, we read his collected works with a renewed sense of joy.[27]

The dimensions of Minakami's comparisons—"yesterday and today, east and west"—owe something to Akutagawa. But the portrait itself is to the point. Kyōka's life and work are about yearning and resistance.

Because it was customary for Kyōka to approve all matters related to the collection, and since Minakami's piece was to appear as an advertisement for the collected works, Minakami had Kyōka read it in Hamano's presence. Kyōka told him it was fine and suggested only a few minor changes. By the next day, however, he had changed his mind. In Minakami's words, Kyōka was a *sotozura*, someone easy on others but hard on himself and those in his most intimate circle. "He was affable. But because he was a perfectionist, he was also uncompromising. He would always say, 'Its up to you.' But then he would censure any decision regarding the collected works."[28] Apparently Kyōka was more often displeased than pleased with decisions regarding the collected works. Upon scrutinizing Minakami's essay a bit more, Kyōka decided he did not like the line "Authority, vulgarity, inelegance, greed, the unshaven face—these are fated to receive his ridicule and scorn" and asked Minakami to strike it out. Minakami, shocked by the sight of the red line that obliterated the sentence, finally protested Kyōka's heavy-handedness. He argued that since he was writing in parallels, the deletion of one side of the longing-or-resistance dyad would ruin the balance of the piece. But Kyōka, who was always sure about aesthetic matters, held firm.

Angered by the request to delete the line, Minakami rewrote the piece. What he finally produced was a prosaic listing of Kyōka's outstanding novels, stories, and plays. It was perfectly unremarkable, but he submitted it for Kyōka's approval, along with a note saying that if this was not good enough, then Kyōka should come up with something himself. The truth was that Kyōka, and no one else, was the one editing the collection. The author consulted the committee only on a small portion of what went on. And he did all the final proofreading and correction by himself.

Kyōka accepted the rewrite, and Minakami was surprised. Upon further reflection, he realized that Kyōka had done so only out of deference to their friendship. Embarrassed about having lost his temper, Minakami suffered because of the high standard that Akutagawa had established and because of Kyōka's similar desire for perfection. For these same reasons, Satomi Ton, who tried numerous times to provide another editor's introduction to the collected works, never wrote anything.

Akutagawa's Death and the End of an Era

Assisting in the publication of Kyōka's work was one of the last things that Akutagawa accomplished during his short life. Unable to rid himself of an "anxiety" about living that had plagued him for many years, he timed his suicide to coincide with the issuing of the fifteenth and final volume of Kyōka's complete works. On July 24, 1927, he took an overdose of sleeping pills and was found dead in the cottage behind his house. Having identified the proletarian movement as the future of Japanese letters and having found the common thread of "an ethics based on poetic justice" that supposedly tied Kyōka to this vigorous critique of capitalism that had come to supplant naturalism as a cultural movement, Akutagawa chose to end his life, no longer capable of believing in such justice himself.

Kubota Mantarō called to relay the news. That evening, Kyōka attended the wake that was held at the Akutagawas' home. There he saw the dead writer's desk still in disarray, cluttered with piles of the two types of sleeping pills that he had taken. In the study, he also found a volume of his collected works. "There is a brazier, its ashes cold because of the summer weather, and on it an iron water kettle still resting in place. My book is next to it, its cover taken off. I cannot hold back the tears that come to my eyes" (1: xi). It seemed that Akutagawa had waited for Kyōka to gain his "victory over his critics" before ending his life.

The funeral was held on July 27, at 3:00 P.M. It had been raining steadily since the morning of July 25, but the skies cleared on the morning of July 27. It was a hot day. Along with Kikuchi Kan and Kojima Masajirō, Kyōka walked along with the coffin as it was taken from Akutagawa's home to the Yanaka Crematorium, where the funeral was held. Kyōka sat in the space reserved for friends. At the appropriate moment, he rose and read in a high, formal voice the following eulogy.

Melodious and bright are your words and your character, you, dear one, who could make the mountains and seas shine like pure jade. Turning your back on this hot and steamy summer, you have left us to wander alone in another, more bearable world. Suddenly you are a giant sun in the heavens. Your light falls upon the literary world, never to go out. While you were still with us here as our friend, we never tired of seeing your face or of hearing the sound of your voice. What are we to do without you? The autumn of our thoughts is deep, our tears are like the dew. Gazing at the moon, as if it were your very countenance, which one among us could express the pain of separation? Noble spirit. Return to us if only for a moment. Return to us, we who linger here on earth. Besides your lovely, intelligent children and your gentle and virtuous wife, there are others who long to see you once again. (28: 600)

For Kyōka, Akutagawa's death came as a shock. This young man's death came at the end of an era, for Kyōka and for Japanese letters in general. Although he would continue to work for twelve more years, Kyōka's best days as a writer were over.

CHAPTER 15

Crisis and Salvation

~

1928–1939

The Nines Club

If Akutagawa felt that his aestheticism was no longer relevant to the dawning age of proletarian writing, the issue of relevance had long since ceased to concern Kyōka. Not one to assert a public political position, he withdrew into narrowing artistic concerns, despite his supposed sympathies with those of the proletarian movement who were waging class warfare and despite the deterioration of the archetype that had sustained his imagination to this point. Tanizaki would later depict Kyōka as one "forgotten." Kyōka was, however, not the only Meiji-period writer whose reputation suffered because of Taishō-era changes in literary sensibilities. Tanizaki, whose writing and lifestyle changed significantly after the Kantō earthquake of 1923, was perhaps the exception. Others, including leading figures of the naturalist movement such as Shūsei, no longer captured the interest of the greater reading public, although they were allowed to retain their status as cultural authorities and as interpreters of their own time—the point of honor being, certainly, that their own time had passed.

As we have seen, Kyōka's nostalgic sense of history extended back beyond the birth of the Meiji state to at least the age of gesaku, as he imagined it reaching him through his mother's texts. No wonder, then, that the dedicated and closely knit group that formed around him during his later years defined itself not by the seriousness and truth-seeking of the Meiji esprit but by the playfulness of the Edo cultural regime. On May 23, 1928, the Nines Club was reorganized after a long hiatus. The club originally formed in fall 1916, soon after Minakami returned from abroad. Once again, Kyōka was the nucleus of the group, whose agenda was simply to gather together for banter and drunken amusement. They called themselves the Nines because the monthly dues were 9 yen 99 sen. Their establishment of choice was the Fujimura in Nihonbashi, whose management always had a pile of polished 1 sen coins prepared for the occasion. In exchange for a ten-yen bill, each member of the club would get one small, shiny coin.

The meetings were official only in the sense that attendance records were kept. The roster, bound in the traditional Japanese manner and titled in Kyōka's own hand, remained at the Fujimura. The first entry reads, "May 23, 1928. Rain. Person in charge: Abe Shōzō [Minakami Takitarō]." Listed in order are Izumi Kyōtarō, Satomi Ton, Komura Settai, Kubota Mantarō, and Okada Saburōsuke.[1] This familiar group includes many who worked on the editorial committee for the complete works. Absent are Tanizaki, who had moved to the Kansai area, and Osanai Kaoru, whose health was failing. (Osanai would die a few months later, in December 1928.) Miyake Shōtarō joined the group in September 1930, and in March 1934 the name of the Nihonga painter and illustrator of many of Kyoka's works Kaburagi Kiyokata was added to the roster, thus bringing the number of regular members to eight. Among them, Miyake was an anomaly. A judge by profession, he was the only one in this group who was neither a writer nor a painter.

The comfort this group found in one another's company was extraordinary. Increasingly cut off from the mainstream of the bundan, Kyōka appreciated this small group of friends who liked his writing, were willing to indulge his fussiness about food, and saw to it that he got home safely after drinking himself into oblivion. Treating themselves to wine and wit, they met without fail at the Fujimura on the twenty-third of each month. Their final meeting was in August 1939. In all, they met 138 times without interruption. They would have met 139 times, had Kyōka not passed away on September 23, 1939.

Kyōka was not an alcoholic. It was just that sake was one of the few things he felt good about consuming in public places. Rice wine could be prepared to his specifications by practically anyone, and it could be done almost anywhere. All that was required was that it be heated to near boiling to ensure its safety.

In contrast, other types of food posed insuperable problems. That was why, besides the Fujimuraya, there were only a few establishments that Kyōka could trust. For him, the proper preparation of food was something only Suzu, who knew his habits thoroughly, could do.

As Kyoka's provider, Suzu knew his daily schedule by heart and was an indispensable part of it. During his later years, his day was a model of regularity. Upon waking, he would wash his face, pray before the *kamidana* (god shelf) and the *Butsudan* (Buddhist altar), and then hurry upstairs to his study to pay his respects to Kōyō by bowing before the calligraphy scroll written by his mentor. Having dispatched these formal matters, he would come down to the tea room for a smoke and a cup of salted tea. Kyōka's tea was always served with salt, put into the cup before, not after, the brewing. So insistent was Kyōka on this particular way of preparing tea that, after his death, Suzu had a dream in which his ghost appeared to her. "He reached his hand out and told me to hand over the bottle of salt that I happened to be holding. I gave it to him. Then he disappeared into the distance. Since he passed away, I hadn't been putting salt in the tea that I offered before the Buddhist altar every morning. He was obviously craving salt and had come to get some."[2]

Kyōka always ate breakfast, which invariably included rice and miso soup with two egg yolks in it. After eating, he would go up to his study and read, mostly Chinese books but also kusazōshi and other works of gesaku, especially those written by Ryūtei Tanehiko and Jippensha Ikku. A photograph shows him at work in his study (see Fig. 17). For snacks, he favored *yōkan* (sliced squares of sweet jelly) and *manjū* (rounded cakes with sweet fillings) of various sorts. He also liked the Western-style rolls that he could buy at the Kimuraya on the Ginza. When eating these, he would pinch the roll with two fingers and eat everything except the part his fingers had touched. That part he would throw away. As a rule, he never ate lunch. For dinner, he would always drink two small carafes of boiled sake and eat a little chicken or white fish. Like the wine, the poultry and fish had to be well cooked, literally purified with fire. Sashimi and sushi were out of the question. For dessert, he always had an apple, eaten in much the same way as the rolls. First, Suzu would wash her hands thoroughly. Then she would carefully pare the apple, making sure not to touch any part of the fruit that was to be eaten. He would receive the peeled apple with equal caution, holding it on the ends between his thumb and index finger. He would then eat the apple while rotating it, careful not to let his lips come close to either end.

We must wonder if Kyōka would have been able to manage such a routine without Suzu's patient dedication. Their relationship, it seems, was close and cordial. He usually got her attention by simply calling out "Hey" (*oi*), avoiding all nominals, as was the common practice. Suzu claimed after his death that when they were alone and he was in good spirits, he would address her with the exalted "thou" (*gokiden*). And on those occasions when he was in even higher spirits, he reverted to the informal "you" (*sokomoto*).[3] By all accounts, she was vitally important to him. He could not live without her. A photograph shows Suzu and Kyōka on an outing picking wild brackens (see Fig. 18).

Of the Mountains and the Sea

Kyōka's last major novel was *Of the Mountains and the Seas* (*Sankai hyōbanki*), serially published in 125 installments in the evening edition of *The New Times* (*Jiji shinpō*) from July 2 to November 26, 1929. Reflecting a late and particularly troubled stage of Kyōka's never-ending battle with fear, the work is uneven and rambling, posing tremendous problems for even the most dedicated readers. Given the difficulties of this piece, it is interesting to note the variety of strategies employed by Japanese critics to fit an obviously flawed piece of work into a larger, sympathetic consideration of Kyōka's career as a writer. As one critic later put it, "I don't read this novel as a novel per se. I listen to it as I would enjoy a piece of music. . . . The story's lack of clarity is irrelevant."[4] This forgiving regard for a baffling lack of structure tries hard to avoid admitting the obvious truth that the work is a failure. As an apology, it necessarily precludes a query into the reasons why this should be the case, reasons that reveal an important, and heretofore largely hidden, chapter in Kyōka's life.

Kyōka's earlier efforts to force the energy of his obsessions into some sort of meaningful structure are abandoned in *Of the Mountains and the Sea*. It is as if he finally tired of the formula that had guaranteed coherence, even though many of the deeper emotional issues that required the archetype were still in force. Like "How Beautiful Without Eyebrows," this novel is based on the author's travels. And, as in many of the later works, the biographical elements that emerge are retrospective and even bitter formulations of the past. A trip to the Wakura Hot Springs, on the Nōtō Peninsula, in May of the same year provided a setting that is both littoral and mountainous, as expressed in the title. This rambling novel is an evaluation (*hyōbanki*) of his homeland, not precisely Kanazawa but places such as Wakura, Wajima, and Hakusan that lie just to the north and east. Unsurprisingly his regard for the entire region was unfavorable. Even to the aging Kyōka, his home province remained a place of defeat and powerlessness, since he associated the Hokuriku region with certain experiences of his youth that he was never able or willing to overcome.

Despite a sense of pride and accomplishment that characterize the protagonist Yano Chikau, a well-known and respected novelist who is obviously Kyōka's proxy in fiction, the protagonist of this work continues to be plagued by local apparitions, legends, songs, and beliefs that sharpen his memory of past folly. As presented as a flashback in the novel, Yano's greatest mistake was to witness a well-viewing ritual (*i nozoki*) in which three young women approached a well from different directions and peered down into the water, as if seeing into another world. All three were pregnant, and their purpose was to divine if their pregnancies would progress successfully. The price for such a guarantee was the lives of young sparrows, dropped down the well to drown in the water below. Not understanding the significance of this sacrifice, the young Yano saved the birds, with the result that all three women and their babies died before childbirth. Struggling with the burden of this guilt, Yano is cursed with childlessness and lives in fear of other forms of retribution.

Doubtless, Kyōka employed this image of the well because of its associations with the womb. The act of looking into some form of passage in order to know the future occurs at three other points in the story—once in the form of a play, once in a vision as Yano gazes out over the breakwater, and once when three women appear together before him. Its periodic, haunting occurrence is matched by repeated allusions to a legend that similarly underlines the theme of immanent punishment and gives voice to the dead women. The allusion is introduced as a legend in the second chapter of the novel and is repeated throughout. According to the original legend, a young woodcutter named Chōta moves into a mountainous area, builds a hut, and begins to log the timber there. He is challenged by a badger (in Kyōka's version it is a *tanuki*, or raccoon dog) who is the lord of the mountain. Manifesting itself in various forms, it is finally killed by Chōta's equally persistent efforts to hold his ground. Seven years later, Chōta hears a voice beckoning him to come out of his hut. "Is Chōta there?" To this he answers, "Who do you say is here?" The voice then replies, "The enemy of my husband, whom you killed seven years ago." The monster is the victim's wife, who has come to exact revenge.

We have witnessed many vengeful women in Kyōka's works, beginning with figures such as Otan in "The Poverty Club" and continuing throughout the author's career as a searcher for psychological buffers who, more often than not, employed female characters as deuteragonists. As noted above, Kyōka built upon the gesaku trope of vengeful spirits (*onryō*) by reconfiguring it in a personal way, just as he gave practically all traditional images a distinctly private value. In essence, he accomplished this by placing society's wronged and insulted within the meta-story's structure so that protagonist and heroine are joined in a battle against the brutish and unjust. Typically they are allies, and the heroine pays the price of the hero's salvation. In this story, however, something fundamental has changed. The archetype has weakened, and Yano is clearly one of the guilty. The voice calling "Is Chōta there?" implicates Yano as an offending party; having caused much suffering out of youthful ignorance, he is not to be excused but is to suffer the spiritual consequences of murder. When Yano hears this story of Chōta and the badger, "a strange voice that had practically disappeared within a sea of blood suddenly erupted like a volcano and exploded within his memory" (24: 18). Unlike Kyōka's previous heroines, the wronged women of this final novel do not forgive, nor do they bear their suffering without complaint.

Driven by a sense of doom and plagued by the voice that seems to be calling for him, Yano can hardly enjoy his stay in Wakura. His reunion with his niece Rie and a former schoolmate only seems to deepen his feelings of regret and inadequacy. He is a vulnerable man who expects tragedy to strike even in an idyllic place, famous for its views of water and mountains. To be sure, the hot springs are soothing, even healing, but from the beginning of the novel, Yano finds his circumstances as an accomplished writer "lonely" and "gloomy." He jokes with the maid. "I think I can find the bathing room by myself. . . . But if I get lost, I'll yell for help. Come running down the hall to save me" (24: 10).

The need is familiar. However, because the integrity of the archetype is compromised, it is not clear who could save a man such as Yano. As we read on, we sense that Kyōka was nervously aware of this question. In the rambling and disconnected scenes of this bewildering narrative, it becomes obvious that he knew *what* he needed to write but that he no longer knew *how* to. Obviously, he felt compelled to address his sense of guilt and the futility of his life as a novelist. Indeed, the very meaning of the act of writing changed as he searched on paper for some sort of solution. He repeated the themes of doom, revisiting variations of the well-viewing scene, allowing the voice "Is Chōta there?" to assert itself again and again. Yet he did not seem to be working toward a confident processing of this profound emotion.

This explains why there are actually two conclusions in *Of the Mountains and the Sea*, one intended and the other not. The second (unintentional one) comes in the penultimate chapter. Yano is with Rie, touring the area in an automobile. On the road, they are surrounded by a number of horsemen who demand that Rie be handed over to them as a sacrificial victim. Unable to save her and once again reminded of his powerlessness, Yano is reduced to tears.

Filled with thoughts of his mother's breasts, Yano bit his—no, he wouldn't be able to bite his chest—his arm. He bit into his left arm and tried to rend it.

He tried to protect his right hand, his writing hand.

Ah, my friend Tanizaki Jun'ichirō of Okamoto in Hyōgō Prefecture! And those still in Tokyo. Minakami, Satomi, Kubota. If you were here, with your talent, your wit, and your courage, we could get them out of this crisis with ease. Or some other friend, anyone. Or perhaps in another sense—I believe this woman's mother, Hanayanagi Kazue, or my wife Sumi would be able to save Rie. If it came to that, they would turn the world upside down to rescue her. Even against these brutes, they would be able to save Yano's sweetheart.

It's just that I've made a mistake in my approach. I've forgotten what comes before and what follows after. I've lost my composure.

Now my eyes will have to witness the limbs of Rie's fair body trampled by the wild hooves of horses, torn by the poisonous fangs of wolves. Close your eyes, tear open your chest! Would that be enough? What does it mean to have skill as a writer?

If I can't save Rie, what good is writing? What good is a novel? What good is a writer? (24: 369)

This remarkably frank admission of the author's powerlessness reveals a cataclysmic breakdown of Kyōka's authorial stance. Many Japanese critics have tried to minimize the importance of this passage by calling it a *gakuya ochi*, or inside joke, that failed. But in the larger context of the author's life, it is a bad joke that means a great deal. Having written passionately for decades and having depended on language and literature to help maintain an emotional balance against the forces of fear, Kyōka finally reached a dead-end and this devastating moment of disequilibrium. As suggested in this and other texts of this period, he seems to have come to doubt his accomplishments as a writer. The shift away from the fictive archetype and toward more autobiographical writing is perhaps explainable as an admission of the essentially exploitative nature of his craft and the implausibility of his lifelong attempt to save himself through fiction. His call for help—from Tanizaki Jun'ichirō, from Minakami Takitarō, from Satomi Ton, and from Kubota Mantarō, from anyone who could come to his rescue—marks a point of real crisis for both Yano the character and Kyōka the writer. The fictive distance between artist and character has been reduced to almost nothing. Consequently, Kyōka found himself trapped in something like a confessional I-novel and in danger of becoming just the sort of artless artist that he had so often derided. Not only did he face his usual fears about life, but now he also confronted the doubly disturbing horror of an art without artifice and of language without magic.

But this is the first of two conclusions. The novel continues for another chapter and discovers another, more familiar way of finding closure. In this alternative ending, all are saved by a messenger from Hakusan, who just happens to be riding with Yano and Rie in the same automobile. Perhaps because of this second ending, Japanese critics have been willing to ignore Kyōka's alarming admission of futility. Unfortunately, such attempts to find ways of appreciating this work by focusing on the legends from which Kyōka worked, like the strategy of dwelling on the metaphoric constants that pervade the work, merely state what is obvious. The problem is not that Kyōka did not know what to write: on a thematic level, the work holds together well enough. Rather, the crisis and deeper significance of this late novel can be traced to a fundamental change in the sexuality of his characters and how this reorientation dislocates the usual relationships between men and women. With the admission of guilt comes a very different state of awareness, a maturity that is almost paralyzing since it corrodes the more formal and mythic construction of meaning that had served Kyōka so well for so long. Having given up on the paradigm, Kyōka was flushed from the ideal world of his imagination. Intimated in earlier works, the crisis finally plays itself out here. In the end what destroyed the usefulness of the archetype was the tendency, in Kyōka's final years, for his men to be more sharply aware of sexual appetite.[5] The men become men.

Given the consistency of Kyōka's artistic vision, this development might seem puzzling. But coherence itself might be the best explanation for what has happened. The emergence of this new sexuality resulted from precisely that idealism which had for so long suppressed its development. It followed, in other words, from the author's continuing attempt to remain constant in the face of change, to compensate for that which was ineluctably slipping away. As Minakami put it, "In his attempt to retain his sexual vigor, Izumi-sensei did his best to retain a youthful spirit in all that he did. In doing so, he tended to force things so that he lost the purity of feeling and the sincerity of youthful passion that he once possessed. The fineness of his sensibility waned. And the quiet maturity that should have replaced a more youthful understanding never seemed to develop."[6] When it finally started to come, this development caused catastrophic changes, eventually nullifying the usefulness of the archetype. Romantic purity (as visualized in the relationship between the mother figure and the weak male) was lost, and the "once possessed" of this aging author was no longer a mother's nurturing care but an aggressive sexual need to have another's body again and again.

A Brother's Death

For Kyōka, the season of loss had already begun. On March 31, 1933, he received news that his younger brother, Toyoharu, had suddenly died of blood poisoning. His relationship with his brother had been strained for many years. By all accounts, Toyoharu was a pleasant, likeable man with an eye for style and flare. He was taller and handsomer than Kyōka, but he achieved neither artistic nor financial success. As a writer, he was a modestly talented novelist whose brother was, as numerous critics put it, a "genius." Had they not shared the same profession, Toyoharu's failures might have been easier for him to bear. For one thing, he would not have had to live with the pen name Shatei, a pun on "live-in disciple" that Kōyō had given him. Kyōka himself was not always kind to Toyoharu. He thought of him as a sponge. Unable to abide his younger bother's inability to manage his financial affairs, Kyōka had all but cut off relations with him. When Toyoharu finally lost his house to creditors, he made the situation more difficult for Kyōka by turning to Tokuda Shūsei, who owned an apartment building in Hongo and agreed to rent out a small apartment to Toyoharu and his wife. It was there, in Shūsei's building, that he died.

Shūsei wrote a short story entitled "Reconciliation" ("Wakai") based on his involvement in the events that followed Toyoharu's death. It is one of the major sources of information we have about Toyoharu, but it is not the only account we have of the problems that plagued his relationship with Kyōka. Twenty or so years after the fact, Satomi Ton would write of an occasion when Toyoharu, desperate for money, suddenly visited his home (across the street from Kyōka's). Toyoharu did not dare approach his brother for help, and so he asked Satomi to ask his brother for a loan of fifty yen. Satomi honored his request. Kyōka immediately and abruptly rejected the idea. Satomi returned home, thinking the matter had ended there. Later that evening, Kyōka came visiting. As if he had forgotten what had happened earlier that day, he handed Satomi five 10-yen bills and asked that they be delivered to his brother.[7]

By dying in Shūsei's apartment building, Toyoharu had once again placed another member of the bundan between himself and his older brother. This time, however, the mediation was made even more difficult by the falling-out that had occurred between Kyōka and Shūsei upon Kōyō's death. Despite their mutual animosity, Shūsei took care of the necessary arrangements. In Shūsei's "Reconciliation," the character named "K" visits the narrator after the funeral, bearing a number of gifts that he had carefully assembled in order to repay the author/narrator for what he had done for "T" at the time of his death. As related by Shūsei, Kyōka spent most of the time during their visit chatting in his usual entertaining way about his pathological fear of dogs. Shūsei's reaction, as expressed in the concluding line of this story, is hardly free of judgment. "I felt as if I had just taken a light knockdown punch."

The ambiguities expressed by this statement were perfectly understandable to those with a personal knowledge of the situation. Commenting on Kyōka's relationship with Shūsei, Satomi Ton wrote:

Unable to accept the goodwill of an old friend, Kyōka was driven by his timid and prudent nature to settle his debt with Shūsei by amassing a pile of gifts that were calculated to cost roughly as much as the amount that had come out of Shūsei's pocket. By repaying the kindness of another's efforts, Kyōka meant to forgive both himself and all others involved. It was not as though Shūsei, who had eaten for a number of years at the same table with Kyōka, was incapable of understanding this. But he seems to have taken offense at being treated like a stranger. "A light knockdown punch." In these seemingly simple words we can feel a full measure of Shūsei's resentment. What did he mean by titling his work "Reconciliation"? The concluding line skillfully undermines whatever gentleness the word *reconciliation* might possess.[8]

Another reading would be that this distancing ambiguity was, in fact, the most effective way of resolving whatever differences lay between the two men. On another occasion, Shūsei explained that his coolness was common to people from Kanazawa.

I'm rather cold toward people, and Kyōka, who is a Kanazawan in temperament, also shares this trait. Or perhaps it's the selfishness of the artist coming through. Speaking for myself, I often find my mind clouded with self-interest. But more than that, it's a certain kind of sensitivity that causes me to come unhinged when things aren't done properly. That's why . . . I'm exacting about money matters and extremely resourceful about finding ways to fulfill my obligations. Kyōka also understands this reality. Tokyo natives tend to suffer from a vanity that neither of us share.[9]

Despite the irony in "Reconciliation," Shūsei himself probably considered their impasse a thing of the past. After Kyōka's visit, Shūsei even made an effort to attend the Nines. His attempt to belong to Kyōka's fan club, however, was short-lived.

> I thought of joining the group but, since I don't drink, nothing much came of it. I did get the chance to see Kyōka get drunk, however. And it was clear to everyone present that he had a strange fastidiousness about all matters pertaining to food. It comes from his fear of living, which also has something to do with his abnormal dread of dogs. No doubt it has some biological cause. I think the idiosyncratic nature of his writing probably shares the same source.[10]

Ever forthright, Shūsei was to the point about Kyōka's biology. Yet equally direct was Satomi Ton's analysis of why Shūsei came only once. The Nines Club was not a place for rigorous argument but for stylish play and boisterous conversation. Shūsei, who had never cultivated anything like a playful avocation, was simply too dull a man to become a part of their group.[11]

Wanderings

Kyōka continued to write, but he did not write well. In his struggle to construct a world amenable to a more aggressive sexuality, of a sort that had not been an element of the archetype, he continued to produce works that lacked both form and emotional strength. His departure from the paradigm led to a weakening of the imaginative force of his work and to a concomitant strengthening of an autobiographical impulse. Although he never went as far as the I-novelists in baldly recounting details of his private life, it is clear that, when no longer guided by the structure of myth, Kyōka's work reads much more like the naturalist fiction that he earlier despised. This lapse not only raises questions about the enduring sincerity of Kyōka's artistic vision but also highlights the problematic understanding of fiction among modern Japanese writers generally. The fragility and insecurity of this understanding would become the focus of, for instance, Maruyama Masao's severe critique of Japanese novelists in general: they fell to carnality (as did their nation, which fought and lost an absurd war) because they lacked the ability to imagine a world that was different. For Maruyama, fictional strength is a function of a mature sense of politics grounded in a critical feel for historical processes. Japanese writers lacked this faculty and were unable to find a workable substitute.[12]

This, at least, is a reading of literary history by someone who openly admits his lack of experience as a reader of literature. Although not emphasized by Maruyama, the paradox hidden in his argument is clear: to want more imagination is always to require less of it, for the possibilities of political life are sufficiently obvious to those who cannot see the social force of something so powerful as beauty. For Akutagawa, a far more penetrating reader than Maruyama, Kyōka's aesthetics were moral for precisely the same reasons that morality needs to be aesthetic. After all, Akutagawa wanted to believe that good art could lead to good living (as it seemed to be doing in at least Kyōka's case), but he understood that most readers—even those like Maruyama and himself—might not be able to understand the connection between fiction and life, beauty and morality. Perhaps a part of Akutagawa's inexplicable and haunting sense of uneasiness was the premonition that someday even Izumi Kyōka would abandon his obsessive belief in aesthetics. Had he lived to read *Of the Mountains and the Sea*, for instance, he, too, would have been called to the rescue. He, too, would have been listed with Tanizaki, Minakami, Satomi, and Kubota. And it would have been a heartbreaking moment for him because Akutagawa would have seen that the level of intensity made possible by Kyōka's imaginative aesthetics of youthful yearning had become sorely diminished. He would have seen that the redemptive powers of this emotion had become, in fact, severely corrupted. Figure 19 shows Kyōka two years before his death, at this time of abandonment.

The death of the past is set down as history, as the inevitable causal relationships between things. Kyōka went on to write the autobiographical *Plum Blossom* (*Usukōbai*, 1937) as a newspaper novel for the *Tokyo Daily News* and the *Osaka Daily*. Often quoted as a source of biographical information, the work suffers for being a forced recounting of the author's youthful involvement with someone of the opposite sex. It is a reading of the past that is, in other words, lifeless to the extent that it tries to capture what was supposedly true: a real romance between a real man and a real woman. This time Kyōka appears as Tsujimachi Itoshichi, a promising young author still training under his mentor's stern though conscientious direction. Kōyō is Uesugi Eizan, august and above criticism. And the woman with whom Tsujimachi becomes involved is not modeled after Higuchi Ichiyō, who is mentioned in an unflattering light, but Kitada Usurai (1876–1900), one of Kōyō's many students. In the story, her name is Tsukimura Kyōko.

Like *The Plum Blossom*, Kyōka's next work was yet another senescent rendering of what once had been. *The Snow Willow* (*Yuki yanagi*), published in December 1937 in *The Central Review*, is a vague, meandering narrative that makes numerous references to other stories. Some of these are lengthy. Kyōka obviously used this intertextual method to prepare the reader for the strangeness of the story he was about to tell, but this web of indirect quotations and summaries is not, in the end, successful.

Once sifted out from its elaborate context, Kyōka's original contribution to this medley of ghost stories is simple. Koyama Chokushin is a sculptor. At the age of fifteen or sixteen, he left his hometown to study in Tokyo, where he lived with one of his countrymen until he was able to move in with his mentor, Kumohara Meiryū. With Kumohara's help, Chokushin becomes a successful artist. As in *The Plum Blossom*, Kyōka's identification with the protagonist is clearly intended. His own experiences of leaving Kanazawa to study with Kōyō in Tokyo become the basis of the story. A person of great drive and intense desire, Chokushin stands in for the author who was, if we accept Minakami's analysis, straining in his old age to recover the virility of youth. Indeed, Chokushin is lustful. The object of his desire is his friend's second wife, Ofuyu. Although he has only met her once or twice, he is unable to forget her. Years after his friend's death, he learns from his friend's younger sister that Ofuyu is living with her daughter. He visits Ofuyu, gets drunk, and attempts a seduction. Learning of his interest in this woman, the sister curses their relationship. She is a nun, and because she is privy to the fact that Chokushin once slept with Ofuyu's daughter when she was working as a geisha, she does what she can to discourage his progress. As a result, six red spots appear around Ofuyu's breasts, and hair begins to grow from these blotches. Driven mad by this deformation of her beautiful white skin (as intimated by the story's title), she commits suicide. By doing so, she saves herself and Chokushin from sexual pollution and from their inevitable devolution into *chikusho* or beasts, the cursed status of the impure.

This metamorphosis—human life taking on a bestial form—echoes *The Holy Man of Mt. Kōya* and Kyōka's first full expression of the meta-story, thirty-seven years earlier. A comparison of *The Snow Willow* with Kyōka's earlier dependence on the archetype illustrates the seriousness of his dilemma during the years just prior to his death. *The Snow Willow* deviates radically from the paradigm. In contrast to *The Holy Man of Mt. Kōya*, the woman, not the man, is transformed; this change marks a very different register of sexual desire. Unlike that of the young mendicant, Chokushin's appetite is not curbed by inexperience or by religious vows. He is fully sexual and, therefore, inappropriate for a role in the archetype. He does not deserve salvation in the way that the young mendicant does. Furthermore, the women of the story are no longer worthy of the role of alluring yet maternal saviors that so many female characters before them played. The long-maintained alliance of usually conflicted powers has broken down: women are reduced to the more familiar late-modern dyad of either sexual objects or enemies of sexuality. This development explains why the sexless old nun rather than Ofuyu steps in to save Chokushin: the younger woman has become too "real" as a sexual object to be of much help to Chokushin. This is also why the interference is not a beautiful metamorphosis but a hideous transformation of Ofuyu's body that is more shocking for its being partial. Although we might tally Ofuyu as one of a multitude of suffering women, her disfigurement, a metaphor for physical attraction gone awry, is an expression of desire that can only be called ugly. In *The Snow Willow*, aesthetic concerns are not so much replaced as simply abandoned. Having relinquished his recalcitrant claim on beauty, Kyōka was an artist adrift.

The Final Work and Return to the Archetype

Kyōka published nothing in 1938. For the first time since he had begun writing professionally, he allowed an entire year to slip away in inactivity. At sixty-five years old, he was both physically and mentally exhausted. From the fall of this year, his health began to deteriorate rapidly. This decline was partially caused by malnutrition, the result of many long-held phobias about food. He contracted pleurisy and was bedridden for a time. Upon recovery, he made a concerted effort to drink more moderately, but his body was weak, and his fondness for tobacco had led to the deterioration of his lungs. By the end of the year, small amounts of blood began to appear in his sputum, the first signs of the cancer that would eventually take his life.

To those around him, the decline caused great concern. Even those of the bundan who did not know Kyōka intimately noticed he was weakening. In March 1938, Masamune Hakuchō, who happened to be seated directly in front of Kyōka at a party, had an opportunity to observe the author closely for the first time.

No matter how delicious the dishes set before him, the ones he was actually able to eat were extremely few in number. He joked about it with the person sitting next to him. Kyōka's fussiness about food had caused his health to suffer. At his doctor's orders, he had started to eat pork cutlets for the first time. Filled with uneasiness about life, he made the comment "Life after fifty is a burden." Kyōka loathed old age and feared death. Yet how is it possible to avoid either?[13]

Hakuchō happened to meet Kyōka again only a few days later, at the celebration of the twentieth anniversary of the Kaizōsha publishing house. This time he had a chance to talk with the aging author, who discussed a topic he had earlier shared with Shūsei: his inordinate fear of dogs. Hakuchō's conclusion was "For those who are sensitive, their insecurities make themselves manifest in various ways." As judgmental as this might sound, the naturalist critic was moved by the encounter. Although Hakuchō had read and publicly denounced Kyōka's work, for the first time he understood how paranoia had been transformed into an existential principle for the author. "Trembling from an uneasiness about life that not even years of involvement in art had been able to eradicate, this man Kyōka moved my heart. I could sense he was a great artist." Unlike Shūsei, Hakuchō stopped far short of reading Kyōka's writings as scripted symptoms of a spiritual disease. Yet he took an equally radical position in peremptorily declaring that "Kyōka's fears of life and death did not manifest themselves in his novels in any way."[14]

Whatever others felt about his fear, the death that Kyōka had dreaded all his life was moving ever nearer. Tanizaki, who no longer resided in Tokyo, was not present to witness the decline. Perhaps for this reason, he was bold enough to ask Kyōka to be the intermediary for the marriage of his oldest daughter, Ayuko, to Satō Haruo's nephew, Takeda Ryūji. The wedding picture (see Fig. 20) shows a man with gray hair, sitting to the right of the groom. He is looking not at the camera but off to the side, as if his attention was being called away by something that no one else in the room even noticed. Sitting to the left of the bride is Suzu—small and proper looking. Of all the women, she is dressed in the most conservative sash. To her left is Tanizaki, vigorous looking and confident. Of Kyōka's role in the ceremonies, he would later comment:

I discovered that this was the first time for Kyōka-sensei, despite his age, to serve as an intermediary in a wedding, and that from the beginning he was very much looking forward to participating. My original intention was that his role be strictly formal. I planned to use his name only. But he himself understood his involvement differently, going to great lengths to participate in all activities, from the betrothal to the actual ceremony. He took my daughter's welfare very much to heart. According to Kubota Mantarō, this was the first and last time he appeared on such an occasion with his wife.[15]

It is likely that Kyōka agreed to Tanizaki's request over Suzu's objections. She was anxious about his health and did her best to limit his activities. Because she knew it drained his strength, she tried to prevent him from doing more writing. But in the end, she could not stop him. He took up his brush once again and began what would be his last story. "The Heartvine" ("Rukōshinsō") was a project that sapped his remaining energy. The manuscript pages—laboriously written and rewritten, page upon page blackened out as if Kyōka knew that this was his last chance to get it right—remain a moving testament to his renewed faith in language, in literature, and in the archetype that once again, and for the last time, gave shape to his literary quest (see Fig. 21).

Published in July 1939 in *The Central Review*, "The Heartvine" shows how Kyōka, who had spent most of his career trying to discover and then to reaffirm the myth of personal salvation that became clear to him in 1900, finally returned to the archetype. On this final occasion, he employed the myth with the intense passion of the best of his earlier works. Here, however, there is something new: a profound sense of regret and humility. At last, the maturity that Minakami had found lacking finally appears. As a result, "The Heartvine" is sure and confident. Not only have the obfuscating force and troubled waywardness of the late stories disappeared, but the familiar lyricism of yearning makes itself felt again, this time tempered and deepened by a profound sense of resignation. No doubt, this new emotional power came both from an acceptance of his own inescapable and imminent death and from a heartfelt sorrow for having lived so long by spilling the blood of others. Expressing these complicated feelings, his last work is perhaps the best writing that he ever did.

To repeat an earlier point, age drew Kyōka's mind to the past. His several trips back to Kanazawa—in November 1926, May 1929, and November 1930—attest to this need to return to visit Meboso Teru, Yuasa Shige, and his younger sister, Yae, and to remember the place of his birth. In "The Heartvine," Kanazawa is again the setting. Once again, the area along the Asano River that provided the original geography of Kyōka's imagination figures prominently. This time, however, the focus is almost entirely on the dead and the dispossessed who occupy the far bank. It is as if, at this late point in his career, Kyōka is interested in the world of the living only insofar as it affirms the sphere of death and the sacred. As before, there is a strong sense of trespass or crossing over to this marginal place. Yet the timing of the journey has been changed—as the story begins, the protagonist Tsujimachi Itoshichi, who first appeared in *The Plum Blossom*, has already arrived on the other side of the river. The realm of the living is, at least in an emotional sense, already the world of the dead.

At a temple on Mt. Utatsu, Itoshichi is making an afternoon pilgrimage to the grave of his cousin Okyō (who was modeled after Meboso Teru). Okyō has recently passed away, and a visit to the dead is a priority. Kyōka gave the temple that Tsujimachi visits the name Senshōji, but there is no question that the actual setting is the Renshōji, which, even now, is the Meboso family temple. Today, the graves are located in the garden to the right of the main hall.[16] But in 1939, the time of this story and the year of Kyōka's death, they were still placed high on the hill behind the complex. Then as now, access to the grave-yard was over a long, steep flight of moss-covered stones. Tsujimachi is halfway up these steps, well committed to the dead, when the story begins. He pauses to rest with Oyone, Okyō's daughter, a typical heroine—physically attractive, spirited, intelligent, tastefully dressed, twenty or so years old. In accordance with the archetype, Oyone is both attractive and unavailable to Tsujimachi, who is not blind to her beauty but is too *old* to think of becoming intimate with her. She is married, after all. So to her, Tsujimachi is an avuncular, perhaps even grandfatherly, figure.

Despite the age difference, their conversation is lively. She has heard from her mother about Tsujimachi and knows much more about him than he at first realizes. As they sit together, she teasingly suggests that the grave he most wants to visit is not her mother's but that of another woman to whom he owes as much, possibly more. Her suggestion takes him aback. Suddenly, the event that he has nearly erased from his memory returns to him.

"I'll forgive you this time," she said to Tsujimachi. "You acted so innocent, I had to scare you. But you know what I'm talking about, don't you? That spring night, the cherry blossoms in full bloom. You were there by the castle gate, at the edge of the dark moat, walking back and forth."

The way Oyone flitted her fingers as she moved her hand made Itoshichi see in his mind's eye the shadowy figure of a small man emerging from the distant woods that surrounded the distant castle. He was walking slowly, arms folded, his eyes focused on the ground. Without enough to wear, not having eaten for several days, he was deter-mined to end his life there. He was that young man. Tsujimachi.

And there was someone else—a sad, beautiful woman, who appeared as if she had alighted from the blossoming clouds. Hidden in the dark shadows, she came slowly to the edge of the same moat, down the hill that divides the city. Her eyes cast down at the ground, the sleeves of her kimono folded softly over her bosom, and the skirts of her kimono floating in midair, she turned away from him. He caught a glimpse of the nape of her neck—a whiteness—as she walked quietly, with a refined grace, into the black night. Around them, the spring flowers were ablaze with color, and the earth beneath his feet began to move like a raft upon water as he watched her walk down the slope beneath the canopy of cherry blossoms in full bloom.

Oh, Oyone. Lift those dangling sleeves. The whiteness of your neck and the graceful lines of your shoulders make you resemble that unfortunate woman!

She, this woman walking down the slope of his memory, was only twenty years old on that night when she threw herself into the abyss. By sacrificing her life, she saved his. Unlike her, he—the young man standing at the edge of the black water—was nothing but a coward. He went on to live, shamelessly. And now he was an old man, the one who had stopped to rest halfway up the graveyard path at the Senshō Temple. (24: 672–73)

Sensing the nearness of death, Kyōka returns once again to this memory, his darkest moment. Hearing Oyone's account of his near-suicide, Tsujimachi feels as though "he has awoken from a dream." In this case, the dream is far more than a momentary lapse of consciousness. This final remembrance of the suicide of another woman, Hatsuji, liberates him from what has been a lifelong pursuit of beauty and salvation. Although "The Heartvine" marks a final return to the meta-story, its somber, elegiac tone tells us that Kyōka had finally allowed himself to awake from the very fiction that had sustained his life. It reveals that he finally could be old. This final, profound affirmation of the archetype is a declaration of its *falseness* rather than its truth. Or perhaps we should say it narrates the truth of its falseness: the trespass is a palliative for the harshness of reality rather than reality itself. At the same time, it is language *at* the end (and *as* the end) of language. For equally undeniable is the truth that the falseness of fiction allowed Kyōka to live a long, full life. And the significance of that life is that the real is never available except through the world of signs and never without the lies that emerge by virtue of the imagined relationships between things. Otherwise, there can be no possibility of structure, pattern, and truth. The emotional tenor, then, of "The Heartvine" is not one of regret and denial but of sadness and apology, an openly admitted indebtedness to the necessity of language and literature that simultaneously asserts and undermines the power of art.

Awakened by Oyone's rehearsal of his past, Tsujimachi's mind turns not only to the young seamstress, who appeared in the earlier "The Night Bell Tolls," but also to Oyone's mother, Okyō. She is modeled after one of a few people who knew the author well enough to understand the true depth of his fear. As described in the story, Okyō knows all, including Tsujimachi's feelings of guilt and his indebtedness to this woman who saved him by taking her own life. Her omniscience and sympathy are compelling aspects of her character. They match the ability of the seamstress, who threw herself into the castle moat, to suffer on Kyōka's behalf. Taken together, these three women—the beautiful Oyone, the understanding Okyō, and the suffering Hatsuji—complete Kyōka's private sense of the feminine ideal.

Previously, this ideal was almost always highlighted against a backdrop of people whose sensibilities are too coarse to appreciate it. Here, Kyōka returns to this familiar pattern. Hatsuji, whose distinguished past sets her apart from the hoi polloi, was driven to suicide by the persecution of her fellow workers, people envious of her ability to embroider so well. Her sewing a design of two dragonflies joined together in flight is used as an excuse to castigate and shun her. Of course, this public display of prudery by her enemies merely camouflages their lack of aesthetic and moral integrity. Even her suicide does not change their hearts: she is buried in an unmarked grave and forgotten. Yet, just as he came to admit his own guilt at having exploited the suffering of his heroines, Kyōka was finally willing to allow the world of the mundane to achieve its own deeper understanding of what he had been trying to accomplish. This becomes clear when Tsujimachi learns from Oyone that, many years after her death, the people of Kanazawa have decided to memorialize Hatsuji by replacing her simple grave with an elaborate monument.

The city's repentance is not without ulterior motives. Hatsuji's monument—a spool of crimson thread atop a white stone base—is designed to play off the grave of the founder of Kaga *yūzen* (silk dying), which is located at a temple not far from the Renshōji. This pair of monuments will affirm Kanazawa's sense of itself as a center for the traditional arts, and the tourism implicit in this attempt to honor Tsujimachi's personal savior establishes an irony that is impossible to miss: Hatsuji finally means something to Kanazawa only because the city has found a way to exploit her death. By mentioning this commemoration, Kyōka is attacking the commercial use of tradition. Yet the bitterness with which Kyōka earlier attacked the crass and unfeeling world of commerce and politics is missing, perhaps because his own history as one who exploited the feminine image is now clear.

The magical power of Hatsuji's art, expressed in the appearance of dragonfly spirits in both Tokyo and Kanazawa, ultimately dominates the narrative with its visual power. Strongly and beautifully, the imagery asserts the salutary thrust of the archetype one last time. Even the workers who attempt to carry Hatsuji's old gravestone without first wrapping its nakedness with a blanket are stopped when two dragonfly spirits appear and send them fleeing in fright. The men are, in a sense, chastened by Hatsuji's unappreciated beauty. Yet, here again, Kyōka's judgment of them was lenient because in his regard for the banal he was also feeling contrition for his own shortcomings. Admitting his own failures, he could accept the brutish for who they are. That is to say, on the brink of his own extinction, he was finally able to accept the world for what it is and not for what he wanted it to be.

Despite this subtle but important change in the use of the meta-story, Kyōka presented an archetype that is still identifiable and intact. The subtle eroticism of earlier writing re-emerges as well. Hatsuji's gravestone is her body. Although roughly handled by the workers, who bind it with ropes and are later made to repent of this indiscretion, it is a surface that is fragrant and soft to Tsujimachi's touch. It is tenderly dressed with Oyone's coat, which she un-hesitatingly offers because she shares the gallant and generous spirit of her mother. Indeed, her sympathy for Hatsuji's plight touches Tsujimachi's heart, making him remember Okyō and the thoughtfulness she once extended to him. Oyone is young and beautiful, as Okyō once was. He is attracted to her as he was once attracted to her mother. Above all, Oyone's presence is comforting. It proves that the good, the just, and the beautiful are followed by children who are similarly good and just and beautiful. Here (and perhaps only here) in this genealogy of morals is there hope for those who live in this evanescent world of dust.

If this were still the universe of *The Snow Willow*, Tsujimachi might attempt to act aggressively on this feeling, causing Oyone to become hideously disfig-ured. But because this protagonist, Kyōka's final hero, is firmly situated within the narrative structure of the archetype, he cannot do so. Precisely for this reason, his feelings toward Oyone are made erotic in the restrained way to which we have become accustomed.

> "I'll put it on."
> "But it's covered with moss from the stone . . ."
> "She had such a sad life. Look at my coat. The grass pattern."
> Tsujimachi was moved by Oyone's kindness. He offered to help her with her coat. "Here. Give me your shoulder."
> "Tsujimachi-san!"
> "To me, you're the same as your mother. How could there be anything wrong?"
> "I suppose it's all right."
> When she turned, her hair brushed against his chest. A chill ran through his body. "I . . . miss your mother."
> Tsujmachi had been involved with the theater and with moviemaking. A moment ago, he had been thinking that he could take a scene like this and exploit it for a profit,

an evil thought secretly sprouting in his heart. But this time there was no such allure, no desire. Tears came to his eyes.

*

"Thanks for waiting." A woman came out from the priests' living quarters, holding a firepan in one hand and a small, flickering candle in the other. "I'll leave this for you at the monument. Please don't forget to bring it back. You know what they say about crows playing with fire."

Oyone had already reached the platform.

"I see. The time has already come. But what's there to be afraid of? The birds are sleeping in the woods near the Thousand-Wing Abyss."

Still standing on the steps, Tsujimachi looked out over the darkened castle town lying below. Flickering through the willow trees, the lights of the city were flowing upon the surface of the river. Stepping down the long flight of steps, he and Oyone descended into the darkness. The spirits of the slums had yet to come out.

Tsujimachi suddenly stopped, as if he had almost run into a tōfu peddler making his way home in the dark. "Dragonflies!"

Oyone immediately fell to her knees and pressed her hands together in prayer.

Above them in the air, the paper lantern they had left at Hatsuji's monument passed through the temple gate, slowly rose into the night sky, then moved away upon a single gust of wind that blew down from the mountain. Two dragonflies quietly moved, and the images of two women appeared. (24: 715–17)

These final words brought Kyōka back to his point of departure: to a sense of helplessness, to feelings of dependence on women, and finally to the same linguistic patterns that made concretely visible the powerful feelings that demanded his steady and careful concern. In the end, Kyōka's faith in language and fiction prevailed, even though he had departed temporarily from the myth that made the images of belief powerful and real. If anything, that departure required him to depend upon the powers of make-believe even more profoundly than before, to see art as the truthful lie that it is, and then to reaffirm it again with a deeper, more sorrowful appreciation. In the end, the strongly felt historical impulse of his later years forced Kyōka to live the meta-story (and thus face his death and his role as a writer) in a way that he never had before. As a young man, the discovery of the archetype had been exhilarating, an adventurous and often violent artistic joy that compelled him to send multitudes of women to their deaths without compunction. This was the price of salvation, exacted by the ephemeral nature of fiction's ability to mollify horror and to express the awesome, as well as the awful. Although the need for death never changed, the awareness of sorrow grew and deepened. It led him first to forsake myth and then finally to embrace this final statement of indebtedness and responsibility that followed from a life of writing and rewriting a fiction that had to be true.

Fiction is false, but what other possibility is available to us so long as meaningful life coalesces around narrative structures? And if the truth is always a story, a necessary fiction, so, too, is a life of value always made beautiful because of its provisional certainty. To echo the concerns of the much earlier "One Day in Spring," what can we live for, if not for the narration of our dreams? In the end, the pursuit of beauty and goodness might be nothing but a constant state of make-believe, an ongoing conversation with the dead that makes us feel as though we are alive for a season and for a purpose. The crucial difference separating fantasy from truth is simply the degree to which we realize that belief is always constructed and that dreams are real to the extent that we understand the ways in which they require our responsibility. With his own death now clearly in the offing, Kyōka cast off all pretending in order to fulfil his need to get the story right one last time. Or perhaps we should say that he wrote in order to get it right for the *first* time. Dying from the cancer spreading in his lungs, he allowed himself to be perfectly honest so that the fiction of his life and his long life of fiction could meld and extinguish themselves together. The struggle, both physical and spiritual, is apparent in the blackened pages of the story's manuscript (see Fig. 21).

Perhaps this explains why the serene yet strikingly visual "Heartvine" is also one of Kyōka's most intensely erotic stories. As Noguchi Takehiko has expressed it, the sexuality here flows from the manner in which life and death are presented as shades of each other.[17] In the world of this story, stone is flesh and flesh stone. The living daughter is the dead mother. And the water that claims the despondent also spurs the coward. Standing at the veil between life and death—a flowing surface of red playing upon white—Kyōka was utterly alive because he was altogether aware that his time in the flesh was nearly over, and that his literary quest and his very reason for being had been the truth built of lies.

More than any writer since Akutagawa, Mishima Yukio opened the way for Kyōka's critical resurgence. Of course, at the time of the story's writing, Mishima had yet to discover his literary soulmate, even though his grandmother, who planned for practically every facet of his life, already had their friendship in mind. At her bidding, the fourteen-year-old Mishima was sent to a bookstore in Shibuya to get the story. Upon asking at the counter, "'Rukō-shinsō' o kudasai," ("The Heartvine" please), the clerk looked at him as if he were crazy.[18] For Mishima, this story would become the very embodiment of Zeami's aesthetic ideal of the flower or *hana*. In his discussion of it, he would quote directly from Zeami's treatise *On the Flower* (*Fūshikaden*). "Because it truly has attained the Flower, [it] will put out many branches and leaves, and its blossoms will remain on the tree until it becomes an ancient one. This is proof before our very eyes of the Flower as it lingers in the bones of an old man."[19] Extending Zeami's metaphor, Mishima would refer to Kyōka's writings in general as "a garden of peonies that steadily blossomed amid the anemic desert of modern Japanese literature."[20]

Parting

After completing the manuscript for "The Heartvine," Kyōka began to deteriorate rapidly. From August, he complained of pains in his chest, abdomen, and pelvic region. He also began to have difficulty breathing. The Banchō house was fully exposed to the sun in the summer. And in the oppressive, sultry heat of Tokyo, Kyōka suffered horribly. Suzu prayed and stayed at his side even through the night. From the backyard she picked a single sprig of dayflower (*tsuyukusa*) and brought it to his bed. The plant with its small blue flowers delighted Kyōka, who repeatedly praised its beauty. He picked up a pencil and scribbled a haiku in the notebook by his bedside.

> I will miss
> The dayflower,
> And the flowering knotweed.

These were the last words he wrote.

On the evening of September 6, Kyōka's heart began to fail. Satomi Ton suggested he be given oxygen and injections of glucose. Kyōka at first refused, but Satomi persisted and finally persuaded him to receive the treatments. Upon receiving the oxygen, Kyōka is said to have responded, "Oh, this feels good. But if I could have one wish, I would wish that this air be chilled, cool as the ocean wind."[21] On the morning of the seventh, he was feeling better. After receiving an injection for his heart, he was able to enjoy a breakfast of miso soup and boiled rice with barley. He asked for the usual egg, but Suzu told him to wait until lunch so he would have something to look forward to. When his regular eleven o'clock examination came around, however, the end was near. The attending physician whispered the dreaded words into Suzu's ear, and she relayed them to Satomi Ton, who immediately left to make calls from his home. Sasakawa Rinpū, Yanagita Kunio, Kubota Mantarō, and Komura Settai arrived within minutes. Satomi Ton joined them shortly thereafter.

Kyōka's bed had been set up in the four-mat room off the entrance. Seeing his closest friends crowd the room, Kyōka realized that he would soon be a dead man. He suggested that he be moved to the next room in order to accommodate everyone. No sooner had everyone moved into the eight-mat room, than Kyōka's heart started to fail. The doctor gave him four shots in quick succession, but to no avail. He died at 2:45 in the afternoon, September 7, 1939.

Telegrams announcing his death were immediately sent to family and friends. Kaburagi Kiyokata and Minakami Takitarō, who had missed Satomi's phonecall, learned of Kyōka's death by telegram. Upon receiving the news, they came immediately to the Banchō house, and were soon joined by Kōyō's widow, Shunyō's widow, Shiga Naoya, Kitamura Rokurō, and others. The job of contacting the newspapers fell to the novelist and editor Sasaki Mosaku. Kubota Mantarō phoned the radio stations. By four o'clock that afternoon, the news of Kyōka's death was already being broadcast to the nation. By that evening, the first obituaries appeared in the papers, telling the Japanese that the eccentric writer Izumi Kyōka had at last passed away. Mourners immediately began to visit the Banchō house to pay their respects, coming in a steady stream that continued through the night and throughout the next day. At the wake, sutras were intoned by clerics from the Enpukuji, the Izumi family temple. The funeral, held on September 10 at the Seishō Temple,[22] was attended by approximately five hundred people, including a contingent of geisha from Nihonbashi. The ceremonies were conducted by Teraki Teihō, Kyōka's principal biographer and one of Kyōka's only two students (who both turned to other professions). At six o'clock that evening, as the entourage carrying Kyōka's cremated remains started out for the graveyard, a heavy rain and thunderstorm began. Those who had known Kyōka well were reminded that of the many natural phenomena that he had feared, thunder was one of the things that horrified him the most. His ashes were buried in Zoshigaya. Sasakawa Rinpū provided the calligraphy for his gravestone. Komura Settai designed the grave.

Eulogies

Numerous obituaries and essays appeared immediately after Kyōka's death and then again a year later. Tokuda Shūsei, who had outlived his hometown rival, wrote of a "genius type" who revered Kōyō to the point of worship, someone who struggled financially until "a great patron of the arts" (Minakami Takitarō) appeared to give comfort and stability to his later years. He described a man of peculiar habits—a modern novelist who sanctified his manuscript pages with drops of water and dipped his fingertips into the ashes of his *hibachi* in order to disinfect them.

When he was young, Kyōka continually sought maternal love and the love of women, so that whenever a beautiful woman became his admirer, he would most always consider that woman's husband to be a fool, whether he was a scholar or a man of wealth. This was an expression of resistance against the ruling class, the attitude of someone who had grown up poor, and a commoner. It would be interesting to study his work from this angle: in all his writings he caricatures people as though he were sitting inside a dark cave, staring out with sharply observant, piercing eyes. His method was much like that of a child who, from a state of innocence, naturally makes fun of adults. As he matured, this tendency became a predilection, a type of amusement that finally lapsed into a sort of self-indulgence. As an artist he could not have been happier, entrusting all to virtuosity and immersing himself in only that which held his interest.[23]

Despite their rapprochement, the tone of Shūsei's memorial is more critical than friendly. Shūsei remembered a man who was always too entertaining in conversation, someone who made others laugh by ridiculing Shun'yō's rise from rags to riches. He spoke of how he had been personally "boycotted" by Kyōka and Fūyō over his manner of chronicling Kōyō's death. Although they reconciled in the end, he admitted his skepticism regarding Kyōka's true feelings. It was as Satomi Ton and others suspected. To the end, Tokuda Shūsei disapproved of Kyōka, both the way he lived and the way he wrote.

But perhaps Shūsei was only trying to counter the dizzying apotheosis that had already begun with the publication of Kyōka's complete works. Kyōka had been a writer who had trained few students but had gained many fans, and with his death many were prompted to place him among the gods. Tanizaki was one. Reflecting the nationalistic tenor of the day, he found a purity in Kyōka's work that he deemed to be essentially Japanese.

Quite frankly, I believe that during the final years of his life, Izumi Kyōka was largely left behind and forgotten. But I also think that because he had accomplished so much as an artist, he was not particularly bothered by this neglect. To me, it didn't seem as though he suffered from loneliness, although we cannot deny that the aging Kyōka was excluded from the mainstream of the bundan. Now that he has passed away, however, a new historical significance and classical luster should accrue to his writings. We should read Kyōka in the way we read Chikamatsu or Saikaku, exploring the unique world of this great writer whose life spanned the Meiji, Taishō, and Shōwa periods.

I use the word *unique* with good purpose. In truth, few other authors have spent their lives within a world so strikingly different from any other. Great artists resemble each other in their extreme individuality. . . . Sōseki, Ōgai, and Kōyō each occupied his own world. But the difference between these men is less than that which separates Kyōka from them all. . . .

Often mystical, bizarre, and obscure, his writing is essentially bright, florid, elegant, even artless. Its most laudable quality is its pure "Japaneseness." Although Kyōka lived during the high tide of Western influence, his work is purely Japanese. All the values that appear in it—the beautiful, the ugly, the moral, the immoral, the chivalrous, the elegant—are native-born, borrowed neither from the West nor from China. . . . He is at once the most outstanding and the most local writer that our homeland has produced.

Shouldn't we then boast of this writer who couldn't have possibly come from another country?[24]

Beyond paying homage to a friend and exemplar, Tanizaki obviously was expressing more than simply personal loyalty. This memorial was written in 1940, the year the second Konoe cabinet formed the New National Structure (*Shintaisei*) that forced the dissolution of Japan's political parties in an attempt to shore up "imperial objectives." Although the banning of his *Makioka Sisters* (*Sasame yuki*) and his preoccupation with translating *The Tale of Genji* give an impression of Tanizaki's mute resistance to Japan's brutal war efforts, we can see why he might have had compelling reasons in 1940 to call Kyōka's work "purely Japanese." Not only had the cult of the emperor made Japaneseness a pressing and enduring issue, but we have only to read "In Praise of Shadows" ("In'ei raisan") to understand how much of a cultural chauvinist Tanizaki would eventually become.

His attempt to find what is unique about Kyōka followed from an understanding of Japanese language and culture that he shared with other authors, notably Kawabata Yasunari and Mishima Yukio. All three admired Kyōka as a protector of a tradition that was embodied in the Japanese language. Their shared admiration can be expressed in a simple syllogism: Japan is made available through the Japanese language; Kyōka, whose distinctive style set him apart, understood and exploited the possibilities of Japanese as no other writer had done; therefore, of all Japanese writers, Kyōka was the most Japanese. Of course, the problem with this sort of essentializing is that it both denies the details of Kyōka's life and ignores the wider context in which he had to work. The tendency to erase the particulars of his life is expressed by the obvious contradiction that runs through Tanizaki's words of praise. If great art is a matter of "extreme individuality," why would anyone want to make any individual the bearer of something so vast (and so vacuous) as a Japanese essence? As this book shows, it simply is not true that Kyōka "borrowed neither from the West nor from China." He borrowed from both and was the richer for it.

Whatever the distortion, this sort of nationalism marks an important critical moment that needs to be addressed. Tanizaki's desire to find greatness in a purely Japanese author is a solipsistic rendering of the authoritative self as it emerges from an awareness of just how deeply Japanese culture has, in fact, been compromised by numerous foreign influences. Tanizaki's praise is disingenuous. It fails us on this account and on two others. It does not admit that culture is in flux and never a purity. And it flees from the truth that language is similarly hybridizing and self-translating. In the end, Tanizaki's claim of Kyōka's uniqueness is either blandly circular—who is not unique?—or an ideologically forced reaction to the cultural context of what we have come to call modern Japanese literature.

Still, the issue he raised is a seductive one, and a study of Kyōka's life and works must deal with this notion of him as modern Japan's most Japanese writer. Although marginalized in his own day, Kyōka was an important figure precisely for those reasons that have made his work so controversial. Was his visual style and dependence on a personalized myth evidence that he was lagging behind or racing ahead of his time? Did he love women or hate them, and how would we be able to decide? Was he an inspired artist or simply mad? Was the fear that drove him on more often akin to horror or to reverence?

Few Japanese writers compel us so forcefully to rethink the notions of "modern," "Japanese," and "literature" with such rigor. This is because few writers, to return to Kobayashi Hideo and our starting point, so effectively persuade us to consider in a serious way the utter opacity of language and the importance of figurality in expressing "the truth made from lies."[25]

Epilogue

Shortly after Kyōka's death, an updated version of his complete works was published by Iwanami shoten. This collection, *Kyōka zenshū*, which appeared from April 1940 to November 1942, was updated in 1973, and again in 1989. The most recent version contains thirty volumes.

Suzu died on January 20, 1950. Before passing away, she donated the bulk of her husband's manuscripts to Keiō University in Tokyo, where they are still kept. She also saw to it that a significant number of his personal effects—including his library, his writing desk and implements, and his folding screen covered with images from Ryūtei Tanehiko's *False Murasaki, Rustic Genji*—were donated to the same university, and that a special room was built in the old library on the Mita campus to display these artifacts. While his belongings were being catalogued, a single sheet of paper was found in the drawer of his writing desk. On it was written in Kyōka's hand, "The power of letters (*iroha*) is immeasurable. Use them with care" (see Fig. 22).

As Tanizaki Jun'ichirō proposed, Kyōka's work has indeed come to have "a new historical significance and classical luster." But the question of whether his stories and plays are read "in the way we read Chikamatsu or Saikaku" still remains to be answered. What *can* be said about Kyōka's present reception is that, as before, his stories continue to be read and taken seriously by a small but devoted group of readers. As Donald Keene has put it,

"The difficulties of his style have kept him in recent years from obtaining a mass audience . . . but in another sense surely no other author of modern Japan is less likely to be affected by the changing tastes of the times. Like the Noh plays he loved and emulated, Kyōka's works partake of a mystery that transcends any particular place and time."[1] Certainly, the difficulty of Kyōka's writing only increases as written Japanese continues to become more simple and clear, and as the objects and experiences of late-modern Japan fade into the past.

As mentioned above, Mishima Yukio correctly predicted that a new, postwar "reading" of Kyōka's work would be mediated by performance. The staging of plays such as *The Castle Tower* and *Demon Pond*, which were too openly affirming of the world beyond to be easily acceptable in their own time, have led to a resurgence of interest in his work. From about the 1970s and the beginning of the so-called Kyōka boom, a number of his pieces have also been adapted for the screen, thus making available to contemporary audiences cinematic interpretations of the archetype—this story of erotic trespass in which the dead are remembered by a fearful journey toward love, salvation, and visual wonder. Of the interpreters of this archetype, it is perhaps the kabuki *onnagata* and film director Bandō Tamasaburō who has played the most decisive role in making Kyōka's work popular.[2] As reflected in both his performances of Kyōka's plays and his choices as a film director, Tamasaburō's understanding of Kyōka's emotional concerns and artistic methods is profound and refreshing.

As for Kyōka's reputation within the academy, this has changed as modernization theory has become critiqued and supplanted by other, multicultural and post-structural approaches to the modern. To a large degree, the phonocentric force of Japan's late-modern era has given way to the flourishing of visually oriented systems of expression—photography, film, dance, theater, television, *manga*, magazines, computer graphics, and the like. Consequently, the figural (and "retrograde") elements of Kyōka's work have in many cases come to be seen as "newer" than the modernity that rejected them. One important aspect of Kyōka's present relevance, then, is how it helps us answer the question of what actually was "new" or "modern" about Japan's late-modern era.[3] In a word, Kyōka's obvious ties to Edo period texts and to Noh drama narrow the gap that supposedly separates *kinsei* (early-modern) from *kindai* (late-modern). To the extent that Kyōka is able to emerge as an important figure of late-modern Japan, a revisionist literary history that discloses rather than suppresses the continuities between Edo period culture and contemporary Japan becomes possible.

For contemporary Japanese writers, Kyōka's relevance lies in how his writing informs the post-modern, figural search for sympathy that has supplanted the late-modern, phonocentric pursuit of truth. For writers such as Kōno Taeko, Tsushima Yūko, and Murakami Haruki, his stories and plays continue to inspire by pointing toward the "potential of the Japanese language" of which Mishima spoke.[4] In the final analysis, Kyōka's most important contribution was to demonstrate the possibility of literature by disturbing the (perceived) stability of language enough to push the written word toward its roots in pure vision, on the one hand, and in pure sound, on the other. To the extent that he was able to isolate and then reintegrate the grapheme and the phoneme in new ways, we might say that his accomplishment was in a broad sense cinematic or pictorial. As such, its resonance with the visually oriented sensibilities of contemporary audiences makes sense, despite the inaccessibility of his prose.

Given the difficulties of reading Kyōka in the original, any significant increase in the number of his readers may occur among those who will have only the mediated access of translated texts on which to rely. Among Meiji period writers, Kyōka lags behind many others in the number of translations into various languages. Mori Ōgai, Koda Rōhan, Higuchi Ichiyō, Natsume Sōseki, Shimazaki Tōson, and Tanizaki Jun'ichirō all have an established presence in the minds of educated English readers, for example. In recent years, however, Kyōka's stories and plays have begun to be translated into Chinese, English, Italian, and French. Needless to say, the difficulties for the translator are legion, not so much because the author is, as Tanizaki put it, so purely Japanese, but because he is accomplished. Although the challenge of producing language that resembles his convoluted and cryptic style is daunting, the opportunity to pour over Kyōka's work a word at a time is its own reward. As illuminated by the details of his life and works, Izumi Kyōka is an artist whose work stands up well to the closest scrutiny. His need for language and art was genuine.

Appendixes

APPENDIX A

Major Titles and Dates of Publication

"Ai to kon'i"	"Love and Matrimony"	1895
"Baishoku kamonanban"	"Osen and Sōkichi"	1920
"Bake ichō"	"Maidenhair"	1896
"Bunindō"	"The Hall of Bunin"	1911
"Chūmonchō"	"The Order Book"	1901
"Funin rishōki"	"Blessings of the Holy Mother"	1924
Fūryūsen	*The Elegant Railway*	1903–4
"Gekashitsu"	"The Surgery Room"	1895
Giketsu kyōketsu	*Noble Blood, Heroic Blood*	1894
"Ichi no maki"– "Chikai no maki"	*The Maki Cycle*	1896–97
"Iki ningyō"	"The Living Doll"	1893
"Higedaimoku"	"The Grave Writer"	1897
"Himin kurabu"	"The Poverty Club"	1895
"Kagerō za"	"The Gossamer Stage"	1913
Kaijin besso	*The Sea God's Palace*	1913
"Kakegō"	"Will-o'-the-wisp"	1915
Kanmuri Yazaemon	*Crowned Yazaemon*	1892
"Katsushika sunago"	"The Sands of Katsushika"	1900
"Kechō"	"A Bird of Many Colors"	1897

"Kindokei"	"The Gold Watch"	1893
Kōya hijiri	*The Holy Man of Mt. Kōya*	1900
"Kuina no sato"	"Water Rail Village"	1901
"Kunisada egaku"	"The Kunisada Prints"	1910
"Kuro yuri"	"Black Lily"	1899
"Kusa meikyū"	"The Grass Labyrinth"	1908
"Machi sugoroku"	"A Throw of the Dice"	1917
"Mayu kakushi no rei"	"How Beautiful Without Eyebrows"	1924
"Meienki"	"Chronicle of a Famous Princess"	1900
"Mine jaya shinjū"	"The Teahouse Suicides on Mt. Maya"	1917
"Minodani"	"Mino Valley"	1896
"Misago no sushi"	"The Osprey's Sushi"	1923
Momijizome Taki no Shiraito	*Taki no Shiraito of the Crimson Leaves*	1915
"Muyūju"	"The Flowering Paulownia"	1906
Nihonbashi	*Nihonbashi*	1914
"Oizuru zōshi"	"The Traveler's Cloak"	1898
Onna keizu	*A Woman's Pedigree*	1907
"Onna kyaku"	"A Female Visitor"	1905
"Ōkakei"	"In Nightingale Hollow"	1898
Oshinobi	*The Spy*	1936
"Rukōshinsō"	"The Heartvine"	1939
"Ryūtandan"	"Of a Dragon in the Deep"	1896
Sankai hyōbanki	*Of the Mountains and the Sea*	1929
"Sasagani"	"The Spider's Web"	1897
"Seishin an"	"Seishin's Nunnery"	1897
Sengoku chazuke	*Warring States, Rice with Tea*	1926
"Shamisen-bori"	"Shamisen Moat"	1910
Shakuyaku no uta	*The Peony's Song*	1918
Shinja Daiō	*Shinja the Great*	1904
"Shirakijo monogatari"	"The White Witch's Tale"	
"Shirasagi"	"The White Heron"	1909
"Shōsei yahanroku"	"The Night Bell Tolls"	1895
"Shunchū"/"Shunchū gokokū"	"One Day in Spring"	1906
Tashinkyō	*Polytheism*	1927
"Tae no miya"	"Shrine of Wonder"	1895
"Tatsumi kōdan"	"A Tale of the Southwest Quarter"	1898

Tenshu monogatari	*The Castle Tower*	1917
Teriha kyōgen	*Teriha Kyōgen*	1896
"Tsunbo no isshin"	"A Deaf Man's Single-mindedness"	1895
Tsuya monogatari	*The Vigil*	1899
"Umi no shisha"	"A Messenger from the Sea"	1909
Usu kōbai	*The Plum Blossom*	1937
Uta andon	*A Song by Lantern Light*	1910
"Yakō junsa"	"The Night Patrol"	1895
Yamabuki	*Wild Roses*	1923
Yashagaike	*Demon Pond*	1913
"Yuna no tamashii"	"The Bather"	1900
"Yōken kibun"	"The Blood-Tempered Sword"	1920
Yukari no onna	*Women of Acquaintance*	1919
Yuki yanagi	*The Snow Willow*	1937
Yushima mōde	*Worship at Yushima*	1899
"Yushima no keidai"	"The Yushima Temple Grounds"	1914

Titles of Journals and Newspapers

Bungakkai	*Literary World*
Bungei kurabu	*Literature Club*
Bunko	*Library*
Bunshō sekai	*Writing World*
Fujin gahō	*Women's Pictorial*
Hototogisu	*The Cuckoo*
Jiji shinpō	*The New Times*
Fujo kai	*Woman's World*
Kokumin no tomo	*Citizen's Friend*
Kokumin shinbun	*Citizen's News*
Mita bungaku	*Mita Literature*
Okujō no teien	*The Roof Garden*
Osaka mainichi shinbun	*Osaka Daily*
Seinenbun	*Literature for Today's Youth*
Seitō	*Blue Stockings*
Shin shichō	*The New Current*
Shin shōsetsu	*New Fiction*
Shigarami zōshi	*Tangled Tales*
Shōnen sekai	*Boy's World*
Subaru	*Pleiades*

Taiyō	*The Sun*
Teikoku bungaku	*Imperial Literature*
Tokyo hibi shinbun	*Tokyo Daily News*
Yamato shinbun	*Yamato News*
Yomiuri shinbun	*Yomiuri News*

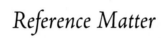

Reference Matter

Notes

For complete author names, titles, and publication data for works cited here in short form, see the Selected Bibliography, pp. 375–88.

Introduction

1. Kobayashi Hideo, "Kyōka no shi, sono ta," *Bungaku* 2 (November 1930). Reprinted in *Bungei tokuhon: Izumi Kyōka*, p. 16.

Chapter 1

1. Murō Saisei, *Dai ni shishū*, p. 66.
2. *Taiyō*, no. 325, p. 11 (1988).
3. James McClain, *Kanazawa: A Seventeenth-Century Japanese Castle Town*, p. 102.
4. This nomenclature is not standard. I place late modern against early modern, which would include that point during the seventeenth century at which urbanization stimulates the reflexiveness that leads to the conceptualization of the self. Writers such as Ejima Kiseki (1666–1735) and Ihara Saikaku (1642–93), for instance, would already be proto-modern, as the Japanese term *kinsei* suggests. What many literary scholars have taken to be the beginning of Japan's modern era in the nineteenth century, as expressed by the Japanese term *kindai*, is more precisely a second, accelerated stage of processes that began much earlier. I choose to extend the reach of the modern period as far back as possible since it becomes impossible to under-

stand Meiji-period authors such as Izumi Kyōka without a knowledge of Edo-period texts. Until now, the difference between Edo and Meiji fiction has been emphasized, largely because of the Eurocentric bias common in the study of modern Japanese literature (*kindai bungaku*), whether done in the West or in Japan. As our knowledge of the Edo period improves and as it becomes less tenable to posit a single, Western source of modernity, this periodization will come to be challenged. I tentatively set the date for the end of the late-modern period at the suicide of Mishima Yukio (1925–70) and the subsequent rise of certain narrative structures and semiotic trends that show a weakening of modern phonocentrism.

For more on the expansion of the term *modern*, see Earl Miner, "Inventions of the Literary Modern"; and Dennis Washburn, *The Dilemma of the Modern in Japanese Fiction*.

5. Izumi Natsuki, "Hanetsuki, tegara, tsutsumi no o," *Gendaishi techō* (bessatsu), p. 128; reprinted in *Shin bungei tokuhon Izumi Kyōka*, pp. 20–21.

6. Gamo Kin'ichirō, *Mō hitori no Izumi Kyōka*, pp. 149–50.

7. Muramatsu Sadataka, *Izumi Kyōka*, p. 37.

8. The numbers in parentheses refer to volume and page numbers in the 1973–76 *Kyōka zenshū* (Collected works of Izumi Kyōka). In some instances, these numbers differ from those in the most recent (1989) edition. These two Iwanami editions were preceded by a twenty-eight-volume set that appeared in 1940–42; all three Iwanami editions roughly follow the fifteen-volume *Kyōka zenshū* published by Shun'yōdō in 1925.

9. Kyōka was proud of his family's connections to the Noh theater and would make a point of mentioning his maternal uncle Matsumoto Kintarō, a well-known Noh actor, in his autochronology. Yoshida Seiichi ("Izumi Kyōka no hyōgen") and numerous others have rightly noted the influence of Noh: not just in obvious intertextual situations, as in *A Song by Lantern Light* (*Uta andon*, 1910), which quotes the play *The Diver* (*Ama*), but also as it informs the narrative tempo and structuring, as in such stories as "How Beautiful Without Eyebrows" ("Mayu kakushi no rei," 1924), "Of Flowers and Herbs" ("Yakusō tori," 1903), and *Women of Acquaintance* (*Yukari no onna*, 1919).

10. Izumi Natsuki, pp. 16–17.

11. For a photograph of this record, see Noguchi Takehiko, ed., *Shinchō Nihon bungaku arubamu: Izumi Kyōka*, p. 14. Kobayashi Teruya (ed., *Izumi Kyōka*, p. 511) argues that if Suzu died of smallpox, it is strange that no one else in the family, including the baby Yae, suffered from the disease. Other than this stamped record, there is no written account of the actual cause of death.

12. This is the chronology first prepared by Kyōka for the *Izumi Kyōka shū*, Gendai Nihon bungaku zenshū, 14 (Kaizōsha, 1928). After his death, Komura Settai added to it for inclusion in the *Kyōka zenshū* (1940–42). The earlier chronology was

prepared by Izumi Toyoharu, Kyōka's younger brother, for the *Kyōka zenshū* (1925). Both are contained in the current *Kyōka zenshū*, published by Iwanami—the first in vol. 1, and the second, earlier one, in vol. 29. The one partially prepared by Kyōka himself is mentioned more often. Both contain errors.

13. The increasing phonocentrism that occurs during the Tokugawa period is the subject of Naoki Sakai's useful *Voices of the Past: The Status of Language in Eighteenth-Century Japanese Discourse*.

14. This is a point I have come to understand more clearly in my discussions with Masao Miyoshi. See his *Off Center: Power and Culture Relations Between Japan and the United States*.

15. A number of studies in English lay out the general contours of this period. An older, nearly forgotten literary history by Okazaki Yoshie has been translated by V. H. Viglielmo as *Japanese Literature in the Meiji Era*. More recently, Donald Keene has given us the similarly encyclopedic *Dawn to the West: Japanese Literature in the Modern Era*. More tightly focused are Masao Miyoshi, *Accomplices of Silence*; Edward Fowler, *The Rhetoric of Confession*; James Fujii, *Complicit Fictions: The Subject in the Modern Japanese Prose Narrative*; and, again, Dennis Washburn, *The Dilemma of the Modern in Japanese Fiction*. The secondary literature in Japanese is voluminous. But a sampling of the most helpful works on the general characteristics of this period would include Maeda Ai, *Kindai dokusha no seiritsu*; Noguchi Takehiko, *Shōsetsu no Nihongo*; Karatani Kōjin, *Nihon kindai bungaku no kigen*; Kamei Hideo, *Kansei no henkaku*; and Takashina Shūji, *Nihon kindai no biishiki*.

16. I have addressed this problem of beginnings in "Pictocentrism—China as a Source of Japanese Modernity," in Sumie Jones, ed., *Imaging/Reading Eros*, pp. 148–52; and also "Modern Japanese Literature on Its Own Terms," in Eiji Sekine, ed., *Revisionism in Japanese Literary Studies: Proceedings of the Midwest Association for Japanese Literary Studies*, pp. 230–52.

17. Osanai Kaoru, "Geki to naritaru Kyōka-shi no shōsetsu," *Yomiuri shinbun*, June 21, 1908; reprinted in Tanizawa Eiichi and Watanabe Ikkō, eds., *Kyōka ron shūsei*, pp. 135–38.

18. For the theoretical implications of picture-centered versus word-centered narrative, see my "Pictocentrism," *Yearbook of Comparative and General Literature* 40: 23–39 (1992).

Chapter 2

1. Gamo Kiichirō, in his *Mō hitori no Izumi Kyōka*, argues that Taka's transfer to the Kotake family would have had to have happened much earlier, since Izumi Seiji's second marriage occurred just a year after Suzu died.

2. Quoted in Iwaya Daishi, *Ningen Izumi Kyōka*, p. 20.

3. Gamo, p. 164.

4. Whether or not Izumi Seiji married yet again is a point of debate, still unresolved.

5. Kobayashi Teruya, "Izumi Kyōka to Kirisutokyō," in idem, Izumi Kyōka, p. 243.

6. From her obituary, as reproduced in Cody Poulton, "Benten of the West: Izumi Kyōka's Image of an American Missionary."

7. From her obituary, furnished by the New York Secretariate of the American Presbyterian Church; reproduced in Kobayashi, p. 243.

8. Muramatsu Sadataka, Izumi Kyōka, p. 14.

9. Satomi Ton, "Sensei no kōaku kan." In pointing out the disparity between Kyōka's respectful treatment of women and his obviously gratuitous use of them in his stories and plays, Satomi raised an important question. In what sense were his literary characters characters? And in what sense are they connected with "real" people?

Teraki Teihō (Hito Izumi Kyōka, p. 143) answered Satomi Ton's plea. "You and I appreciate women in our own way. But even without their company, air would still pass in and out of our lungs and we would still go on living. The sort of love that Sensei possessed, however, was such that he could not survive for a minute, or even for a second, in a world without women. His attachment to them was not to their flesh (niku) but was a simple appreciation of the feminine spirit (tamashii)."

Nina Cornyetz, in Dangerous Women: Phallic Fantasy and Modernity in Izumi Kyōka, Enchi Fumiko, and Nakagami Kenji, argues that the issue of real or imagined is irrelevant. What is significant is that Kyōka, too, like most other male writers of the Meiji period, created a masculine subject through the abjection or "othering" of female identity.

10. Muramatsu Sadataka, Izumi Kyōka kenkyū, p. 14.

11. From p. 3.

12. Eigo kyōiku shiryō (Tōkyō horei shuppan, 1980), 3: 15.

13. Yanagida Izumi, "Kyōkaden kakigaki," p. 125.

14. Ibid., p. 126.

15. For Nishi's proposal, see William Reynolds Braisted, trans., Meiroku zasshi: Journal of the Japanese Enlightenment, p. 9.

16. Quoted from Ivan Hall, Mori Arinori, p. 189.

17. Mishima Yukio, "Ozaki Kōyō, Izumi Kyōka," p. 560.

18. In the journal New Fiction (Shin shōsetsu), January 1901, Kyōka gave a brief account of his favorite authors and texts. Besides these three works, he named several Edo-period writers including Bakin, of whom he eventually tired, Shikitei Sanba (1776–1822), Santō Kyōden (1761–1816), Jippensha Ikku (1765–1831), and Ryūtei

Tanehiko (1783–1843), who would remain favorites. In the way of contemporaneous fiction, Kyōka noted newspaper novels, Morita Shiken's translation of "The Blind Messenger" ("Ko shisha"), Ozaki Kōyō's *Confessions of Love* (*Iro zange*), and Rohan's *The Buddha of Art* (*Fūryū Butsu*).

19. Tezuka Masayuki, "Izumi Kyōka to Morita Shiken."

20. Kyōka was open about his indebtedness to Morita Shiken. In an interview with Muramatsu Sadataka (see *Izumi Kyōka*, p. 93), he stated that the style of "The Surgery Room" ("Gekashitsu") was modeled after the translatese of Shiken's work.

21. Tokuda Shūsei, *Hikari o otte*, pp. 81–82. School records indicate that Tokuda Shūsei matriculated in April 1988. Kyōka misremembered the year.

22. Shinbo Chiyoko, "Shin shiryō shōkai," p. 77.

23. Maruoka Akira, "Kōyō no bungakuteki isan," p. 302. Quoted in Donald Keene, *Dawn to the West*, p. 129.

24. Ozaki Kōyō, *Ninin bikuni iro zange*, in *Ozaki Kōyō shū*, pp. 3–4.

25. Muramatsu Sadataka, *Kindai Nihon bungaku no keifu*, I, p. 33.

26. "Shinchō hyakushu no *Iro zange*," *Kokumin no tomo* (*Citizen's Friend*), 4, no. 48: 35 (1889). Also quoted in Ikari Akira, *Ken'yūsha no bungaku*, p. 90.

Chapter 3

1. The date of Kyōka's departure for Tokyo has long been a point of debate. But Kobayashi Teruya ("Kaga zōgan no shokunin-tachi: Kyōka no shosaku o hitotsu no shiten toshite") has recently produced documents in the possession of the Mizuno family that indicate that 1890 is correct.

2. Izumi Kyōka and Oguri Fūyō, "Kōyō-sensei,"in Ozaki Kōyō, *Ozaki Kōyō-shū*, p. 362.

3. Ibid., p. 363.

4. Ibid.

5. Reproduced in Muramatsu Sadataka, *Izumi Kyōka*, p. 357.

6. Quoted in Iwaya, p. 36.

7. Arakawa Hōshō, *Izumi Kyōka den*, p. 45.

8. Okazaki Yoshie (p. 218), for example, wrote that "Oguri Fūyō (Kōyō gave him the name Fūyō, using the *yō* portion of his own name) emerged from Kōyō's school, and the general opinion was that he surpassed his master Kōyō in the intensity of his erotic description and in the brilliance of literary style."

9. Tokuda Shūsei, Chikamatsu Shūkō, et al., p. 48.

10. Tokuda, *Hikari o otte*, pp. 127–28.

11. Tokuda, "Bō Kyōka-kun o kataru," quoted in Yoshimura Hirotō, *Izumi Kyōka no sekai: gensō to byōri*, p. 255.

12. Arakawa, p. 46.

13. Muramatsu, *Izumi Kyōka*, p. 78.

14. The date of publication given in the second chronology is May 1893. Both month and year are incorrect.

15. From Kyōka's second chronology: "Not wanting to nip the bud at first blossom, Kōyō-sensei valiantly negotiates for its continuation. I didn't find out about this until afterward. It was made possible only by sensei's great charity" (1: v).

16. The most readily available version of this work is in *Meiji kaika-ki bungaku shū*, in the *Meiji bungaku zenshū* (Chikuma shobō, 1969), 2: 212–27. For a study of other possible texts upon which Kyōka might have based this work, see Akiyama Minoru, "Kanmuri Yazaemon kō—Izumi Kyōka no shuppatsu."

17. Koike Masatani ("Izumi Kyōka—*Kanmuri Yazaemon* to *Shinkyoku gyoseki dōji kun*") suggests that Kyōka learned this regard for the underclass from Bakin, and that *Kanmuri Yazaemon* shows thematic and structural similarities with *Kinsei setsu bishōnen roku* and its sequel *Shinkyoku gyokuseki dōji kun*.

Chapter 4

1. A letter to Toyoharu; quoted in Arakawa Hōshō, p. 50.

2. Tobari Chikufū, *Ningen shugyō*, pp. 28–32.

3. All three letters quoted in Iwaya Daishi, pp. 42–43.

4. Quoted in ibid., p. 44.

5. Kōyō mentions this manuscript, then entitled "Kame no saiku," in a letter dated March 17, 1894. Alhough the piece was not published until January 1895, we know it was written in the months shortly after Seiji's death.

6. Reproduced in Muramatsu Sadataka, *Izumi Kyōka*, pp. 85–86.

7. The articles are reproduced in Takakuwa Noriko, "Ikai to gensō," p. 106.

8. Kobayashi Teruya, who interviewed Kanbara, has not yet published this information. He was kind enough to relate this anecdote to me at his home in Kanazawa, February 18, 1996.

9. Keene, "Izumi Kyōka," in idem, p. 206.

10. For a detailed study of the dating of the several *Noble Blood, Heroic Blood* manuscripts, see Mita Hideaki, "*Giketsu kyōketsu* kenkyū" in idem, *Izumi Kyōka no bungaku*, pp. 145–75.

11. Keene, p. 207.

12. Teraki, *Hito Izumi Kyōka*, pp. 212–13.

13. Mita, *Izumi Kyōka no bungaku*, pp. 146–59.

14. Muramatsu Sadataka, *Izumi Kyōka jiten*, p. 27.

15. The encyclopedia was probably Otowa's idea (see Ikari Akira, "Kyōka to Ichiyō," p. 2).

16. Tokuda Shūsei, *Hikari o otte*, p. 230.

17. Ibid., p. 231.

18. Ibid.

Chapter 5

1. For Kyōka's recounting of this process, see "Shojosaku dan" (28: 674–77).

2. This is the opinion of Noguchi Takehiko (*Izumi Kyōka*, pp. 9–10).

3. Seki Ryōichi, "Yakō junsa."

4. Muramatsu, *Izumi Kyōka kenkyū*, p. 232.

5. "Bungei kurabu," *Seinen bun* 1, no. 4: 10 (May 1895).

6. Taoka Reiun, "Jibun: *Taiyō* dairokugo no shōsetsu—'Gekashitsu.'"

7. *Bungakkai*, no. 31, p. 32 (July 1895).

8. *Teikoku bungaku*, no. 8, pp. 105–6 (August 1895). As for the work's faults, the review says the story is "overdone," and its characters are "unnatural."

9. Shimamura Hōgetsu, "Shōsetsukai no shinchō o ronzu."

10. Noguchi, *Izumi Kyōka*, p. 8.

11. Translation quoted from Keene, p. 196.

12. Yoshiya Nobuko, "Izumi-sensei no kakareru josei." In Kyōka's day, the term "feminist" would often have meant something like "a lady's man." Its usage here, however, is close to the one familiar to us today: someone who is aware of and speaks out against the oppression of women.

13. August 1895: quoted in Muramatsu, *Izumi Kyōka jiten*, p. 34.

14. Akutagawa Ryūnosuke, "*Kyōka zenshū* ni tsuite."

15. Mori Ōgai, "Sannin jōwa," esp. pp. 418–19.

16. Reproduced in Yoshida Seiichi, *Higuchi Ichiyō kenkyū*, p. 99.

Chapter 6

1. Quoted in Muramatsu, *Izumi Kyōka jiten*, p. 40.

2. Quoted in Muramatsu, *Izumi Kyōka*, pp. 363–66.

3. Arakawa Hōshō, p. 64.

4. Honma Hisao, "Kyōka tsuioku hitotsu, futatsu," p. 2.

5. Quoted in Muramatsu, *Izumi Kyōka*, p. 119.

6. "Shōkai," *Meiji Taishō bungaku zenshū* (Shun'yōdō, 1928), p. 644.

7. This dependency is the subject of numerous (though often schematic) studies. See Carmen Blacker, *The Catalpa Bow*; Doi Takeo, *Amae no kōzō*; Miyata Noboru, *Hime no minzokugaku*; Yamaguchi Yasuo, *Bunka jinruigaku e no shōtai*, pp. 136–48; Yanagita Kunio, *Imōto no chikara*.

8. Mishima Yukio, "Ozaki Kōyō, Izumi Kyōka," p. 561.

9. Teraki Teihō, *Hito Izumi Kyōka*, p. 79. The other is Kaburaki Kiyokata (1878–1978). Sasakawa's real name was Taneo. While a student, Sasakawa helped start a

magazine, to which Kyōka contributed a story. He went on to become the principal of Utsunomiya Middle School in 1901, then returned to Tokyo to work on Sanseidō's *Encyclopedia of Japan* in 1907. It was then that he began teaching at Meiji University.

10. For an insightful reading of this story, see Hashimoto Yoshi, "*Teriha Kyōgen* ni tsuite," pp. 120–27.

11. Written to Maeda Takeo, March 24, 1907; quoted in Mita, *Izumi Kyōka no bungaku*, pp. 137–38.

12. For a development of this argument, see ibid., pp. 138–41.

13. This is a reading put forward by Takakuwa Noriko, "*Teriha Kyōgen*—koji ni narubeki kizashi."

14. Noguchi Takehiko, "Kyōka no onna," p. 139.

15. Mita, *Izumi Kyōka no bungaku*, p. 134.

16. Ibid.

17. I discussed this matter with Professor Muramatsu, who suggested I omit discussion of this matter.

18. Masao Miyoshi, *Off Center*, esp. pp. 37–61.

19. Susan Napier (*The Fantastic in Modern Japanese Literature: The Subversion of Modernity*) understands the fantastic elements in Kyōka's work as a subversion of modernity. The pairing with modernity is a reasonable one, but giving value to each side of this binarism is an ongoing problem.

20. Cody Poulton, *Of a Dragon in the Deep*, pp. 96–97. Poulton also points out that "the ethnologist Yanagita Kunio wrote as late as the 1920's that 'in a certain large city along the Hokkoku line' (i.e. Kanazawa) the townspeople would still make rounds at night banging bells and drums to ward off evil spirits from their children."

21. For more on this point, see Taneda Wakako, "'Ryūtandan'—Izumi Kyōka no yōnen sekai."

22. Orikuchi Shinobu, "Kodai kenkyū."

23. Arakawa Gyorō, "Saikin no sōsakkai," p. 181.

24. Quoted in Hashimoto, p. 121.

25. Togawa Shūkotsu, "Saikin no sōsakkai"; quoted in Nakatani Katsumi, *Izumi Kyōka: shinzō e no shiten*, p. 49.

26. *Jogaku zasshi*, no. 431, p. 37 (December 1896).

Chapter 7

1. Oka Yasuo ("Izumi Kyōka to Ozaki Kōyō") argues that Kōyō's rapid fall from popularity was in large part due to his willingness to please his readers. According to Oka, Kyōka set himself apart from his mentor in exactly this respect. Stubbornly pursuing his own artistic vision rather than pandering to his audience, Kyōka never

gained the popularity of Kōyō, but his work has generally come to be more highly regarded as a result.

2. For a study of the social setting of "The Poverty Club," see Akiyama Minoru, "Jizen no jidai no bungaku: 'Himin kurabu' no kokoromi."

3. Yoshimura, *Izumi Kyōka no sekai*, p. 245. For a statement on Kyōka's feudalistic obedience, see Tokuda Shūsei, "Izumi Kyōka to iu otoko."

4. Yoshimura, *Izumi Kyōka no sekai*, p. 248.

5. Ibid., p. 248.

6. Yoshimura, *Izumi Kyōka no sekai*, p. 270.

7. Tokuda, "Bo Izumi Kyōka-kun o kataru"; quoted in Yoshimura, *Izumi Kyōka no sekai*, p. 270.

8. Tokuda Shūsei, "Ozaki Kōyō," in *Meiji Taishō bungō kenkyū*; quoted in Yoshimura, *Izumi Kyōka no sekai*, p. 270.

9. For a discussion of Toyoharu's writings, see Ikari Akira, "Shatei Izumi Toyoharu ron."

10. P. F. Kornicki, "The Survival of Tokugawa Fiction in the Meiji Period."

11. For more on language reform, see Nanette Twine, *Language and the Modern State: The Reform of Written Japanese.*

12. Kasahara Nobuo (see the chapter "Yūka suru jikan," in *Izumi Kyōka—bi to erosu no kōzō*, pp. 118–35) discusses the change in tense as a negotiation of the incest taboo. In the present, the mother is real; consequently, reunion with her is forbidden. In the past, she becomes the fantasy mother, a viable object of the young boy's erotic desire.

13. Yoshida Masashi, "Izumi Kyōka to kusazōshi: *Shaka hassō Yamato bunko* o chūshin toshite."

14. See "Sono goro" (28: 692–93) and "Mukashi no ukiyoe to ima no bijinga" (28: 790–94). Presently, Kyōka's collection of kusazōshi is housed in a specially appointed room for Kyōka memorabilia at Keiō Gijuku's old library on the Mita campus and is available for perusal. The prewar bibliographies for this material are found in two monthly bulletins (*geppō*) appended to original Iwanami *Kyōka zenshū* (1940–42): "Izumi Kyōka zōsho mokuroku" (A bibliography of Izumi Kyōka's private library), and "Kyōka sensei no 'kusazōshi' mokuroku" (A bibliography of Kyōka's kusazōshi), *Kyōka zenshū geppō*, nos. 14 and 19, respectively. For a bibliography of the collection as it exists today, see "Izumi Kyōka zōsho mokuroku," *Izumi Kyōka zenshū geppō*, no. 29.

15. *Shigarami zōshi*; quoted in Hashimoto, pp. 120–27.

16. Taoka Reiun, "Seinen bun jibun."

17. Muramatsu, *Izumi Kyōka kenkyū*, p. 268.

18. Ibid., p. 266.

19. Ozaki Kōyō, "Ren'ai mondō."

20. Kasahara Nobuo, "Erosu, kanjō, soshite yume."

21. For more on Kyōka's relationship to the brothels, see Tezuka Masayuki, "Karyūkai."

22. Muramatsu, *Izumi Kyōka*, p. 408.

23. Reproduced in ibid., p. 403.

24. Again, for a development of this concept, see my "In the Scopic Regime of Discovery."

25. *Yomiuri News*, April 22, 1901; quoted in Muramatsu, *Izumi Kyōka jiten*, p. 63.

26. Masamune Hakuchō, "Tsuioku ki"; quoted in Muramatsu, *Izumi Kyōka jiten*, p. 63.

27. Tayama Katai, *Kindai no shōsetsu*, p. 96.

28. This is the opinion of, for instance, Kasahara Nobuo (*Bi to eros no kōzō*, p. 170).

Chapter 8

1. Teraki (*Hito Izumi Kyōka*) records the date incorrectly, as Meiji 34 (1901).

2. Ibid., p. 30.

3. This argument was first presented in my "Water Imagery in the Work of Izumi Kyōka."

4. Takahashi Tōru, "Monogatarigaku ni mukete: kōzō to imi no shudaiteki na henkan."

5. Yoshida Seiichi, "*Kōya hijiri* kenkyū."

6. Kasahara Nobuo, "*Kōya hijiri* no shinwateki kōsō ryoku."

7. Napier, pp. 26–37.

8. Kasahara Nobuo, *Bi no erosu no kōzō*, pp. 180–212.

9. Maeda Ai, "Izumi Kyōka *Kōya hijiri*—tabibito no monogatari."

10. Matsubara Jun'ichi, "Kyōka bungaku to minkan denshō to."

11. Mita Hideaki, "*Kōya hijiri* nōto," in idem, *Izumi Kyōka no bungaku*, pp. 260–78.

12. Tōgō Katsumi, "*Kōya hijiri* no suichūmu."

13. For an inquiry into the nature of this seriousness, see Hosea Hirata, "The Emergence of History in Natsume Sōseki's *Kokoro*."

14. "Kyōka no kingyō" *Bunko*, April 1900; reproduced in *Kyōka zenshū geppo*, no. 5 (March 1974).

15. Mishima, "Ozaki Kōyō, Izumi Kyōka," pp. 559–60.

16. Marilyn Ivy's (*Discourses of the Vanishing: Modernity, Phantasm, Japan*) metaphor of the "vanished" is useful when thinking about the structure of the modern and role of nostagia in the formation of modern consciousness. To couch the reappearance of a lost essence as the reproduction of a "voice" is at first surprising, a mixed metaphor. It represents a diluting of the figure of speech in favor of speech, a

phonocentric model by which to understand a phonocentric process. Within literary texts, what actually vanished was not what could be heard but what could be seen.

17. The dating of this manuscript varies widely. Muramatsu Sadataka places it as early as 1889 or 1890 in his "Shoki shōsaku 'Shirakijo monogatari' to *Kōya hijiri no seiritsu*" in idem, *Izumi Kyōka*, pp. 263–69. However, in an earlier essay, he tentatively placed it much later, at 1893 or 1894. Mita Hideaki ("'Shirakijo monogatari' seiritsu kō," in idem, *Izumi Kyōka no bungaku*, pp. 279–84) places it at 1893. Oka Yasuo ("*Kōya hijiri* seiritsu no kiban," p. 157) dates it to 1893; and Matsumura Tomomi ("Kyōka shoki sakuhin no shippitsu jiki ni tsuite—'Shirakijo monogatari' o chūshin ni") to June–November 1895. Kasahara Nobuo (*Izumi Kyōka: erosu no mayu*, p. 33) now follows Matsumura.

18. Much of Kyōka's personal library was destroyed during the bombing of Tokyo during World War II. But his collection of kusazōshi is kept in a specially appointed room for Kyōka memorabilia at Keiō Gijuku's old library on the Mita campus, and is available for perusal. A prewar bibliography of the entire library as it existed prior to the bombings enables us to reconstruct what is now missing. See note 14 to Chapter 7. For an account of the transfer of Kyōka's books, manuscripts, and effects to Keiō Gijuku, see Itō Yanosuke, "Izumi Kyōka no ihin to genkō."

Chapter 9

1. "Kyōka ni atau," *Teikoku bungaku*, p. 73 (July 1900).
2. From Kyōka's introduction to the work. *Meiji Taishō bungaku zenshū: Izumi Kyōka hen* (Tokyo: Shun'yōdō, 1928); quoted in Muramatsu Sadataka, Asada Yōjirō, Mita Hideaki, eds., *Izumi Kyōka-shū*, p. 575.
3. Quoted in Muramatsu et al., eds., *Izumi Kyōka-shū*, p. 572.
4. Although not expressed in exactly these terms, these points are taken up in Takahashi Tōru, "Monogatarigaku ni mukete"; see also his *Monogatari bungei no hyōgenshi*.
5. Quoted in Muramatsu, *Izumi Kyōka jiten*, p. 73.
6. Masamune Hakuchō, "Bundan kanken."
7. Quoted in Yoshimura Hirotō, *Izumi Kyōka: geijutsu to byōri*, p. 150.
8. Teraki, *Hito Izumi Kyōka*, p. 36.
9. Ibid., p. 47.
10. Ibid., pp. 48–49.
11. Ibid., p. 34.
12. Quoted in Iwaya, pp. 73–74.
13. See Muramatsu, *Izumi Kyōka kenkyū*, pp. 273–74.
14. Ibid., p. 274.

15. Muramatsu agrees with Yoshimura Hirotō, who reads this story not as revenge but as a confession of Kyōka's psychological trauma. Having had to equivocate before his mentor, he waited until Tobari Chikufū came along not only to request a story for publication but to supply him with the anecdotal material that jarred his memory and provided him with the opportunity to express his anguish.

16. Teraki, *Hito Izumi Kyōka*, p. 43.

17. Muramatsu, *Izumi Kyōka*, p. 150.

18. Ibid., p. 148.

19. Quoted in ibid., p. 151.

20. Fujisawa Yukihide, "'Yakusō tori'—Izumi Kyōka no sōzōryoku to *Myōhō-rengekyō*."

21. For an account of Kyōka's hunt for herbs, see "Hakkutsu saiki" (Picking the tetterwort; 28: 345–46).

22. Quoted from Richard Torrance, *Tokuda Shūsei and the Emergence of Japan's New Middle Class*, 101–8.

23. Teraki, *Hito Izumi Kyōka*, p. 44.

Chapter 10

1. Tayama Katai, *Tōkyō no sanjū nen*, p. 273.

2. Tayama Katai, "Rokotsu naru byōsha," p. 157.

3. Quoted in Muramatsu, *Izumi Kyōka*, p. 161.

4. Tezuka Masayuki, "Izumi Kyōka to Morita Shiken," p. 231.

5. For a contemplation of this inversion of good and evil, see Matsumura Tomomi, "Aku no sekai."

6. Quoted in Kasahara, *Erosu no mayu*, pp. 63–64.

7. Quoted in Muramatsu, *Izumi Kyōka jiten*, p. 81.

8. This is the interpretation of Kasahara Nobuo (*Erosu no mayu*, pp. 63–159).

9. Kasahara Nobuo ("*Suikōden* no keifu—*Fūryūsen* made," in idem, *Erosu no mayu*, pp. 161–206) argues that Kyōka's work most resembles Takebe Ayatari's *A Japanese Water Margin* (*Honchō suikōden*, 1773) in its "mutinous spirit and in the directionality of its mythical structuring." For an argument against the influence of *The Water Margin*, see Tezuka Masayuki, "*Fūryūsen* purotto kō."

10. For more on the contribution of this text to the development of modern consciousness in Japan, see my "Pictocentrism—China as a Source of Japanese Modernity."

11. Muramatsu, *Izumi Kyōka*, p. 155.

12. Takakuwa Noriko, "'Shunchū' 'Shunchū gokoku' ron."

13. Yoshimura Hirotō, *Izumi Kyōka: geijutsu no byōri*, p. 35.

14. Quoted in ibid., pp. 35–36.

15. Ibid., p. 41.

16. Yoshida Masashi, "Izumi Kyōka, sobo no shi to 'Onna kyaku.'"

17. Ibid., p. 124.

18. Ibid., p. 125.

19. Quoted in Yoshimura Hirotō, "Kyōka mandara," p. 53.

20. Teraki Teihō, *Hito Izumi Kyōka*, pp. 51–52.

21. Kimijima Yasumasa, "Izumi Kyōka no sunda Zushi," p. 45.

22. Ibid., p. 45.

23. Ibid., pp. 45–46.

24. Teraki, *Hito Izumi Kyōka*, p. 52.

25. Ibid., p. 53.

26. Mita Hideaki, "'Shunchū/Shunchū gokoku' to hankindai," p. 130.

27. It is this passage in particular that convinces the psychiatrist and literary critic Yoshimura Hirotō (*Izumi Kyōka: geijutsu to byōri*, esp. pp. 227–49) that Kyōka was suffering from depersonalization (*rijinshō*). Tamawaki Mio apparently displays the proper symptoms. She lacks a sense of her existence. She does not feel at home in her own body. She does not feel the reality of the world that surrounds her.

28. Only a month earlier than the publication of "One Day in Spring," Hasegawa Tenkei (1876–1940), one of the principal advocates of naturalism, published "Art in the Age of Disillusion" ("Genmetsu jidai no geijutsu") in the *Sun*. His essay declares all illusory images of the past done away. No one believes in the things of the spirit. All that remain are "temples, shrines, landscape."

29. Takakuwa, "'Shunchū' 'Shunchū gokoku' ron," p. 131.

30. The doppelgänger occurs in two other works, "Starlight" ("Hoshi no akari," 1898) and "How Beautiful Without Eyebrows" ("Mayu kakushi no rei").

31. Yoshimura, "Kyōka mandara."

32. Matsumura Tomomi, "'Shunchū' no sekai," p. 121.

33. Takakuwa, "'Shunchū' 'Shunchū gokoku' ron," p. 137.

34. Mita, "'Shunchū'/'Shunchū gokoku' to hankindai," pp. 146–52.

35. Ibid., pp. 147–48.

Chapter 11

1. Yoshimura, *Izumi Kyōka no sekai*, p. 224.

2. I have not seen this playbill and am relying on Matsumura Tomomi, "*Onna keizu no haikei*: 'Shizuoka' no imi suru mono," p. 162.

3. Yoshimura, *Izumi Kyōka no sekai*, p. 205.

4. Ibid., p. 204.

5. Wadatsu Kiyoo, "Konjiki yasha no koro," p. 67; quoted in Yoshimura Hirotō, *Makai e no enkin hō* (p. 139).

6. Wadatsu Kiyoo, "Kyōka-san no koto"; quoted in Yoshimura, *Makai*, p. 145.

7. "*Onna keizu* no moderu," *Gakushikai kaihō*, no. 693 (October 1966); quoted in Muramatsu, *Izumi Kyōka jiten*, p. 92.

8. Katsumoto Seiichirō, "Izumi Kyōka saku *Onna keizu*," pp. 11–12.

9. Itō Sei, "Izumi Kyōka," p. 83.

10. Muramatsu, *Izumi Kyōka*, p. 125.

11. Katsumoto, p. 13.

12. The writer and Kyōka's close friend Minakami Takitarō finally persuaded Kyōka to register her name so Suzu could receive royalties after he died.

13. Katsumoto, p. 11.

14. Mishima Yukio, *Sakkaron*; quoted in Noguchi Takehiko, "Sōzōryoku no gengo kūkan," in idem, *Shōsetsu no nihongo*, p. 223.

15. Mishima Yukio, *Bunshō tokuhon*, p. 49.

16. Noguchi, p. 223.

17. Mita Hideaki, "'Kusa meikyū,'" p. 79.

18. Mishima Yukio, "Shōsetsu to wa nani ka," in *Mishima Yukio zenshū*, vol. 33; quoted in Shibuzawa Tatsuhiko, "Ranpu no kaiten: 'Kusa meikyū,'" pp. 156–58.

19. For an account of the interview with the editor, novelist, and critic Nakamura Murao, see Itō Sei, *Shizenshugi no saiseiki*, pp. 188–89.

20. Noguchi, *Shōsetsu no Nihongo*, p. 221.

21. Ibid., p. 233.

22. Ibid., p. 215.

23. This is Noguchi Takehiko's point; see ibid., p. 216.

24. For a fuller discussion of this interpretation, see Takakuwa Noriko, "'Kusa meikyū' ron: Kyōkateki sōzōryoku no tokushitsu o megutte," p. 113.

25. Kobayashi Teruya, "'Kusa meikyū' no kōzō: temari uta genshi dan," p. 74.

26. Orikuchi Shinobu, "Ishi ni deiru mono."

27. Nakatani Katsumi ("'Kusa meikyū': Meikyū no naijitsu to dasshutsu no kokoromi ni tsuite," in idem, *Izumi Kyōka*, p. 135) argues that because Ayame is a replacement for Akira's mother, her heightened eroticism (and the promise of sexual fulfillment) requires such a heightened sense of the supernatural.

28. This is the interpretation of Shibuzawa Tatsuhiko (p. 166).

29. "Shincho shōkai," *Shinchō* 8, no. 4: p. 46 (April 1908).

30. *Bungei kurabu* 14, no. 3: 316 (February 1908).

Chapter 12

1. Noguchi Takehiko, "Gensō no bunpōgaku."

2. Koshino Itaru, "Izumi Kyōka bungaku hihyō-shi kō (I)."

3. "Umi no shisha" was canonized in the Shun'yōdō *Kyōka zenshū* upon being published for the fourth time. The Shun'yōdō version was followed by the later Iwanami *zenshū*. The four stages of this story's evolution are as follows:

Writing World 4, no. 9 (1909)

Kunisada egaku [anthology] (Shun'yōdō, 1912)

Ginshoku shū [anthology] (Shun'yōdō, 1920)

Kyōka zenshū, vol. 7 [complete works] (Shun'yōdō, 1925)

Changes in punctuation (and wording) can be noted in each of these stages. Consequently, the story did not assume its final form until sixteen years after Kyōka completed the manuscript. We cannot say whether Kyōka himself is responsible for all these alterations, although it is likely that, especially at the *Writing World* stage, editors and printers took liberties with the text.

This point can be illustrated by the editor's choice of the reading *nigoriniku* for the compound 濁肉 in *Writing World*. The manuscript reads *nigorimi*, and for the *Kunisada egaku* anthology the reading was changed back to *nigorimi*. In the final Iwanami version, the reading given is *nigorijishi*. Given Kyōka's sensibilities, it is doubtful that he would have read the second character as *niku*. While this alteration was no doubt the work of editors or typesetters, other alterations are surely Kyōka's, such as changing the name of the Jinmu Temple to Genmu Temple. This modification did not take place until the final stage of the story's evolution.

4. There is also a limit to limits. This is demonstrated by Kyōka's treatment of his narrator walking the plank thrown over the tidal pool. He pauses to look into the pool "as if sitting on a bench" (*suzumidai ni kaketa yō ni* 納涼臺[すずみだい]に掛[か]けたやうに; 217. 14). The full idiom is *koshi o kakeru* (腰を掛ける to sit on a chair or on a raised surface). But here *koshi* is deleted, leaving the sentence less clear but still comprehensible. An example of being slightly beyond the limit of spareness is *nobashite mo todokanu mukō de, kururi to mawaru fū shite, sumashite mata oyogu* (伸[の]ばしても届[とど]かぬ向[むか]うで、くるりと廻[まわ]る風[ふう]して澄[す]まして又[また]泳[およ]ぐ), to which Kyōka felt it necessary to add a direct object and *ude o* (腕[うで]を arm), so the sentence would make sense: "Beyond the reach of my arm, the jellyfish seemed to make a spinning motion, rise up to the surface, then swim calmly again" (219. 5).

5. Edwin McClellan, "The Impressionistic Tendency in Some Modern Japanese Writers."

6. Gotō Chūgai, "Meiji bundan kaikoroku" (1933); quoted in Nakatani, pp. 150–51.

7. Quoted in Nakatani, p. 152.

8. Kyōka mentions the incident in "Nōgaku zadan" (28: 787).

9. For many years, the whereabouts of the manuscript was unknown. Recently, it was donated to the Ishikawa Museum of Modern Literature by members of Sasakawa Rinpū's family.

10. Muramatsu, *Izumi Kyōka*, pp. 320–21.

11. Shinoda Hajime, *Nihon no kindai shōsetsu*, p. 34.

12. For a reading of the cinematic style of this story, see Izawa Atsushi, "Uta andon ni okeru eigateki hyōgen." Izawa is right to point out the visually associative nature of the work's narratology, but in declaring Kyōka a predecessor to Eisenstein, he gives little credit to Japan's long and sophisticated visual tradition that preceded Kyōka's work.

13. Tōgō Katsumi, *Izumi Kyōka: hito to bungaku*, p. 124.

Chapter 13

1. Muramatsu, *Izumi Kyōka kenkyū*, p. 46.

2. Quoted in ibid., p. 46.

3. Teraki Teihō, *Hito Izumi Kyōka*, pp. 238–39.

4. Ibid., p. 71.

5. Kawakami's *Taki no Shiraito* was actually a twisting together (*naimaze*) of two strands: *Noble Blood, Heroic Blood* and "The Reservist" ("Yobihei," 1894).

6. *The Capital News* (*Miyako shinbun*), November 7, 1895; quoted in Cody Poulton, "Spirits of a Different Sort," p. 9. Throughout this chapter, I have benefited greatly by Poulton's study of the plays as well as from his translations of them.

7. *Asahi News* (*Asahi shinbun*), December 11, 1895; quoted in Poulton, p. 11.

8. For more on this play, see Ochi Haruo, *Kyōka to gikyoku*, pp. 21–44. This includes a discussion of the sequel, *Taki no Shiraito of the Crimson Leaves* (*Momijizome Taki no Shiraito*), that Kyōka wrote in 1915. Based on the premise that both Kin'ya and Taki no Shiraito survive, he has Kin'ya marry the daughter of the Chinese knife thrower, whom Shiraito murdered in the original story. Shiraito suddenly visits them and expresses her disappointment.

9. Quoted in Iwasa Shin'ichi, "Kyōka mono to jōen," p. 38.

10. The letter is mentioned in Kyōka's missive to Kitamura, as contained in *Bundan meika shokan shū* (Shinchōsha, 1918), p. 2.

11. Ōe Ryōtarō, "Kitamura Rokurō kikigaki," *Shinpa* (November 1978); quoted in Kasahara Nobuo, *Hyōden Izumi Kyōka*, p. 303.

12. Kasahara, *Hyōden Izumi Kyōka*, p. 303.

13. Ibid., p. 301.

14. Poulton, "Spirits of a Different Sort," p. 102.

15. For Kyōka's description of the theater of his day, see "Hongō no Kōya hijiri ni tsuite," 29: 160–63.

16. See, e.g., Muramatsu, *Izumi Kyōka*, pp. 304–19. Or Kasahara, *Bi to erosu no kōzō*, pp. 345–64.

17. Cody Poulton makes this point in his study of the plays.

18. Tayama Katai wrote reviews of the play: "Yama naka no kōsui," *Taiyō*, March 30, 1902, p. 5; and "Hauputoman ga *Chinshō*," *Mannengusa*, no. 4, pp. 1–4 (February 21, 1903); quoted in Poulton, "Spirits of a Different Sort," p. 96.

19. Hasegawa Tenkei, "*Chinshō* no hon'yaku"; quoted in Muramatsu, *Izumi Kyōka jiten*, p. 159.

20. Tobari Chikufū, "*Chinshō* no honyaku ni tsuite."

21. Tayama Katai, "Inki no tsubo." Yanagita Kunio's regard for Katai was similarly dismissive. He avoided Tayama's writings because he knew beforehand what they would contain. He felt that the autobiographical force of *The Quilt* compromised the literary potential of the novel, for instance. And he especially took offense at *The Wife* (*Tsuma*, 1909) in which Yanagita's marriage is discussed.

For more on Yanagita's interactions with the members of the literary world, see Robert Morse, *Yanagita Kunio and the Folklore Movement: The Search for Japan's National Character and Distinctiveness*, esp. pp. 22–23.

22. Muramatsu, *Izumi Kyōka*, p. 311. Kasahara Nobuo (*Bi to erosu no kōzō*, pp. 345–63, esp. p. 357) similarly finds the division of natural and supernatural a problem. Sugimoto Suguru ("Izumi Kyōka no gensō geki: *Yashagaike no fukken*") counters these positions, finding the two stories complementary.

23. Muramatsu Sadataka, Miyoshi Yukio, and Kasahara Nobuo, "Kyōka to hankindai," p. 13.

24. Kasahara, *Hyōden Izumi Kyōka*, p. 319.

25. The influence of Oscar Wilde's *Salome* is evident. For a discussion of Wilde and his significance to the late-modern period, see Poulton, "Spirits of a Different Sort," pp. 174–79.

26. Regarding Kyōka's heroines, Noguchi Takehiko ("Kyōka no onna," pp. 143–44) writes, "The agony of death is that which allows women to pass from this world to the next and to take upon them a glorified, supernatural state. It is the torture of death experienced in their former life that is given as a type of almost religious trial, allowing them finally to acquire the mysterious ability to pass in and out of both life and death as magical figures, as monstrosities, as princess-like goddesses dwelling in the mountains."

27. For more on this connection with nature, see Ochi Haruo, *Kyōka to gikyoku*, pp. 14–15.

28. In the original version of *Women of Acquaintance* (1919) a similar figure, obviously based on Kyōka's memories of his father, appears. As in the play, his ability as an artisan is measured by his being able to make eyes.

29. Muramatsu, *Izumi Kyōka*, p. 193.

30. Ikuta Chōkō, "Kyōka-shi no shōsetsu o ronzu," p. 93.

31. For a discussion of Kyōka's theatrical regard for space, see Gunji Masakatsu, "Kyōka no geki kūkan," p. 44.

32. Usami Yoshikazu, "Intabyū *une heure avec* Akutagawa Hiroshi."

33. *Kitamura Rokurō nikki*, March 13, 1923; quoted in Kasahara, *Hyōden*, p. 297.

Chapter 14

1. He later wrote *Wild Roses* (1923), as already mentioned, and three other plays: *Warring States, Rice with Tea* (*Sengoku chazuke*, 1926), *Polytheism* (*Tashinkyō*, 1927), and *The Spy* (*Oshinobi*, 1936).

2. Kasahara, *Bi to erosu no kōzō*, p. 315.

3. Yoshida Masashi, "Izumi Kyōka *Yukari no onna* no seiritsu o megutte," p. 27.

4. Ibid., p. 30, quoting "Kyōka no omoide," *Kyū Iwanami zenshū*, vol. 27, *Kyōka zenshū geppō* no. 27 (October 1942).

5. For an explanation of social critique implicit in this work, see Yoshitani Hiroya, *Minzoku kenkyū no shikaku*, pp. 40–41.

6. Ibid.

7. Kawabata Yasunari, "*Kushige shū* to *Shisei oni*"; quoted in Yoshida Masashi, "Izumi Kyōka *Yukari no onna*, " p. 30.

8. Kawabata Yasunari, "Izumi Kyōka no *Kushige shū* nado," p. 205.

9. Ibid., p. 206.

10. Ibid., p. 207.

11. Tanizaki Jun'ichirō, *Seishun monogatari*, p. 382

12. Muramatsu Sadataka, "Kyōka o meguru Taishō sakka gunzō," pp. 218–19.

13. Nomura Shōgo, "Kyōka, Jun'ichirō zakkan," p. 15.

14. Iwaya, p. 172.

15. Muramatsu, "Kyōka o meguru Taishō sakka gunzō," p. 219.

16. I develop this idea more fully in my "In the Scopic Regime of Discovery."

17. The lack of tense in Japanese is noted by Ono Susumu, *Bunpō* II, p. 11

18. Takakuwa Noriko, "Mayu kakushi no rei."

19. Minakami Takitarō, "*Kyōka zenshū* no ki," pp. 189–90.

20. Ibid., p. 191.

21. Komura Settai, "Minakami Takitarō-shi no omoide"; quoted in Kasahara, *Hyōden*, pp. 328–29.

22. "Kyōka kai kiji," *Shinshōsetsu* 30, no. 5: 1 (May 1925). This volume was hastily put together. Despite the page number, this article is one of the last.

23. Kasahara, *Hyōden*, p. 326.

24. Sasakawa Rinpū, "Yaji kara Kidahachi-san e," p. 24.

25. Akutagawa Ryūnosuke, "*Kyōka zenshū* mokuroku kaiko."

26. Akutagawa Ryūnosuke, "*Kyōka zenshū* ni tsuite."
27. Minakami, "*Kyōka zenshū* no ki, " p. 194.
28. Ibid.

Chapter 15

1. Kasahara, *Hyōden*, p. 334.
2. Quoted in Teraki Teihō, "Kyōka no ichinichi," p. 66.
3. Ibid., p. 69.
4. Shinoda Kazushi, "Izumi Kyōka no ichi," *Subaru*, no. 4 (1971); quoted in Takakuwa Noriko, "Izumi Kyōka *Sankai hyōbanki*: anyu ni yoru tenkai toshite," p. 37.
5. This is a point suggested by Noguchi, *Izumi Kyōka*, p. 40.
6. Minakami Takitarō, "Kyōka sekai bekken," p. 279.
7. Satomi Ton, "Futari no sakka," pp. 90–91.
8. Ibid., p. 92.
9. Tokuda Shūsei, "Izumi Kyōka to iu otoko," p. 122.
10. Ibid., p. 125.
11. Kasahara, *Hyōden*, p. 350.
12. Maruyama Masao, "From Carnal Literature to Carnal Politics," p. 251.
13. Masamune Hakuchō, "Zatsubun chō," *Kaizō* (April 1940); quoted in Kasahara, *Hyōden*, p. 352.
14. Masamune Hakuchō; quoted in Kasahara, *Hyōden*, p. 352.
15. Tanizaki Jun'ichirō, "Izumi-sensei to watakushi"; quoted in Kasahara, *Hyōden*, p. 353.
16. In preparing the manuscript for this book, I made several visits to this temple over a number of years. All were memorable, but none more so than when I visited with Nagae Teruyo during the Kanazawa Obon. Climbing up the moss-covered steps, we saw black and orange butterflies, as large as swallows, the empty shells of cicadas clinging to the gravestones. The loud droning of summer insects reinforced the thought that we had stepped into another world, where the dead return to remember those who come to feel their presence.
17. Noguchi, ed., p. 96.
18. Mishima, "Ozaki Kōyō, Izumi Kyōka," p. 566.
19. Ibid., p. 567.
20. Ibid., p. 559.
21. Arakawa Hōshō, p. 277.
22. Kyōka belonged to the Nichiren Sect, although the Seishō Temple is a Sōtō temple. Originally, the use of another temple was planned, but a change was made purely because of scheduling problems.

23. Tokuda Shūsei, "Kyōka tsuioku."

24. Tanizaki Jun'ichirō, "Junsui ni 'Nihonteki' na 'Kyōka sekai.'"

25. Kobayashi Hideo, "Kyōka no shi sono ta," p. 16.

Epilogue

1. Keene, p. 217.

2. For Bandō Tamasaburō on Kyōka and his positive reception in contemporary Japan, see his interview with Gunji Masakatsu, "Taidan: Kyōka geki o megutte."

3. This is the focus of my next research project. By tracing the evolution of the word-image relationship in Edo- and Meiji-period texts, I hope to understand the fundamental characteristics of the "visual tradition" to which Kyōka belonged, especially as it developed during modernity's phonocentric sweep.

4. Kōno Taeko's appraisal of Kyōka—"I know no writer who surpasses Kyōka in his power of expression"—can be found in "Kyōka no seimei." For Tsushima Yūko on Kyōka, see "Masei no sekai"; and "Pari no Izumi Kyōka." Murakami Haruki has not actually written on Kyōka's work, to my knowledge, but he has mentioned the author several times in my talks with him.

Selected Bibliography

Unless otherwise indicated, the place of publication of Japanese-language works is Tokyo.

Primary Texts

Kyōka zenshū (The complete works of Izumi Kyōka). 15 vols. Shun'yōdō, 1925.
Kyōka zenshū (The complete works of Izumi Kyōka). Iwanami shoten, 1940–42 (28 vols.); 1973–76 (29 vols.); 1989 (30 vols.).
Kyōka zenshū (The complete works of Izumi Kyōka). Emutei shuppan, 1994. 15 vols. Reprinting of the 1925 Shun'yōdō edition.

Annotated Texts

Asada Yōjirō, annotator. *Chūkai Kyōka shōsetsu* (The works of Izumi Kyōka, annotated). Sōkensha, 1967. Consists of *Uta andon*, "Katsushika sunago," and "Chūmonchō."
———. *Chūkai kōsetsu Izumi Kyōka Nihonbashi* (The annotated *Nihonbashi*). Meiji shoin, 1974.
Kasahara Nobuo, annotator. *Hyōshaku Tenshu monogatari*. (The annotated *Tenshu monogatari*). Kokubunsha, 1991.
Muramatsu Sadataka, Asada Yōjirō, Mita Hideaki, annotators. *Izumi Kyōka-shū* (Collected works of Izumi Kyōka). Nihon kindai bungaku taikei, 7. Kadokawa shoten, 1970. Consists of *Giketsu kyōketsu*, "Yakō junsa," "Gekashitsu," "Kaijō hatsuden," *Teriha Kyōgen*, *Yushima mode*, *Kōya hijiri*, and "Chūmonchō."

Muramatsu Sadataka, Kasahara Nobuo, Mita Hideaki, Tōgō Katsumi, annotators. *Izumi Kyōka*. Ōfūsha, 1983. Consists of "Ryūtandan," "Kechō," "Katsushika sunago," and "Rukōshinsō."

English Translations

Inouye, Charles, trans. *Japanese Gothic Tales by Izumi Kyōka*. Honolulu: University of Hawaii Press, 1996. Consists of trans. of "The Surgery Room" ("Gekashitsu"), *The Holy Man of Mt. Kōya* (*Kōya hijiri*), "One Day in Spring" ("Shunchū" and " Shunchū gokoku"), and "Osen and Sōkichi" ("Baishoku kamonanban").

————. *The Tale of the Wandering Monk*. New York: Limited Editions Club, 1995. Trans. of *Kōya hijiri*.

————. *Three Tales of Mystery and Imagination, Japanese Gothic by Izumi Kyōka*. Kanazawa: Takakuwa bijutsu insatsu, 1992. Trans. of "The Surgery Room" ("Gekashitsu"), "One Day in Spring" ("Shunchū" and " Shunchū gokoku"), and "Osen and Sōkichi" ("Baishoku kamonanban").

Kohl, Stephen, trans. *The Saint of Mt. Koya and The Song of the Troubadour*. Kanazawa, Takakuwa bijutsu insatsu, 1990. Trans. of *Kōya hijiri* and *Uta andon*.

Poulton, Cody, trans. *Of a Dragon in the Deep*. Kanazawa: Takakuwa bijutsu insatsu, 1987. Trans. of "Ryūtandan."

————. *Spirits of Another Sort*. Unpublished manuscript. Trans. of *Demon Pond* (*Yashagaike*), *The Sea God's Palace* (*Kaijin besso*), *Castle Tower* (*Tenshu monogatari*).

Seidensticker, Edward, trans. "A Tale of Three Who Were Blind." In Donald Keene, ed., *Modern Japanese Literature*, pp. 242–53. New York: Grove Press, 1956. Trans. of "Sannin mekure no hanashi."

Important Bibliographies

"Izumi Kyōka zōsho mokuroku" (A bibliography of Kyōka's private library). *Izumi Kyōka geppō*, no. 29 (1976). Reprinted in Tōgō Katsumi, ed. *Izumi Kyōka: bi to gensō* (Izumi Kyōka: beauty and fantasy), pp. 221–23. Nihon bungaku kenkyū shiryō shinshū, 12. Yūseido, 1991. A list of the books in Kyōka's private library as it exists today.

Shōwa joshi daigaku, Kindai bungaku kenkyū shitsu. *Kindai bungaku kenkyū sōsho* (A researcher's bibliography for modern literature), vol. 47. 1977. Contains reviews of Kyōka's work at the time of publication.

Tanaka Reigi. "Izumi Kyōka sankō bunken mokuroku (zasshi no bu)" (A bibliography of reference works on Izumi Kyōka [journal articles]). *Dōshisha kokubungaku*, no. 13: 102–36 (1978). This and the following three bibliographies compiled by Tanaka contain recent articles and reviews.

————. "Izumi Kyōka sankō bunken mokuroku (zasshi no bu) hoi" (A bibliography of reference works on Izumi Kyōka [journal articles], supplement). *Izumi Kyōka kenkyū*, 5: 72–83 (1980).

————. "Izumi Kyōka sankō bunken mokuroku (zasshi no bu) hoi 2" (A bibliography of reference works on Izumi Kyōka [journal articles], supplement no. 2). In Izumi Kyōka kenkyū kai, ed., *Ronshū Izumi Kyōka* (Collected essays on Izumi Kyōka), pp. 223–61. Yūseidō, 1987.

————. "Izumi Kyōka sankō bunken mokuroku (zasshi no bu) hoi 3" (A bibliography of reference works on Izumi Kyōka [journals], supplement no. 3). In Izumi Kyōka kenkyū kai, ed., *Ronshū Izumi Kyōka* (Collected essays on Izumi Kyōka), 2: 224–47. Yūseidō, 1991.

Works Cited

Akiyama Minoru, "Jizen no jidai no bungaku: 'Himin kurabu' no kokoromi" (Literature in the age of charity: a tentative look at "The Poverty Club"). In Izumi Kyōka kenkyū kai, ed., *Ronshū Izumi Kyōka* (Collected essays on Izumi Kyōka), pp. 33–50. Yūseidō, 1987.

————. "*Kanmuri Yazaemon* kō—Izumi Kyōka no shuppatsu" (A study of *Crowned Yazaemon*—Izumi Kyōka's point of departure). *Kokugo to kokubungaku* 60, no. 4: 49–62 (April 1983). Reprinted in Tōgō Katsumi, ed., *Izumi Kyōka: bi to gensō* (Izumi Kyōka: beauty and fantasy), pp. 55–68. Nihon bungaku kenkyū shiryō shinshū, 12. Yūseidō, 1991.

Akutagawa Ryūnosuke. "*Kyōka zenshū* mokuroku kaihō" (Preface to the *Complete Works of Izumi Kyōka*). *Shinshōsetsu* 30, no. 5: 1–4 (May 1925). Reprinted in *Akutagawa zenshū* (Complete works of Akutagawa), 12: 198–200. Iwanami shoten, 1996.

————. "*Kyōka zenshū* ni tsuite" (On the *Complete Works of Izumi Kyōka*). Reprinted in *Akutagawa zenshū* (Complete works of Akutagawa), 12: 203–4. Iwanami shoten, 1996.

Arakawa Gyorō, "Saikin no sōsakkai" (Recent publications). *Taiyō* 2, no. 12: 180–84 (December 1896).

Arakawa Hōshō. *Izumi Kyōka den* (A biography of Izumi Kyōka). Shōwa tosho shuppan, 1981.

Bandō Tamasaburō and Gunji Masakatsu. "Taidan: Kyōka geki o megutte" (A dialogue: on the plays of Izumi Kyōka). *Kokubungaku kaishaku to kyōzai no kenkyū* 36, no. 9: 6–25 (August 1991).

Blacker, Carmen. *The Catalpa Bow*. London: Allen & Unwin, 1975.

Braisted, William Reynolds, trans. *Meiroku zasshi: Journal of the Japanese Enlightenment*. Cambridge: Harvard University Press, 1979.

Cornyetz, Nina. *Dangerous Women: Phallic Fantasy and Modernity in Izumi Kyōka, Enchi Fumiko, and Nakagami Kenji* (forthcoming from Stanford University Press).

Doi Takeo. *Amae no kōzō*. Kōbundō, 1981. Trans. by John Bestor as *Anatomy of Dependence*. New York: Kodansha International, 1973.

Fowler, Edward. *The Rhetoric of Confession*. Berkeley: University of California Press, 1988.

Fujii, James. *Complicit Fictions: The Subject in the Modern Japanese Prose Narrative*. Berkeley: University of California Press, 1993.

Fujisawa Yukihide. "'Yakusō tori'—Izumi Kyōka no sōzōryoku to *Myōhōrengekyō*" ("Picking Herbs"—Izumi Kyōka's Creative Imagination and the *Lotus Sutra*). *Kokubungaku kaishaku to kyōzai no kenkyū* 36, no. 9: 97–103 (August 1991).

Gamo Kin'ichirō. *Mō hitori no Izumi Kyōka* (Another Izumi Kyōka). Tōbi shuppan, 1965.

Gunji Masakatsu. "Kyōka no geki kūkan"(Kyōka's theatrical space). *Kokubungaku kaishaku to kyōzai no kenkyū* 30, no. 7: 44–49 (June 1985).

Hall, Ivan. *Mori Arinori*. Cambridge: Harvard University Press, 1971.

Hasegawa Tenkei. "*Chinshō* no hon'yaku ni tsuite" (On the translation of *The Sunken Bell*). *Shin shōsetsu* 12, no. 7: 135 (July 1907).

Hashimoto Yoshi. "*Teriha Kyōgen* ni tsuite" (On *Teriha Kyōgen*). In Tōgō Katsumi, ed., *Izumi Kyōka*, pp. 120–27. Nihon bungaku kenkyū shiryō sōsho. Yūseidō, 1980.

Hirata, Hosea. "The Emergence of History in Natsume Sōseki's *Kokoro*." Unpublished paper.

Honma Hisao. "Kyōka tsuioku hitotsu, futatsu" (One or two memories of Kyōka). *Kyōka zenshū geppō*, no. 21: 1–3 (1975).

Ikari Akira. *Ken'yūsha no bungaku* (Writings of the Ken'yūsha school). Hanawa shobō, 1961.

———. "Kyōka to Ichiyō"(Kyōka and Ichiyō). *Izumi Kyōka kenkyū*, no. 5: 1–19 (1980).

———. "Shatei Izumi Toyoharu ron" (A study of Shatei, Izumi Toyoharu). *Meiji Taishō bungaku kenkyū* 21: 18–26 (March 1957).

Ikuta Chōkō. "Kyōka-shi no shōsetsu o ronzu" (An explication of Kyōka's fiction). *Shin shōsetsu* 16, no. 6: 75–95 (June 1911). Reprinted in Tanizawa Eiichi and Watanabe Ikkō, eds., *Kyōka ron shūsei* (A collection of critical writings on Izumi Kyōka), pp. 168–80. Rippū shobō, 1983.

Inouye, Charles. "In the Scopic Regime of Discovery: Ishikawa Takuboku's *Diary in Roman Script* and the Gendered Premise of Self Identity." *Positions: East Asian Cultures Critique* 2, no. 3: 542–69 (1994). Reprinted in Tani Barlow, ed., *Formations of Colonial Modernity in East Asia*, pp. 223–47. Durham, N.C.: Duke University Press, 1997.

———. "Modern Japanese Literature on Its Own Terms." In Eiji Sekine, ed., *Revisionism in Japanese Literary Studies: Proceedings of the Midwest Association for Japanese Literary Studies*, pp. 230–52. West Lafayette, Ind.: Purdue University Press, 1996.

———. "Pictocentrism." *Yearbook of Comparative and General Literature* 40: 23–39 (1992).

———. "Pictocentrism: China as a Source of Japanese Modernity." In Sumie Jones, ed., *Imaging/Reading Eros*, pp. 148–52. Bloomington: Indiana University, East Asian Studies Center, 1996.

————. "Water Imagery in the Work of Izumi Kyōka." *Monumenta Nipponica* 46, no. 1: 43–68 (Spring 1991).

Ishihara Ningetsu. "Shincho hyakushu no *Iro zange*" (New writing—Kōyō's *Confessions*). *Kokumin no tomo* 4, no. 48: 35–36 (1889).

Itō Sei. "Izumi Kyōka." In *Itō Sei zenshū* (Complete works of Itō Sei), 19: 81–98. Shinchōsha, 1973.

————. *Shizenshugi no saiseiki* (Naturalism at its zenith). Nihon bundan shi, 12. Kōdansha, 1971.

Itō Yanosuke. "Izumi Kyōka no ihin to genkō" (Izumi Kyōka, memorabilia and manuscripts). *Juku* (Keiō Gijuku), no. 62: 12–13 (December 1973).

Ivy, Marilyn. *Discourses of the Vanishing: Modernity, Phantasm, Japan.* Chicago: Chicago University Press, 1995.

Iwasa Shin'ichi. "Kyōka mono to jōen" (Performances of Kyōka's work). *Kokubungaku kaishaku to kanshō*, no. 156 (special issue on Izumi Kyōka): 37–45 (May 1949).

Iwaya Daishi. *Ningen Izumi Kyōka* (A biography of Izumi Kyōka). Tōkyō shoseki, 1979.

Izawa Atsushi. "*Uta andon* ni okeru eigateki hyōgen" (Cinematic method in *A Song by Lantern Light*). *Kokubungaku shiryō to kanshō*, no. 156: 80–82 (May 1949).

Izumi Kyōka kenkyū kai, ed. *Ronshū Izumi Kyōka* (Collected essays on Izumi Kyōka). Yūseidō, 1987.

————. *Ronshū Izumi Kyōka* (Collected essays on Izumi Kyōka), vol. 2. Yūseidō, 1991.

Izumi Natsuki. "Hanetsuki, tegara, tsutsumi no o" (A Kyōka miscellany). *Gendaishi techō* (bessatsu), January 1972, pp. 124–37. Reprinted in *Shinbungei tokuhon: Izumi Kyōka* (New literature reader: Izumi Kyōka), pp. 16–21. Kawade shobō shinsha, 1991.

Kamei Hideo. *Kansei no henkaku* (Altered sensitivities). Kōdansha, 1983.

Karatani Kōjin. *Nihon kindai bungaku no kigen*. Kōdansha, 1980. Trans. by Brett de Bary et. al., *Origins of Modern Japanese Literature*. Durham, N.C.: Duke University Press, 1993.

Kasahara Nobuo. "Erosu, kanjō, soshite yume" (Eros, emotion, dreams). *Hatayo* 10, no. 10: 19–23 (1992).

————. *Hyōden Izumi Kyōka* (A critical biography of Izumi Kyōka). Hakuchisha, 1995.

————. *Izumi Kyōka—bi to erosu no kōzō* (Izumi Kyōka—the structure of beauty and eros). Shibundō, 1976.

————. *Izumi Kyōka: erosu no mayu* (Izumi Kyōka: a cocoon of eros). Kokubundō, 1988.

————. "*Kōya hijiri* no shinwateki kōsō ryoku" (The mythical power of *The Holy Man of Mt. Kōya*). *Bungaku* 55, no. 3: 53–69 (March 1987).

Katsumoto Seiichirō. "Izumi Kyōka saku *Onna keizu*" (Izumi Kyōka's *A Woman's Pedigree*). *Tosho*, pp. 11–13 (March 1951).

Kawabata Yasunari. "Izumi Kyōka no *Kushige shū* nado" (Izumi Kyōka's *Comb Box Collection*, etc.). Reprinted in Tanizawa Eiichi and Watanabe Ikkō, eds., *Kyōka ron shūsei* (A collection of critical writings on Izumi Kyōka), pp. 204–207. Rippū shobō, 1983.

———. "*Kushige shū* to *Shisei oni*" (*The Comb Box Collection* and *The Street Goblin*). *Bungei shunjū* 21, no. 6 (June 1943).

Keene, Donald. *Dawn to the West: Japanese Literature in the Modern Era.* New York: Holt, Rinehart, Winston, 1984.

Kimijima Yasumasa. "Izumi Kyōka no sunda Zushi" (Izumi Kyōka's Zushi). *Kyōka kenkyū*, no. 4: 45–52 (March 1979).

Kobayashi Hideo. "Kyōka no shi, sono ta" (Izumi Kyōka's death and other matters). Reprinted in *Bungei tokuhon: Izumi Kyōka* (Literature reader: Izumi Kyōka), 37: 15–19. Kawade shobō shinsha, 1981.

Kobayashi Teruya. "Izumi Kyōka to kirisutokyō" (Izumi Kyōka and Christianity). In Tōgō Katsumi, ed. *Izumi Kyōka*, pp. 238–248. Nihon bungaku kenkyū shiryō sōsho. Yūseidō, 1980.

———. "Kaga zōgan no shokunin-tachi: Kyōka no shosaku o hitotsu no shiten to-shite" (The Damascene craftsmen of Kaga: a perspective on Kyōka's work). In Kurokawa Taketo, ed. *Howatto izu Kanazawa*, pp. 77–78. Mattō: Maeda insatsu, 1992.

———. "'Kusa meikyū' no kōzō: temari uta genshi dan" (The structure of "The Grass Labyrinth," a fantastic tale of a *temari uta*). *Kyōka kenkyū* 4: 72–86 (1979).

Kobayashi Teruya, ed. *Izumi Kyōka.* Ishikawa kindai bungaku zenshū, 1. Kanazawa: Nōtō insatsu, 1987.

Koike Masatani. "Izumi Kyōka—*Kanmuri Yazaemon* to *Shinkyoku gyoseki dōji kun*" (Izumi Kyōka—*Crowned Yazaemon* and Bakin's *Shinkyoku gyoseki dōji kun*). *Kokubun-gaku kaishaku to kanshō* 44, no. 13: 167–75 (December 1979).

Kōno Taeko. "Kyōka no seimei" (Kyōka's life force). In *Bungei tokuhon: Izumi Kyōka* (Literature reader: Izumi Kyōka), pp. 110–12. Kawade shobō shinsha, 1981.

Kornicki, P. F. "The Survival of Tokugawa Fiction in the Meiji Period." *Harvard Journal of Asiatic Studies* 41, no. 2: 461–82 (December 1981).

Koshino Itaru. "Izumi Kyōka bungaku hihyō-shi kō (I)" (A historical perspective on criticism of Kyōka's literary work). *Hokudai bungakubu kiyō* 29, no. 2: 163–244 (1981).

Maeda Ai. "Izumi Kyōka *Kōya hijiri*—tabibito no monogatari" (Izumi Kyōka's *The Holy Man of Mt. Kōya*—a traveler's tale). In Tōgō Katsumi, ed., *Izumi Kyōka*, pp. 137–140. Nihon bungaku kenkyū shiryō sōsho. Yūseidō, 1980.

———. *Kindai dokusha no seiritsu* (The birth of the modern reader). Yūseidō, 1973.

Maruyama Masao. "From Carnal Literature to Carnal Politics." Trans. by Barbara Ruch, in Ivan Morris, ed., *Thought and Behaviour in Modern Japanese Politics*, pp. 245–67. London: Oxford University Press, 1963.

Masamune Hakuchō. "Bundan kanken" (Personal views of the literary world). *Taiyō*, p. 20 (May 1901).

———. "Tsuioku ki" (A record of memories), *Sandē mainichi*, June 17, 1923.

————. "Zatsubun chō" (A miscellany). *Kaizō*, pp. 368–74 (April 1940).

Matsubara Jun'ichi. "Kyōka bungaku to minkan denshō to" (Kyōka's writings and the oral tradition). In Tōgō Katsumi, ed., *Izumi Kyōka*, pp. 203–15. Nihon bungaku kenkyū shiryō sōsho. Yūseidō, 1980.

Matsumura Tomomi. "Aku no sekai" (The world of evil). *Kokubungaku kaishaku to kanshō* 46, no. 7: 52–54 (July 1981).

————. "Kyōka shoki sakuhin no shippitsu jiki ni tsuite—'Shirajo monogatari' o chūshin ni" (Kyōka's beginnings as a writer, with a focus on "The White Witch's Tale"). *Mita kokubun*, no. 4: 29–39 (November 1985).

————. "*Onna keizu* no haikei: 'Shizuoka' no imi suru mono" (The background of *A Woman's Pedigree*: the significance of "Shizuoka"). *Bungaku* 51: 162–68 (June 1983).

————. "'Shunchū' no sekai" (The world of "One Day in Spring"). In Kasahara Nobuo, Tōgō Katsumi, Mita Hideaki, and Muramatsu Sadataka, eds., *Ronshū Izumi Kyōka* (Collected essays on Izumi Kyōka), pp. 111–25. Yūseidō, 1987.

McClain, James. *Kanazawa: A Seventeenth Century Japanese Castle Town.* New Haven: Yale University Press, 1982.

McClellan, Edwin. "The Impressionistic Tendency in Some Modern Japanese Writers." *Chicago Review* 17, no. 4: 48–60 (1965).

Minakami Takitarō. "Kyōka sekai bekken" (My humble view of Kyōka's world). *Chūō kōron*, pp. 257–79 (March 1929).

————. "*Kyōka zenshū* no ki" (A chronicle of the *Complete Works of Izumi Kyōka*). Reprinted in Tanizawa Eiichi and Watanabe Ikkō, eds., *Kyōka ron shūsei* (A collection of critical writings on Izumi Kyōka), pp. 187–99. Rippū shobō, 1983.

Miner, Earl. "Inventions of the Literary Modern." *CLIO* 21, no. 1: 1–22 (Fall 1991).

Mishima Yukio. *Bunshō tokuhon* (Literary reader). Chūō kōron sha, 1959.

————. "Ozaki Kōyō, Izumi Kyōka." In idem, *Sakkaron* (A study of authors). Chūō kōron sha, 1970. Reprinted in *Bungei tokuhon: Izumi Kyōka* (Literature reader: Izumi Kyōka), pp. 10–14. Kawade shobō shinsha, 1981; and in *Mishima Yukio zenshū* (Collected works of Mishima Yukio), 33: 553–67. Shinchōsha, 1976. (Note: all references in the Notes are to the *Zenshū*.)

Mita Hideaki. *Izumi Kyōka no bungaku.* Ōfūsha, 1976.

————. "'Kusa meikyū'" ("The Grass Labyrinth"). *Kokubungaku kaishaku to kanshō* 46, no. 7: 76–82 (July 1981).

————. "'Shunchū/Shunchū gokoku' to hankindai" ("One Day in Spring" and anti-modernism). In Izumi Kyōka kenkyū kai, ed. *Ronshū Izumi Kyōka* (Collected essays on Izumi Kyōka), 2: 128–55. Yūseidō, 1991.

Miyata Noboru. *Hime no minzokugaku* (An ethnology of noble women). Seidōsha, 1987.

Miyoshi, Masao. *Accomplices of Silence.* Berkeley: University of California Press, 1974.

————. *Off Center: Power and Culture Relations Between Japan and the United States.* Cambridge: Harvard University Press, 1991.

Mori Ōgai. *Mezamashigusa*. February 1896, volume 2.

————. "Sannin jōwa" (Frivolous talk for three). *Mezamashigusa*, no. 4: 413–19 (April 25, 1896).

Morse, Robert. *Yanagita Kunio and the Folklore Movement: The Search for Japan's National Character and Distinctiveness*. New York: Garland, 1990.

Muramatsu Sadataka. *Ajisai kuyōshō—waga Izumi Kyōka* (Hydrangea memorial—my Izumi Kyōka). Shinchōsha, 1988.

————. *Izumi Kyōka*. Bunsendō, 1966.

————. *Izumi Kyōka jiten* (An Izumi Kyōka dictionary). Yūseidō, 1982.

————. *Izumi Kyōka kenkyū* (A study of Izumi Kyōka). Tōjusha, 1974.

————. *Izumi Kyōka—kotoba no renkinjutsushi* (Izumi Kyōka, crafter of language). Shakai shisōsha, 1973.

————. *Kindai Nihon bungaku no keifu, I* (Modern Japanese literature and its traditions, I). Shakai shisō kenkyūkai shuppan, 1956.

————. "Kyōka o meguru Taishō sakka gunzō" (Taishō authors, with a focus on Izumi Kyōka). In Izumi Kyōka kenkyūkai, ed., *Ronshū Izumi Kyōka* (Collected essays on Izumi Kyōka), pp. 204–222. Yūseidō, 1987.

Muramatsu Sadataka, Miyoshi Yukio, and Kasahara Nobuo. "Kyōka to hankindai" (Kyōka and anti-modernism). *Bungaku* 51, no. 6: 1–23 (June 1983).

Murō Saisei, *Dai ni shishū* (Poems, collection II). Bunbudō shoten, 1988.

Nakatani Katsumi. *Izumi Kyōka: shinzō e no shiten* (Izumi Kyōka: a look into the heart). Meiji shoin, 1987.

Napier, Susan. *The Fantastic in Modern Japanese Literature: The Subversion of Modernity*. New York: Routledge, 1996.

Noguchi Takehiko. "Gensō no bunpōgaku" (A grammar of fantasy). *Kokubungaku kaishaku to kyōzai no kenkyū* 30, no. 7: 26–34 (June 1985).

————. *Izumi Kyōka*. Kanshō Nihon gendai bungaku. Kadokawa shoten, 1982.

————. "Kyōka no onna" (Kyōka's women). In *Bungei tokuhon: Izumi Kyōka* (Literature reader: Izumi Kyōka), pp. 138–46. Kawade shobō shinsha, 1981.

————. *Shōsetsu no Nihongo* (The Japanese language and fiction). Nihongo no sekai, 13. Chūō kōron sha, 1980.

Noguchi Takehiko, ed. *Shinchō Nihon bungaku arubamu: Izumi Kyōka* (Shinchō Japanese literary album: Izumi Kyōka). Shinchōsha, 1985.

Nomura Shōgo. "Kyōka, Jun'ichirō zakkan" (Various impressions of Kyōka and Tanizaki Jun'ichirō). *Kokubungaku kaishaku to kanshō* 38, no. 3: 14–21 (June 1973).

Ochi Haruo. *Kyōka to gikyoku* (Kyōka and drama). Sunagoya shobō, 1987.

Oka Yasuo. "Izumi Kyōka to Ozaki Kōyō" (Izumi Kyōka and Ozaki Kōyō). *Kokubungaku kaishaku to kanshō* 38, no. 8: 74–79 (June 1973).

————. "Kōya hijiri seiritsu no kiban" (The foundations of *The Holy Man of Mt. Kōya*).

In Tōgō Katsumi, ed., *Izumi Kyōka*, pp. 153–161. Nihon bungaku kenkyū shiryō sōsho. Yūseidō, 1980.

Okazaki Yoshie. *Japanese Literature in the Meiji Era*, trans. V. H. Viglielmo. Ōbunsha, 1955.

Ono Susumu. *Bunpō II* (Grammar II). Iwanami kōza: Nihongo, 7. Iwanami shoten, 1977.

Orikuchi Shinobu. "Ishi ni deiru mono" (Things emerging from stone). In *Orikuchi zenshū*, 15: 212–55. Chūō kōron, 1955.

———. "Kodai kenkyū" (A study of antiquities). In *Orikuchi Shinobu zenshū* (Complete works of Orikuchi Shinobu), 2: 3–15. Chūō kōron, 1955.

Osanai Kaoru. "Geki to naritaru Kyōka-shi no shōsetsu" (Kyōka's theatrical novels). *Yomiuri shinbun*, June 21, 1908. Reprinted in Tanizawa Eiichi and Watanabe Ikkō, eds., *Kyōka ron shūsei* (A collection of critical writings on Izumi Kyōka), pp. 135–38. Rippū Shobō, 1983.

Ozaki Kōyō. *Ninin bikuni iro zange* (Two confessions of love). Meiji bungaku zenshū, 18. Chikuma shobō, 1969.

———. *Ozaki Kōyō shū* (Collected works of Ozaki Kōyō). Meiji bungaku zenshū, 18. Chikuma shobō, 1965.

———. "Ren'ai mondō" (Questions and answers about romance). *Shinchō gekkan*, January 1897.

Poulton, Cody. "Benten of the West: Izumi Kyōka's Image of an American Missionary." Unpublished paper, 1990.

———. *Of a Dragon in the Deep*. Kanazawa: Takakuwa Bijutsu Insatsu, 1987.

———. "Spirits of a Different Sort." Unpublished manuscript.

Sakai, Naoki. *Voices of the Past: The Status of Language in Eighteenth-Century Japanese Discourse*. Ithaca, N.Y.: Cornell University Press, 1991.

Sasakawa Rinpū. "Yaji kara Kitahachi-san e" (From Yaji to Kitahachi). *Shin shōsetsu* 30, no. 5: 23–25 (May 1925).

Satomi Ton. "Futari no sakka" (Two authors). Reprinted in Tanizawa Eiichi and Watanabe Ikkō, eds., *Kyōka ron shūsei* (A collection of critical writings on Izumi Kyōka), pp. 85–94. Rippū shobō, 1983.

———. "Sensei no kōaku kan" (The master's likes and dislikes). In *Satomi Ton zenshū* (Complete works of Satomi Ton), 10: 322–24. Chikuma shobō, 1941. Also reprinted in *Bungei tokuhon: Izumi Kyōka* (Literature reader: Izumi Kyōka), pp. 72–73. Kawade shobō shinsha, 1981.

Seki Ryōichi. "'Yakō junsa'" ("The Night Patrol"). *Kokubungaku kyōzai to kanshō* 38, no. 8: 112–13 (June 1973).

Shibuzawa Tatsuhiko. "Ranpu no kaiten: 'Kusa meikyū'" (The spinning lamp: "The Grass Labyrinth"). In Tōgō Katsumi, ed., *Izumi Kyōka*, pp. 156–168. Gunzō Nihon no sakka, 5. Shōgakkan, 1992.

Shimamura Hōgetsu. "Shōsetsukai no shinchō o ronzu" (On recent developments in fiction). *Waseda bungaku*, no. 1: 23–27 (January 1896).

Shinbo Chiyoko. "Shin shiryō shōkai" (An introduction to new materials). *Kyōka kenkyū* 2: 77 (1976).

Shinoda Hajime. *Nihon no kindai shōsetsu* (Japan's modern novels). Shūeisha, 1973.

Suda Chisato. "'Shunchū' no kōsō" (The plot construciton of "One Day in Spring"). In Izumi Kyōka kenkyū kai, ed., *Ronshū Izumi Kyōka* (Collected essays on Izumi Kyōka), 2: 108–27. Yūseidō, 1991.

Sugimoto Suguru. "Izumi Kyōka no gensō geki: *Yashagaike* no fukken" (Izumi Kyōka's theater of the fantastic: the revisiting of *Demon Pond*). *Kokugo to kokubungaku* 58, no. 8: 64–75 (August 1981).

Suzuki, Tomi. *Narrating the Self: Fictions of Japanese Modernity*. Stanford: Stanford University Press, 1996.

Takahashi Tōru. *Monogatari bungei no hyōgenshi* (A history of tale narratives). Nagoya: Nagoya daigaku shuppankai, 1987.

———. "Monogatarigaku ni mukete: kōzō to imi no shudaiteki na henkan" (Toward a study of tale literature: subjective change in structure and meaning). In Takahashi Tōru and Itoi Michihiro, eds., *Monogatari no hōhō: katari no imi ron* (The methods of tales: essays on the meaning of narrating), pp. 4–20. Sekai shisōsha, 1992.

Takakuwa Noriko. "Ikai to gensō" (The other world and fantasy). *Kokubungaku kaishaku to kyōzai no kenkyū*, pp. 102–8 (June 1990).

———. "Izumi Kyōka *Sankai hyōbanki*: an'yu ni yoru tenkai toshite" (Izumi Kyōka's *Of the Mountains and the Sea*: narrative progression through metaphor). *Nihon kindai bungaku* 32: 37–48.

———. "'Kusa meikyū' ron: Kyōkateki sōzōryoku no tokushitsu o megutte" ("The Grass Labyrinth": Kyōka's unique imaginative powers). In Tōgō Katsumi, ed., *Izumi Kyōka: bi to gensō* (Izumi Kyōka: beauty and fantasy), pp. 109–20. Yūseidō, 1991.

———. "'Mayu kakushi no rei'" ("How Beautiful Without Eyebrows"). *Kokubungaku kaishaku to kanshō* 46, no. 7: 88–92 (July 1981).

———. "'Shunchū' 'Shunchū gokoku' ron" (A treatise on "One Day in Spring"). In Izumi Kyōka kenkyū kai, ed., *Ronshū Izumi Kyōka* (Collected essays on Izumi Kyōka), pp. 126–46. Yūseidō, 1987.

———. "*Teriha Kyōgen*—koji ni narubeki kizashi" (*Teriha Kyōgen*—premonitory signs of becoming an orphan). *Kokubungaku kaishaku to kanshō* 54, no. 11: 84–89 (1989).

Takashina Shūji. *Nihon kindai no biishiki* (Modern Japanese aesthetics). Seidosha, 1986.

Taneda Wakako. "'Ryūtandan'—Izumi Kyōka no yōnen sekai" ("Of a Dragon in the Deep"—Izumi Kyōka's childhood world). *Bungaku* 51, no. 6: 177–86 (June 1983).

Tanizaki Jun'ichirō. "Izumi-sensei to watakushi" (Master Izumi and I). *Bungei shunjū*, November 1939, pp. 368–70.

———. "Junsui ni 'Nihonteki' na 'Kyōka sekai'" (The purely Japanese world of Izumi Kyōka). In *Tanizaki Jun'ichirō zenshū* (Complete works of Tanizaki Jun'ichirō), 22: 336–38. Chūō kōron sha, 1968.

———. *Seishun monogatari* (Childhood years). In *Tanizaki Jun'ichirō zenshū* (Complete works of Tanizaki Jun'ichirō), 13: 343–440. Chūō kōron sha, 1967.

Tanizawa Eiichi and Watanabe Ikkō, eds. *Kyōka ron shūsei* (A collection of critical writings on Izumi Kyōka). Rippū shobō, 1983.

Taoka Reiun. "Jibun: *Taiyō* dairokugo no shōsetsu—'Gekashitsu'" (A review of contemporary fiction—"The Surgery Room"). *Seinenbun*, July 1895, p. 2.

———. "Seinenbun: jibun" (Contemporary fiction). *Bunko*, May 1897, p. 6.

Tayama Katai. "Hauputoman ga *Chinshō*" (Hauptmann's *The Sunken Bell*). *Mannengusa* no. 4: 1–4 (February 1903).

———. "Inki no tsubo" (The ink pot). *Bunshō sekai* 5, no. 9: 14–19 (July 1910).

———. *Kindai no shōsetsu* (The modern novel). Daitō shuppansha, 1941.

———. "Rokotsu naru byōsha" (Straightforward description).*Teihon Katai zenshū* (The official complete works of Tayama Katai), 26: 154–59. Rinsen shoten, 1995.

———. *Tōkyō no sanjū nen* (Thirty years in Tokyo). Hakubunkan, 1917.

———. "Yama naka no kōsui" (Lakewater in the mountains). *Taiyō*, July 28, 1902, p. 5.

Teraki Teihō. *Hito Izumi Kyōka* (Izumi Kyōka the person). Kindai sakka kenkyū sōsho, 18. Nihon tosho sentā, 1983.

———. "Kyōka no ichinichi" (A day in the life of Izumi Kyōka). Reprinted in Tanizawa Eiichi and Watanabe Ikkō, eds., *Kyōka ron shūsei* (A collection of critical writings on Izumi Kyōka), pp. 65–69. Rippū Shobō, 1983.

Tezuka Masayuki. "*Fūryūsen* purotto kō" (A consideration of the plot of *The Elegant Railway*). In Izumi Kyōka kenkyū kai, ed., *Ronshū Izumi Kyōka* (Collected essays on Izumi Kyōka), 2: 91–107. Yūseidō, 1991.

———. "Izumi Kyōka to Morita Shiken" (Izumi Kyōka and Morita Shiken). In Tōgō Katsumi, ed., *Izumi Kyōka*, pp. 226–37. Nihon bungaku kenkyū shiryō sōsho. Yūseidō, 1979.

———. *Izumi Kyōka to sono shūhen* (Izumi Kyōka and company). Musashino shobō, 1989.

———. "Karyūkai" (The gay quarters). *Kokubungaku kaishaku to kanshō* 46, no. 7: 48–51 (July 1981).

Tobari Chikufū. "*Chinshō* no hon'yaku ni tsuite" (On the translation of *The Sunken Bell*). *Shin shōsetsu* 12, no. 7: 134–37 (July 1907).

———. *Ningen shugyō* (Training to be human). Chūō kōron sha, 1934.

Tōgō Katsumi. *Izumi Kyōka: hito to bungaku* (Izumi Kyōka: the man and his work). Tōkyō denroku, 1990.

————. "*Kōya hijiri* no suichūmu" (The underwater dream of *The Holy Man of Mt. Kōya*). In Tōgō Katsumi, ed., *Izumi Kyōka*, pp. 141–52. Nihon bungaku kenkyū shiryō sōsho. Yūseidō, 1980.

Tōgō Katsumi, ed. *Izumi Kyōka*. Gunzō Nihon no sakka, 5. Shōgakkan, 1992.

————. *Izumi Kyōka*. Nihon bungaku kenkyū shiryō sōsho. Yūseidō, 1980.

————. *Izumi Kyōka: bi to gensō* (Izumi Kyōka: beauty and fantasy). Nihon bungaku kenkyū shiryō shinshū, 12. Yūseidō, 1991.

Tokuda Shūsei. *Hikari o otte* (Pursuing the light). Shinchōsha, 1939.

————. "Izumi Kyōka to iu otoko" (Izumi Kyōka the man). *Bungei shunjū*, December 1935, pp. 116–25.

————. "Kyōka tsuioku" (Memories of Kyōka). Reprinted in Tanizawa Eiichi and Watanabe Ikkō, eds., *Kyōka ron shūsei* (A collection of critical writings on Izumi Kyōka), pp. 75–78. Rippū shobō, 1983.

————. "Wakai" (Reconciliation). In *Tayama Katai shū* (Collected works of Tayama Katai), pp. 190–200. Nihon kindai bungaku, 21. Kōdansha, 1962.

Tokuda Shūsei, Chikamatsu Shūkō, et al. "Ozaki Kōyō." In Satō Giryō, ed., *Meiji Taishō bungō kenkyū* (A study of major Meiji and Taishō writers), pp. 35–63. Shinchōsha, 1936.

Torrance, Richard. *Tokuda Shūsei and the Emergence of Japan's New Middle Class*. Seattle: University of Washington Press, 1994.

Tsushima Yūko. "Masei no sekai" (A magical world). In *Nihon bungaku arubamu: Izumi Kyōka* (Album of Japanese literature: Izumi Kyōka), pp. 97–103. Shinchōsha, 1985.

————. "Pari no Izumi Kyōka" (Izumi Kyōka and Paris). In Tōgō Katsumi, ed., *Izumi Kyōka*, pp. 5–12. Gunzō Nihon no sakka, 5. Shōgakkan, 1992.

Twine, Nanette. *Language and the Modern State: The Reform of Written Japanese*. The Nissan Institute / Routledge Japanese Studies Series. New York: Routledge, 1991.

Uchida Tōru. "*Onna keizu* no moderu" (Character sources for *A Woman's Pedigree*). *Gakashikai kaihō*, no. 693 (October 1966).

Usami Yoshikazu. "Intabyū *une heure avec* Akutagawa Hiroshi," (An hour-long interview with Akutagawa Hiroshi). *Higeki/Kigeki* 31, no. 10: 74–76 (October 1978).

Wadatsu Kiyoo. "*Konjiki yasha* no koro" (*The Gold Demon* era). *Bungei shunjū*, February 1965, pp. 65–67.

Waki Akiko. *Gensō no ronri: Izumi Kyōka no sekai* (The logic of fantasy: Izumi Kyōka's world). Kōdansha gendai shinsho, 348. Kōdansha, 1974.

Washburn, Dennis. *The Dilemma of the Modern in Japanese Fiction*. New Haven: Yale University Press, 1995.

Yamaguchi Yasuo. *Bunka jinruigaku e no shōtai* (An invitation to cultural anthropology). Iwanami shinsho, 204. Iwanami shoten, 1982.

Yanagida Izumi. "Kyōkaden kakigaki" (A Kyōka biography, random jottings). *Kokubungaku kanshō to kaishaku*, no. 82: 119–27 (1943).

Yanagita Kunio. *Imōto no chikara* (A younger sister's power). Sōgensha, 1940.

————. *Yama no jinsei* (Life in the mountains). Kyōdo kenkyū sha, 1926.

Yoshida Masashi. "Izumi Kyōka, sobo no shi to 'Onna kyaku'" (Izumi Kyōka— his grandmother's death and "A Female Visitor"). *Gakuen*, January 1989, pp. 120–29.

————. "Izumi Kyōka to kusazōshi: *Shaka hassō Yamato bunko* o chūshin toshite" (Izumi Kyōka and illustrated fiction, especially *The Eight Lives of Siddhartha, a Japanese Library*). In Tōgō Katsumi, ed., *Izumi Kyōka: bi to gensō* (Izumi Kyōka: beauty and fantasy), pp. 172–86. Nihon bungaku kenkyū shiryō shinshū, 12. Yūseidō, 1991.

————. "Izumi Kyōka *Yukari no onna* no seiritsu o megutte" (On the provenance of Izumi Kyōka's *Women of Acquaintance*). *Aoyama Gakuin Daigaku bungakubu kiyō*, no. 23: 25–45 (January 1982).

Yoshida Seiichi. *Higuchi Ichiyō no kenkyū* (Studies on Higuchi Ichiyō). Shinchōsha, 1956.

————. "Izumi Kyōka no hyōgen" (The expression of Izumi Kyōka). *Kikan Meiji bungaku* 2: 54–71 (1934).

————. "*Kōya hijiri* kenkyū" (A study of *The Holy Man of Mt. Kōya*). *Kokugo to kokubungaku* 10, no. 10: 54–78 (1935).

————. *Romanshugi no kenkyū* (On romanticism). Tōkyōdō shuppan, 1970.

————. "Tensai Kyōka" (Kyōka the genius). *Kyōka zenshū geppō* 9: 1–3. Iwanami shoten, 1974.

Yoshimura Hirotō. *Izumi Kyōka: geijutsu to byōri* (Izumi Kyōka: art and pathology). Kongō shuppan shinsha, 1970.

————. *Izumi Kyōka no sekai: gensō no byōri* (Izumi Kyōka's world: fantasy and pathology). Makino shuppan, 1983.

————. "Kyōka mandara" (Kyōka's mandala). *Kyōka kenkyū*, 4: 53–71 (March 1979).

————. *Makai e no enkin hō* (A perspectival approach to a world of magic). Kindai bungeisha, 1991.

Yoshitani Hiroya. *Minzoku kenkyū no shikaku* (From the point of view of folklore studies). Sugiyama shoten, 1992.

Yoshiya Nobuko. "Izumi-sensei no kakareru josei" (Master Izumi's female characters). *Shin shōsetsu*, pp. 11–14 (May, 1926).

Yura Kimiyoshi. "Kyōka ni okeru chōshizen—'Kechō' shōkō" (The supernatural in Kyōka's "A Bird of Many Colors"). In Tōgō Katsumi, *Izumi Kyōka*, pp. 128–36. Nihon bungaku kenkyū shiryō sōsho. Yūseidō, 1980.

Index

Harvard East Asian Monographs

(* out-of-print)

17. Andrew J. Nathan, *A History of the China International Famine Relief Commission*

*18. Frank H. H. King (ed.) and Prescott Clarke, *A Research Guide to China-Coast Newspapers, 1822–1911*

19. Ellis Joffe, *Party and Army: Professionalism and Political Control in the Chinese Officer Corps, 1949–1964*

*20. Toshio G. Tsukahira, *Feudal Control in Tokugawa Japan: The Sankin Kōtai System*

21. Kwang-Ching Liu, ed., *American Missionaries in China: Papers from Harvard Seminars*

22. George Moseley, *A Sino-Soviet Cultural Frontier: The Ili Kazakh Autonomous Chou*

23. Carl F. Nathan, *Plague Prevention and Politics in Manchuria, 1910–1931*

*24. Adrian Arthur Bennett, *John Fryer: The Introduction of Western Science and Technology into Nineteenth-Century China*

25. Donald J. Friedman, *The Road from Isolation: The Campaign of the American Committee for Non-Participation in Japanese Aggression, 1938–1941*

26. Edward LeFevour, *Western Enterprise in Late Ching China: A Selective Survey of Jardine, Matheson and Company's Operations, 1842–1895*

27. Charles Neuhauser, *Third World Politics: China and the Afro-Asian People's Solidarity Organization, 1957–1967*

28. Kungtu C. Sun, assisted by Ralph W. Huenemann, *The Economic Development of Manchuria in the First Half of the Twentieth Century*

*29. Shahid Javed Burki, *A Study of Chinese Communes, 1965*

30. John Carter Vincent, *The Extraterritorial System in China: Final Phase*

31. Madeleine Chi, *China Diplomacy, 1914–1918*

*32. Clifton Jackson Phillips, *Protestant America and the Pagan World: The First Half Century of the American Board of Commissioners for Foreign Missions, 1810–1860*

33. James Pusey, *Wu Han: Attacking the Present through the Past*

34. Ying-wan Cheng, *Postal Communication in China and Its Modernization, 1860–1896*

35. Tuvia Blumenthal, *Saving in Postwar Japan*

36. Peter Frost, *The Bakumatsu Currency Crisis*

37. Stephen C. Lockwood, *Augustine Heard and Company, 1858–1862*

38. Robert R. Campbell, *James Duncan Campbell: A Memoir by His Son*

39. Jerome Alan Cohen, ed., *The Dynamics of China's Foreign Relations*

40. V. V. Vishnyakova-Akimova, *Two Years in Revolutionary China, 1925–1927*, tr. Steven L. Levine